ANATOMY
OF A
TYPEFACE

ANATOMY
OF A
TYPEFACE

ALEXANDER LAWSON

DAVID R. GODINE, PUBLISHER

BOSTON

First published in 1990 by
DAVID R. GODINE, PUBLISHER, INC.
Horticultural Hall
300 Massachusetts Avenue
Boston, Massachusetts 02115

LIBRARY OF CONGRESS CATALOGING IN PUBLICATION DATA

Lawson, Alexander S.
Anatomy of a typeface.

Bibliography: p.
Includes index.
1. Type and type-founding. 2. Printing—Specimens.
I. Title.
Z250.L34 1990 686.2′ 24   81-47326
ISBN 0-87923-332-X
ISBN 0-87923-333-8 SC

PHOTO CREDITS

p. 46: reprinted by permission of Carolyn Hammer; p. 109: reprinted by
permission of Martino Mardersteig; p. 128: reprinted by permission of Her-
mann Zapf; p. 228: reprinted by permission of the Syndics of Cambridge
University Library; p. 336: reprinted by courtesy of the Trustees of the Boston
Public Library; pp. 119, 348, 404: reprinted by permission from the Melbert
B. Carey, Jr., Graphic Arts Collection, Rochester Institute of Technology.

FIRST EDITION
Manufactured in the United States of America

CONTENTS

PREFACE

It may seem presumptuous to select for this book only thirty contemporary printing types from the many thousands that have appeared since the fifteenth century, but I propose through the discussion of these thirty designs to present an overview of all the rest. As the typographic historian Harry Carter wrote so felicitously, 'Printer's types have generally been studied for the love of them,' and, indeed, most of the books about type have been written from that viewpoint.

Of course, every printer harboring a fondness for types tries to justify this interest by citing practical considerations of use, but in most instances the printer is really seduced by the beauty of the letter forms themselves. The more such a printer becomes involved in the exciting history of typographic development, the more likely it is that he or she will continue to seek that perfection of form that represents the ideal.

This book, then, is *not* written for the printer convinced that there are already far too many typefaces. It is, rather, addressed to the person who believes the opposite – that the subtleties of refinement as applied to roman letters have yet to be fully investigated and that the production of the perfect printing type remains a goal to be desired as much by contemporary as by future type designers.

The reader will note that the specific types listed herein are placed, insofar as the roman forms are concerned, in the sequence of their classification, and that in many cases I have included other typefaces contemporary with those discussed. In two instances – those of script types and decorated letters – I have not singled out a particular face, as both designations contain so many individualized designs.

It must be admitted that the classification of printing types is a controversial subject and one upon which little amicable agreement may be expected. In my short study, *Printing Types: An Introduction* (Beacon Press, 1971), I compared some of the current systems that have evolved internationally during the past forty years, and then I attempted to rationalize a nomenclature that would help to simplify the study of types. It is this method that I have followed in arranging the sequence of types for this book.

The system begins with Blackletter ('Gothic' in European terminology) and continues into the romans with Oldstyle, subdivided into Venetian, Aldine-French, and Dutch-English. The romans conclude with Transitional and Modern, followed by Square Serif and Sans Serif. The listing is completed with Script-Cursive and Display-Decorative. After using this system in the teaching of typography over a thirty-year period, I know that it is reasonably effective in the initial study of printing types. I am not disposed to consider it faultless by any means. A classification system, after all, is simply a tool, extremely useful in sorting out the myriad forms already available, but not an end in itself. Its primary purpose is to help people become familiar with these forms preparatory to putting them to effective and constructive typographic use.

This book has been written during a period of tremendous technological change in the field of typography. Since about 1950, when the first simplified procedure was evolved for the composing of type by photographic methods, printing from metal types has been in decline. This metamorphosis, continuing from simple mechanical typesetting through various stages to high-speed computer-oriented composition, has brought with it a transformation that promises to abrogate five centuries of traditional craftsmanship in the assembling of the printed word.

The typesetting machine is now available in such multitudinous variety that the conventional methods of composing-room apprenticeship are no longer valid. In addition, small firms are increasingly attracted to what is primarily a new industry using 'word processing' techniques. Since all of the new devices are equipped with typewriter keyboards, little is required of an operator except basic typing skills.

Such shifts in customary typographic practice inevitably have resulted in a decline of quality. This is particularly noticeable in book typography. Any comparison of contemporary trade books with those produced twenty or more years ago will reveal a retrogression in the standards of production, affecting such details as the proper selection of type style and size, the use of italics and small capitals, legible spacing between words and lines, and the like. Formerly the responsibility of skilled craftsmen, these aspects of design are now too often disregarded. Frequently, these niceties of typographic design are not even *available*.

Some of these difficulties, which are to be expected in a transitory situation, may be alleviated through the efforts of trade associations to evolve and sponsor training procedures and promote standards of quality. To this end, there is an increasing need for the study of the history of printing types. Certainly, the current technology of typesetting has resulted in the manufacture of composing machines capable of maintaining all that is best in traditional typography.

One other concern remains to be mentioned in this introductory note: the current lack of copyright protection for contemporary type designers and manufacturers of composing devices, who are understandably reluctant to underwrite and produce new designs, fearing the immediate pirating of their more popular offerings. Such difficulties have been faced by designers over the past hundred years, but they have been intensified by the mushrooming of equipment manufacturers during the past two decades and the mechanical ease with which such copying can be done. Once again, this is an industry-wide problem, requiring the most intensive effort on the part of all practitioners to seek reasonably ethical standards. The alternative is clear: a serious decline in the number of new designs and, even more important, a reluctance on the part of designers to attempt the creation of new letter forms.

Since 1966 I have conducted a department, 'Typographically Speaking,' in the periodical *Printing Impressions*, in which the content of much of the present book appeared in greatly abbreviated form. I am most grateful to Irving Borowsky, publisher of *Printing Impressions*, for his kind permission to reprint these articles. I am also appreciative of the support of James F. Burns, Jr., the magazine's former editor.

Archie Provan, associate professor in the School of Printing at the Rochester Institute of Technology, and long my colleague there, has been very helpful with suggestions for improving the original articles. I have also been singularly fortunate in having for my publisher David R. Godine, who, almost unique among his contemporaries, is most knowledgeable about typographic matters and in addition maintains a personal involvement in the format and design of his books. I am also grateful for the support provided by my editor, Hilary Douglass Horton, who has humanized my journalistic prose. David Pankow, librarian of the Melbert B. Cary, Jr., Graphic Arts Collection at R.I.T., has been most helpful with the bibliography and in the selection of illustrations. Finally, my wife, Evelyn T. Lawson, has struggled valiantly in the preparation of the manuscript to overcome the numerous inconsistencies, particularly between American and British usage, that exist in typographic nomenclature.

ALEXANDER S. LAWSON
Jekyll Island, Georgia

ANATOMY
OF A
TYPEFACE

GOUDY TEXT
AND THE BLACK-LETTER TYPES

Frederic W. Goudy, prolific type designer though he was, came rather late to the design of a black-letter type, just about midway, in fact, in his prodigious output of approximately 123 type designs. Goudy's late arrival at such a basic type style was undoubtedly affected by the rather low esteem in which black-letter types, except as display, were held by the fraternity of printers in the United States during much of his active career as a type designer (1895–1945). But once his Village Letter Foundery was reasonably well established in Marlborough, New York, in 1927, Goudy came to realize that he possessed 'no black-letter type among my stock of designs.'

Although there was in the 1920s no lack of black-letter types generally available to the trade, Goudy's inclination was to provide one that followed the tradition established by Johann Gutenberg about 1440, which had since been much deviated from, particularly during the nineteenth century. And though the use of black letter had declined, most American printers recognized that for general commercial printing they required at least one such style. It was Goudy's intention to provide the perfect example of it.

A glance at some of the types of the genre then being displayed in printers' specimen books indicates the astonishing variety of black-letter styles obtainable from typefounders and composing-machine manufacturers early in the century. The two American foundries then in operation, American Type Founders Company and Barnhart Brothers & Spindler, offered respectively five and six different models, and the composing-machine firms each had three or more.

Several of these faces were reasonably sound interpretations of the historic black letters, but too many were hangovers from the nineteenth century, in which typefounders had apparently lost sight of the traditional forms and become possessed with the need to add superfluous embellishments for the sake of novelty.

Goudy Text

ABCDEFGHIJKLMNOP

QRSTUVWXYZ

abcdefghijklmnopqrstuvwxyz

& fffiffiflffl

Goudy Text

Goudy, however, was anchored to typographic tradition and consistently sought to honor its precepts. And since he had earned his living at hand-lettering and had become a teacher in the subject (about 1900), he was of course completely familiar with every style of letter form. As a type designer he favored the romans, but his skill with the pen along with his knowledge of historic letter structure assured the felicity of his approach to a black letter.

In his textbook *Elements of Lettering*, published in 1922, Goudy had drawn a black letter that he called Goudy Black. He returned to this virile alphabet for the foundation of the type that was completed in 1928. While Goudy Black had originally been cut for distribution through the designer's own small foundry, its use in a Christmas card prompted the president of the Lanston Monotype Machine Company, Harvey Best, to request Goudy's cooperation in making it available as a Monotype face, thus giving the new type distribution far beyond the confines of the tiny shop in Marlborough. In the intervening years Goudy Text, the name suggested by the Monotype firm, has become the most widely used type of its kind in the United States.

To modern readers black-letter types are difficult to read. The illegibility stems primarily from unfamiliarity – the types are infrequently used today – but in addition the form has certain peculiarities, particularly in the construction of the capitals. During its long period of development, from the eleventh to the fifteenth century, the dual alphabet – the combination of majuscule (capitals) and minuscule (lowercase) characters – became fully established in manuscripts. Because capitals were frequently used for decorative initials, the scribes chose to embellish them; they also added lines and flourishes to fill in the counters (enclosed white spaces) of the capitals that appeared to be excessively open in relation to the narrower and heavier lowercase characters. This practice, although creating an art form, reduced the cohesiveness of the letters as units of an alphabet and made them difficult to distinguish.

A study of the manuscripts produced in the late-medieval period discloses the enormous range of decoration in the construction of black-letter capitals, resulting in almost no consistency of style. In the age of typography, the designers of printing types based on the scribal hands were thus faced with a problem, and their inability to come up with a uniform style meant that many of the contradictions of the copyists persisted.

Goudy approached the problem by creating a second series of capitals, based on the roman scripts common to book hands of the eighth to the eleventh century. These he named Lombardic Capitals, and they were made available as an alternate for the standard Goudy Text capitals. Their romanized style permits greater legibility and at the same time they add a decorative touch otherwise lacking. Most

Lombardic Capitals

printers who purchased Goudy Text also acquired the Lombardic Capitals, which are useful both as initials and also for the occasional headings for which a standard black letter would be inappropriate.

Goudy Text adheres quite closely in overall appearance to the true textura letter of mid-fifteenth-century Italy. *Textura* is an Italian term derived from the 'woven' appearance of a page of black letter; it is quite condensed and avoids the excessive ornamentation that was later applied to the black-letter types. Goudy was evidently also influenced by French models, however, as he refrained from using the traditional diamond at the foot of the perpendiculars, except for the lowercase *i* and *l*. Here again, the result is increased legibility.

In his autobiography, *A Half-Century of Type Design and Typography, 1895–1945*, published in 1946, just a year before his death, Goudy confessed to a typographic faux pas in the addition of a tiny pointed projection at the left side of the stems of the letters *b*, *h*, *k*, and *l*; this spur belongs properly only to the letter *l*, to differentiate it from the figure 1. He noted that no one had mentioned the historic error to him since the type had been produced in 1928.

Goudy need not have been overly concerned, as the recognition and proper identification of black-letter types has always been a subject of great confusion among printers and even typographers. The classification of printing types is at best an imprecise subject, and in the area of black-letter types it can be chaotic, requiring an intensive study of sources not readily accessible to most typographers. As even paleographers and bibliographers have always found themselves at odds on the matter, it is unlikely that ordinary printers of the present era – when such types are rarely seen – will ever be able to arrive at satisfactory conclusions regarding black-letter nomenclature. Neither has there been agreement concerning the numerous appellations given to the letter form; in addition to black letter, it has been called gothic, text letter, textur, textura, English, and Old English.

Nevertheless, it is worthwhile to trace in outline the development of black letter, since at least there is general agreement among printing historians on the essential facts.

The northern-European gothic manuscript hand that in the mid-fifteenth century became the inspiration for the first printing types was the product of some four hundred years of change in the structure of letters. It is not necessary to go back further than the ninth-century reforms in writing promulgated by Charlemagne, for black letter evolved from this early book hand, now called Carolingian minuscule.

The 42-line Bible of Johann Gutenberg, Mainz, 1455

Carolingian writing was round and open, and indeed was the fundamental inspiration for the style formulated by the humanist Italian
scribes in the late fourteenth and early fifteenth centuries. Eventually
this humanist style resulted in the roman types of the closing decades
of the fifteenth century.

Letter of Indulgence, Mainz, 1455

North of the Alps, in the twelfth century, the roundness of the Carolingian script was giving way to letters considerably more condensed and far heavier in stroke. This was because the monasteries, long dominant in the making of books, were at that time being displaced by the universities, which had different requirements, particularly the production of textbooks. By the thirteenth century it had become customary for the university scribes, in the interest of conserving space and materials, to invent contractions, or joined letters, a practice that also decreased the time spent on lettering an entire text; in the letters themselves stub endings began to replace tapering strokes. By the fourteenth century the terminals of many lowercase characters were being ended in a compact diamond.

Further standardization of the alphabet occurred when craftsmen outside the university writing rooms employed the written word. These were the architects and artisans, such as goldsmiths and medallists, who produced inscriptions in stone, wood, and metal. Economy of letter production was essential to these crafts, and the resultant systematization affected the styles of the scribes. Architectural fetish in letter forms, rigidly adhered to, made the textura character so narrow as to be almost illegible. It was believed, for example, that the letter *i* could be employed as the unit of width on which to build almost the entire minuscule alphabet.

Thus, by 1440 – the date upon which most historians agree that Gutenberg began the experiments that resulted in the invention of movable type – the accepted form of writing had become reasonably standardized. Moreover, Gutenberg realized the importance, in printing the Bible and other liturgical works with which he initiated his art, of employing the particular textura of his own time and place, fifteenth-century Germany. When it became the punchcutters' task to reproduce his letters in metal, they quickly recognized the standardized forms he had used.

In addition, during this long period of the development of the gothic forms, there were a number of other variations that affected the construction of black letter. Depending on the text to be copied, for example, scribes had been using different scripts: works of law, writings of the church fathers, commentaries of all kinds, and literature in the vernacular, each requiring its own style. It soon became apparent to the printers that they too would be expected to supply different styles for particular applications.

Evidence of this influence on type was almost immediate. In fact, during the period of the production of Gutenberg's first Bible, he printed two indulgences that were set in slightly different types, though both had a textura for headings. (These Mainz Indulgences, incidentally, represent the first dated printing, 1454–55.) The types followed two variants of the style used by law clerks, and were excellent renderings of this almost cursive script; the letters are much more open and free of the conventions of the textura. The English typographic historian Harry Carter has called them *bastardas*, another term used in the classification of gothics, which will be discussed below. Carter has high praise for the Mainz Indulgence types.

The earliest attempt to create what might be called a book type – that is, a type more useful for classical (Greek and Roman) as opposed to liturgical works – was the letter cut by Peter Schoeffer for use in the *Rationale* of Durandus, printed in 1459. Now termed the Durandus type, this was the first gothic to be cast in a small size, a large pica. It has the rounded form of roman but lacks the serifs of that style. The

ut confolarent eas ðe fratre fuo. Martha
ergo ut audiuit ꝗ iḣefus veit occurrit illi:
maria aūt ðomi fedebat. Dixit ergo martha
ad iḣefū. Domine:fi fuiſſes hic frater meus
nõ firiſſet moꝛtuus. Sed a nūc fcio:ꝗ que-
cūꝗ popofceris a ðeo ðabit tibi ðeus. Dicit
illi iḣus. Refurget frater tuus. Dicit ei martha. Scio ꝗ refurget in refurrectõe in no-
uiſſimo ðie. Dicit ei iḣs. Ego fū refurrectõ
et vita. Qui credit in me etiam fi moꝛtuus
fuerit viuet:et omnis qui viuit a credit in
me:nõ moꝛiet in eternū. Credis hoc Ait
illi. Vtiꝗ ðne. Ego credidi ꝗ tu es criftus

et facies illius fudario erat ligata. Dixit ei
iḣefus. Soluite eum: a finite abire. Multi
ergo ex iuðeis qui venerat ad mariā et mar-
thaꝫ viderant que fecit iḣefus: credideꝛt
in eum. Quidaꝫ aūt ex ipis abieꝛt ad pha-
rifeos:et dixerūt eis que fecit iḣefus. Colle-
gerūt ergo pontifices a pharifei concilīū: et
dicebant. Quid facimus Quia hic homo
multa figna facit. Si dimittimus eum fic:
omes credét in eū. Et veniét romani: a tollét
locū noftrū a genté. Vnus auteꝫ ex ipis cai-
phas nomine:cū eſſet pontifex āni illius dixit eis Vos nefcitis qcꝗ nec cogitatis:ꝗ

A a B C D E F ʜ ʜ ᴊ ʀ ᴌ M ᴏ ɴ ᴏ P ᴘ ᴏ Q q ᴏ

ʀ ꝫ ꜱ ᴛ ʙ ᴠ ꝫ x ʏ ꝫ

a ã ȧ b bͤ bͤ bo b̃ c ć ȧ cͣ cã ce cͤa co cõ cꝛ cͣu cü ᴅ d ð ð̄ ðͤ ðͦ e ė ē ec et

f fͤ ff fi fo fr fra fu g g gͤ g̈ g̈ g̈ g̈' b ʜ bͤ bͤ bo i i i ı ī ī n̈ m m̄ m ü l lͤ llm

m mi n ñ n̈ ñ o õ õ œ ø p p̄ p̄ pͣ pͤ pͦ po põ pp pͦp pp ꝑ ꝓ q q q̄ q̄ q̄ q̄ q̄q̄

cꝗ ꝗ ꝗ r rͣ rͣ ra rä ru rū ꝫ s ꝭſ fi ꝭſſ fh ft fu fū ꝼ ꝶ t tͤ tͤ te tͤ tͤ ti tͤ to tu tͤi u

ü ü ui ui v ꝟ ꝩ vꝫ w x x̄ ꝫ ꝫ ɑ ꝗ . · ꝫ o ꝥ ꝯ

Blackletter of Peter Schoeffer in his 1462 Bible

lowercase *g* with an upper and lower bowl and an 'ear' makes its first
appearance in a printing type in this font.

Schoeffer apparently wished to break away from the formal textura
and return to the later book letters of the preceding century. Historians
still differ about the provenance of the Durandus type and its classification, but it is most frequently referred to as gotica-antiqua, or
gothic-antique, with *antique* here used in its European sense, meaning
'roman': hence, a type with both gothic and roman characteristics.
Harry Carter, however, is of the opinion that since the Durandus
type was a re-creation of a fourteenth-century northern-European
book hand, it was not influenced by the roman forms, and thus he
prefers to use *gothic-antique* only for those faces in which the designer
definitely leaned to the roman models.

Schoeffer later improved upon this type and used it for the edition
of the Bible he printed in 1462. Hellmut Lehmann-Haupt, Schoeffer's
biographer, has called this Bible type Schoeffer's masterpiece. It was

widely copied during Schoeffer's time by such printers as Ulrich Zell and Günther Zainer, but by the end of the century the style had given way to the rotundas, or round gothics. Nevertheless, its influence as a gothic book type persisted: four centuries later William Morris in England used it as the inspiration for his Troy and Chaucer types at the Kelmscott Press.

Another group of gothics to sanction a breakaway from the formal texturas came under the heading southern gothic, also called *rotunda*, or round gothic. As a letter form, emerging about the thirteenth century, rotunda had been favored by the Italian and Spanish scribes. Based like the textura on the Carolingian minuscule, the rotunda, however, took a different direction south of the Alps, retaining the openness of its progenitor but affirming the strength of the gothic stroke.

When printing came to the Italian peninsula, in 1465, and quickly spread to numerous locations, rotundas were cut by many of the printers. The Venetian Nicolas Jenson, particularly – known in our time for his roman type – was highly praised by his contemporaries for his fine rotunda, which he used for law texts. His fellow Venetian Wendelin da Spira, along with several other Italian printers, also cut rotundas for books on canon law, making it difficult to determine which printer was actually responsible for establishing the rotunda for such texts.

Colophon of Schoeffer's 1462 Bible

Almost immediately the rotundas found favor with the northern printers, quite possibly owing to the general admiration for Italian humanism. The style was adopted for a great variety of printing uses, particularly for works in Latin, and by the end of the fifteenth century it was being employed in Germany, the Low Countries, and France, as well as in Italy and Spain.

The final development of the gothic hand as a printing type occurred with its adaptation to the cursive, or written, form, although this was restricted to northern Europe. During the last three decades of the fifteenth century, when the market for printing had been much enlarged, the printers turned to the vernacular hands that abounded, especially in Germany, as a source for types that departed from the formal gothics and semiformal rotundas. The great demand for inexpensive books – almanacs, dream books (interpreting dreams as omens), household books, and other popular literature – prompted the cutting of these easily recognized types, which had broad appeal among the increasing numbers of people who could read.

The classifiers of type place all the informal gothics under the French heading *lettre bâtarde*. However, numerous authorities believe that this term should be used only in reference to the French national hand of the fifteenth century, which was converted to type soon after printing came to France, in 1470, and spread to the Low Countries and England when William Caxton began printing at Westminster, in 1476. A. F. Johnson, the English expert on early types, prefers simply to use the term *bastard*, although the Latinized *bastarda* is more generally employed by historians.

The 1454–55 Mainz Indulgences exhibit the first types of this group. Nothing is known of these particular faces beyond that time, but by 1490 bâtardes were in wide use in Germany, where the name applied

---

Therefore J, William Carton, a symple personne, have endevopred me to wryte fyrst over all the said Book of Polycronycon, and sommewhat have chaunged the rude and old Englisshe that is to wete, Certain words which in these days be neither usyd ne understanden.

Flemish Blackletter types used by William Caxton

to them, apparently arbitrarily, was Schwabacher (there is no evident reason why the Bavarian town of Schwabach was thus memorialized, as there was no typefounding or even printing at that location).

Until almost the middle of the sixteenth century the Schwabacher style was what was most used for German-language printing; it was saliently used at Basel in Switzerland, then a center of scholarly printing. The next important bâtarde to be developed in Germany was the Fraktur design, which for the following four centuries served as the German national type.

Fraktur is a more condensed letter than the Schwabacher, and varies from the earlier type in being more pointed, with sharply tapered ascenders; printers naturally had a fondness for this narrower form, which made the type more economical in book work. The design of Fraktur is credited to the Nuremberg calligrapher Johann Neudörfer, and at the request of Emperor Maximilian it was cut in metal for type in 1513. Within the next decade a number of other Frakturs were produced, and by the 1540s it was beginning to replace Schwabacher as the preferred letter for German printing.

At the same time that the Schwabacher types were emerging for vernacular printing in Germany, a French bâtarde was coming into popularity in western Europe. It remained a little closer than the Schwabacher to the textura, but with the rounder features of the bâtarde letters. Its first appearance dates from about 1475, and within the next few years it came into wide use in Paris and Lyons and also spread to Switzerland and the Low Countries. It was this design, originally employed at Bruges by William Caxton, that became the first type to be used in England, when Caxton established his press there in 1476. For about sixty years it was almost the English national type, but by the middle of the sixteenth century the influence of the roman designs had begun to dominate English as well as French printing.

One other French innovation in the design of black letter, occurring during the last decade of the fifteenth century, had a strong influence in England, and it remains up to the present a basic contribution to the style of textura types. This design forgoes the narrowness of the original German models, and substitutes curves for the rather inflexible vertical strokes of the first texturas. One of the finest examples of this French textura was used by the Paris printer-publisher Antoine Verard. Caxton had acquired the type by 1490, and Wynkyn de Worde, who took over Caxton's business after his death, used a similar textura, as did the English printer Richard Pynson. It was employed in the first printing of the Book of Common Prayer, in 1549, and in 1611 for the Bible printed at the command of King James.

Joseph Moxon, in his *Mechanick Exercises* of 1683 – the first English manual of printing – called this type the Black English Letter; his reproduction of it closely follows the Verard textura. In the eighteenth century William Caslon's classic Black Letter was almost identical to that of Moxon, thus continuing the tradition of the fifteenth-century French textura into the standardized black letter of our own times.

In the long run it was the classical influence of the Renaissance that spelled the end of the prevalence that the gothic hands had maintained in northern Europe since the twelfth century. Only in Germany did it remain a convention, where it survived as a text type even into the twentieth century. Elsewhere, by the close of the eighteenth century black letter was being used primarily for headings and for specialized liturgical printing. In every other instance the roman letter forms had taken over the world of printing.

Even in Germany, where Fraktur was for so long the national type, the black letter has had a curious history. During the middle years of the nineteenth century, a great period of European nationalism, the use of Fraktur was inevitably strengthened – sufficiently, in fact, to offset the modernizing influence of the Industrial Revolution, particularly through the dominance of German technical and scientific literature. With the growth of international advertising in the early years of the present century, the use of roman type in Germany increased, but even as late as 1930 almost sixty percent of the new books being published were still composed in the German black letter (also called Deutsche Schriften), and almost every newspaper stayed with the Fraktur.

When Adolf Hitler came to power, his National Socialist Party decreed that the Fraktur be considered the only appropriate letter form for the German language. This resulted in a wider use of Fraktur in the twentieth century than in earlier times. In 1940, however, it was officially determined that Fraktur interfered with the German plan of world domination, since outside Germany the roman forms prevailed. Thus, the Nazis then issued a proclamation that roman would henceforth be the German standard type, the explanation given being that Fraktur was a 'Schwabacher-Jewish type.'

In postwar Germany roman has become the standard type, although with some difficulty, as the schoolbooks through which all

Fraktur type in the *Prayer Book of Maximilian I*, Augsburg, 1513

adults had learned their alphabet were composed in black letter. But there is little likelihood that Fraktur will ever again be the national type; now less than one percent of German books appear in that hand. As a display letter, however, the face has been revived.

Urely vaine are all men by nature, who are ignorant of God, and could not out of the good things that are seene, know him that is : neither by considering the workes, did they acknowledge the worke-master,

*Rom. 1.9.
deut. 4.19.
and 17.3.

2 *But deemed either fire, or wind, or the swift aire, or the circle of the stars, or the violent water, or the lights of heauen to be the gods which gouerne the world :

3 With whose beautie, if they being delighted, tooke them to be gods: let them know how much better the Lord of them is; for the first Author of beautie hath created them.

4 But if they were astonished at their power and vertue, let them vnderstand by them, how much mightier he is that made them.

5 For by the greatnesse and beautie of the creatures, proportionably the Maker of them is seene.

6 But yet for this they are the lesse to bee blamed : for they peraduenture erre seeking God, and desirous to finde him.

*Rom. 1.21
|| Or, seeke.

7 For being * conuersant in his workes, they || search him diligently, and beleeue their sight : because the things are beautifull that are seene.

8 Howbeit, neither are they to bee pardoned.

9 For if they were able to know so much, that they could aime at the world; how did they not sooner finde out the Lord thereof?

10 But miserable are they, and in dead things is their hope, who called them gods which are the workes of mens hands, golde and siluer, to shewe arte in, and resemblances of beasts, or a stone good for nothing, the worke of an ancient hand.

*Isai 44.13.
|| Or, timber-wright.

11 *Now a || carpenter that felleth timber, after hee hath sawen downe a tree meet for the purpose, and taken off all the barke skilfully round about, and hath wrought it handsomely, & made a vessell thereof fit for the seruice of mans life :

|| Or, chips.

12 And after spending the || refuse of his worke to dresse his meat, hath filled himselfe :

13 And taking the very refuse among those which serued to no vse (being a crooked piece of wood, and ful of knots)

hath carued it diligently when hee had nothing else to doe, and formed it by the skill of his vnderstanding, and fashioned it to the image of a man :

14 Or made it like some vile beast, laying it ouer with vermilion, and with paint, colouring it red, and couering euery spot therein :

15 And when he had made a conuenient roume for it, set it in a wall, and made it fast with yron :

16 For he prouided for it, that it might not fall: knowing that it was vnable to helpe it selfe, (for it is an image and hath neede of helpe :)

17 Then maketh hee prayer for his goods, for his wife and children, and is not ashamed to speake to that which hath no life.

18 For health, hee calleth vpon that which is weake : for life, prayeth to that which is dead : for aide, humbly beseecheth † that which hath least meanes to helpe : and for a good iourney, hee asketh of that which cannot set a foot forward :

† Gr. that hath no experience at all.

19 And for gaining and getting, and for good successe of his hands, asketh abilitie to doe, of him that is most vnable to doe any thing.

CHAP. XIIII.

1 Though men doe not pray to their shippes, 5 Yet are they saued rather by them then by their Idoles. 8 Idoles are accursed, and so are the makers of them. 14 The beginning of Idolatrie, 23 And the effects thereof. 30 God wil punish them that sweare falsely by their Idoles.

Gaine, one preparing himselfe to saile, and about to passe through the raging waues, calleth vpon a piece of wood more rotten then the || vessell that carieth him.

|| Or, ship.

2 For verely desire of gaine deuised || that, and the workeman built it by his || skill :

|| Or, vessell or ship.

3 But thy prouidence, O Father, gouerneth it : for thou hast * made a way in the Sea, and a safe path in the waues :

*Exod.14. 22.

4 Shewing that thou canst saue from all danger : yea though a man went to Sea without arte.

5 Neuerthelesse thou wouldest not that the workes of thy wisedome should be idle, and therefore doe men commit their

The King James Bible printed by Robert Barker, London, 1611

Capitulū Quartum.

ad gratie donū suscipiēdū ē actus liberi arbitrij moti a do. Et ꝗtū ad hoc dicitur homo se p̃pa rare: ꝓm illud ꝓuer. xvi. Dois e preparare aiuz. Et est a deo pnciplr mouente liberu arbitrium. Et ꝯm hoc oi a deo voluntas hois p̃parari: et gressus hois dirigi. ¶ Sciēdū ē ꝙ duplex ē pre paratio hois ad gratiá. Una ē que est simul cum gratie infusione Et talis p̃paratio est meritoria nō quidē gratie que iā hr̄ur: sed gr̃e que nōdum habetur. i. augmētatōis eius. Est alia p̃paratio que ē gr̃e gratú faciētis: que tn̄ ē a deo mouente sed non sufficit ad meritū hois nōdū per gr̃am iu sificati: qr̄ nullū meritū pōt esse nisi ex gr̃a. Item ista preparatio ad donū gratie recipiendū nōduz habite: contingit duplr. Cum. n. ut dictū ē: sit a deo p̃ueniente mouente voluntatem ho. s ad bo nū. Q̃nꝗ̃ deus mouet hoiem ad bonū: nō tame p̃fectū: ꞇ talis preparatio precedit gratiá gratum facientem ēt tp̃re. Sicut mouet frequenter p̃ma nentes in peccato: ad faciēdū elemosynas: ieiuia: oratōes ꞇ h̃mói. Sicut mouit. b. Aug. añ couer satione ad audiēdū p̃dicatōes Ambrosij exbor tatōes simpliciū: exēpla Antonij. Un dicit ō pe. di. v. Admonem̃ de p̃seuerante in odio uel alio crimine ꝙcꝙ bōi poterit: ꝙ faciat. S. elemosynas ie iunia: oratōes: ꞇ h̃: ut dē̃ cꝯ cor illustret. S. p gra tiā gratú faciēte. Q̃nꝗ̃ vo dē̃ statim mouet ho minē ad perfectū bonū: ꞇ subito hō accipit gra tiam. vñ dicit Ecci. xi. Facile est in oculis dei subi to hō estare pauperē. Et Jo. vi. O is ꝙ audit a pa tre ꞇ didicit uenit ad me. Sic accidit in Saulo: qui cū actu p̃sequeretur ecclesiā ꞇ iter agēt ad capiē dum christianos: subito luce circūfultus recepit gratiá: Act. ix. Lū g̃ a do sit ista p̃paratio: n̄ refert ꝙ fuit statim uel paulati. Agens. n. infinite vtutis deus: sicut exigit māz vel disp̃ōez m̃e: quasi p̃sup posita et alterius cā̃e actōe: ita ꞇ sine eo: sed in su bito pōt māz disp̃ōe ꞇ formā introducē: ꞇ ꞇt pal ius tpe disp̃ōe māz paulati ꞇ postea formā indu cere: sicut in sanitate contingit que aliqñ paulati i̓utroducif: aliqñ. i̓ subito in sanatōe miraclosa.

Quātū ad tertiū. S. §. II.

ꝙ preparatio hois ad gratiá: n̄ necessitat ad gra tiā p̃ hoc ex eo ꝙ hō cōparat ad deū: sicut lutū ad figuli: ꝓm illud. Diere. xviij. Sicut lutū in ma nu figuli: ita ꞇ uos i̓n manu mea ait dñs. Lutū at nō accipit ex necessitate formā a figulo: ꝙtúcúꝗ sit figurati. Pro cui' declaratoe dr̄. b. Tho. p̃ ma ꝑe. q. cxij. ar. iij. ꝙ p̃paratio hois ad gratiá est a deo sicut a mouente: ꞇ a libero arbitrio sic mo to. Pōt igif gratie cōsiderari duplr accipi. Uno mó. put ē a libero arbitrio: ꞇ ꝓm hoc nulla neces sitate h̄z ad gr̃e cōsecutiōem: qr̄ donū gr̃e excedit oēm p̃parationē vtutis hũane. Alio mó pōt con siderari ꝓm ꝙ ē a deo mouente: ꞇ tunc h̃z necessi

tatem ad id ad qō ordinatur: nō ꝙdē necessitatez coactōis: sed infallibilitatis: qr̄ intentio dei deficie nō pōt: ꝓm qō dicit. b. Aug. de p̃destinatōe sctor̃z ꝙ per beneficia dei liberátur certissime quicūꝗ liberantur. Un si i̓ ex i̓ntentione dei mouentis ē: ꝙ hō cuius cor mouet gratia cōsequatur: infallibi liter illam cōsequatur: ꝓm illud Jo. vi. Ois ꝙ audit a patre ꞇ didicit uenit ad me. Qō dr̄ dicit glo. ad Ro. v. De' recipit eū qui cōfugit ad se aliter cēt i eo iniquitas: i̓ntelligitur de illo qui confugit ad eū per actum liberi arbitrij : iam per gr̃am i̓formati quem si non reciperet: esset ꝫ iusticiá quá ipse sta tuit. Et sciendum ꝙ defectus gratie prima cā ē ex nobis. Sed collatōis prima causa est ex deo: scōz illud Osee. xiij. Perditio tua isr̃l: tm̃ ex te: ex me auxilium tuum.

Quātū ad quartū. §. III.

S. ꝙ non sit in oibus equaliter gratia: manifestat ex hoc qō dic aplus ad ephe. iiij. Unicuiꝗ uestrū datur gratia ꝓm mensuram donatōis xp̃i. S3 qō mensuratur: non equaliter datur ꞇc. Et hoc sic ō clarat. b. Tho. p̃ma secunde. q. cxij. art. iiij. Dabi tus duplicem habitudinem habē pōt. Unum ex parte finis vel obiecti: ꝙ dicitur vna virtus nobilior altera: qr̄ ad maius bonum ordinatur. Alio modo ex parte subiecti: qō magis uł minus ꝑticipat habitum inherentem. Secundū ergo p̃mam habitudinem : gratia non potest esse ma ior ꞇ minor: qr̄ gratia ꝓm sui rationem: coniūgit hominem summo bono quod est deus. Sed ex parte subiecti pōt suscipere magis ꞇ minus prout S. min' vel perfectius illustratur a lumine gratie vnus ꝙ alius. Cuius diuersitatis ratio ē: ex aliqua parte preparantis se ad gratiam. Qui eniz se ma gis ad grām preparat plenore3 grām recipit. S3 ex hac parte non potest accipi prima ratō diuer sitatis hui'. qr̄ preparatio non est hois nisi i quan tum liberum arbitrium eius preparatur a deo Unde prima causa huius diuersitatis est ex parte dei: qr̄ diuersimode sue gratie dona dispensat: ad hoc ꝙ ex diuersis gradibus gratie pulchritudo ecclesie consurgat ꞇ perfectio. Sicut etiam et di uersos gradus rerum instituit ut esset perfectum vniuersum. Unde aplus ad ephe. iiij. enumeratis pluribus gratie subdit: ad consumarionem sanc torum edificationem corporis xp̃i. Qō autez di citur sap. vi. Equaliter ipsi est cura de omnibus: non intelligitur ꝙ det dona gratie equaliter: sicut nec nature gradus: sed quia unico actu ꞇ simplici maiora ꞇ minora dispensat. Cyprianus: de cōse. di. iiij. sic ait. Plane eadem gratia spiritualis: ꝙ a baptismo equaliter a credentibus sũmif: i̓ puer satōe atꝗ actu nostro postmodu uel minuit uel augetur: ut i euāgelio dñico. Cum semen equalit seminatur: sed p uarietate terre: aliud absumitur

To return to Goudy Text, in the half century since its initial appearance it has become the standard for the use of black letter in the United States. One other type, however, has also been extremely popular, and this is Cloister Black, cut by Morris Benton and Joseph W. Phinney for the American Type Founders Company in 1904.

Cloister Black is a true English black letter, deriving from the late-fifteenth-century French style that was taken to England before 1500 and became so well established that it was used for the first setting of the King James Bible. Then through the later influence of William Caslon it continued in popularity. This is the type most frequently called Old English, a term more widely employed in the United States than in any other country. Like Goudy Text, Cloister is frequently used for newspaper titles, diplomas, certificates, and the like.

In addition to Goudy Text and Cloister Black the most commonly seen black letter is Wedding Text, another Benton design (1906). It may be said of Wedding Text that in its time it was the best-selling black letter of all, and absolutely no printing shop would have done without it. If the definition of embellish is 'to enhance with fictitious additions,' then truly Wedding Text is a black letter with embellishment to spare. Its use was de rigueur for well over a generation of printers until it was superseded in the twenties by Park Avenue Script.

Returning to the purer black letters, there are two that have received wide critical acclaim on the part of discerning typographers, and no account of black-letter types would be complete without them. Both are bâtardes but contain individual anachronisms that make it difficult to pinpoint their classification.

The first of the pair, and undoubtedly the most admired all over the world, is Jessen Schrift, the design of which was begun in 1924 by Rudolf Koch. Originally named Koch Bibel Gotisch ('Bible gothic') – for its first use in a magnificent edition of *The Four Gospels*, printed privately at the Klingspor Foundry in Offenbach, Germany – Jessen is an individualistic black letter that follows no particular historic model. A feature that has probably contributed much to its popularity is the romanized capital alphabet: these letters may be used independently as capitals, giving the font a strong utilitarian value, yet they blend so well with the lowercase that their roman form is not distracting.

The initial use of Bibel Gotisch in the United States was by the Grabhorn Press in San Francisco. The Grabhorn brothers, Edwin and Robert, may also claim this as the first commercial use of the type

winded close without, and thereafter came the clatter of arms about the door, and exceeding tall weaponed men came in, one score and five, & strode two by two up to the foot of the dais, and stood there in a row. ⟨And Hallblithe deemed their war-gear exceeding good; they were all clad in ring-locked byrnies, and had steel helms on their heads with garlands of gold wrought about them and they bore spears in their hands, and white shields hung at their backs. Now came the women to them and unarmed them; & under their armour their raiment was black; but they had gold rings on their arms, and golden collars about their necks. So they strode up to the dais and took their places on the high-seat, not heeding Hallblithe any more than if he were an image of wood. Nevertheless that man was next to him who was the chieftain of all and sat in the midmost high-seat; and he bore his sheathed sword in his hand and laid it on the board before him, and he was the only man of those chieftains who kept a weapon. But when these were set down, there was again a noise without, and there came in a throng of men armed and unarmed who took their places on the endlong benches up & down the hall; with these came women also, who most of them sat amongst the men, but some busied them with the serving: all these men were great of stature, but none so big as the chieftains on the high-seat. NOW came the women in from the kitchen bearing the meat, whereof no little was flesh-meat, and all was of the best ⟨Hallblithe was duly served like the others, but still none spake to him or even looked on him; though amongst

The Chaucer type of William Morris, 1891

outside the Klingspor Foundry. It was selected for *The Voiage and Travaile of Sir John Maundevile, Kt.*, a medieval text printed in 1928, which was illustrated by Valenti Angelo, who also hand-illuminated the initials. It is an altogether beautiful book. The artist tells an amusing

gefinde nachfolgen vnſerm wege
mit ſenfftem gang mitſambt dem
er hauß frawe·vñ mit dem vyhe·
Vnd do diſes gefiele das ſÿ gien/
gen·raphael ſprache zů thobiam·
Nym̄ mit dir von der gallen des
fiſches·wañ ſÿ wirt notdürfftig
Darumbe thobias name võ der
gallen·vnd ſÿ giengen hyn·Vnd
anna ſaß täglich bey dem wege·
auff der höhe des berges·dauon
ſÿ mocht geſehen võ ferre·Vnd
do ſÿ wartet võ der ſelben ſtat·ſÿ
ſahe ſein zůkunfft võ ferre·vñ ze
handt erkañt ſÿ zůkömen jren ſu
ne·ſÿ lieff vñ verkündet jrē mañ
ſagend·Siehe dein ſune kumbt·
Vnd raphael ſprach zů thobiam
So du wirſt eingeen in dein hauß
zůhandt anbete deinem herrē got·
vnd ſage jm genad·vmb nähne
dich zů deinem vater·vñ küß jn
Vnd zůhandt ſalbe auff ſeine au/
gen võ der gallen des fiſches· die
du tregſt mit dir·Wañ wiſſe daz
zůhandt werdent auffgeton ſeine
augen·vnd dein vater wirt ſehē
das liecht des hÿmels·vñ freüet
ſich in deinem angeſicht· Do für
lieſſ der hund der mit jm was ge
weſen an dem wege als ein bott·
vñ freüet ſich mit der wadlung
ſeines ſchwanⱬes·Vnd ð blÿnd
vater ſtůnd auff·er begunde zů
lauffen vnd zů ſtoſſen mit den füſ
ſen·er gabe die handt dem kynde
vnd lieffe entgegen ſeinem ſune·
Er empfienge jn·vnnd küſſet jn
mit ſeiner hauß frawen·vñ ſÿ be
gunden beyde zů weynē vor freü
den·Vnd do ſÿ heten angebet got
vnd heten geſaget·ſÿ ſaſſen ſa zů

men· Do name thobias von ðr
gallen des fiſches·er ſalbet die au
gen ſeines vaters·Vnd er gedul
det es ſchier ein halbe ſtund· vnd
ein weyſſe als ein heüdtlein eins
eyes·begunde außgeen võ ſeinen
augen·vnd zůhandt empfieng er
die geſicht·Vnd ſÿ loberen got er
vnd ſein hauß fraw· vnd alle die
die jn erkantten·Vnd thobias ſp
rach·O herre got iſrahel·ich ge/
ſegne dich·wañ du haſt mich ge
keſtigt· vnd haſt mich behalten·
Siehe·ich ſiehe thobiam meinen
ſune·Vnd nach ſiben tagen·ſara
das weyb ſeines ſuns gieng ein
geſundt·vnd alles jngeſinde· vñ
auch vyhe·vnd die kämelthyer·
vnd gar vil gůts des weybs·vñ
auch das gelt das er het empfan
gen võ gabelo·Vnd er ſaget ſein
em vater vnd můter alle gůttat
gotes·die er het geton bey jm·du
rch den man der jn hette gefüret·
Vnd achior·vnd nabath·die ſch/
wöſterſüne thobie·kamen freü
wend zů thobiam·Sÿ freüetend
ſich mit jm von allen gůten din/
gen die got het geton bey jm·Vñ
ſÿ wirtſchafftten mit freüden du
rch ſiben tage·vnd wurdē erfreü
wet mit groſſer freüde·

Das xii Capitel

Wie Thobias vnd ſein ſune das
halbteyl jres gůtz Raphaeli wol
ten geben·Vnd wie er ſich offen/
baret·vnd von jn ſchiede·

Schwabacher type of Hans Schönsperger, Augsburg, 1490

ĀBCDEFGHIJKLMNO
PQRSTUVWXYZ &.,='`:;()!?

Lowercase Fonts

abcdefghijklmnopqrstuv
wxyz.,='`:;()!?

Figure Fonts

1234567890

EXTRA CHARACTERS

DEFK

Rudolf Koch's Jessen type

Rudolf Koch's Wilhelm Klingsporschrift

Incoming Officers Pledge Improved Quality and Design Change

Cloister Black (ATF)

story involving this book, indicative of the whimsical existence of Edwin and Robert Grabhorn: 'Ed had a Stutz car, which he had bought to drive to California, selling his Kelmscott *Chaucer* to get the money. I bought it from him for $600. Bob used some of that money to go to Indiana for a visit. Later I sold the car to Bill Wheeler for $100 and a copy of the *Maundevile*.'

Finally there is Goudy Thirty, so named to represent the final Goudy type (the figure –30– on newspaper copy designates the end of a story). Requesting this last type design, Harvey Best, President of the Lanston Monotype Machine Company, wrote Goudy on March 31, 1941: 'This face of course would not be used in your lifetime, but would be used by Monotype as a tribute to you.' Goudy accepted the commission, although even at the age of 76 he was in no hurry to do a 'last' type.

During the next few years Goudy worked up his ideas and by 1945 he had delivered his drawings to the Lanston office in Philadelphia. His design was for a rotunda, or southern gothic, with romanized capitals, such as in Koch's Jessen but lacking the 'gothic' weight. The type could thus lend itself to a broader application in book work. Of it, the designer wrote, 'The type pleases me; it will please some readers; it may be execrated by others; I wish that I might know how it will be received – and maybe I shall!'

But at Goudy's death on May 11, 1947, the type had still not been produced, the primary reason being that it didn't even come close to what the Monotype firm had wanted – a book type in the spirit of W. A. Dwiggins's Caledonia, an extremely popular type patterned on

THIS TYPE, SO FAR UNDER COVER AND IN COURSE OF REVISION TO ADAPT IT TO THE MONOTYPE DIE CASE, PATTERN MAKING, ETC., WAS BEGUN A YEAR or two ago to submit to a college in the West which was then seeking a type for its press; but due to war restrictions the commission fell through. When Mr Best of the Monotype Company suggested that the Company might bring out a type after I had passed on, to be called "Goudy Thirty," this design, which I had been working on at odd times, struck me as particularly adapted for the purpose. As I worked on it I had determined to make it, as far as I was able, my last word in type design, a type in which I would give my imagination full rein, and a type by which as a designer of types I would be willing to stand or fall, even though not here in the flesh to defend its possible vagaries or idiosyncrasies.

The type pleases me; it will please some readers; it may
be execrated by others; I wish that I might know
how it will be received, and
maybe I shall!
F·W·G

A B C D E F G H I J K L M N O P Q R S T U V W X Y Z

℃ This insert, which tells in Mr Goudy's own words the origin of Monotype Goudy Thirty, was printed especially for the Graphic Arts Review on mould-made Nideggen paper furnished through the cooperation of Stevens-Nelson Paper Company, New York.

12345 a b c d e f g h i j k l m n o p q r s t u v w x y z 67890

Goudy Thirty

Gold Rings

Silk Hosiery

Brightest Star

Regular Diplomat

Wedding Text (ATF)

Scotch Roman. The Thirty drawings remained in the firm's files until John Anderson, proprietor of the Pickering Press and consultant to Monotype, decided to act as Goudy's advocate. This effort resulted in the issuing of the design in 1953.

That Goudy Thirty was not a financial success for Lanston was owing to several factors: it was cut in only two sizes, 18- and 60-point (the latter for initial letters), the times were not right for a round gothic, and Monotype use in the United States was in a serious decline.

Nevertheless, the face did attract the attention of many fine printers, particularly those who still occasionally hand-set books. The Grabhorn Press bought it, as did Dorothy and Lewis Allen for their California press. Bruce Rogers in his last years admired it and purchased fonts for a series of books he planned to produce; although only one of these (*The Life of St. George*) was printed before his death in 1957, Rogers stated that he believed Thirty to be one of Goudy's best types.

2

HAMMER UNCIAL

'With this uncial type face, I am aiming at a letter form which eventually may fuse roman and black letter, those two national letter forms, into a new unity. The impulse leading to this attempt came from a strong recognition of the difference between old and modern languages, as a fact which becomes obvious to anyone who tries, as I did, to write modern languages in an antique hand, acquired from the study of old manuscripts.'

So wrote Victor Hammer in 1943. Painter, sculptor, calligrapher, wood engraver, punchcutter, and printer, Hammer was in all these activities first of all a craftsman, and he preferred to be so described. The type that Hammer was discussing was American Uncial, the design of which he had completed at Wells College in Aurora, New York. An Austrian, he had come to the United States in 1939, fleeing the Nazi tyranny.

The American Uncial of Victor Hammer was his fourth type in this form, emerging twenty-three years after his initial tentative approach to type design. Its first appearance was in 1946 in *A Dialogue on the Uncial Between a Paleographer and a Printer*, written by Hammer and printed on his hand press for Chicago's Society of Typographic Arts. This *Dialogue* is essential to an understanding of Hammer's philosophy, both as a printer and as a type designer. One sentence from it perhaps sums up the essence of his thought: 'It is my conviction that the type designer should do his work in the service of the language.'

Such an ideal to Hammer was represented by a single letter form – the uncial, which stems from the medieval writing hands of the fourth to ninth centuries. A transition from the early rigid inscriptional majuscules to the informal hand of the Carolingian minuscule (created in response to Charlemagne's writing reforms and revived by the humanists in the fifteenth century, resulting finally in the roman printing types), the uncial had a rounder, more open appearance than the

The art of book-producing was on the highest level at the time of the invention of printing. ABCDEFGHIJKLMNOPQRSTUVWXYZabcdefghijk lmnopqrstuvwxyz1234567890ff&/$.-:;!?'

ABCDEFGHIIJKLM NOPQQRSTUVW XYZ

Hammer American Uncial

Half-uncial manuscript hand, 7th-8th century

Uncial manuscript hand, 9th century

black-letter forms, which were developed after the eleventh century in northern Europe. As a young man Hammer had adopted a broad pen for his personal writing, and his fondness for this period in history had influenced his desire to duplicate the manuscript hand of the era.

The term *uncial* is somewhat obscure, having no precise definition helpful to its description as a letter form. The Latin derivation is 'ounce' or 'inch,' the latter of which has been suggested as the amount of space an uncial character originally occupied, but no such specification exists. The letter was the principal book hand of the scribes in the period mentioned above. By the seventh century, in its evolution toward the Carolingian minuscule, the form was called half-uncial, in which the development of ascenders and descenders appears. The most notable extant example is the ninth-century *Book of Kells*, highlight of the golden age of Irish monasticism.

Early in his life Hammer had been guided by the example of William Morris, and this influence was to be important in his development as a printer. Hammer's first approach to type design was the

ΡRATER IACOBI & IOSEPH & IUDAE & SIMONIS
NONNE SORORES EIUS HIC NOBISCUM SUNT &
SCANDALIZABANTUR IN ILLO ∴
DICEBAT ILLIS IHS QUIA NON EST PROFE
PHETA SINE HONORE NISI IN PATRIA SUA & IN
COGNATIONE SUA & IN DOMO SUA & NON PO
TERAT IBI VIRTUTEM ULLAM FACERE NISI PAU
COS INFIRMOS UT POSSIT AS MANIBUS CURA
VIT & MIRABATUR PROPTER INCREDULITA
TEM EORUM ⸎ DOCEBAT IS ∴
CIRCUMIBAT CASTELLA IN CIRCUITU
& CONVOCAVIT DUODECIM & COEPIT
EOS MITTERE BINOS & DABAT EIS
POTESTATEM SPIRITUUM IMMUNDORUM & PRAE
CIPIT EIS NE QUID TOLLERENT IN VIA NISI VIRGAM
TANTUM NON PERAM NON PANEM NEQUE
IN ZONA AES SED CALCIATOS SANDALIIS & NE

The Book of Kells, c. late 8th–early 9th century

drawing of an uncial letter that was cut for him in 1921 by a Viennese punchcutter, A. Schuricht, and later produced by the Klingspor Foundry in Offenbach, which named it Hammer Unziale. But although the type was successful for the foundry, Hammer never liked or used it. The collaboration with Schuricht was fruitful, however,

OF DISCOURSE·

OME IN THEIR DISCOURSE DE-
SIRE RATHER COMMENDATION
OF WIT IN BEING ABLE TO HOLDE
ALL ARGUMENTS/THEN OF
IUDGEMENT IN DISCERNING
WHAT IS TRUE/AS IF IT WERE A
PRAISE TO KNOW WHAT MIGHT
BE SAID/AND NOT WHAT SHOULDE BEE
THOUGHT·SOME HAUE CERTAINE COM-
MON PLACES AND THEAMES WHEREIN
THEY ARE GOOD/AND WANT VARIETIE/
WHICH KINDE OF POUERTIE IS FOR THE
MOST PART TEDIOUS/AND NOWE AND
THEN RIDICULOUS·§THE HONOURABLEST
PART OF TALKE/IS TO GUIDE THE OCCASION/
AND AGAINE TO MODERATE AND PASSE
TO SOMEWHAT ELSE·§IT IS GOOD TO VARIE
AND MIXE SPEECH OF THE PRESENT OC-
CASION WITH ARGUMENT/TALES WITH
REASONS/ASKING OF QUESTIONS/WITH
TELLING OF OPINIONS/AND IEST WITH EAR-
NEST·§BUT SOME THINGES ARE PRIUI-
LEDGED FROM IEST/NAMELY RELIGION/
MATTERS OF STATE/GREAT PERSONS/
ANY MANS PRESENT BUSINESSE OF IM-
PORTANCE/AND ANY CASE THAT DESER-
UETH PITTIE·§HE THAT QUESTIONETH
MUCH SHALL LEARNE MUCH/AND CON-
TENT MUCH/SPECIALLY IF HEE APPLIE HIS

Samson

for Hammer observed with great interest the punchcutter's techniques and determined to acquire his own skill in the cutting of type.

During the 1920s Hammer resolved to add the craft of printing to his artistic endeavors. He set up his first printing press in his home in Florence, Italy, beginning what eventually became his paramount

ABCDefghijklmnopq
RStuvwxyz
ÄÖÜ ch ff 1234567890
pARSiFAL tANNhÄUSER MeiStERSINGER

Unziale

interest, and one that was to bring him considerable renown. In 1929 he moved to a larger house, the Villa Santuccio, which gave its name to his press – Stamperia del Santuccio, an imprint Hammer retained for all his books – in which he used only uncial types. The first work produced under this imprint – the first of thirty that Hammer designed and published – was Milton's *Samson Agonistes*, composed in Hammer's second uncial type, which received the name Samson.

Samson was cut by Paul Koch, son of the famous German type designer Rudolf Koch, who was to become a longtime friend of Hammer's. As in 1921, Hammer chose to be the observer. He made his initial effort as a punchcutter in the production of several Greek characters for use in the Milton volume, and finally he put his punch-cutting apprenticeship to the test in the production of a third uncial, named Pindar, for the book in which it was first used, the *Fragmente des Pindar* of Hölderlin. Hammer later wrote that he had cut the letters without any previous attempt at drawing them and made only slight corrections after smoke proofs of the punches indicated necessary changes.

Before his arrival in the United States in 1939, Hammer had been appointed to teach art and lettering at Wells College in upstate New York. There he turned again to the design of an uncial type, producing a set of punches that he took to the American Type Founders Company. The foundry was not at all prepared to market an uncial type, but it did cast a font from which the designer printed a specimen showing. Although this uncial was never to be produced, Hammer was already at work on the design for another one, his American Uncial.

Hammer first cut the American Uncial steel punches by hand and then sought a founder who could prepare the matrices and cast

ðet würðen/ðann handelt es sich um mehr als
Unholðenaswehr unð Bannzauber wie ðen
ganzen Tag über vor ðen Sippen-Behausungen/
Bei solch feierlichstem unð ðringlichstem An-
rufe aller guten Geister ðes Wachstums/aller
segnenðen unð spenðenðen Kräfte ðes Las-
sings gewinnt ðas metaphysische Beðürfnis ðer
Stammesgemeinschaft Ausðruck im Ursymbol
arischer Anschauung ðes Weltwerðens·

Da wirbelt unter frostgrauem Winterhim-
mel in ebenso großartiger als abweisenðer Um-
gebung ðräuenðen Schneegebirgs unð nacht-
ðunkler Wälðer ðas uralte Sinnbilð ðes Sonnen-
raðes vierfach geschlungen seinen tönenðen
Kreis/ðie männliche Gewalt ðes Gestirnes be-

Pindar

---

fu piero/ come si e ðetto/ studiosissimo ðell' arte/ e si esercito
assai nella prospettiva/ eð ebbe buonissima cognizione
ð'euclide/ in tanto che tutti i giri tirati ne' corpi regolari/
egli meglio che altro geometra intese/ eð i maggior lumi che
ði tal cosa ci siano sono ði sua mano/

Andromaque

the type. His search ended with the Society of Typographic Arts in
Chicago, which with the help of type designer R. Hunter Middleton
raised funds for the project and suggested a founder, Charles Nuss-
baumer, of the Dearborn Type Foundry. Another American who was

A TYPOGRAPHIC SOLECISM
✿

✠ THIS TYPE FACE has been designed by Fred W. Goudy for his own amusement. ✠ It is, in a manner of speaking, a typographic solecism. ✠ For his lower case letters he has drawn on the half-uncials of the fourth, fifth, sixth and seventh centuries, eighth century uncials, suggestions from types of Victor Hammer, Rudolf Koch and others. With these he has attempted to combine majuscules based on square capitals of the fourth century, and the rustic hands of the scribes, to which he has added his own conceits. ✿ If

Goudy Friar

most helpful to Hammer's subsequent career in the United States was Joseph Graves of Lexington, Kentucky. Sufficient type was thus cast for the press at Wells College. It was in appreciation of the Society's help that Hammer produced as a keepsake his *Dialogue* mentioned earlier, set in American Uncial, in the 12-point size on a 14-point body.

No American firm, however, was interested in marketing the new uncial, so Hammer returned to Klingspor, which produced it for sale in both Europe and the United States. In 1955 a 16-point size was added, along with a set of 30-point initials. Much of Hammer's magnificent printing has been produced from this cutting, which for the first time gave American printers the opportunity to use a type with an authentic medieval feeling. Although mostly employed by private presses, Hammer's uncial has also been frequently selected by commercial designers whenever an uncial is required. When the

A WAY TO ETERNITY
GODS OF EGYPT

Solemnis

aBcdefGhijklmn
opqrstuvwxyz
1234567890

Libra

German Stempel foundry took over the operation of Klingspor the type was dubbed Neue ('new') Hammer Unziale, as the very first Hammer Unziale of 1921 was still available.

Finally, in the 1950s Victor Hammer began work on his fifth uncial type. Called Andromaque (after the Greek legend), it is the first of the Hammer types to depart from the strong medieval letter forms with which the designer had been experimenting for more than thirty years. Andromaque is reminiscent of Greek cursive characters. It is also a truly minuscule form and may very well have been what Hammer had always been striving toward. It was cut in 1959 by the Paris foundry Deberny et Peignot in a 10-point size, and was first shown in specimen in Hammer's *Digression on the Roman Letter*, printed the same year.

Before Hammer's death in 1967, a 14-point cutting was begun, but it was only partially completed. Since then Dr. Middleton, working

SAPIENTIA FILIIS SUIS VITAM IN-

Wisdom breathes life into her children

spirat et suscipit inquirentes se

and shelters those who seek her and she

et præibit in via justitiæ: et qui

will go before them in the way of justice: and he

illam diligit diligit vitam: et qui

who loves her loves life: and those

vigilaverint ad illam complec-

who watch for her will embrace

tentur placorem ejus. Qui tenu-

her delight. They that hold

erint illam vitam hereditabunt:

her fast shall inherit life

et quo introibit benedicet Deus.

and where she enters God will bless.

Qui serviunt ei obsequentes er-

They that serve her shall serve

unt sancto: et eos qui diligunt

the Holy one: and God loves those

eam diligit Deus. Investiga illam

who love her. Study her

et manifestabitur tibi et contin-

and she shall be revealed to thee and

American Uncial, from Victor Hammer's *Chapters on Writing and Printing*, Lexington, 1963

with Hammer's wife, Carolyn Reading Hammer, has completed the font. Mrs. Hammer plans to use the type for work that she continues to produce in her husband's tradition.

The anachronism of American Uncial as a representative of the eighth-century style may be readily noticed by students of letter forms. The historical uncial alphabet was chiefly a minuscule, that is, there was no distinction between capitals and lowercase letters. Hammer's uncial, however, has both forms for each letter, embodying his attempt – fundamental to his dedication to legibility – to bring about the fusion of the black-letter and roman alphabets.

The need for this fusion, Hammer said, derives from the fact that a language such as German makes abundant use of consonants, letters that often have ascenders and descenders. In printing this kind of language an open type with short strokes makes it easier to read than does, for example, the narrow, tight black letter (Fraktur) that evolved from the 'vertical' German. Latin languages, by contrast, make greater use of vowel letters, which are rounded, so that the more open roman form was the natural outcome. In being combined with the constricted black letter, the roman serves as a relaxer.

The majuscule alphabet that Hammer thus devised for his American Uncial is very close to the humanist sans serif. It combines well with the rest of his font – so much so, in fact, that the reader is hard put to notice the incongruity of standard capitals in an uncial alphabet.

Frederic W. Goudy designed an uncial font similar to Hammer's, named Friar, in 1937. Goudy, however, considered the mixing of capitals and lowercase in an uncial alphabet a 'typographical solecism,' and so attempted a 'pure' version. Nevertheless, he credited the Hammer uncials as the inspiration for his design. Unfortunately, but few fonts of Friar were cast before the fire that in 1939 destroyed the contents of Goudy's workshop.

In addition, there are two other uncial types seen in contemporary printing. Libra, designed by S. H. de Roos for the Typefoundry Amsterdam in 1939, is probably the most widely used of all uncials. A minuscule alphabet with no accompanying set of capitals, Libra gives the effect of pure lowercase. The other uncial is Solemnis, designed by G. G. Lange in 1953 for the Berlin foundry Berthold. Also a twenty-six-letter alphabet, Solemnis differs from Libra in that most of the characters favor the majuscule form.

The Hammer type has become the first choice among the available uncials for book printing, since it seems to represent the uncial character at its best. It has been used by numerous private-press printers for short works that call for a medieval appearance. Although it is obvious that today the uncial letter is a distinct departure from the standards by which we measure typographic legibility, we can nonetheless admire the vigorous character of Hammer's interpretation. It has provided modern bookmakers with the opportunity to produce period printing of authentically orthodox flavor but more legible – hence accessible – than its prototype.

And Victor Hammer himself led the way, by virtue of a lifetime of devotion to standards of craftsmanship that, alas, seem to be, like his type, anachronistic in the world of contemporary printing.

Victor Hammer

3

CLOISTER OLD STYLE

When printing became established on the Italian peninsula in about 1465, the first types to emerge were transitional between the black-letter (gothic) northern-European manuscript hands and those forms now called roman. It was owing to the humanist influence early in the fifteenth century that the scribes who were engaged in copying the ancient Greek and Roman texts turned to the letter styles that had emerged as early as the eighth century in the writing reforms insti-gated by Charlemagne (from which developed the writing style now known as Carolingian minuscule).

By the mid-fifteenth century the tradition had been set for the later printed editions of the classics to appear in this transitional form: the early printers, naturally enough, were guided by readers' familiarity with certain letter styles in the development of their types. It was thus logical for the Italian printers to turn to the humanist manuscripts as models, and to use these models to continue the manuscript tradition via typography.

It is rarely possible for modern observers to determine which manuscript models were used by the first fifteenth-century punch-cutters; those printers who entered the craft after it had been estab-lished simply copied the type that had already proved successful. By contrast, the task of identifying more recent sources is much simpli-fied, for types, rather than manuscript hands, serve as the inspiration for later revivals.

The creator of such a revival – the first step in the evolution of Cloister Old Style – was William Morris. Writing in 1895, a year before his death, he summed up his ideals as a printer in *A Note by William Morris on His Aims in Founding the Kelmscott Press*, in which he dis-cusses the rationale behind his first choice of a type for his printing venture:

By instinct rather than by conscious thinking it over, I began by getting myself a font of Roman type. And here what I wanted was a letter pure in

CLOISTER LIGHTFACE IS THE LATEST ADDITION TO THE CLOISTER FAMILY AND IS AN HISTORIC TYPE DESIGN

CLOISTER LIGHTFACE is formed after the original type model of Nicolas Jenson of France, created and used by him in his printing house in Venice in the year 1470, whom it made celebrated in his own time and famous for all time. Now, in this year 1925, it has been conscientiously adapted to twentieth century uses and for many kinds of papers unknown to the said illustrious Nicolas Jenson by the chief type designer of the American Type Founders Company, Morris F. Benton. Cloister Lightface will be acclaimed by many authorities as being the ideal Jenson type face. It is incomparable for rich beauty combined with great dignity. Mr. Benton has very faithfully adhered to the Jenson model, maintaining its original purity insofar as possible.

Cloister Oldstyle (ATF)

form; severe, without needless excrescences; solid, without the thickening and thinning of the line, which is the essential fault of the ordinary modern type, and which makes it difficult to read; and not compressed laterally, as all later type has grown to be, owing to commercial exigencies. There was only one source from which to take examples of this perfected Roman type, to wit, the works of the great Venetian printers of the 15th century, of whom Nicolas Jenson produced the completest and the most Roman characters from 1470 to 1476.

It may be observed that Morris had an extreme dislike for the roman types of his own era, types that indeed lacked individuality

KINGDOM
Encounters Soldier
OBNOXIOUS
Question Announced

Lining Jenson Oldstyle No. 2 (ATF)

and character, and resulted from the diminished aesthetic standards of type design that accompanied the inexorable demand for cheap, fast printing engendered by the Industrial Revolution. These late-nineteenth-century types, generally referred to in our time as 'modern romans,' were the product of the newly industrialized atmosphere of the printer's craft, representing decades of deterioration in the printing process.

Morris named the design that resulted from his study of fifteenth-century typographic letter forms the Golden type. The name is associated with the three-volume edition of the medieval manual *The Golden Legend*, which had been planned as the first production of his Kelmscott Press (although its ambitious length delayed its publication).

For the model of his design, Morris turned to a pair of Venetian books, the *Historia naturalis* of Pliny, printed by Nicolas Jenson in 1476, and Aretino's *Historia Florentina*, printed by Jacobius Rubeus in the same year. Morris has stated, however, that his inspiration stemmed from the types of several Italian printers of the same period. The cutting of the type was turned over to the English punchcutter Edward Prince. It may also be noted that Morris depended for technical advice on his friend, the commercial engraver Emery Walker.

49

What sprang from this collaboration was not, as Morris remarked, a 'servile' copy of Jenson, but one that suited the concept Morris had evolved for the individualized printing he planned to produce. The Golden type and that of Nicolas Jenson are alike only in generalized details; the Golden is noticeably heavier. So successful, however, was this use of the Jenson-inspired type in the magnificently printed Kelmscott editions that it stimulated other private-press printers to embark on similar efforts. More important, it aroused an interest on the part of type designers in general in reexamining fifteenth-century sources for models upon which to base new typefaces.

The commercial typefounders, for example, took note of the wide-spread appeal of the Golden type and began to produce, not versions of the original Jenson, but undeviating imitations of Morris's type. But whereas William Morris required only one size of the Golden type, the founders, to meet the demands of their printer customers, had to cut a complete range of sizes, and it is here that the eccentricities inherent in this type – the slanted serifs, for instance – became most noticeable. These copies, obtainable under a variety of names (Jenson, Kelmscott, Ancient Roman, and others), were nevertheless purchased in great quantity. The Golden design also influenced numerous similar styles cut for printers, mostly amateur, who wished to produce books in the Morris manner, but none of these types (Vale, Essex, Merrymount, Village, and so forth) had any lasting effect on the typefounders.

The next step in the process that eventually resulted in the cutting of Cloister Old Style came about with the establishment in 1900 of the Doves Press in London by T. J. Cobden-Sanderson, who was also animated by the Morrisonian ideal. The Doves type began, like the Kelmscott, with Jenson, and was cut by the same punchcutter, Edward Prince. It should be noted that a partner in this press was Emery Walker, who had earlier advised Morris on the selection of a type. But Cobden-Sanderson eschewed the strongly decorated Kelmscott pattern and turned instead to pure typography. This breakaway from the medievalism of Morris better suited the requirements of the nascent twentieth-century art of the book.

Still another development leading to the more modern aesthetic judgment of the types of Nicolas Jenson occurred about the same period. The American typographer Bruce Rogers – then designing books for the Riverside Press in Cambridge, Massachusetts – had examined in the Boston Public Library a copy of the great Jenson

fidem supplices confugimus. Nihil nrā intereft vtrum
sub illo legato sub illo præsidio locros ee sinatis an ira
to hā et poenis ad supplicium dedatis. Non postulam
ut extemplo nobis de absente in dicta ca credatis Corā
ipse audiat veniat ipse diluat si qcq sceleris quod
homo in homines edere pot in nos prætermisit non
recusamus qn et nos omnia eadem iterum si pati possu
mus patiamur et ille omni diuino humanoq, liberetur
scelere. Hæc cum a legatis dicta eent quæsissetq, ab
iis. Q. fabius. detulissentne eas querelas ad P. scipio
nem responderunt missos legatos ee s; eum belli ap
paratu occupatum ee in africam aut iam traiecisse.
aut intra paucos dies traiecturum. et legati gratia
qta eet apud impatorem exptos ee cum inter eum et
tribunos cognita ca tribunos in uincula coniecerit. le
gatum æque sontem aut magis et in ea potate reliq
rit. lussis excedere extemplo legatis. non pleminius
m. s; et scipio principum orōnibz lacerari. Ante omis
Q. fabius natum eum ad corrumpendam disciplinam
militarem arguere. Sic et in hispania plus ppe p sedi
tionem militum q bello amissum externo et regio mo
re et indulgere licentiæ militum et seuire in eos. Sen
tentiam dein æque trucem orationi adiecit pleminiū
uinctum romam deportari placere. et ex uinculis cam

Fifteenth-century humanist manuscript hand

possem dicere. Porro cū duæ sint cōsuetudines quæ uirtuti
subīcidunt: alia qdem quid quodq3 entiū sit ispicit: alia ue
ro quid uocetur: atq3 in hunc modū de rōali philosophiæ p
te differunt. Enimuero moralē philosophiæ ptē i subiectos
diuidunt locos: uidelicet de appetitione: de bonis & malis :
de pturbationibus: de uirtute: de fine: deq3 prima extimatō
ne: & de actibus ac de officiis: de adhortationibus & hortati
onibus: in hunc autem modū subdistingūt Chrysippus ar
chedemus Zeno tarsensis Apollodorus Diogenes Antipa-
ter & Possidonius. Nā cittieus Zeno & cleanthes ut antiq-
ores simplicius ita tractarunt. At hi & rōnalē naturalemq3
philosophiæ ptē diuiserunt. Primā autē hanc aīantis appe
titionē fuisse dicunt seipsum tuendi atq3 seruandi : natura
sibi ipsū ab initio ita cōciliāte: ut chrysippus ait i prio de fi-
nibus: primū ͵pprium cuiq3 aīanti dicēs sui ipsius fuisse cō-
mendationē huiusq3 notionē. Neq3 eni fas erat aīal ipsum
uel ab se alienū fieri: uel oīo id fieri: uel non sibi maxie ͵ppi
quū fieri. Restat ut dicamus hanc ipsum sibi maxīa concor
dia & caritate deuīxisse. Ita enī & noxia propellit: & quæ ad
sui constantiā sunt utilia suscipit. Quod autē dicunt quidā
primā appetitionē animātibus ad uoluptatē fieri falsum ͵p
fecto est. Accessionē enim dicunt si quid sit uoluptatē esse :
cū ipsam p se natura inqsierit: & quæ cōmendatōi suæ sūt
accomodata pcepit : quēadmodū exhilarescunt aīalia uire
scuntq3 arbores: Nihilq3 aiunt differt natura in arboribus
& aīalibus quādo de illis absq3 motu uoluntatis ac sēsu dis
ponit: & in nobis quædā eadē ratōe fiunt. Cū uero ex super
fluo appetitio animantibus accesserit: qua uteutes pagant
quæ sua sunt: in eis quidē naturali cōstātia appetitionē illā
disponi. Cæterū cū rōalibus pfectiore præcepto data sit rō
secundū eā uiuere. s. recte fieri his quæ secundū naturā sūt
ea qppe artifex accidit moderatrixq3 appetitōis . Quocirca

Roman type of Nicolas Jenson, Venice, 1475

in her bely, and remayned vyrgyn after the chyldyng. And when he had so sayd, he was anone all hoole parfightely. And thenne saide peter to hym ☙ Take that palme of the honde of oure broder Johan, and leye it on the peple that be blynde, and who that wylle bileue shalle receyue his sight ageyne. And they that wylle not byleue shall neuer see. And thenne thappostles bare marye vnto the monument, and satte by it, lyke as our lord had commaunded, and at the thyrdde day Jhesu crist cam with a grete multytude of Angels and salewed them and saide pees be with yow. And they answerd, god, glory be to the whiche only makest the grete myracles and merueyles. And oure lord sayd to thappostles ☙ What is now youre aduys that I ought now to doo to my moder, of honour and of grace? Syre, it semeth to vs thy ser-uauntes that lyke as thou hast vanquysshyd the deth & regnest world withoute ende, that thou reyse also the body of thy moder, & sette her on thy ryght side in perdurabylyte. And he graunted it. And thenne Mychael the angel cam & presented the sowle of Marye to oure lord. And the saueour spacke and sayde ☙ Aryse vp, haste the my culuer or douue, tabernacle of glorye, vessel of lyf, Temple celestyal, and lyke as thou neuer feltest conceyuing by none atouchement, thou shalt not suffre in the sepulcre no corrupcion of body. And anon the sowle cam ageyne to the body of marye and yssued gloryously oute of the tombe, and thus was receyued in the heuenly chambre, and a grete companye of angels with her. And saynt Thomas was not there, and whan he cam he wolde not byleue this. And anone the gyrdell with whiche her body was gyrde cam to hym fro the ayer, whiche he receyued, and therby he vnderstode that she was assumpt in to heuen. ☙ And alle this here to fore is sayd & called Appocriphum. Whereof saynt Jerom sayth in a sermon to paula and Eustochium her doughter ☙ That book is said to be apocryfum, sauf that somme wordes whiche ben worthy of feyth & ben approued of seyntes as touchyng nyne thynges, that is to wete, that the comforte of thappostles was promysed and

The Golden type of William Morris, 1892

book, Eusebius's *De Praeparatione Evangelica*, printed in 1470. Excited by the desire to re-create this beautiful design, Rogers then sought out other Jenson books. He reproduced their pages in what he later described as 'the search for what I fondly thought would be the ideally perfect type; not knowing then that it was something like the quest of the Holy Grail.'

In 1901 Rogers had progressed to the point of having the Riverside Press authorize the cutting of his designs, which was done by John Cumming, a punchcutter working in Worcester, Massachusetts. Origi-

oxen. So the service was prepared, and the priests stood in their place, and the Levites in their courses, according to the king's commandment. And they killed the passover, & the priests sprinkled the blood from their hands, and the Levites flayed them. And they removed the burnt offerings, that they might give according to the divisions of the families of the people, to offer unto the Lord, as it is written in the book of Moses. And so did they with the oxen. And they roasted the passover with fire according to the ordinance: but the other holy offerings sod they in pots, and in caldrons, and in pans, & divided them speedily among all the people. And afterward they made ready for themselves, & for the priests: because the priests the sons of Aaron were busied in offering of burnt offerings and the fat until night; therefore the Levites prepared for themselves, and for the priests the sons of Aaron. And the singers the sons of Asaph were in their place, according to the commandment of David, and Asaph, and Heman, and Jeduthun the king's seer; and the porters waited at every gate; they might not depart from their service; for their brethren the Levites prepared for them. So all the service of the Lord was prepared the same day, to keep the passover, and to offer burnt offerings upon the altar of the Lord, according to the commandment of king Josiah. And the children of Israel that were present kept the passover at that time, and the feast of unleavened bread seven days. And there was no passover like to that, kept in Israel from the days of Samuel the prophet; neither did all the kings of Israel keep such a passover as Josiah kept, and the priests, and the Levites, and all Judah and Israel that were present, and the inhabitants of Jerusalem. In the eighteenth year of the reign of Josiah was this passover kept. ¶ After all this, when Josiah had prepared the temple, Necho king of Egypt came up to fight against Carchemish by Euphrates: and Josiah went out against him. But he sent ambassadors to him, saying, What have I to do with thee, thou king of Judah? I come not against thee this day, but against the house wherewith I have war: for God commanded me to make haste: forbear thee from meddling

The Doves type, in the English Bible of the Doves Press, 1903–05

nally intended for a notable edition of the *Essays* of Montaigne, and thus named Montaigne, the Rogers type was actually used for the first time in another book designed by Rogers, Sir Walter Raleigh's *Last Sea Fight of the Revenge*, published in 1902. Rogers, however, was not satisfied with the face and some years later improved on it in a new design named Centaur, which will be discussed in the next chapter.

The activities of the numerous private presses of the period 1900–1910 aroused the interest of both commercial printers and typefounders – William Morris's concept of returning to the historic typefaces had begun to take effect. The earliest big venture in type

IN PRINCIPIO CREAVIT DEUS CŒLUM, ET

terram. Terra autem erat inanis et vacua, et tenebræ erant super faciem abyssi; et Spiritus Dei ferebatur super aquas. Dixitque Deus: Fiat lux. Et facta est lux. Et vidit Deus lucem quod esset bona; et divisit lucem a tenebris. Appel-lavitque lucem Diem et tenebras Noctem; factumque est vespere et mane, dies unus. Dixit quoque Deus: Fiat fir-mamentum in medio aquarum, et dividat aquas ab aquis. Et fecit Deus firmamentum, divisitque aquas, quæ erant sub firmamento, ab his, quæ erant super firmamentum. Et factum est ita. Vocavitque Deus firmamentum, Cœ-lum; et factum est vespere et mane, dies secundus. Dixit vero Deus: Congregentur aquæ, quæ sub cœlo sunt, in lo-cum unum, et appareat arida. Et factum est ita. Et voca-vit Deus aridam, Terram, congregationesque aquarum appellavit Maria. Et vidit Deus quod esset bonum. Et ait: Germinet terra herbam virentem, et facientem semen, et lignum pomiferum faciens fructum juxta genus suum, cujus semen in semetipso sit super terram. Et factum est ita. Et protulit terra herbam virentem, et facientem se-men juxta genus suum, lignumque faciens fructum, et ha-

Merrymount design of Bertram Grosvener Goodhue

revivalism, the recutting of Bodoni by Morris Benton for the American Type Founders Company, occurred in 1910, and it proved such a suc-cess that the foundry planned further such projects. One of these was Benton's Cloister Old Style, first produced in 1913. This face fulfilled the broad demands of the trade for a type employing the same historic sources as those of the esteemed private presses.

Morris Fuller Benton had become a type designer through the circumstance of having for a father Linn Boyd Benton, a typefounder and the inventor, no less, of the pantograph device, patented in 1885, which had mechanized the craft of punchcutting. It was this machine that freed typefounding from the laborious procedure of cutting by

'the world knoweth, and especially such things as have drawne-on
'publike effects, and of such consequence, it is an inexcusable defect,
'or as I may say unpardonable oversight.[65] To conclude, whosoever
'desireth to have perfect information and knowledge of King Fran-
'cis the first, and of the things hapned in his time, let him addresse
'himselfe elsewhere, if he will give any credit unto me. The profit he
'may reap here, is by the particular deduction of the battels and ex-
'ploits of warre, wherein these Gentlemen were present ; some privie
'conferences, speeches or secret actions of some Princes that then
'lived, and the practices managed, or negotiations directed by the
'Lord of Langeay, in whom doubtlesse are verie many things well-
'worthie to be knowne, and diverse discourses not vulgare.'

THE ELEVENTH CHAPTER.

Of Crueltie.

 E thinks vertue is another manner of thing,
and much more noble, than the inclina-
tions unto goodnesse which in us are ingen-
dered. Mindes well borne and directed by
themselves follow one same path, and in
their actions represent the same visage that
the vertuous doe. But vertue importeth and
soundeth somewhat, I wot not what, greater
and more active, than by an happy com-
plexion, gently and peaceably, to suffer it selfe to be led or drawne
to follow reason. He that through a naturall facilitie and genuine
mildnesse should neglect or contenme injuries received, should no
doubt performe a rare action and worthy commendation; but he who,
being touch and stung to the quicke with any wrong or offence received, should arme himselfe with reason against this furiously-blind
desire of revenge, and in the end, after a great conflict, yeeld himselfe
master over-it, should doubtlesse doe much more. The first should
doe well, the other vertuously ; the one action might be termed goodnesse, the other vertue. For it seemeth that the verie name of vertue
presupposeth difficultie and inferreth resistance, and cannot well exercise it selfe without an enemie. It is peradventure the reason why
we call God good, mightie, liberall and just, but we terme him not

Montaigne type designed by Bruce Rogers in *Essays of Montaigne,* 1902

hand every letter in a font of type, a practice that had not changed since Johann Gutenberg invented it in 1440. Before Benton, the only other procedure used for the production of matrices was electrotyping, which was developed about 1840. Electrotyping, however, was employed primarily for the copying of existing typefaces rather than for original designs; the method in fact encouraged the pirating of type designs (a custom common in our own time when phototypesetting machines were being developed).

When the younger Benton graduated from Cornell in 1896 as a mechanical engineer, he went to work for the American Type Founders Company as assistant to his father. The senior Benton had been given the responsibility of organizing the type-production facilities of that recently formed combine, put together in 1892 – despite loud protests in the printing trade – by the merging of some two dozen separate typefoundries. Morris Benton's duties were related to the mechanical aspects of typefounding, particularly the adaptation of the American Point System of typographic measurement, which had been instigated in 1886. But as the chaos and pressures that resulted from the vast amalgamation subsided, the young engineer began to develop an interest in letter forms themselves. As early as 1898 he produced the first of what ultimately became a list of more than 180 types, making him the most prolific type designer who has ever lived. This first type was originally named Buddy, but when it was employed by Elbert Hubbard it was renamed Roycroft, after Hubbard's craft center and printing establishment in upstate New York.

Benton next became involved in the development of the various additions to the Century family of types, on which his father had collaborated with the great scholar-printer Theodore L. De Vinne.

By 1904 Benton was fully established in type design with the production of the Cheltenham family of typefaces, based on the original face drawn by the architect Bertram Goodhue, which became the most widely known of all American types. In 1909 Benton turned to his first important revival of a classic type, that of Bodoni. Then, attracted to the Venetian letter forms favored by the private presses, he came to an appreciation of the work of the fifteenth-century Italian printers.

Cloister Old Style became the hallmark design in the revival of the Venetian old-style types in the present century. The face followed the spirit of its Jenson original in the blunt, solidly constructed serifs, but it had fuller bracketing than is apparent in the earlier letter. In

Cloister Italic, available in fourteen sizes ranging from six up to seventy-two point, sounded a new note in italic design. As no italic types were made in the first century of printing which would harmonize with the roman type of Jenson, it was necessary in designing this series to follow the shapes of the earlier sixteenth century italics of Aldus of Venice and certain French italics of a third of a century later. The resulting design is a vigorous italic that harmonizes excellently with the Cloister Oldstyle and is an admirable series on its own account

Cloister Oldstyle Italic (AFT)

this respect Stanley Morison, the English typographic historian, has discussed the lack of brackets (often called fillets) in all Venetian types before 1495; he wonders whether the craftsmen lacked the proper tools with which to refine serifs. More recently another English typographic historian, Harry Carter, has suggested that the invention in the 1470s of the jeweler's eyeglass provided the means of more exact seeing and therefore cutting.

Another feature of the Venetian types captured in Cloister Old Style is the avoidance of strong contrast between thick and thin strokes. Some authorities believe this shows that the Italian punchcutters during the first thirty years of printing were attempting to reproduce exactly the pen-drawn humanistic roman, rather than striving to cut original type letters.

The most distinctive of Jenson's lowercase letters is *e*, with its angled crossbar, a style followed by practically every Italian designer of the period until the appearance of the types of Francesco Griffo, cut for the press of Aldus Manutius in 1495.

67 And both I and my Sages grew aware
   of sunset, by my shadow vanisht thence,
   when we had made brief trial of the stair.
70 And ere within one dim circumference
   the wide horizon mingled sea and shore,
   and Night held sway with all her influence,
73 Each of us on a stair was bedded; for
   the mountain-law deprived us of the will
   and of the power of there ascending more.
76 Just as, while ruminating, goats grow still,
   however bold and nimble they had run
   over the heights before they browsed their fill,
79 Husht in the shade while blazes hot the sun,
   watcht by the herdsman leaning on his rod,
   who, leaning thus, attends them every one;
82 And as the shepherd, stretcht upon the sod,
   watches by night his quiet flock beside,
   that no wild beast may scatter it abroad:
85 Even so did we at such an hour abide,
   I like the goat, they shepherdlike, all three
   hemmed in by lofty rock on either side.

Cloister Lightface, in the edition of Dante printed by John Henry Nash,
San Francisco, 1929

   The capitals of Cloister retain the full height of the Jenson font, a
factor criticized by Morison as detracting from the legibility of the
face. Both *M* and *N* have the slab serifs typical of the Venetian types;
that is, the upper serifs center on the stems of the letter. In many of

ABCDEFGHIJKLMNOP
QRSTUVWXYZ&
abcdefghijklmnopqrstu
vwxyz 1234567890

Eusebius (Ludlow)

the types favored by the Italian printers this feature was also carried over to the *A*.

In his design of the italic for Cloister Old Style, Benton encountered the problem faced by all modern type designers who return to the Venetian letter forms: there is no model to follow. Italic type was not cut until 1500, and when it finally did appear, in the *Virgil* of Aldus printed in 1501, it was used as a type completely independent of roman. It was not until the 1540s in France that italic was cut in a form that was complementary to the roman, and a good deal later before the two styles became, as they are today, inseparable.

Thus, type designers have had to invent and design italics to go with any roman that appeared between 1470 and 1500. Benton was among the first to confront this difficulty, the early private-press printers having ignored it by employing roman alone. He elected to create a cursive form that he believed to be in the spirit of the roman. Other type designers, by contrast and as will be discussed later, have preferred an italic with a strictly historic relationship to the upright form. This has resulted in the italics called chancery, based on Renaissance calligraphic sources, in which the letters are narrow and spiky. Cloister italic, by comparison, is a pleasantly rounded and sloped letter, certainly retaining the feeling of the roman.

Although lacking the aesthetic impact of some of the later Venetian revivals, Cloister has proved to be a most successful cutting, and has found its way into printing offices the world over, either in its foundry

(ATF) version or in the adaptations produced for the various type-setting machines. Those cut for the slug-casting machines (Linotype and Intertype) are identical to the Benton version except for the inevitable lack of kerning – not obtainable in a slug-casting machine matrix – which is most noticeable with the lowercase *f*.

The Ludlow Typograph Company, manufacturer of a slug-casting device used for display typography, brought out a type drawn by Ernst Detterer in 1923 that is quite close in spirit to Cloister Old Style. This face was first called Nicolas Jenson, but later changed to Eusebius. (The name has historic analogy, for Pamphili Eusebius was the author of the book that Jenson so splendidly printed in 1470, thereby establishing the printer's reputation for the design of the roman type that has come to be the standard for all those that followed.)

The italic of Eusebius differs from that of Cloister in that it follows the chancery style. It was drawn by R. Hunter Middleton, who, after Morris Benton and Frederic W. Goudy, has been one of the most prolific American type designers.

Although most American printers were enthusiastic about Cloister when it first appeared, the redoubtable printer-historian Daniel Berkeley Updike treated it somewhat condescendingly in his great work *Printing Types* (1922): 'Cloister Old Style Roman was based on a study of Nicolas Jenson's long-suffering and as yet unrivalled font, and its italic is of an interesting early form. It is a practical type; not very inspired, perhaps, yet quiet and satisfactory because not attempting too much. . . .'

At present, Cloister Old Style as a book type has lost ground to some of the later Venetian old styles. But in commercial printing and for advertising display it continues to be popular, particularly in its boldface version encountered daily in the consumer periodicals.

For examples of its use in distinguished book making, the reader is urged to examine the work of the San Francisco printer John Henry Nash, who was very fond of the type and employed it frequently. The great book from his press, the four-volume *Dante* published in 1929, is completely hand-set in Cloister Light, one of the weights produced by the American Type Founders Company.

4

CENTAUR

In 1915 there was issued from the Montague Press at the Dyke Mill in Montague, Massachusetts, a slim quarto volume printed in an edition of 135 copies. The designer of this book was Bruce Rogers and the printer was Carl Purington Rollins. For bibliophiles who collect the work of Rogers, *The Centaur*, by Maurice de Guérin, is one of the most desirable items. The little volume seldom appears in the booksellers' catalogues, though, as most of the copies are held by institutional libraries.

The reason for the book's demand, aside from being designed by Rogers, is that it represents the first appearance of a type esteemed the world over as one of the finest ever produced in this century. Named for the book, Centaur was its designer's third and final approach to the design of a printing type (the first was the Montaigne of 1901, followed by the remodeling of a Caslon for a book published in 1909). Thereafter Rogers restricted himself primarily to book typography, although from time to time he did alter various characters of the fonts that he had selected for some of his important works.

The reputation of Bruce Rogers is secure as the most accomplished book designer that America has yet produced, and this high regard has spread far beyond our shores. The English typographic authority Sir Francis Meynell has stated unequivocally that Rogers 'was the greatest artificer of the book who ever lived.'

He was born on May 14, 1870, in Linnwood, Indiana. As a boy, Rogers had ambitions to be an artist and enrolled at the age of fifteen at Purdue, then a twelve-year-old land-grant college located just a few miles from his home. Entering with him was his friend John T. McCutcheon, who was later to be a prominent cartoonist. The two boys were the only males in the art course. Although the art curriculum of Purdue at that time was not particularly distinguished, Rogers did manage to become aware of fine books, and he contributed to the design of the publications of the school – the first Purdue yearbook

ABCDEFGHIJKLMN
OPQRSTUVWXYZ
abcdefghijklmnopqrstu
vwxyz 1234567890
fiff fl ffi ffl

Centaur (English Monotype)

was produced in 1889, with Rogers and McCutcheon providing decorations, headings, and illustrations. After several jobs of no consequence following his graduation, in 1890, Rogers became involved in commercial design in 1894, when he was asked by Joseph M. Bowles, publisher of the periodical *Modern Art*, to contribute artwork to that publication. Bowles showed him several books produced by William Morris's Kelmscott Press and like other young designers of this era, Rogers was animated by exposure to these works. For a book published by Bowles, Rogers created an alphabet of initials that, with sundry headbands and tailpieces, was reflective of Morris's work.

Rogers's career began to take direction when the Boston lithographer Louis Prang offered to publish *Modern Art*, a proposal that Bowles accepted, prompting his removal to Boston. At Bowles's suggestion Rogers also went East in 1895. Not long after his arrival in Boston he met Daniel Berkeley Updike, who had recently established his Merrymount Press after having spent a number of years at the Riverside Press of the publishing house Houghton, Mifflin & Company. Updike introduced Rogers to George H. Mifflin, who offered him employment as a designer at Riverside. Rogers remained

Drawings of Centaur type by Bruce Rogers

there until 1912, a seventeen-year stint during which he fully established himself as a book designer of remarkable ability.

About 1900 Houghton, Mifflin engaged in an ambitious publishing program of fine books and placed Rogers in charge of their production. The first opportunity to design a printing type came quickly. As described in chapter three, at an exhibition in the Boston Public Library Rogers had examined a copy of the *De Praeparatione Evangelica* of Eusebius, printed at Venice in 1470 by Nicolas Jenson. Fascinated by the type in which the book was composed, he sought out its owner and received permission to photograph a page. (Rogers eventually acquired a copy of the book, which can be found in the Newberry Library in Chicago, along with the photographs of the type.) He thereupon began work on what he thought would be the ideal type, having no idea that the endeavor would be so difficult.

Rogers soon persuaded his employer to let him proceed with drawings for a new type to be used for an important forthcoming publication, a folio edition of Montaigne's *Essays.* Using the Jenson letter as his model, Rogers completed his design and – at the suggestion of Joseph W. Phinney, manager of the Boston branch of the American Type Founders Company – he secured the assistance of John Cumming of Worcester, Massachusetts, for the cutting of the punches. Rogers was not particularly happy with the outcome of this initial venture into type design, feeling that the punchcutter, though highly skilled, had not quite preserved the flavor of either the Jenson original or his own drawings. But the publisher was most enthusiastic about the new type and Rogers agreed to use it for the Montaigne edition, from which it took its name. Privately, however, Rogers decided that his search for the perfect type would be continued at a later date.

It was to be a dozen years before the opportunity arose to produce another typeface. Midway in his Riverside employment Rogers had come to a decision concerning his career, turning full time to typography at the expense of illustration and painting, fields which had also always attracted him. The decision was doubtless owing largely to the acclaim his Riverside books had brought him, along with numerous new friends who were to influence his subsequent career.

Among these was Emery Walker, whom Rogers finally met in 1912 when, having left Riverside, he made his first visit to England. Walker was the engraver who had been a strong force in the design of the Golden type of William Morris and of the Doves Press type of T. J. Cobden-Sanderson. Rogers had also previously established a friendship with Henry Watson Kent, the Bostonian who in 1903 had become librarian of New York's Grolier Club and two years later was made assistant secretary of the Metropolitan Museum of Art. Walker and Kent were to prove instrumental in the development of Centaur type: Walker for his experience in adapting Jenson's design for Morris and Cobden-Sanderson, and Kent for the support he provided in his capacity at the Metropolitan.

THE CENTAUR. WRITTEN BY MAURICE DE GUÉRIN AND NOW TRANSLATED FROM THE FRENCH BY GEORGE B. IVES.

I Was born in a cavern of these mountains. Like the river in yonder valley, whose first drops flow from some cliff that weeps in a deep grotto, the first moments of my life sped amidst the shadows of a secluded retreat, nor vexed its silence. As our mothers draw near their term, they retire to the caverns, and in the innermost recesses of the wildest of them all, where the darkness is most dense, they bring forth, uncomplaining, offspring as silent as themselves. Their strength-giving milk enables us to endure without weakness or dubious struggles the first difficulties of life; yet we leave our caverns later than you your cradles. The reason is that there is a tradition amongst us that the early days of life must be secluded and guarded, as days engrossed by the gods.

My growth ran almost its entire course in the darkness where I was born. The innermost depths of my home were so far within the bowels of the mountain, that I should not have known in which direction the opening lay, had it not been that the winds at times blew in and caused a sudden coolness and confusion. Sometimes, too, my mother returned, bringing with her the perfume of the valleys, or dripping wet from the streams to which she resorted. Now, these her home-comings, although they told me naught of the valleys or the streams, yet, being attended by emanations therefrom, disturbed my thoughts, and I wandered about, all agitated, amidst my darkness. 'What,' I would say to myself, 'are these places to which my mother goes and what power reigns there which summons her so frequently? To what influences is one there exposed,

While at the Grolier Club, Kent had developed a keen interest in typography that prompted him, after his move to the Metropolitan, to become personally involved in the operation of the museum's small printing plant, which actively produced exhibition labels, posters, announcements, and the like. During his long tenure there, Kent built this little shop into the Museum Press, which achieved renown for the high quality of its productions – many of which were designed by Kent himself. One of the projects that particularly interested Kent was improving the quality of the exhibition labels, and with this in mind he asked Rogers to consider the design of a type exclusively for the use of the Metropolitan. Thus encouraged, Rogers returned to his interpretation of the Jenson type, trying to provide the suitable model he believed had not been accomplished with the Montaigne delineation.

In a letter to Daniel Berkeley Updike written later, in 1922, Rogers explained the reason for his seeming dependence on a single original type:

So much has already been written about Jenson's Roman and its derivations that nothing more seems necessary or even perhaps, advisable – but it is, I believe, much nearer to its MS prototype than most people suspect. When I made the Centaur type I enlarged Jenson's and *wrote* over the prints with a flat pen – just as rapidly as I could – then I selected the best (?) of my characters and touched them up with a brush and *white* – (no black) just about as much as a punch-cutter would do with a graver – and the type was cut from these patterns. It proved to my own satisfaction, at least, that the lower-case (with the exception of the s) of Jenson, was cut directly from a MS hand – and not *drawn* – as the caps of course were. I enclose a bit of the writing and the 'trued-up' letters – I wish now I hadn't 'trued' them so much – Will one *ever* learn?

Rogers now discussed with Frederic W. Goudy the transfer of his drawings to matrices for the casting of type. Goudy recommended commissioning the Chicago matrix engraver Robert Wiebking for this purpose; Wiebking had cut several of Goudy's earlier types most successfully, using the matrix-engraving machine. Rogers agreed, and when the work was completed in 1914, he felt that the new type was a good deal closer to the original Jenson than was the Montaigne for which the punches had been cut freehand. He was also convinced that it came closer to his own ideals of a reconstructed Venetian roman type.

The original size chosen for casting was 14-point, this being the only size for which a lowercase alphabet was required. In addition, the Metropolitan required several sizes of caps for display purposes; these were cut in 12-, 14-, 20-, 24-, 30-, 48-, and 60-point, and were named Museum Press Capitals. Rogers agreed to sell his design to the Museum for $500, the type to become its property except that he would retain the privilege of ordering for his own use (not for sale) such quantities as he required of the 14-point, the only size for which the lowercase had been cut.

Rogers was delighted when in April 1914 the Metropolitan immediately accepted his offer and assented to his terms. He wrote to Kent expressing his pleasure that the trustees liked his type well enough to want to own it. In another letter to Kent, written in May 1914, Rogers mentioned that

the name 'Centaur' was associated with this type only in my own mind; so far and inasmuch as the type and the design is now yours I would be glad to have you label it as you will and not accept 'Centaur' unless you care to. The only point in calling it 'Centaur' would be to print that little piece as its first showing, and as that may have to be indefinitely postponed there is no reason why it should not be called anything you prefer. Why not call it 'Kent,' which is a splendid name for a type and never used to my knowledge. I'll take the responsibility of re-christening it if you have no objections.

Kent apparently did not reply to this suggestion, and the typefoundry that held the matrices for casting dubbed the design Bruce Rogers. When Wiebking had completed the cutting of the matrices they were shipped to the Western Type Foundry in St. Louis, a firm established in 1901 to compete with the American Type Founders conglomerate.

In 1919 Western went out of business, transferring all of its equipment and holdings to Barnhart Brothers & Spindler of Chicago. When Kent received word of the sale of the St. Louis foundry, he became concerned about the Centaur matrices. Officials at BB&S, not at all awed by the prestige of the Metropolitan Museum of Art, replied that they would require proof of ownership and payment for the matrices. They also suggested that the foundry keep them in storage for further casting as required. Following an exchange of letters, all parties agreed to the matrices' remaining in the BB&S vault, although a year and a half later a nervous Kent wrote to Rogers asking him whether he felt it safe to leave the matrices with the foundry. Rogers reassured him on the matter.

However, early in 1925 Rogers received a letter from the well-known Baltimore printer Norman T. A. Munder, stating that he had been asked by Barnhart Brothers & Spindler to write to Rogers on

FRA·LUCA
DE·PACIOLI
O͟F BORGO·S
SEPOLCRO
B·STANLEY
MORISON
THE·GRO-
LIER·CLUB
NEW·YORK
MCMXXXII

A Centaur title page by Bruce Rogers, 1933

that it was manifest to them that looked upon him, what sorrow he had now in his heart. ⟨18 Others ran flocking out of their houses to the general supplication, because the place was like to come into contempt. ⟨19 And the women, girt with sackcloth under their breasts, abounded in the streets, and the virgins that were kept in ran, some to the gates, and some to the walls, and others looked out of the windows. ⟨20 And all, holding their hands toward heaven, made supplication. ⟨21 Then it would have pitied a man to see the falling down of the multitude of all sorts, and the fear of the high priest, being in such an agony. ⟨22 They then called upon the Almighty Lord to keep the things committed of trust safe and sure for those that had committed them. ⟨23 Nevertheless Heliodorus executed that which was decreed. ⟨24 Now as he was there present himself with his guard about the treasury, the Lord of spirits, and the Prince of all power, caused a great apparition, so that all that presumed to come in with him were astonished at the power of God, and fainted, and were sore afraid. ⟨25 For there appeared unto them an horse with a terrible rider upon him, and adorned with a very fair covering, and he ran fiercely, and smote at Heliodorus with his forefeet, and it seemed that he that sat upon the horse had complete harness of gold. ⟨26 Moreover two other young men appeared before him, notable in strength, excellent in beauty, and comely in apparel, who stood by him on either side, and scourged him continually, and gave him many sore stripes. ⟨27 And Heliodorus fell suddenly unto the ground, and was compassed with great darkness: but they that were with him took him up, and put him into a litter. ⟨28 Thus him, that lately came with a great train and with all his guard into the said treasury, they carried out, being unable to help himself with his weapons: and manifestly they acknowledged the power of God: ⟨29 For he by the hand of God was cast down, and lay speechless without all hope of life. ⟨30 But they praised the Lord, that had miraculously honoured his own place: for the temple, which a little afore was full of fear and trouble, when the Almighty Lord appeared, was filled with joy and gladness. ⟨31 Then straightways certain of Heliodorus' friends prayed Onias, that he would call upon the most High

to grant him his life, who lay ready to give up the ghost. ⟨32 So the high priest, suspecting lest the king should misconceive that some treachery had been done to Heliodorus by the Jews, offered a sacrifice for the health of the man. ⟨33 Now as the high priest was making an atonement, the same young men in the same clothing appeared and stood beside Heliodorus, saying, Give Onias the high priest great thanks, insomuch as for his sake the Lord hath granted thee life: ⟨34 And seeing that thou hast been scourged from heaven, declare unto all men the mighty power of God. And when they had spoken these words, they appeared no more. ⟨35 So Heliodorus, after he had offered sacrifice unto the Lord, and made great vows unto him that had saved his life, and saluted Onias, returned with his host to the king. ⟨36 Then testified he to all men the works of the great God, which he had seen with his eyes. ⟨37 And when the king asked Heliodorus, who might be a fit man to be sent yet once again to Jerusalem, he said, ⟨38 If thou hast any enemy or traitor, send him thither, and thou shalt receive him well scourged, if he escape with his life: for in that place, no doubt, there is an especial power of God. ⟨39 For he that dwelleth in heaven hath his eye on that place, and defendeth it; and he beateth and destroyeth them that come to hurt it. ⟨40 And the things concerning Heliodorus, and the keeping of the treasury, fell out on this sort.

CHAPTER 4

THIS Simon now, of whom we spake afore, having been a bewrayer of the money, and of his country, slandered Onias, as if he had terrified Heliodorus, and been the worker of these evils. ⟨2 Thus was he bold to call him a traitor, that had deserved well of the city, and tendered his own nation, and was so zealous of the laws. ⟨3 But when their hatred went so far, that by one of Simon's faction murders were committed, ⟨4 Onias seeing the danger of this contention, and that Apollonius, as being the governor of Celosyria and Phenice, did rage, and increase Simon's malice, ⟨5 He went to the king, not to be an accuser of his countrymen, but seeking the good of all, both publick and private: ⟨6 For he saw that it was

the company's behalf, although 'I am almost afraid to do so.' Munder was to find out if Rogers would be willing 'to give the printers of the country approval to use your Centaur.' He said that the foundry, hoping to supply it nationally, wished to begin immediately advertising the type and hoped that Rogers would accept the commission to design such materials. Alarmed, Rogers sent the letter to Kent, saying, 'It looks very much as though Barnhart Brothers & Spindler were planning to "seize" the Centaur type – by right of eminent domain, if not by any other.'

Rogers added, 'If they decide to do it, I don't know any way of preventing it. Valuable as such a design is in the market, there has never been any satisfactory way of preventing its being stolen.' He recommended that the Metropolitan ask for the return of the matrices, and that in the future it hire a private typecaster to produce the type when required; he pointed out that Fred Goudy might be willing to do this, as he had recently set up his own foundry. Kent was not at all enthusiastic about Centaur's being used by ordinary printers for run-of-the-mill printing, and said so in reply. He immediately requested BB&S to return the matrices to the Museum, and also wrote to Robert Wiebking to send pattern plates to either the Museum or Bruce Rogers. By the end of January 1925 the Centaur matrices were in storage at the Museum Press.

During the next few years there were so many requests that Centaur be made available to the printing trade that Rogers seriously began to consider such a project. So when the Lanston Monotype Machine Company, in Philadelphia, asked permission to cut the letter for machine composition, Rogers decided to allow the transfer, Kent's disapproval notwithstanding. But because Rogers was returning to England for a protracted stay, the decision was made that the Lanston Monotype Corporation of London would undertake the task. This English firm had at one time been fully connected with the American Monotype company, but later became independent of it. The firms had agreed to work together in the matters of machine development and the exchange of types.

When Rogers arrived in England in 1928, the work of adapting Centaur began and was completed the following year. As Rogers had not supplied an italic for his original design, it now became necessary to provide one. The designer, however – referring to himself as 'an indifferent calligrapher' – felt that a proper italic was beyond his ability. He therefore persuaded his fellow American Frederic Warde, who a year or two earlier had produced a very fine chancery italic named Arrighi, to permit its use as the italic for Centaur. Warde acceded and offered his privately cut type to the Monotype firm for this purpose.

Centaur thus entered the domain of the 'ordinary printer,' enabling that person to produce typography that, if not always up to the standards of a Bruce Rogers, did provide a distinguished addition to the type cases. Certainly in the past half century the letter has been used in the production of a good deal of distinctive printing, not the least being some beautiful machine-set books designed by Bruce Rogers himself.

Without doubt the most exalted commercial use of Centaur has been in the magnificent folio Bible produced by Oxford University Press, by all accounts the masterpiece design of Rogers and one of the monumental books in five centuries of English printing. This lectern Bible, begun in 1929 and six years in production, is composed in 22-point, and since it is entirely without decoration there is nothing to interfere with its acceptance as an outstanding example of pure typography. Before the Oxford Bible was completed two other Rogers works were produced, each using Monotype Centaur and each also high on the list of his accomplishments as a designer of books: *The Odyssey of Homer*, in the translation of T. E. Shaw, completed in 1932, and *Fra Luca de Pacioli*, printed at Cambridge University Press for the Grolier Club of New York in 1933. The eminent American printer Joseph Blumenthal, in his chapter on Bruce Rogers in *The Printed Book in America* (1977), wrote of these three books as 'imperishable.'

Centaur has been one of the most widely praised roman types of our time. Even so conservative an observer as D. B. Updike said of it, in *Printing Types*, 'It appears to me one of the best roman fonts yet designed in America – and, of its *kind*, the best anywhere.' And at the level of that 'ordinary' printer, Centaur has been advertised for many years in the trade periodicals by the San Francisco typesetting firm Mackenzie & Harris as 'The Noblest Roman of Them All.' Happily, although considered the finest recutting of Jenson's type, it has never been subjected to the type-family idea so beloved by suppliers. And it is to be hoped that in the transfer to film its grand proportions will not be the victim of the distortions of weight and width manipulation that accompany the concept of the type family.

In 1930 Rogers was beginning to be plagued by financial problems. After his eight-year stay at the plant of William Edwin Rudge in Mount Vernon, New York – which constituted his most active period of book making, with almost a hundred titles designed – he was back to free-lancing. But the books that he was working on in England were lengthy projects, and this kept his income at a minimum. (Such financial strictures were what had, in the end, prompted him to release his Centaur design to the English Monotype firm.) His wife then became very ill, requiring expensive medical care, and so he sought further relief by offering the original matrices for sale. Writing to the San Francisco printer John Henry Nash, he inquired if Nash was interested in buying them, provided that Henry Watson Kent and the Metropolitan Museum agreed to the sale.

Nash replied to Rogers that the matrices would no longer command a high price, since the machine version was now available. Rogers differed, stating that the matrices represented the *real* Centaur and were therefore more valuable than before; he then remarked that after consultation with Fred Goudy he had decided to fix the price at $2,500. But nothing came of this attempt to dispose of the matrices, and thus they remained in storage at the Metropolitan Museum printing office.

Henry Watson Kent retired from the secretaryship of the Metropolitan in 1940, and died in 1948. The Museum Press languished without his guidance, closing its doors in the 1950s. Exactly what became of the Centaur patterns is not known, but the matrices for 12-, 20-, 24-, 30-, 48-, and 60-point are now in the Melbert B. Cary, Jr., Graphic Arts Collection at Rochester Institute of Technology. The drawings are in the Newberry Library in Chicago.

In 1948 Rogers was prevailed upon to modify Centaur for the Justowriter machine, one of the strike-on devices that came into prominence in the immediate post–World War II period. More advanced than other typewriters of the period, this instrument provided three character widths instead of the single unit. Centaur's design refused such strangulation, however, and though key bars were manufactured and the style was renamed Rogers, it is doubtful that many machines were ordered with this particular arrangement.

But Centaur type itself, by virtue of its cutting by the Monotype Corporation, will continue to provide printers with what is probably the most admirable of the numerous revivals of the fifteenth-century type of Nicolas Jenson.

BEMBO

During the 1920s the English Monotype company – Lanston Monotype Corporation – under the direction of Stanley Morison, embarked upon a program that was the most ambitious of any composing-machine manufacturer to date: the recutting of numerous historic typefaces. From this enlightened undertaking came such revivals as Bodoni, Garamond, Poliphilus, Baskerville, Fournier, and Bembo. All of these types have since become part of the repertoire of book printers throughout the world.

The last design of this group, Bembo, appeared in 1929 and has proved to be one of the most popular types of our time for the composition of books. In Europe, where Monotype composition has been the principal method of book typesetting, Bembo quickly became a dominant letter form. In the important Exhibition of British Book Production it continues to be seen in a remarkably high percentage of the books chosen each year. Since well over a hundred titles are selected for each show, it is evident that Bembo receives prime consideration from British designers.

In the United States in a similar exhibition – the Fifty Books of the Year, established in 1923 and sponsored by the American Institute of Graphic Arts – some eighty books composed in Bembo have been chosen since 1938, when the type first appeared in this country. And this despite the great majority of books exhibited having been set on slug-casting machines (Linotype, Intertype), as opposed to the Monotype (single-type) method of composition, from which Bembo is set.

Of the two Italian Renaissance types selected for his typographic revivals, Morison favored Poliphilus (cut in 1923) over Bembo. But he later acknowledged that this opinion was due principally to the then relative obscurity of the types of Aldus Manutius, the Venetian publisher-printer, and the absence of 'critical approval of Aldus's typographic merits.'

The great historic typography resurgence engendered by William Morris and the private-press movement early in the twentieth century had placed such emphasis on the types of the mid-fifteenth-century Venetian Nicolas Jenson that the contributions of other Italian punch-cutters were being ignored. It was not until the quickening interest in printing scholarship during the 1920s – prompted in part by the publication of such books as Daniel Berkeley Updike's superb *Printing Types: Their History, Forms, and Use* (1922) and the seven volumes of the periodical *The Fleuron* (1923–30) – that typographers became more aware of the later Venetian types and especially those of Aldus.

Aldus Manutius (1450–1515) was a scholar of Greek and Latin who had taught at the University of Ferrara before becoming tutor to the Pio family at Carpi. (He had changed his name from Teobaldo

ABCDEFGHIJKL
MNOPQRSTUV
WXYZ&

abcdefghijklmnop
qrstuvwxyz

1234567890

Bembo

explicabo; non tanq̃ recenſeátur.   Igi-
túr;cum illum multa in umbra ſedentem
comperiſſem ; ita initium interpellandi
eum feci. PETRVS BEMBVS FILI
VS. Diu quidem páter hic ſedes:& certe
ripa haec uirens; quam populi tuae iſtae
denſiſſimae inumbrant; & fluuiusalit;ali
quanto frigidior eſt fortaſſe,q̃ ſit ſatis .
BERNARDVS BEMBVS PATER.
Ego uerofili nuſpiam eſſe libentius ſoleo;
q̃ in haccum ripae, tum arborum , tum
etiam fluminis amoenitate:neq; eſt,quod
uereare,nequid nobis frigus hoc noceat,
praeſertim in tanto aeſtatis ardore: Sed
feciſti tu quidem pérbene; qui me ab iis
cogitationibus reuocaſti;quas & libentiſ-
ſime ſemper abiicio , cum in Nonianum
uenitur;et núc quidem nobis neſcio quo
pacto furtim irrepſerant non modo non
uocantibus , ſed etiam inuitis.
BEMBVS   FILIVS .   Derep.ſci
licet cogitabas aliquid , aut certe de trium

Page from De Ætna, Venice, 1495

Manucci to Aldo Manuzio, later Latinized to Aldus Manutius, a
common practice among classical scholars of the time.) His great
love for Greek literature inspired him to print the important Greek
texts, which he planned to salvage, edit, publish in Greek, translate

into Latin, and make available to the growing audience for the classics. The wealthy Pio family agreed to finance the project, which proved to be most costly, since it was necessary to assemble a staff of editors and translators, in addition to commissioning the cutting of Greek types.

Aldus chose Venice as the location of this major venture in Italian publishing, to be called the Aldine Press. The city, the great center of trade between Europe and the East, provided a cosmopolitan market for the books. Another essential factor in this choice was the availability of craftsmen with the skills required to establish a complete printing office in a period when every item required for production had to exist on the premises (as opposed to today's diversified printing operations). Of vital importance, too, was the large Greek colony in Venice from which editors and proofreaders were obtained.

Aldus arrived in Venice in 1490 and began his labors, first assembling a staff that eventually included some of the great scholars of the age, one of them being Erasmus of Rotterdam. It took five years before the first book, a Latin and Greek grammar, issued from the press. But though devoted to the classics, Aldus had no intention of neglecting current literature, and in the same year, 1495, he published *De Ætna*, an account of a visit to Mount Etna written by Pietro Bembo, then but twenty-five years of age. Bembo was destined to become one of the most popular of the Renaissance writers (he later took holy orders and became a cardinal).

Aldus expressed his philosophy as a publisher in an introduction to his edition of Aristotle's *Organon*: 'Those who cultivate letters must be supplied with the books necessary for their purpose; and until this supply is secured I shall not rest.' Indeed he did not rest. He neglected everything but his work, resulting in a decline into poor health that hastened his death in 1515 – he was worn out and not at all enriched by his endeavors, owing primarily to the pirating of his texts by competitors. But his contribution to literature was magnificent. It resulted in the early dissemination of knowledge through the study of the classics. It made available the Aldine innovation of the inexpensive small-format book (so successful that it was widely plagiarized in Italy and France). The pirated editions not only stole the carefully edited texts but imitated the types used by Aldus and even affixed his pressmark, the famous dolphin and anchor – the dolphin signifying speed and the anchor stability. The pirate editions even frequently included Aldus's motto, *Festina lente*, 'make haste slowly.'

THE ROMAN TYPE OF THE POLIPHILO (ALDUS) 1499 DESIGNED BY FRANCESCO GRIFFO. NOW RECUT FOR USE WITH THE "MONOTYPE" COMPOSING MACHINE

ETTER design owes much to the famous types cut by Nicolas Jenson in 1470 and used by him to such magnificent effects. A remarkable and permanent influence upon the whole of subsequent typography resulted. Within a year or two of its appearance his roman was copied all over Italy. Nevertheless it is possible that some exaggeration has crept into our estimate of its influence and that we have not taken into sufficient account the importance of Aldus. The latter's activities as a scholar and a publisher have perhaps to some extent overshadowed his merit as a printer and we have contented ourselves with recognising the importance of his usage of the first italic, 1501. It should be noted however that from the time of his establishment as a printer until his death he never employed types which were immediately based on the Jenson model. Whether or not the Aldine letters are an improvement upon those of his illustrious predecessor is a matter of taste, but it will at least be agreed that they differ in such important respects as set and cut of serif. The type of this present announcement is a "Monotype" reproduction of the famous letter used in the Poliphilus of 1499, and it may be in place to emphasize its producer's claim to credit for a design beautiful in itself and important in its influence. To our eyes it possesses a much more "present day" feeling than is conveyed in the letters of the earlier master. It symbolises

Poliphilus (English Monotype)

The roman type in which *De Ætna* was composed (called simply the De Ætna type), on which Bembo is based, was cut by Francesco Griffo, sometimes styled Francesco da Bologna. Aldus was most fortunate in obtaining the services of such an inventive punchcutter, who produced all of the types for the Aldine Press, including the famous italic of 1500–1. A former goldsmith, like many of the early punchcutters, Griffo had already cut types for several other Venetian printers – the brothers di Gregorii in particular – since arriving in the city from Padua about 1480.

·I·

QUOT SINT GENERA PRINCIPATUUM ET
QUIBUS MODIS ACQUIRANTUR

Tutti li stati, tutti e' dominii che hanno avuto et hanno imperio sopra li uomini, sono stati e sono o republiche o principati. E' principati sono o ereditarii, de' quali el sangue del loro signore ne sia suto lungo tempo principe, o e' sono nuovi. E' nuovi, o sono nuovi tutti, come fu Milano a Francesco Sforza, o sono come membri aggiunti allo stato ereditario del principe che li acquista, come è el regno di Napoli al re di Spagna. Sono, questi dominii cosí acquistati, o consueti a vivere sotto uno principe, o usi a essere liberi; et acquistonsi, o con le arme d'altri o con le proprie, o per fortuna o per virtú.

·II·

DE PRINCIPATIBUS HEREDITARIIS

Io lascerò indrieto el ragionare delle republiche, perché altra volta ne ragionai a lungo. Volterommi solo al principato, et andrò tessendo li orditi soprascritti, e disputerò come questi principati si possino governare e mantenere.

Dico, adunque, che nelli stati ereditarii et assuefatti al sangue del loro principe, sono assai minori difficultà a mantenerli che ne' nuovi, perché basta solo non preterire l'ordine de' sua antinati, e di poi temporeggiare con

II

Use of Bembo type by Giovanni Mardersteig, Verona, 1967

When jobs have type sizes fixed quickly margins of error widen unless the determining calculations are based upon factual rather than hypothetical figures. No variation in the amount of copy can affect the degree of error once that error has been made. If instead of the required ten point the ABCDEFGHIJKLMNOPQRSTUVWXYZ

Bembo Condensed Italic (English Monotype)

Griffo also cut the roman type that was used for *Hypnerotomachia Poliphili* by Francesco Colonna, printed by Aldus in 1499. This remarkable work, believed by many bibliophiles to be the finest printed book of the entire Renaissance, was, ironically, far removed in content from the scholarly texts normally published by Aldus. It was evidently a job he had taken on, in the manner of countless printers who followed him, merely to keep his shop busy. The type of the *Poliphili* was long considered superior to that of the Bembo book, but during the last half century typographic taste has favored the latter design.

Most Venetian types from the time of Jenson had been rather closely adapted from the humanist manuscript hand, and therefore tended to be somewhat heavy in stroke and serif. (It was of course this feature that so much attracted William Morris when he sought a replacement for the anemic book types of the nineteenth century.) Francesco Griffo must receive much of the credit for the departure of the punchcutter from slavish dependence on the pen-drawn characters. The engraving of a steel punch, utilizing files and gravers, requires precision skills and allows refinements beyond the scope of the reed or the pen. It is evident that Griffo realized the potential of his tools in the creation of letter forms at once livelier and more precise than those of the scribes.

Another significant departure from the Jenson type is noticeable in Griffo's capitals, which he shortened in relation to the lowercase ascenders. Serving as his model, however, were the same majuscules cut in stone by the Romans that Jenson had followed.

Griffo's concepts apparently took several years to develop. The

WHEREVER CIVILIZATION EXTENDS
TYPOGRAPHERS WILL BE REQUIRED
ABCDEFGHJKLMNOPQRSTUVWXYZ

OF ALL DOCUMENTS JUDGED
SIX WERE GIVEN AN AWARD
ABCDEFGHJKLMOPQRSTUYZ

THE BANK RECOGNIZES
OUR CLAIMS AS VALID
ABCDEGHJLMNPQWXY

ABDEGHJKMNQRST
ABCDFHLNOPUVW

Bembo Titling (English Monotype)

great twentieth-century printer-scholar Giovanni Mardersteig noted
of the Griffo types that they were first a modification of the Jenson
letters but then they showed a 'gradual evolution from the earliest
Venetian types, and they constantly improve until they reach their
finest shape in the Bembo type which he cut for Aldus.'

The Monotype cutting of the *De Ætna* type, although an excellent
rendering, could not be other than an approximation of the original.
There are always both aesthetic and economic problems in the adaptation of the early types. For example, there is the difficulty of
determining the allowance to be made for ink squeeze in the original
(owing to the weight of the impression), or the exact shape of characters that were badly printed or poorly cast in metal. In the redesign

PROFESSIONAL TYPOGRAPHY
In All Classes Of Printing Reflects Merit
in the product advertised and yields $12345

Bembo Italic

of Griffo's type there was also the problem of which variant of certain characters to select. For it must be remembered that during the incunabula period printers were still in competition with scribes in the production of books, and they frequently followed the scribe's inclination to provide several variations of a particular character.

Discussing these variations in his essay on the *De Ætna* types, Dr. Mardersteig listed eight lowercase characters for which Griffo provided alternates. For example, there were five variants of *e* and three of *a*. These alternates have proven useful in determining the origin of some of the French types, modeled on those of Griffo by Claude Garamond and Antoine Angereau some thirty-five years after Griffo had designed them.

In addition, the modern pantograph machine necessarily mechanizes a design, particularly in its inability to vary a face from size to size, a factor that to the eye of the typographic purist removes much of the individual charm of the historic fonts.

Finally, a major predicament in the production of Monotype Bembo was the selection and cutting of an italic to complement the roman, a quandary previously discussed in the chapter on Cloister Old Style. A partial solution in this case was to supply two italic forms for Bembo.

The first, cut by the noted English calligrapher Alfred Fairbank, was judged too independent of the roman, a decision deplored by its designer. It has since been marketed as a separate type, a true example of the chancery style. Originally named Narrow Bembo Italic, now called Bembo Condensed Italic, it is an exceedingly fine type in its own right and justly popular as such. Upon the rejection of the Fairbank italic the drawing room of the company prepared a more conventional italic, based on the designs of the Venetian printing master Giovantonio Tagliente.

Bembo was a slow starter in the United States, even though the Lanston Monotype Machine Company of Philadelphia made it available in the 1930s. (The American and English Monotype firms, as noted earlier, were separate but maintained a working arrangement until the demise of the American branch several years ago.) The problem was the strong competition in the United States from the slug-casting machines, Linotype and Intertype, which obtained much the larger share of the market for composing machines. Thus, the single-type-casting Monotype system was not nearly so well represented in American books as it was in English and European.

But with the recent increase in phototypesetting for book composition such types as Bembo will undoubtedly see wider use. Several of the manufacturers of film-setting devices have already made the type available, which assures its continuing success almost five centuries after its appearance.

ARRIGHI

One of the finest examples of the early use of italic types appears in *Coryciana* (1524), a collection of Latin poems written by Blodius Palladius. Like many another printed book, this volume is admired today primarily as an example of printing rather than for the beauty of its thought or language – justifying the observation of George Bernard Shaw that the survival of a book can more frequently be credited to its printer than to its author.

The elegance of the *Coryciana* type was not just happenstance. It was the product of a printer who had already established his reputation as a writing master and who was the author of the first book that taught the nonprofessional writer how to pen the style known as the chancery cursive: the justly famous *Operina*, published in 1522 by Ludovico degli Arrighi. Employed as a scribe in the secretariat of papal briefs, Arrighi had written his text in pen and then had it copied in a wood engraving for printing. The work is still used as a basic calligraphic text, owing largely to the skill of John Howard Benson, who translated the work from Italian, lettered the English translation in Arrighi's style, and matched the original line for line.

The chancery cursive was a calligraphic development stemming from the humanist revival of the fifteenth century. In the various chanceries, or administrative offices, of both church and court, the responsibility of the scribes was the preparation of letters of communication. In the papal chancery in Rome these communications were called bulls, so termed because of their round seals, *bullae*. The bulls, written in a gothic hand, frequently required supplementary information in separate form, which was written in a contemporary style of 'round hand,' a cursive form of roman.

This informal 'round hand' became standardized for less important papal business, and the documents themselves became known as briefs. The sloped writing – *cancelleresca cursiva* ('chancery cursive') – common to these briefs was to become the model for the styles that

ABCDEFGHIJ

KLMNOPQRST

UVWXYZ

abcdefghijklmno

pqrstuvwxyz

fifffflffifflgggyzy

$&.,-:;!?

1234567890

Arrighi

obtained the name italic in 1501, when they were first reproduced as printing types by Francesco Griffo for the Venetian publisher Aldus Manutius.

The historic development of italic itself has long been known to modern printers, but the more distinctive *cancelleresca cursiva* was practically unknown in printing types until the 1920s – that most productive and innovative period of typographical research. Daniel Berkeley Updike's *Printing Types*, first published in 1922, mentioned Arrighi not at all, but in the second edition of 1937, the author acknowledged the Italian printer-scribe in the notes in which he described the increasing interest in typographic history that had developed since 1922.

But despite the efforts of modern scholars (Stanley Morison, for one), many printers remain confused about the distinctions between the ordinary italic types and those sloped forms based on the chancery cursive. Both styles are currently in use, but the chancery is generally restricted to accompanying roman types modeled on forms that developed before 1500.

It was at that time that Aldus Manutius had begun the production of editions of the classics that would find a ready market among scholars and students. To accomplish such an objective he necessarily had to depart from the established practice of printing books in large format, a practice making them both bulky and expensive. To conserve space it appeared reasonable to use a type that was closer fitting than the roman, or upright, character. His punchcutter, Francesco Griffo, chose the informal cursive writing styles as a model, producing a font that was used by Aldus to print a small-format edition of Virgil in 1501. This was the first book to be set in an inclined letter, a style later given the name italic, from 'Italy,' its place of origin. This earliest italic differs from later models in the lack of the sloped form of capitals, roman being used in their place.

Probably the need for being economical with space, especially space related to character width, was foremost in Griffo's mind when he selected the cursive style. But another theory, and a fairly logical one, holds that earlier editions of the classics were beyond the means of penurious scholars, who frequently resorted to copying the books themselves. As their style of writing was the cursive, cursive print to them would be as legible as roman print.

It is immaterial which theory is correct. The fact remains that italic immediately became extremely popular for composing books,

design of Ludovico degli Arrighi, is used; it has never appeared before. An earlier version of the face, called Arrighi, was used in the small privately printed edition of the Poet Laureate's new verses, "The Tapestry," published in London last year.

The "Crito" will be printed at the Officina Bodoni at Montagnola di Lugano, Switzerland, a press which by reason of its perfection of technique is justly considered to rank among the foremost in Europe. Later there will appear the interesting

MEMOIRS OF THE AUTHOR
OF A VINDICATION OF THE RIGHTS
OF WOMEN
by
William Godwin,

transcribed and with an Introduction by John Middleton Murry. The reprint follows exactly the rare second edition of this important "Memoir" published in 1798.

The details of design and production have been entrusted to Frederic Warde who is well-known to amateurs of fine printing on both sides of the Atlantic.

The first cutting of Arrighi, called Vicenza, as used in the announcement for an edition of *Plato's Crito*, printed by Giovanni Mardersteig, 1926

DE FALSA SAPIENTIA.

se, suaq; confirmet: nec ulli alteri sapere concedit; ne se
desipere fateatur. sed sicut alias tollit ; sic ipsa quoq; ab
alijs tollitur omnibus . Nihilo minus enim philosophi
sunt , qui eam stultitiæ accusant . Q uancunq; lauda-
ueris, ueram'q; dixeris; à philosophis uituperatur, ut sal
sa. Credemus ne igitur uni sese suam'q; doctrinam lau-
danti; an multis unius alterius ignorantiam culpan-
tibus? Rectius ergo sit necesse est, quod plurimi sentiunt,

The italic cut for Aldus by Francesco Griffo, 1501

and entire works, especially classics, were set in italic. The Aldine Press, carried on by Aldus's sons following his death in 1515, continued this tradition. The English bibliographer A. F. Johnson called the sixteenth century the Age of Italics, stating that south of the Alps, particularly in Italy, almost as many titles were produced in that style as in roman.

Owing to its use in the influential Aldine classics, italic soon became established elsewhere, first in the pirating of the Venetian printer's texts, and then for other original books. By 1525 italics were being employed by German printers and had appeared in the scholastic center in Basel. Following a cutting by Simon de Colines in Paris about 1525, they were taken up by other French printers. Further impetus was given to the use of the italic letter in French printing by the appearance of Arrighi's book, whose types were a great aesthetic advance over the 1501 italic of Aldus.

It was probably the combined influence of the Aldine and the Arrighi italics that led French punchcutters after 1530 – Colines, Claude Garamond, Robert Granjon – to create an italic different from both, one that would complement the roman instead of being an independent type. From the mid-fifteenth century this increasingly became, and remains, the accepted practice everywhere.

Harry Carter, the late typographic historian, in his Lyell lectures at Oxford in 1968, assigned to François Guyot of Antwerp the credit for actually matching romans with italics. Guyot was for many years a supplier of type for the famous French printer Christopher Plantin, and had in addition justified many of the matrices that Plantin had purchased in France for use in his Antwerp shop. Guyot died in 1570.

In this area A. F. Johnson takes issue with Updike, who had originally stated that the Aldine italic was the model for all subsequent italic types. Aldus, however, in his dedication to publishing inexpensive texts, was under no compulsion to demand a beautiful model for his cursive type, nor did he make any attempt to produce 'beautiful' books with it. As a scholar, his principal concern was with the subject matter, and as a publisher, with the economics of the market for books, particularly textbooks. Thus, the Virgil of 1501 shows a somewhat cramped page, made even more difficult to read by the employment of numerous ligatures; Updike noted some sixty-five tied letters in this one book alone. The case for the Aldine italic as the one model for all subsequent italics is therefore weak.

The full development of type in the chancery form had to await the awakened interest of the writing masters whose talents were manifested in the numerous books on letter forms that appeared during the first half of the sixteenth century. The newly ubiquitous nature of the printed word had, naturally enough, created keen interest on the part of scribes in the alphabetic forms being utilized by printers: the English calligrapher James Wardrop has written, 'Printing, which killed writing as a trade, favored its development as an art.' It is in this respect that we now recognize the contributions of the Italian writing masters, who inspired the cutting into printing type of the finest of all italic forms, the chancery cursive.

In our own time, a number of excellent copies of this style are available and the best of them, named Arrighi, properly calls attention to the man who first used such a design – the calligrapher Ludovico degli Arrighi, originally from Vicenza, who hence occasionally styled himself Vicentino.

Having become interested in the printing craft during the production in 1522 of his *Operina*, Arrighi set up a press at Rome with the intention of doing fine printing. For his type he drew an italic letter patterned on those same chancery forms shown in his calligraphy book. He employed an engraver of seals, Lautitius Perusinus, for the cutting of his punches. The delicate kerning of so many of the written characters required outstanding skill on the part of the engraver, and Perusinus, whose talents have been praised by no less an authority than Benvenuto Cellini, supplied such skill.

Page from the *Operina of Arrighi*, Rome, 1522

The initial use of Arrighi's new cursive was in the *Coryciana* of 1524. Apart from being composed in one of the finest italic types ever drawn, the book is also notable for the first appearance of those capitals we know today as swash. A second italic type of Arrighi, produced in 1526, eliminated the swash capitals and affixed standard serifs to the ascenders: in the first type, the ascenders had been rounded (or pear-shaped, to some authorities), in the style of the pen-drawn cursives, and it is evident that in his second version Arrighi was attempting to produce a type of greater utility than the original design. It must be remembered that all types were hand-cast and that the composition of type metal produced a relatively soft type whose quality cannot be compared to the more solidly cast types achieved in the twentieth century. This weakness particularly affected the casting of kerned letters that project from the body of the type and are a prominent feature of italic.

That Arrighi had succeeded as a printer and as a type designer may be noted from a letter written to Pope Clement VII by Giangiorgo Trissino, an author whose work was printed by Arrighi: 'These new letters have been made here in Rome by Ludovico Vicentino, who, as in calligraphy, has surpassed all other men of our age, so, having recently invented this most beautiful method of doing in print all that was formerly done with the pen, in his beautiful types he has gone beyond all other printers.'

Arrighi printed successfully until 1527. That year it is believed he lost his life in the Sack of Rome, since he was not heard from following that outrage.

His death notwithstanding, Arrighi's chancery cursive subsequently became well established and was cut by other engravers in Italy and France, where it served as a model for the development in the seventeenth century of the italic forms of the French punchcutters. Thereafter, however, it went out of style, not to be revived until the twentieth century.

Probably the first modern type to be based on the *cancelleresca* was designed by the English calligrapher Edward Johnston. It was his classes in the study of calligraphy early in this century that were so very important to the revival of interest in the work of the Italian Renaissance writing masters, and which in turn encouraged the present interest in classic handwriting and the prestige enjoyed by calligraphers.

Johnston began work on a chancery cursive about 1914, but his experiments were not widely known. His designs were cut by the noted punchcutter of the Kelmscott and Doves Press types, Edward Prince, with the aid of George Friend. Johnston's type, to be used in conjunction with a roman for Count Kessler's Cranach Press at Weimar, was laid aside during the First World War when this fine press ceased its activities, not to resume production until 1925. The cursive was thus first used in 1926, for the colophon of an edition of Virgil, but it was not cast for text composition until 1931.

In the meantime, the type revival program by the English Monotype firm had already begun under the direction of Stanley Morison. For Poliphilus, cut in 1923, it became necessary to supply an italic that had some affinity with the roman, and Morison decided on a chancery cursive. Consequently, he turned to the second type of Arrighi. Morison later acknowledged his debt for 'discovering' this design to Johnston in the latter's influential text, *Writing and Illuminating and Lettering* (1906). The Monotype version was named Blado, as it constituted the first revival of such a letter to be made available to printers since the time of Antonio Blado, who had acquired the Arrighi types in 1526. The italic of Poliphilus is thus an independent type, although Blado and Poliphilus complement each other.

The next chancery to be revived was designed by a young American typographer, Frederic Warde. It was named Arrighi, since its model was the type of *Coryciana*. Warde was an enigmatic figure in American typography of the early 1920s. He began working at the Printing House of William Edwin Rudge in Mount Vernon, New York, during the great period when Bruce Rogers was active in that firm. The reputation of Rogers was instrumental in attracting many aspiring young typographers to Mount Vernon, where they had the opportunity to rub elbows with the most famous book designer of the century; this group, later known as the Rudge Alumni, included such prominent figures as Joseph Blumenthal and Peter Beilenson.

Warde next became director of printing at Princeton University Press and married Beatrice Becker, then an assistant librarian to Henry Lewis Bullen at the library of the American Type Founders Company. In 1924 the young couple decided to travel to Europe to devote their time to typographic studies. Beatrice Warde was to remain in England for the rest of her life, establishing a worldwide reputation as a writer and publicist for typography.

In England, Frederic Warde met Charles Hobson of the Cloister Press in Manchester, and through him, Stanley Morison. The Wardes

Corytius voto reddidit ista suo

H ausit enim illius mentem Deus , et dedit arti

Q uod non humanæ est , fingeret artis , opus .

A delon

Uirgo parens , nec virgo parens , natusq̃ , neposq̃

I dem qui cunctis est pater hic residet

E sse potest quicq̃ maius , te iudice , rerum ?

S unt hæc de cœlo mystica missa tibi .

Philippus Beroaldus Iunior

Uobis Corycius maxima numina

H as ponit statuas , non sibi flagitans

A mpli arbitria regni ,

M aiorem aut titulum ambiens ,

N am quæ vestra homini sancta dedit manus

S at lætum faciunt . Vos rogat vt diu

H is quæ possidet , vti

& vita incolumi queat ,

A udi sacra cohors cœlitum , et accipe

Q uas fert Corycius suppliciter preces

S i æuum puriter egit ,

& si vos coluit pie .

Page from *Coryciana*, printed by Arrighi, Rome, 1524

MARCI HIERONYMI VIDAE CREMONENSIS SCACCHIA LVDVS.

l

V dimus effigiem belli, simulataque ueris

P rælia, buxo acies fiEtas, et ludicra regna .

V t gemini inter se reges albusque, nigerque

P ro laude oppositi certent bicoloribus armis.

D icite Seriades Nymphæ certamina tanta

C arminibus prorsus uatum illibata priorum.

N ulla uia eſt. tamen ire iuuat, quo me rapit ardor,

I nuiaque audaci propero tentare iuuenta.

V os per inacceſſas rupes, et inhospita euntem

S axa Deæ regite, ac secretum oſtendite callem .

V os huius ludi imprimis meminiſſe neceſſe eſt.

V os primæ ſtudia hæc Italis monſtraſtis in oris

K

The second italic of Arrighi, Rome, 1527

and Morison struck up an instant, if short-lived friendship (at least on Frederic's part). But it was through Morison that Warde became acquainted with Arrighi's *Coryciana*, obtaining a copy from a bookseller in Paris. It was also at Morison's suggestion that Warde undertook the design of a modern version of the Arrighi type.

Warde turned apparently to the Parisian punchcutter Charles Plumet for the engraving of the punches from his designs. There has been, however, some controversy concerning the cutting of the punches. Morison wrote in 1953 that Charles Malin, another French punchcutter of the period, had made them; Morison stated, 'I think that I was solely responsible for the negotiations and began discussion with Malin. . . .' Yet in 1934 Warde had written a letter to Henry Watson Kent of the Metropolitan Museum in New York (which had purchased Warde's matrices and punches) saying that Plumet had cut the punches; this is corroborated by Morison's biographer, Nicolas Barker, who in his 1972 study of Morison quoted from letters between Plumet and Warde. Moreover, in the only biographical article written on Warde after his death, in 1939 (published in *Print* magazine), Will Ransom declared that Plumet was the punchcutter. The matter was cleared up in 1981 when the Melbert B. Cary, Jr. Graphics Arts Collection at the Rochester Institute of Technology acquired the punches and matrices for Arrighi. The name of Charles Plumet is inscribed at the foot of each punch in the font.

Arrighi type was first used in 1926 in a book entitled *The Calligraphic Models of Ludovico degli Arrighi, Surnamed Vicentino*, printed by Hans (later Giovanni) Mardersteig at the Officina Bodoni, then located in Montagnola di Lugano, Switzerland. The introduction to this book was written by Morison.

Warde then produced a second version of Arrighi, with standard treatment of serifs on the ascenders. In the colophon of the first book in which this new type was used, in 1926 – *Crito: A Socratic Dialogue by Plato*, also printed by Mardersteig – the face was called Vicenza.

The final version of Arrighi, and the one that is best known, is that of England's Lanston Monotype Corporation. In 1929 Bruce Rogers had gone to Oxford to plan the printing by the University Press of his great masterwork, the lectern Bible (which was finally completed in 1935). It was composed in his own Centaur type in the 22-point size. Centaur – first cut as a private type in 1914 – did not, however, possess a companion italic. Thus, when the Monotype firm adapted Centaur to machine-casting for use in the Bible, it was

THE FIRST ELEGY

ho would give ear, among the angelic host,
Were I to cry aloud? and even if one
Amongst them took me swiftly to his heart,
I should dissolve before his strength of being.
For beauty's nothing but the birth of terror,
Which we endure but barely, and, enduring,
Must wonder at it, in that it disdains
To compass our destruction. every angel
Is terrible, and thus in self-control
I crush the appeal that rises with my sobs.
Of whom, alas, of whom shall we have need?
Neither of angels nor of men: already
The sagacious animals have found us out,
How little at our ease we live and move
In this intelligible world. maybe
We keep the image of some tree that hangs
Above a slope, that daily we behold;
Or we recall the path of yesterday,
And our indulgence to the constancy
Of some dear habit, that remained with us

4

Edward Johnston's italic type in the Cranach Press edition of Rilke's *The Duineser Elegien*, Weimar, 1931

necessary to provide an italic. Rogers was of the opinion that he lacked the skill to produce a competent chancery cursive to accompany his roman, and he therefore persuaded Frederic Warde to design such a type. Warde thereupon made a third version of his Arrighi design, this time supplying inclined capitals, which had not been available in the first two cuttings, which followed the Aldine tradition of roman capitals. He also shortened the ascenders to conform more closely with Centaur, a type that Rogers had adapted from the 1470 original of Nicolas Jenson.

Since its introduction as a Monotype face, Arrighi has been considered by many typographers to be the best current example of the chancery-cursive style, and thus has been widely used by many of the great printers of our time. Rogers called it 'one of the finest and most legible cursive letters ever produced,' and proclaimed it a fitting companion for such a calligraphic roman as Centaur.

Warde sold his original punches and matrices to the Metropolitan Museum in 1934 (his critics have since claimed they were not his to sell). More recently, the English printer Will Carter requested the matrices and received permission to recast several fonts, which was done at the foundry of the Oxford University Press. The whereabouts of the punches is now unknown.

Arrighi in its best-known adaptation, the Monotype cutting, has many of the features of all the chancery italics: the compact set width, the wide kerning, and a slighter incline than the conventional italics. However, several distinctions may be noted. Perhaps the easiest characteristic of this type to remember is the lowercase *g*, in which the ear has been removed.

DANTE

Readers may very well be mystified as to why such a handsome roman letter as Dante has not achieved the degree of popularity in the United States accorded other Renaissance printing types, such as Bembo, Centaur, and Palatino. This less-frequently encountered revival was designed in 1954 by Giovanni Mardersteig.

Although the craft of the printer contributes to the scholarly aptitude of most of its practitioners, the fact remains that since the first century and a half following Johann Gutenberg's invention of movable type, the appellation scholar-printer could be reasonably applied to very few people who labored in the printing office. And this is particularly true in the present century. Only three American exceptions come immediately to mind – Theodore L. De Vinne, Daniel Berkeley Updike, and Joseph Blumenthal. All these men were first practical printers, in the sense that they were responsible for the operation of printing plants (although only one of them, De Vinne, had learned the trade as an apprentice). But long after their firms have been disbanded their names remain widely known for their singular contributions to the printing craft itself, in which each of them tran-scended the mere management of a business.

A European example of this genre was Dr. Mardersteig, whose name is instantly associated with the great traditions of typography by those who have known him, and whose work at his Officina Bodoni has provided constant and distinguished service to scholarly printing. Future typographic historians will probably be surprised that his efforts to maintain the scholarly heritage came at a time when tech-nological change was creating an atmosphere uniformly antithetic to the continuance of this old printing tradition: it is because of the success of his efforts that this great tradition was preserved.

What are Mardersteig's credentials as a scholar-printer? In the course of a lecture on his work presented several years ago, Alan Fern, of the Library of Congress, put them into a succinct statement:

'His profound scholarship was reflected in the choice of works he printed. His texts were the result of his reading in a number of languages. Upon them were bestowed the most careful editorial attention and the finest possible typographic form.'

The printer preferred anonymity, but he did write a short exposition of his philosophy, which might be defined as a credo: 'First, service to the author, searching for the form best suited to his theme. Second, service to the reader, making reading as pleasant and light for him as possible. Third, the giving of the whole an attractive appearance without imposing too much self-will.'

In an account of his first six years as a printer, Mardersteig wrote: 'All texts before being set up are thoroughly examined. The best critical edition is chosen and if it does not agree with the latest research, a new revised text is established by comparison with the original manuscript or the first edition.' Few private printers could even begin to match such rigorous standards of production.

Born in Goethe's city of Weimar in 1892 and christened Hans Mardersteig, he was fortunate to be a member of an extremely literate and artistic family. Although he earned a degree in law, he declined to follow that profession and instead became a teacher. However, an association with Count Harry Kessler, proprietor of Weimar's distinguished Cranach Press, turned Mardersteig's thoughts to publishing. He then became an editor and production supervisor for the publishing house of Kurt Wolff, first in Leipzig and later in Munich.

In 1922, because of declining health, Mardersteig moved to Montagnola di Lugano in Switzerland to establish himself as a printer. Upon his arrival he commissioned the construction of a hand press; for his type he was most fortunate in having obtained permission from the Italian government to resurrect matrices produced by the great eighteenth-century printer Giambattista Bodoni. Mardersteig was given exclusive use of the original types, which had been preserved at Parma.

During the next five years he produced twenty-one books, most of which were hand-set in Bodoni. Of these early volumes, two became landmarks in Mardersteig's progress as a printer of scholarly attainments, and both were in fact a departure from the Bodoni pattern. First was *The Calligraphic Models of Arrighi* (1926), written by Stanley Morison, set in a cutting of the Arrighi cursive by the American type designer Frederic Warde. A year later Mardersteig produced *A Newly*

Discovered Treatise on Classic Letter Design Printed at Parma by Dami-anus Moyllus circa 1480, edited and introduced by Stanley Morison and composed in the Poliphilus and Blado types. Several of these early editions were produced for other publishers, and in doing this Mardersteig established a tradition that he followed for the rest of his life – printing on commission as well as to please himself.

Mardersteig's work at Montagnola was interrupted in 1926 when he won a competition to produce the entire works of the Italian poet Gabriele D'Annunzio. For this huge project he found it necessary to remove his establishment, Officina Bodoni, to the large modern press of Arnoldo Mondadori in Verona, where the D'Annunzio work was to be printed. The forty-nine volumes took five years to complete, a trying time for the printer, as the theatrical poet often demanded to see the work page by page at his home on the shores of Lake Garda. Some of these books ran to more than five hundred pages, all hand-set in Bodoni types. Two hundred ninety copies of the set were printed, all on the hand press.

Following this rather harrowing experience, Mardersteig spent 1933 in Glasgow, Scotland, as adviser to the Collins Cleartype Press. When he returned to Verona, he refused an offer from Mondadori to become art director and chose instead to take his press into his own home, on a hillside overlooking the city. He now expanded his typographic resources to include such historic faces as Garamond, Baskerville, Bembo, Janson, and Centaur.

Mardersteig had met the English typographic historian Stanley Morison as early as 1924. The two shared an interest in the fifteenth-century Italian letter forms, particularly the types of the punchcutter Francesco Griffo, who had produced for Aldus Manutius the types of two of the great works to issue from the Aldine Press, Bembo's *De Ætna* and the *Poliphili* of Colonna. About 1929, at Morison's urging, Mardersteig began his research into the Griffo types that resulted in a new design. He secured the assistance of Charles Malin, a highly skilled punchcutter residing in Paris, who had cut the trial size of Eric Gill's Perpetua design. For the next twenty-five years Malin was to collaborate with Mardersteig in the cutting of all of his types, offering numerous suggestions in their design that proved invaluable to the printer.

This initial venture into type design in 1929 was named Griffo. Similar to the Monotype Bembo, which was also inspired by the *De Ætna*, Griffo may very well be a closer rendition of the original.

DANTE

Charles Malin, Paris

abcçdefghiɪjklmnopqrstuvwxyzæœ ff fi fl ffi ffl ß   1 2 3 4 5 7 8 9 0 — ? ! ' , ;

ABCDEFGHIJKLMNOPQRSTUVWXYZÆŒ   *ABCDEFGHIJKLMN*

Madame & Monsieur Charles Malin
présentent au Docteur Giovanni MARDERSTEIG
et à sa famille leurs meilleurs vœux & souhaits de

abcdefghiìjklmnopqrstuvwxyzʒʒ æœ ç &   *fi fl ff ffi ffl ß ä é è ô ü*

ECHO BOCCACE OIEH Æ Œ

ABCDEFGHIJKLMNOPQRSTUVWXYZ
abcdefghijklmnopqrstuvwxyz ff fi fl ffi ffl Æ æ Œ œ ç 1 2 3 4 5 6 7 8 9 0
à è ì ò ù á é í ó ú â ê î ô û ä ë ï ö ü À È Ì Ò Ù É Ä Ö Ü . , ' : ; ? ! ([- —

ABCDEFGHIJKLMNOPQRSTUVWXYZ
abcdefghijklmnopqrstuvwxyz   ff fi fl ffi ffl Æ æ Œ œ ß ñ ç &   1 2 3 4 5 6 7 8 9 0
à è ì ò ù á é í ó ú â ê î ô û ä ë ï ö ü À È Ì Ò Ù É Ä Ö Ü . , ' : ; ? ! (-

ABCDEFGHIJKLMNOPQRSTUVWXYZ
abcdefghijklmnopqrstuvwxyz   1 2 3 4 5 6 7 8 9 0
ff fi fl ffi ffl Æ æ Œ œ Ç ç ß ñ & ⋆ « » . , ' ; : ! ? ([- —
à è ò ù á é í ó ú â ê î ô û ä ë ï ö ü À È Ì Ò Ù É Ä Ö Ü

ABCDEFGHIJKLMNOPQRSTUVWXYZ
abcdefghijklmnopqrstuvwxyz   1 2 3 4 5 6 7 8 9 0
ff fi fl ffi ffl Æ æ Œ œ ç ñ ß ʒ & « » . , ' : ; ? ! ([- —
à è ì ò ù á é í ó ú â ê î ô û ä ë ï ö ü È Ì Ò Ù É Ä Ö Ü

ABCDEFGHIJKLMNOPQ
RSTUVWXYZ ÆŒ

Dante Monotype, Officina Bodoni

et tu reuerſi ſumus; ut de Aetnae incendi-
is interrogaremus ab iis, quibus notum
eſt illa nos ſatis diligenter perſpexiſſe; ut
ea tandem moleſtia careremus; placuit mi
hi eum ſermonem conſcribere'; quem
cum Bernardo parente habui paucis poſt

Unaccountably, it was not used at the Officina Bodoni until 1939, for the edition of *Due Episodi della Vita di Felice Feliciano*, the forty-first book produced at the press. After the war the type was revised. In 1967, when Mardersteig printed his own edition of *De Ætna*, he chose Griffo for setting the original Latin and Monotype Bembo for the English translation, making for a most interesting juxtaposition of the two types. He also wrote an erudite account of the types' origin.

The association with Stanley Morison, as well as the one with Frederic Warde, had definitely increased Mardersteig's desire to investigate the development of classic typefaces. But though his predisposition was to remain in the era of Aldus for inspiration, he did break away on at least one occasion. During his year's residence in Scotland with the Collins Cleartype Press, Mardersteig had super-vised the production of a type for that firm that was based on the English Roman No. 1 of the nineteenth-century Scottish typefounder Alexander Wilson. It was named Fontana and was cut for Monotype composition. Fontana was used by Collins for thirty years before the firm released its exclusive rights.

About 1934 Mardersteig drew Zeno, which was cut in Paris by Malin in 1936–37. The design harks back probably to one of Nicolas Jenson's contemporaries of mid-fifteenth-century Venice; it retains the solid strength of the Venetian types but without the somewhat cumbersome slab serifs so prevalent in those styles. In the 16-point

THE GOSPEL ACCORDING
TO SAINT MARK

CHAPTER I

THE BEGINNING OF THE GOSPEL of Jesus Christ, the Son of God; as it is written in the prophets, Behold, I send my messenger before thy face, which shall prepare thy way before thee. The voice of one crying in the wilderness, Prepare ye the way of the Lord, make his paths straight.

John did baptize in the wilderness, and preach the baptism of repentance for the remission of sins. And there went out unto him all the land of Judæa, and they of Jerusalem, and were all baptized of him in the river of Jordan, confessing their sins. And John was clothed with camel's hair, and with a girdle of a skin about his loins; and he did eat locusts and wild honey; and preached, saying, There cometh one mightier than I after me, the latchet of whose shoes I am not worthy to stoop down and unloose. I indeed have baptized you with water: but he shall baptize you with the Holy Ghost.

And it came to pass in those days, that Jesus came from Nazareth of Galilee, and was baptized of John in Jordan. And straightway coming up out of the water, he saw the heavens opened, and the Spirit like a dove descending upon him: and there came a

III

Mardersteig's Zeno design as used in *The Four Gospels*, Verona, 1962

PACIOLI

Charles Malin, Paris

ABCDEFGHILMNOPRSTUVZ BOLZANO

CHARLES MALIN   MARDERSTEIG

ABCDEFGHIJKLMNOPRSTUV

FILOSOFIA CRITICA STORIA
MŒURS ZUKUNFT

ABCDEFGHIJKLMNOP

RIME TRIONFI POESIE
CORSO LIRE

ABCDEFGHIJKLMNOPQRSTUVWXYZ

ABCDEFGHIJKLMNOPQRST
UVWXYZ

ABCDEFGHIJKLMNOP
QRSTUVWXYZ

Pacioli Titling

A B C D E F G H I J K L M
N O P Q R S T U V W X Y Z
Æ & Œ

a b c d e f g h i j k l m n o
p q r s t u v w x y z æ œ fi
1 2 3 4 5 6 7 8 9 0

A B C D E F G H I J K L M
N O P Q R S T U V W X Y Z
Æ & Œ

a b c d e f g h i j k l m n
o p q r s t u v w x y z æ œ
1 2 3 4 5 6 7 8 9 0
ffi ffl

Fontana

size, Zeno was first used in an edition of *San Zeno Vescovo, Patrono di Verona*, by Lorenzo Montano, printed in 1937. Later Mardersteig revised this face and employed it in one of the great books of his press, *The Four Gospels*, printed in 1962.

Still another Renaissance type came from Mardersteig's hand, in

1950–51. Named Pacioli, it was a titling font for which the model was the majuscule alphabet drawn in the fifteenth century by Fra Luca de Pacioli. Mardersteig first used this beautiful rendition, appropriately, in his edition of Pacioli's *De Devina Proportione*, published in 1956.

Dante was Mardersteig's last and finest type, cut in 1954. Here again, the Verona printer became involved with the fifteenth-century Italian types. It is unfortunate that Mardersteig never managed to find the time to write extensively about his five types; it would be interesting to compare the drawings, for example, with the models that he was adapting for his personal use at the Officina Bodoni. Without such explication, we must look to the letters themselves, and Dante appears to have been influenced by the Aldine types, although it retains some of the vigor of the earlier Venetians.

Malin completed the punches for the 12-point size just one year before his death, in 1956. Unlike Griffo and Zeno, which were not used immediately, Dante was chosen for, and received its name from, the edition of Boccaccio's *Trattatello in Laude di Dante* that Mardersteig printed in 1955. The type quickly became a favorite of its designer, being selected for another two dozen books during the next twenty years.

Although produced for a private press, Dante is by no means over-refined, a condemnation that may be applied to so many types of similar conception. As a book type it has few idiosyncrasies to inter-fere with its readability. Its crisp and sparkling contrast of stroke is eminently suited both to the antique finish of most book papers and to the dull-coated stocks, used for illustrations. The height of the capitals falls slightly below that of the ascenders, but the reduction is not quite so abrupt as in the Bembo series.

Recognizing its usefulness as a book type, the Monotype Cor-poration of London arranged in 1955 to issue Dante for machine-composition. The firm used the 12-point size as produced by Charles Malin, which with but few changes was adapted for the range of sizes that would make the design most serviceable to printers. The italic is a chancery, matching beautifully the spirit of the roman; in this case Mardersteig departed from the earlier concept of the cursive form he had given to Griffo, which is more closely related to the first italic cut for Aldus (in 1501) than to the chancery style associated with the designs of Arrighi. Since the introduction of Dante, Monotype has added a semi-bold weight, along with a series of titling capitals, both of which broaden its usefulness in book production.

its poet. Even our aforementioned D'Annunzio, by training perfectly equipt, cannot do much more than moan ornately.

> O sinuous, moist and burning mouth, where my desire is intensified when I am sunk in deep oblivion, and which relentlessly sucks my life. O great head of hair strewn over my knees during the sweet act. O cold hand which spreads a shiver and feels me shivering.

Yet in the moment that our situation seems to have become impossible (as bereft of hope as Virginia Woolf's Orlando has imagined it to be), *deus ex machina*: we recollect the honest masters of our tongue, and in them, on occasion, we find the problem solved, the tribute paid, the vision pure, the writing done. In Ben Jonson, for instance:

> *Have you seene but a bright Lillie grow,*
> *Before rude hands have touch'd it?*
> *Ha' you mark'd but the fall o' the Snow*
> *Before the soyle hath smutch'd it?*
> *Ha' you felt the wooll of Bever?*
> *Or Swans Downe ever?*
> *Or have smelt o' the bud o' the Brier?*
> *Or the Nard in the fire?*
> *Or have tasted the bag of the Bee?*
> *O so white! O so soft! O so sweet is she!*

Initially I wrote of displacement as if it went from thing to thing—phallus to flower:

> *Full gently now she takes him by the hand,*
> *A lily prison'd in a gaol of snow,*
> *Or ivory in an alabaster band;*
> *So white a friend engirts so white a foe . . .*

but I have been dropping hints all along like heavy shoes that the

[42]

Page of Monotype Dante from *On Being Blue* by William Gass, 1976

107

American book designers regret the restricted availability of Dante, in which mechanical composition is confined to the Monotype, a type-setting machine no longer in wide use. Up to the time of this writing it has not been adopted for phototypesetting by any of the American manufacturers, although it seems only a matter of time before a licensing agreement will be worked out with the Monotype Corporation that will add the face to the library of fine book types currently obtainable on phototypesetting machines.

Although Dante was the last type to be designed by Giovanni (as he was now called) Mardersteig, his career as a scholar-printer continued unabated. It was in the last three decades of his life that his reputation extended far beyond the circle of connoisseurs of fine printing.

An astute observer of the changes that were bound to come in printing technology, Mardersteig had realized that he could not depend on the hand press for economic survival, and in 1949 he founded a modern printing plant. Located in Verona, his Stamperia Valdonega quickly established itself in the production of first-quality printing. The Officina Bodoni, meanwhile, continued in Mardersteig's home, issuing distinguished books, every edition of which was sold out upon the announcement of its publication.

There now followed exhibitions of Mardersteig's work in the major cities of Europe, along with honors in profusion on both sides of the Atlantic. He received the Gutenberg Prize of the City of Mainz in 1969; his biographer, Hans Schmoller, commenting on this fitting award, has stated, 'If ours is to be the last century of the traditionally printed book, how fortunate that a printer like Mardersteig lived in it and created such an incomparable body of work.' In 1968 the American Institute of Graphic Arts awarded Mardersteig its Medal, which has gone to most of the great printers of our time. Then in 1972 the School of Printing of Rochester Institute of Technology brought him to the United States – for what he knew would be his last visit to these shores – to receive its Frederic W. Goudy Award. R.I.T.'s Melbert B. Cary, Jr., Graphic Arts Collection contains one of the most complete holdings of Officina Bodoni books in the United States, a number of which were obtained in Verona by Cary in the early days of that press.

During the visit of 1972 Dr. Mardersteig addressed an enthusiastic audience at the Morgan Library in New York City. His concluding remarks were: 'What the future of typography will be, nobody knows.

The invention of phototypesetting will have a decisive influence. But we who don't belong to the big industry believe that it is necessary to aim for the highest standard, which could be a model for others, so that our crafts will not lose their importance. The art of printing should never die.'

Giovanni Mardersteig died on December 27, 1977. It is perhaps fitting to remember him as, in the words of his good friend Stanley Morison, a printer who 'acted on the belief that to confer fine typographical form upon a fine piece of literature is a justifiable use of time and labor, material and skill.' It may be noted here that Martino Mardersteig is continuing the tradition of his father in both printing establishments in Verona, the Officina Bodoni and the commercial press, Stamperia Valdonega.

Giovanni Mardersteig

GOUDY OLD STYLE

'If there were an individual, readily recognized quality or characteristic which the type designer could incorporate in drawings that would make any one type more beautiful, legible, or distinguished than another, it is obvious that only type of that kind would be designed.'

This statement was made by Frederic W. Goudy, a man who spent more than fifty years of his life in pursuit of that 'recognized quality' in a printing type. Nobody seems to know exactly how many types Goudy produced (even he couldn't recall every design), but a reasonable estimate would be upwards of 125. Many of them are now nearly forgotten, a factor due probably to his persistence in 'going his own way' and designing letters primarily for hand-composition, rather than to the quality of the types themselves. Another circumstance was the loss by fire in 1939 of the accumulated drawings and matrices of many years of his type production. In addition, those types that he produced for the composing machine were limited to the Monotype single-type system, which in the United States never attained the popularity of the linecasting machines.

Frederic Goudy died in 1947, and since then the appreciation of his types has been in decline. There has also been a tendency to disregard his influence as one of the great type designers of this century, although few disputed this reputation during his most active years of type production, 1915 to 1940.

Indeed, the name Goudy was, during the last quarter century of his life, a household word in printing offices in every part of the United States and in a number of other countries as well. A primary reason for this fame was not just his numerous types but also the fact that Fred Goudy was a very accessible man, who willingly appeared on countless lecture platforms from coast to coast to discuss the great love he had for letter forms. His warmheartedness toward his fellow printers caused him rarely to refuse a request to talk about type.

ABCDEFG
HIJKLMN
OPQRSTU
VWXYZ

abcdefghij
klmnopqrst
uvwxyz

1234567890

Goudy Oldstyle (ATF)

FRED · W · GOUDY AND WILL · H · RANSOM
THE VILLAGE PRESS · PARK RIDGE · ILLINOIS

THIS is the first showing of a new type designed by Mr. Goudy for the exclusive use of the Village Press. The matrices were cut and the type cast by Wiebking, Harding & Co. of Chicago, to whom credit is due for the faithful rendering of Mr. Goudy's drawings. ❦The designer's aim was to produce a letter generous in form, with solid lines and strong serifs, and "without preposterous thicks and thins." Legibility of the text as a whole was the first consideration, & the founders of the Press trust that the letter will prove acceptable to the readers of their productions.

❦ABCDEFGHIJKLMNOPQRSTUV WXYZ & $ ❦abcdefghijklmnopqrstuvwxyz & æœ ff fi ffi fl ffl ct st—1234567890.,:;'!?⸗ 123 ( )

❦Of seventy-six impressions—the first production of the Press—this is number ₍ ₃

Park Ridge, July 24th, 1903.

The Goudy Village type, 1903

Born in Springfield, Illinois, in 1865, Goudy was over thirty before he designed his first typeface, Camelot, in 1896. By 1900 he was an instructor of lettering in Chicago and beginning to make a reputation as an advertising designer. With the establishment in Chicago of his

Village Press, in 1903, he also became active as a printer and gradually began to build his reputation as a type designer.

Goudy's earliest types were display faces, reflecting his commercial-lettering experience. Even the type he called Village, first used for his own Village Press, was originally created in 1903 for Kuppenheimer & Company, a Chicago clothing manufacturer. In 1908 he ventured to design a book type for the old *Life* magazine. Cut for Monotype composition by the Lanston Monotype Machine Company, it was officially named 38-E, although it is often called Goudy Light or Goudy Old Style (*not* to be confused with the subject of this chapter).

Possibly Goudy enjoyed this excursion into the design of a commercial type for a periodical and the challenges it brought (such as the need to study Renaissance forms), but there is no doubt that he was also excited by the private-press movement – then at its height – in which he took an active part. In any event, in 1911 for the New York publisher Mitchell Kennerley he produced Kennerley, his first important book type and first popular success. This effort was immediately followed by the titling letter Forum, which was enthusiastically

OLD STYLE TYPES
will always be $67890

USE THIS OLD
style letter in ads

NEW TYPES
print far better

Goudy Light Old Style No. 38 (Monotype)

received and fully established his reputation as a type designer. Both of these types were cut for private use.

The American Type Founders Company thereupon became interested in Goudy, commissioning him to do a type. He agreed, on the condition that his original drawings would not be subjected to 'interference by the foundry's drawing room.' Goudy then began work on the face, which eventually became the most widely used type he ever designed. Called Goudy Old Style by ATF, it first appeared in 1915 and was an instant best seller for the foundry.

There have been numerous accounts of the origin of the type. One of the reasons for its success was the renewed interest in the classic typefaces, which Goudy had already begun to satisfy with Kennerley and Forum, and which ATF had fed with the Bodoni revival in 1910, followed by Cloister Old Style two years later. Goudy at one time stated that his inspiration derived from the lettering on a Hans Holbein painting, but he later admitted that he couldn't trace the exact source. Most type designers would sympathize with Goudy in this, as it is easy to grow enthusiastic about a letter form and then when a type idea germinates to be confused about its specific sources.

One of Goudy's biographers, Peter Beilenson, said of Goudy Old Style that it was a 'happy blend of French suavity and Italian fullness, marred by the supposed commercial practicality of shortened descenders.' Goudy apparently agreed with this criticism, for just before his death he wrote that he had – albeit under protest – 'allowed ATF to inveigle' him into using such abbreviated descenders.

It was, however, these short descenders that helped endear the type to the commercial printers, allowing as they did an economical use of vertical space, particularly for the composition of advertising.

ABCDEFGHIJKLMNOPQ
RSTUVWXYZ
abcdefghijklmnopqrstuvwxyz
1234567890   .,-;:'!?$&

Goudy Bold (Morris Benton-ATF)

ABCDEFGHIJKLMNOPQR
STUVWXYZ   abcdefghijklm
nopqrstuvwxyz   .,´;:'!?$&fffiffi
flffloeœæŒÆctst   1234567890

Kennerley Old Style

Goudy Old Style was thus an immediate success in the 'ad alley,' as newspapers refer to their advertising section. In the 1917 supplement to the famous 'Big Red' ATF specimen book of 1912, an addition to the Goudy 'family' was announced – Goudy Title. The 1920 supplement introduced Goudy Bold. In 1921, Goudy Catalogue was ready, followed by Goudy Handtooled in 1922. Goudy Extrabold was added in 1927, and that year ATF issued a separate 124-page specimen book containing nothing but Goudy Old Style and its derivatives.

Although this promotion of the Goudy types was most remunerative for the foundry, it didn't enrich the designer, for Goudy had sold the original design for just fifteen hundred dollars instead of entering into a royalty agreement based on sales. His relationship with the American Type Founders Company naturally deteriorated, particularly after 1920, when Goudy was named art director of the Lanston Monotype Machine Company and he began to produce a notable group of types for that firm. For ATF he designed but one other face, Goudytype, plus a series of initial letters named Cloister Initials.

All of the variants of Goudy Old Style were cut for ATF by its resident type designer, the talented Morris Benton. Wadsworth A. Parker, another ATF house designer, aided Benton in the cutting of Goudy Handtooled.

In its original form, Goudy Old Style was widely used for advertising and job printing. Its beautifully drawn classic capitals became a favorite of book designers for title pages and chapter headings, but it has not generally been used for book-text composition, although it later became available for Monotype composition. In the fifty years between 1923 and 1973 only once has it appeared for an entire book in the annual Fifty Books of the Year Exhibition, in 1933. It has, however, been selected for innumerable title pages during the same period.

It is the boldface version that keeps Goudy Old Style alive and healthy, despite the chagrin of the designer at 'not being allowed to draw the boldface.' The American typographer Lester Douglas showed the writer a drawing Goudy had given to him, captioned: 'How I would have drawn Goudy Bold.' In actuality there was not a great deal of difference between this sketch and that of the bold's designer, Morris Benton. Goudy was justifiably piqued, of course, by ATF's refusal to give him further compensation for the huge success of the Goudy family.

In his autobiography, *A Half-Century of Type Design and Typography, 1895–1945*, Goudy mentions a visit to ATF by members of the American Institute of Graphic Arts. While leading a tour, Henry Lewis Bullen, the typographic historian and librarian of ATF's Typographic Library, stopped at a casting machine. Bullen informed the group that the types being cast there had been designed by one of the Institute's own members and further stated, 'Here is where Goudy goes down to posterity while the American Type Founders Company goes down to prosperity.'

EXPERIENCES WHICH REVEAL DISCOURAGING DIFFICULTIES
PRIMITIVE NEWSPAPER PUBLISHER HAD TO CONTEND WITH

My father had already been a printer for a number of years, and some time in the early thirties had led a forlorn editorial struggle in a West Virginian hamlet, with the monthly periodical which he printed himself and edited with the help of his sister. As long as he remained in business he remained simply country editor and country printer. He had started the study of medicine when quite young but in due time abandoned it for his life's calling, without much regret, and though with his inventive and speculative nature he was often tempted to experiment in a number of other things, I do not think that he would ever have thought of forsaking his newspaper work. In truth, the call of printing was in our blood, though it brought to us neither honor nor profit and we were planning and dreaming most of the time how we could break away from it

ABCDEFGHIJKLMNOPQRSTUVWXYZ
abcdefghijklmnopqrstuvwxyz
$1234567890

Goudy Handtooled (Morris Benton-ATF)

There appears over the past decades to have been a noticeable reliance on Goudy Bold in the advertising of distillers: this writer has listed some fifteen different alcoholic beverages promoted by Goudy Bold. But the type also remains a prime favorite for all advertising appearing daily in consumer periodicals at every level. In fact, it seems that whenever the requirements are for a solid, legible roman letter, the layout is marked for Goudy.

All of the photographic devices currently available for the setting of display composition offer fonts of Goudy Old Style, assuring its wide use for a long time to come.

Frederic W. Goudy and his types may seem dated to the younger typographers of today, but there is not much question about his influence during a good part of this century. He was never an ivory-tower designer, always retaining the common touch, even though in his later years he designed fewer display types and became more and more involved in his personal investigations into the purity of the Italian Renaissance letter forms.

All of Goudy's types were drawn freehand – without the use of compass, straightedge, or French curve. Early in his career of designing types for the composing machine, Goudy objected to the methods employed by the Monotype firm to transfer his drawings to matrices; he believed that this compromised his artistic principles. He therefore in the midtwenties withdrew to his workshop in Marlborough, New York, to produce his own matrices for what he called the Village Letter Foundery.

Here for some fifteen years he turned out many of his best designs, but offered them only in fonts for hand-composition. In 1939 the workshop was destroyed by fire, with the result that the types produced here during this prolific period were lost. Fortunately, however, the types Goudy had continued to draw for Monotype, such as Deepdene and Goudy Text – two of his most successful designs – were not among these.

Thus, during the last quarter century of his life, although Goudy maintained his connection with the Lanston Monotype company, he spent more time on his own production of types. These were of less commercial application than his earlier designs, but they satisfied his instincts as an independent type designer.

The many romans Goudy designed in his home workshop during the period up to 1939 have been rejected by his critics as look-alikes. His numerous friends and admirers, however, could distinguish them

THIS is sixteen pt. Deepdene Roman, designed and cut by
Fred W. Goudy. It was first shown in September, 1927.
ABCDEFGHIJKLMNOPQRSTUVWXYZ&
abcdefghijklmnopqrstuvwxyz
fi ffi ff fl ffl 234567890 JjjJ QQQ

THIS is Deepdene Italic designed and cut by Fred W. Goudy in
February, 1929. ABCDEMPRIRQNR J
ABCDEFGHIJKLMNOPQRSTUVWXYZ &
abcdefghijklmnopqrstuvwxyzz
ff fi ffi fl ffl ff f ffi ff fl ffl ffi gg k z a gy g gg

Deepdene and Deepdene Italic

as the products of his continuing quest for perfection of the roman
letter forms. The fruits of that quest were destroyed in the fire.

The idealistic Goudy's essential practicality is evident in a lecture
he gave before the annual convention of the International Club of
Printing House Craftsmen in New York in 1939. He stated:

My craft is a simple one. For nearly forty years I have endeavored constantly
to create a greater and more general esteem for good printing and typography,
to give printers and readers of print more legible and more beautiful types
than were hitherto available. Printing essentially is a utilitarian art, yet even
utilitarianism may include distinction and beauty in its type forms. To meet
the demands of utility and preserve an esthetic standard is the problem I set
myself years ago, and now, at 74, with over one hundred and eight different
type designs to my credit, I am proud to say that I have never consciously
permitted myself to use the print presenting a worthy message to serve as a
mere framework or scaffolding upon which to exploit my own skill, or even
to allow my craft to become a means in itself, instead of a means only to a
desirable and useful end.

During his lifetime Frederic W. Goudy made a lasting contribution
to American typography, and though never adequately rewarded
financially, he received broad personal recognition, resulting in three
honorary degrees from American colleges and numerous medals,
including that of the American Institute of Graphic Arts.

More important, Goudy acquired countless friends, who never ceased to respond to his humanity. Attesting to this are the three biographies published during his lifetime and four others that remain unpublished. There is also a Goudy Society, which meets annually to celebrate his birthday, March 8. No other designer of printing types in our times has been so warmly remembered.

Frederic Goudy

PALATINO

In 1950, with the design of Palatino, a young German calligrapher–type designer named Hermann Zapf came to the attention of the world's typographers. Although the type took a year or two to circulate, its thirty-one-year-old creator made an immediate impact. For that year *Feder und Stichel* (*Pen and Graver* in its English version) was published, employing the new type in its introductory text. A product of the Stempel typefoundry of Frankfurt am Main, for which Zapf was serving as art director, this book consisted of twenty-five pages of alphabet designs. These had been lettered by Zapf in 1939 and were cut in lead printing plates by August Rosenberger in his spare time during the war years (it was Rosenberger who had introduced the young designer to the cutting of punches).

Feder und Stichel was published in an edition of only 80 copies on Japan paper and in 500 copies on Fabriano. The supply was quickly exhausted, as the revival of calligraphy that had begun in London early in the century under the influence of Edward Johnston was well under way, and most practitioners were avid for fine examples – the magnificently printed slim volume quickly achieved renown as an outstanding manual of the calligrapher's art. The introduction in the new Palatino font, representing the type's first use, was hand-set. A further personal touch was that all the copies of this edition were hand-bound by Gudrun von Hesse, Mrs. Hermann Zapf.

In 1951, Cooper Union in New York became the first American institution to recognize Zapf's talents, and mounted an exhibition featuring his work along with that of Fritz Kredel, the famous wood engraver and book illustrator. Zapf at this time made his first visit to the United States, captivating American audiences with his charm and his very obvious love for and skill with letter forms. Through the efforts of the American calligrapher Paul Standard, who had arranged the show, the English edition of *Feder und Stichel* was planned (the German edition had gone out of print). Thus in 1952 the printing

ABCDEFGHIJKLMNOPQRS TUVWXYZ abcdefghijklm nopqrstuvwxyz 1234567890 .,-;:!?""''$&fffifl=Qu

Palatino

office of Stempel produced 2,000 copies of the new version, which, like the first edition, were disposed of very rapidly. Both editions now command high prices from booksellers fortunate enough to locate copies.

What is considered remarkable is that this beautiful, classic book was lettered by a man just twenty years of age and self-taught as a calligrapher. Apprenticed at fifteen as a color corrector in a lithographic plant, Zapf a year later visited an exhibition of the lettering of Rudolf Koch. He was so much inspired that he immediately purchased supplies and began the experiments that quickly brought him to professional competence. Later he described his long hours of practice, when he was frequently admonished by his parents for overuse of the electric lights in the small hours of the night. He sometimes despaired from lack of guidance – discovering, for example, that after three years of effort, he was holding his pen in the wrong position.

In 1950, Zapf was extremely busy in the production of printing types. To accompany the Palatino, he added a titling font, which was named Michelangelo. He also drew two italics, one to serve as a complement to the Linotype version and the other for single-type composition in foundry type. This second italic, closer fitting than the first, is a chancery cursive and is one of the best available types in this category. The next addition to the Palatino family was a bold titling letter called Sistina, soon followed by a boldface version of Palatino itself and a font of swash capitals for the foundry italic. Michelangelo and Sistina today enjoy frequent use, independent of Palatino, wherever fine capitals are required.

Zapf calligraphy, from Pen and Graver, 1952

This vast output within such a short time recalls the virtuosity of Frederic W. Goudy, and Hermann Zapf would be quick to recognize and appreciate such a consanguinity. He has long harbored great admiration for Goudy's ability as a type designer and also for his espousal of craftsmanship. In still another way Zapf has followed Goudy – in his readiness to be of help to his fellow typographers, no matter how inconvenient to his personal life.

Zapf did not begin his career as a type designer with the creation of Palatino. After three years of his apprenticeship as a color etcher the creative urge was so strong in him and his lettering studies had progressed to such a point that in 1938 he applied for employment with a Frankfurt lettering studio. Shortly thereafter he became a free-lance letterer, at which time he began the serious study of printing types that would lead to the experiments resulting in his first type by 1939. Understandably, this was a Fraktur, for much of Zapf's early calligraphy had been in that style. Zapf later wrote that it was through his reading of *Writing and Illuminating and Lettering*, Edward Johnston's famous manual of 1906, that he drew away from the 'highly individual' style of Rudolf Koch's lettering and expanded his knowledge of the wider tradition of letter forms.

Gustave Mori, the German historian of European typefounding, who was directing the Stempel foundry, learned of Zapf's presence in Frankfurt and in 1939 retained his services for the firm. The punchcutter August Rosenberger took Zapf's drawings and hand-cut the test size of the type, which was called Gilgengart (honoring a German sixteenth-century book of religious texts). The type was not ready for distribution until 1941, and it unfortunately coincided with the government decree branding Fraktur a 'Jewish concoction.' It was not until after the war – during which Zapf served as a map designer – that he produced a roman type, drawn with a broad pen, which was named Novalis. However, after the cutting of a normal weight, a boldface, and an italic, the decision was made for commercial reasons not to issue this type; nevertheless, its designer had acquired invaluable experience in the effort.

In 1948 Zapf started work on another roman, but one that he felt was more attuned to the times. This was the design that finally became Palatino. In its drawing Zapf applied the rationale he was to bring to many of the fine types he has produced since that time: the concept of adapting types to printing processes, as well as to their methods of manufacture, from that of single-type casting to composing-machine matrices. He later employed this approach to meet the exigencies of transfer to film grid and disk, and eventual digitizing for cathode-ray-tube (CRT) typesetting devices.

The open counters that make Palatino such a legible letter were provided to overcome a then current printing problem in Germany, poor-quality paper. The weight of the type was also thickened beyond that of a normal roman in order to adapt to the lithographic and gravure printing processes of that period.

As a boy Hermann Zapf had been determined to become an electrical engineer. Although he was won over to the practice of calligraphy, his scientific bent has kept him sympathetic to the technical requirements of modern type design – he strongly believes that the

ABCDEFGHIJKLMNOPQRS
TUVWXYZ   abcdefghijklmnop
qrstuvwxyz   1234567890
.,-;:!?'''' $&ffffifl=e ThQu

Palatino Italic with swash characters

DON CARLOS
HEIDELBERG

Michelangelo

designer must temper artistic judgment with technical understanding. Because he has pursued a study of the newest technologies, engineers in turn respect his capabilities and are most willing to collaborate with him. As a result, his types remain true to his concepts of typographic harmony. Zapf also believes that the typographer, and not just the type designer, must in the future become 'an analytical designer who must hew to strictly logical sequences in the course of his work.'

Along with many of the best type designers of this century, Zapf returned to the letter forms of the Italian Renaissance in the preparation of Palatino. Although he wished to call the new face Medici, it was the decision of the foundry staff that it be named Palatino, after Giovanbattista Palatino, a sixteenth-century calligrapher and con-temporary of the punchcutter Claude Garamond. Palatino's writing manual, *Libro Nuovo d'Imparare a Scrivere*, was published in Rome in 1540. Although a controversial figure among his fellow scribes, Palatino has been called by the historian of calligraphy James Wardrop a 'calligrapher's calligrapher.'

Following his work on Palatino, Zapf went to Italy, visiting Florence, Rome, and Pisa in order to study firsthand the Roman inscriptional letters found there in such profusion. The sketches he made at this time later became the basis for the Palatino titling fonts Michelangelo and Sistina. The influence of the classical lapidary majuscules is evident throughout the Palatino family, markedly in *E*, *F*, and *L*, which retain the narrow proportions. The swash variants he produced for Palatino italic stem particularly from studies in the Laurentian Library in Florence and the Vatican Library in Rome.

Zapf has steadily maintained that as he did not create Palatino as a book type but rather as a commercial face, he has always been somewhat distressed by its use for book work. As his intent was to produce a display type, he leaned to a calligraphic treatment of certain letters, which to some extent interferes with the legibility of Palatino when considered as a type for continuous reading. Nevertheless, such a stricture has seemingly not discouraged book typographers in the United States. One response to the legibility factor was the suggestion of the well-known American type designer William A. Dwiggins to design a number of 'alternate' though normal characters to replace the elaborate letters in question (*E*, *F*, *S*, *v*, *w*, *y*, and others), a process that of course represents a reversal in the usual procedure of cutting alternate letters – it is the fancier characters that are ordinarily cut as alternates to the original ones. In addition, Zapf conceived of a weight to be called Palatino Book, which he cut, but the salespeople at Stempel and German Linotype preferred to produce it as a separate type, to be called Aldus Buchschrift (a decision that annoyed Zapf, as the basic design had little relationship to the types of the scholar-printer Aldus Manutius). Never cut in display sizes, Aldus has been used primarily in Germany for machine-composition.

The success of Palatino was international, despite some modest criticism of the serif endings of such letters as *h*, *n*, and *m*, and the unusual lowercase *t*, which rises to almost full ascender height. In Aldus, this letter was brought back to normal proportions.

The favorable opinion of typographers unfortunately brought

MALKUNST

LEONIDAS

Sistina

with it difficulties that have plagued Zapf's artistic life ever since, and for a time had him at the verge of quitting his work as a type designer. Plagiarism seems to be the price of popularity. The unauthorized copying of types has harassed type designers throughout the 500-year history of printing, and it seems destined to remain one of the hazards of the profession.

Palatino appeared simultaneously with the emergence of photo-typesetting as a replacement for the standard hot-metal operations. While the composing-machine manufacturers were themselves adapting to this trend, a number of firms with no previous exposure to the printing trade decided that this changeover represented an opportune time for them to become involved in the growing graphic-arts market. The newer firms quickly equipped themselves with facilities for the preparation of types, but they had little interest in the development of their own styles. Printers who purchased the new devices naturally wanted to have the popular type styles, and this demand inevitably resulted in a wave of imitation of existing types. Under the law, the name of a type could be registered but the design itself was unpatentable, and therefore considered by the new entrepreneurs to be in the public domain. Palatino is thus currently known as Elegante, Malibu, Andover, Paladium, and Pontiac, depending upon the supplier. The designer receives no financial return from any of these 'adaptations.'

Unquestionably, Hermann Zapf is the most conspicuous victim of the widespread pirating of type styles in the post–World War II era. His later types, Melior and Optima in particular, were also broadly appropriated. To add insult to injury, the new composing equipment not only stole the designs but also invaded the market of conventional machines, further reducing the designer's income from his royalties in the sale of matrices and foundry types. Since Zapf received no remuneration from the firms that usurped his designs, it was manifest that type design could not be profitable for him, which discouraged him from pursuing his calling. Moreover, he had to suffer the artistic anguish of witnessing the wide use of badly produced renditions of his creations.

For a time during the 1970s there was speculation that these abuses of artistic property would be curtailed by the passage of a new copyright act, but the United States Congress refused to give protection to the design of printing types. However, within the industry itself there have been heartening signs that unauthorized appropriation of types will at least be discouraged. A firm representing designers, the International Typeface Corporation, was founded in 1970 and has been most successful. Its method is to work with a type designer in the preparation of a new font and to license the font's use to the various composing-machine manufacturers. ITC will supply the original art, obviating the manufacturer's need to produce – often inadequately – its own copies, thus assuring the integrity of the original. The subsequent sales by the manufacturers will bring royalties to the designer through an arrangement with ITC. This concept has been accepted by the great majority of firms engaged in the production of typesetting equipment with the wholesome result that the design of printing types may once again offer a reasonable financial return to their creators.

mit 1 p durchschossen   L 1140 10 p

The art of book-producing was never on a higher level than at the time of the invention of printing. The power and harmony of what Gutenberg and his associates in strict adherence to the sound tradition of Gothic scripts cut, founded, set and printed has been surpassed by none of their followers either in their own country or in other countries. A second culminating point of German graphical art was reached in the early Renaissance when masters like Dürer, Holbein, and Cranach were using the woodcut which had had its origin and been put TO THE TEST IN GERMANY, FOR BOOK-ILLUSTRA

mit 1 p durchschossen   L 1141 12 p

Die Kunst, ein Buch als Ganzes schön zu gestalten, hat nie höher gestanden als zur Zeit der Erfindung des Buchdrucks. Was Gutenberg und seine Genossen im Anschluß an die sichere Tradition der gotischen Handschriften geschnitten, gegossen, gesetzt und gedruckt haben, hat keiner ihrer Nachfolger daheim oder im Ausland an Kraft und Harmonie übertroffen. Den zweiten Höhepunkt erreichte die deutsche Buchkunst zur Zeit der frühen Renaissance, als Meister WIE DÜRER, HOLBEIN UND CRANACH

Aldus (Linotype)

Hermann Zapf worked closely with ITC, producing a number of new types. He now works out of his home, designing typefaces and type programs for a number of companies, bringing his unique skills in the construction of beautiful letters to a marketplace in which traditional inventiveness is far too often in short supply.

Hermann Zapf

GARAMOND

The types that currently bear the name of the great sixteenth-century French punchcutter Claude Garamond have been in popular demand for about seventy years and are thus available from a variety of sources, including foundries and composing-machine manufacturers. These many versions do not always have the same characteristics, a disconcerting factor that interferes with their ready identification.

The Garamond types have a rich past, stemming as they do from the most influential era of French typography, the 1500s. New interpretations of the historic sources continue to appear from time to time, and though these may be confusing to younger typographers, they do attest to the universality of the French old-style types and offer a challenge in the pursuit of their origin.

During the first century of the printer's craft, each printing office was more or less independent, there being practically no outside source for supplies other than paper. In order to secure a supply of type, it was necessary for the master printer to hire a punchcutter and a typecaster. (The two occupations could be embodied in the same person, but the cutting of a punch required both technical and artistic ability, whereas the caster's job demanded less skill and was lower on the scale of printing-office employment.) After punches had been cut, it was necessary to drive matrices of copper or brass, and these had to be carefully justified in order to achieve the proper fitting of the character struck and assure its alignment with the other letters of the font. A mold had to be constructed, and following the casting operation each letter had to be dressed, which included removing the jet caused by the type metal entering the mold, the rubbing of each character to remove burrs, and finally the planing of the foot to eliminate the jet break.

The printer also had to obtain a supply of type metal, consisting of tin, lead, and antimony, and such supplies were difficult to procure in many localities.

ABCDEFGHIJKLMNO
PQRSTUVWXYZ
abcdefghijklmnopqrstuvwxyz
1234567890

ABCDEFGHIJKLMNOPQRSTUVWXYZ
abcdefghijklmnopqrstuvwxyz 1234567890

Garamond (ATF)

It was sometimes possible to purchase punches and matrices from the spouse of a deceased printer or, on occasion, to bargain for them with a competitor. This practice, however, provided no guarantee of a sufficient supply of type if the cutting and casting skills were not available within the shop. Another method of obtaining matrices was to purchase strikes from another printer who would, of course, be reluctant to sell the punches. Such sales often took place at fairs where printers congregated to trade and sell their books.

Punchcutting, along with matrix adjustment, was a skill that required a good deal of training and experience. There never seemed to be an adequate number of such craftsmen to keep printers happy until the establishment of typefounding as a completely separate craft, in the 1500s.

By the mid-sixteenth century typefounding was making a tentative start, primarily in the form of shops that had accumulated stocks of punches and matrices and which employed casters who produced types for other printers without such facilities.

Into this printing scene entered Claude Garamond, who had been born about 1500, the exact date being uncertain, as are the facts of his early years. It is probable that he was apprenticed to the punchcutter

& parem inibi cum ofsibus fuperficiem conftituentes,illorum gibbum,quod
depreſſum magis,ac planum,quàm teres cernitur,ne minimum quidem exce
dunt.adeò,ut quemadmodum ulnam & radium attenſis ipſis cedere oſtendi-
mus muſculis,ſic quoq; poſtbrachialis oſſa ſecundùm lōgitudinem anguloſa,
&lineis quibuſdam pulchrè extuberantia ſpectentur, pro muſculorum uidelicet,qui ipſis exporriguntur,ratione.uti etiam poſtbrachialis os,indicem ſuſti
nens, in internā manus ſedem, quà brachiali articulatur, notatu dignum edu-
cit[k] proceſſum,cui[l] muſculus brachiale mouentium ſecundus inſeritur.Dein
poſtbrachialis os,paruo præpoſitum digito,quà brachiali committitur,exter-
no ſuo latere, ueluti à brachiali[m] protuberat, ut cōmodè tendinis inſertionem
admitteret[n] muſculi brachiale mouentium tertij.Inſuper oſſa indicem & me
dium digitos ſuffulcientia,ipſorum externa ſede ad brachiale[o] ampla quoq; &
aſpera ſunt, ut bifidum excipiant tendinem[p] muſculi brachiale mouentium
quarti,qui ideo potiſsimum uidetur bipartiri, & dein lateſcere, quòd ſimplex
& teres uni alicui proceſſui parù aptè inſereretur, qui extra brachialis & poſtbrachialis exteriorem gibbamq; ſedem extuberaſſet.

k 1 fi.cap.
25 ſupra
charact. 6
& 7.
l 3 muſc.
tab. A.
m 1,3 fig.
cap. 25 ſu-
prà N.
n 9 muſc.
tab. Ξ.
o 2 fi.cap.
25 ſupra
charact.5,
6,7.
p 11 muſc.
tab. A.

DE OSSIBVS DIGITORVM MANVS.
Caput XXVII.

FIGVRA VIGESIMI SEPTIMI
CAPITIS, TRES CON-
tinens tabellas.

PRIMA TA- SECVNDA. TERTIA.
bella.

TRIVM TABELLARVM HVIVS CAPITIS
figuræ,& earundem characterum Index.

 *Ossivm digitorum ſeriem duæ priores figuræ, ad initium uigeſimi quinti Capitis repoſitæ, common-
ſtrant : quemadmodum & tres integrum oſsium contextum exprimentes figuræ, ad huius libri calcem locan-
dæ. Figura autem hic occurrens, ac in tres ueluti tabellas digeſta,digitorum articulos oculis ſubijcit. Harum e-*
A. *nim prima,duo exprimit oſſa: quorum alterum A inſigniui,eſtq́; poſtbrachialis os,indicem ſuſtinens.alterum*
B. *B indicatur, eſtq́; primum indicis os ab externa ſede, quemadmodum & illud poſtbrachialis os, delineatum.*
C. *Præſenti itaq; tabella,primi digitorum articuli effigies proponitur. C enim caput rotundum notat poſtbrachia-*
D. *lis oſsis.D uerò ſinum primi oſsis,quo caput C inſignitum excipitur.*
E.F. *Secunda tabella primum indicis quoq; os notat, E notatum,& ſecundum pariter F inſignitum: ut horum*
G,H. *oſsium delineatio ſecundi quatuor digitorum articuli ſpeciem proponeret. G itaq; & H duo indicant capitula*
I,K. *primi indicis oſsis. I uerò & K ſinus ſecundi oſsis,quos duo primi oſsis capitula ſubintrant.L autem ſinum ſi-*
L. *gnificat, in medio capitulorum primi oſsis conſiſtentem, ac in quem tuberculum ſecundi oſsis inter duos ſinus I*
M. *& K notatos prominens,& M inſignitum ſubingreditur.*
N.O. *Tertia tabella ſecundum indicis os N inſignitum, & tertium O notatum proponit, tertij cuiuſq; digiti ar-*
 ticuli

A B C D E F G H I J K L M N
O P Q R S T U V W X Y & Z
abcdefghijklmnopqrstuvwxyz
1 2 3 4 5 6 7 8 9 0

Garamond Roman (Stempel)

Antoine Augereau, from whom he learned the craft that was to establish his reputation into the twentieth century. Garamond apparently then worked with other punchcutters before embarking on an independent career.

It was probably in the late 1520s that Garamond was approached by the Parisian scholar-printer Robert Estienne to cut a series of new roman types. Estienne was continuing the press founded by his father, Henri, about 1502, and he was turning it into one of the establishments that helped mark the era as noteworthy in the history of typography.

Garamond's roman first appeared in *Paraphrasis in Elegantiarum Libros Laurentii Vallae*, by Erasmus, printed by Estienne in 1530. That year Estienne produced several other books with Garamond's type. The first complete showing of the types came in 1531.

Typographic scholars have long debated the design origins of Garamond's types, but there is general agreement now that they derive from the types cut for Aldus Manutius in Venice by Francesco Griffo. Of particular interest in this respect is the 1495 edition of *De Ætna* by Pietro Bembo, much more than, for instance, the Aldine *Hypnerotomachia Poliphili* of 1499. Garamond was a friend of Geoffroy Tory, the first French *imprimeur du roi* (royal printer) and a notable force in the aesthetic development of the printed book. It is known that Tory possessed a copy of *De Ætna*, which could have been passed to the punchcutter for study. The matter becomes complicated as three others – Simon de Colines; Antoine Augereau, Garamond's former master; and the printer Christian Wechel – produced similar types at about the same time. There is no conclusive evidence that

Colines was a punchcutter, but he was certainly a good printer, who, having married Henri Estienne's widow, had continued to produce the fine Estienne books. According to Nicolas Barker in an article in *The Library* on the Aldine romans in Paris, Garamond's and Augereau's versions were almost identical.

There is no doubt, however, that the *De Ætna* type was the inspiration for the French copies. The reader will recall, in the chapter on Bembo type, that it possessed eight variants of certain lowercase letters. In the type that he cut for Estienne, Garamond used seven of these variants, in all instances selecting the more eccentric renderings, according to Barker. Since these alternate characters appeared only in *De Ætna* and not in later Aldine publications, the evidence points to this type as the model for Garamond.

In later romans, Garamond frequently departed from his earlier copy and refined the type to better reflect his own artistic concepts. One particular such letter is the capital *M*, which in the early models lacked the serif at the top of the right stem.

The relationship that Garamond maintained with Robert Estienne was mutually beneficial. The punchcutter was most fortunate to be working in a cultural climate that encouraged scholarly printing – it

ABCDEFGHIJKLMN
OPQRSTUVWXYZ
abcdefghijklmnopqrstuvwxyz
1234567890

ABCDEFGHIJKLMNOPQRSTUVWXYZ
abcdefghijklmnopqrstuvwxyz 1234567890

Garamond (Ludlow)

was the regime in France of Francis I, who enthusiastically promoted the art of the book – but Garamond could scarcely have advanced his reputation without the assistance of a printer such as Estienne, of marked superiority in the practice of his craft. And Garamond's growing skill gilded Estienne's name.

The Garamond types brought attention to their designer, prompting the king to commission from him a font of Greek. Garamond's Grec du Roi further enhanced his celebrity, although later Greek scholars deplored his models, which continued the tradition of the informal Greek script originally cut for Aldus Manutius. Nevertheless, the Garamond Greek served as the standard until the present century.

Upon Garamond's death in 1561, his punches and matrices were sold, a principal purchaser being Christopher Plantin, whose printing office in Antwerp was to become the largest and finest in Europe before the end of the century. This establishment still exists as the Plantin-Moretus Museum, where during the past thirty years typographic scholars have catalogued the thousands of punches and matrices in its possession. Many of these are now attributed to Claude Garamond.

The Garamond punches also found their way to the typefoundries being established in the sixteenth century. In 1592 the Frankfurt foundry of Egenolff-Berner issued a broadside specimen that has since become an important source of information concerning the types of the era, and in it are several fonts ascribed to Garamond. There is some doubt whether these punches were acquired directly

---

Qui sequitur me, non ambulat in tenebris: dicit Dominus. Haec sunt verba Christi, quibus admonemur, quatenus vitam ejus & mores imitemur, si velimus veraciter illuminari, & ab omni caecitate cordis liberari. *Summum igitur studium nostrum sit, in vita Jesu Christi meditari.*

ABCDEFGHIJKLMNOPQRSTUVWXYZ
abcdefghijklmnopqrstuvwxyz & st

Garamond (English Monotype)

A B C D E F G H I J K L M N O P Q
R S T U V W X Y Z & Æ Œ Q U Ç [(
a b c d e f g h i j k l m n o p q r s t
u v w x y z æ œ fi fl ff ffi ffl Q u st ct
$1234567890   . , - '':;!? $1234567890

(Lining Figures supplied with all Fonts unless Hanging Figures are specified.)

DIGNIFIED FOR
Broadsides, Booklets
and folders as well as

Frederic W. Goudy's Garamont (Monotype)

from Garamond's widow or were brought to Frankfurt from Antwerp by the punchcutter Jacob Sabon.

Sabon, upon the death of the printer Christian Egenolff in 1555, had become associated with Egenolff's widow in the maintenance of the typefoundry that was part of the printing office. Having later worked with Christopher Plantin at Antwerp, Sabon might well have helped in the subsequent acquisition of the Garamond punches and matrices from Plantin by the Frankfurt foundry, of which he had become owner by virtue of his marriage to Christian Egenolff's grand-

ABCDEFGHIJKLMN
OPQRSTUVWXY&Z
abcdefghijklmnopqrstuvwxyz
1 2 3 4 5 6 7 8 9 0
ABCDEFGHIJKLMN
OPQRSTUVWXY&Z
abcdefghijklmnopqrstuvwxyz
1 2 3 4 5 6 7 8 9 0

Caractères de l'Université (Imprimerie Nationale)

daughter. Upon Sabon's death in 1580, his widow married Konrad Berner, the foundry then being styled Egenolff-Berner. The Egenolff-Berner casting established the Garamond designs as the principal roman types used by European printers during the next century. It is the 1592 specimen, which also contains italics designed by Robert Granjon, that has served as the source of several of the current revivals of the Garamond types.

Another important derivation of the present-day Garamonds is the type that was cut by the French printer Jean Jannon and first shown in his specimen sheet dated 1621. Jannon, who was printer to the Protestant academy at Sedan, suffered the misfortune of having his typefounding materials confiscated by the king's forces at the instigation of Cardinal Richelieu. His punches and matrices were later placed under the care of the Imprimerie Royale – the royal printing office – which had been established by Richelieu in 1640 (and still exists as France's national printing office). The first use of these Jannon types was in the 1642 production of the cardinal's memoirs.

Although cut some sixty years following the death of Claude Garamond, the Jannon types contain many characteristics that are obviously patterned on his designs. However, as 'M. Beaujon' (Beatrice Warde) points out, in the authoritative article on the Garamond types in volume five of *The Fleuron* (1925), the angle of the serifs of such letters as *s*, *m*, *n*, *p*, and *r* in the Jannon model is much greater than in the Garamond original. Obviously Jannon, though influenced by Garamond, did exercise his artistic prerogative to alter a number of individual features.

The style represented by the Jannon designs lost favor, and his types were ignored for about two hundred years. When they were 'discovered' in the vaults of the French national printing office, in 1825, they were attributed, not to their designer, who had been long forgotten, but to Claude Garamond. Printed in 1845 in a specimen of the historic types owned by the office, the Jannon types were not used again until revived by Arthur Christian, director of the printing office, for a history of that establishment published in 1901.

The Jannon types were again used with distinction in Anatole Claudin's four-volume *Histoire de l'Imprimerie en France au XVᵉ et au XVIᵉ Siècle*, of 1900 to 1920. This work – called by D. B. Updike 'probably the finest book on printing that has ever been published' – brought international renown to the *caractères de l'Université*, as the type was known.

The use of 'Garamond' in these books called attention once again to French typography of the sixteenth century. Here in the United States in the early 1900s, the American Type Founders Company, looking to continue the success it had enjoyed with the revivals Bodoni and Cloister Old Style, turned its attention to that period.

The foundry was of course fortunate to have as its librarian the typographic historian Henry Lewis Bullen, and the ATF library was the best of its kind in the United States. With Bullen's encouragement, Morris Benton commenced a redrawing of Garamond. The foundry was also fortunate to retain as adviser the typographic designer T. M. Cleland, who lent invaluable assistance to the project.

The model selected was the *caractères de l'Université* group of types. But it was not for several years, after the Garamond revival was well under way, that Beatrice Warde (a former assistant to Bullen

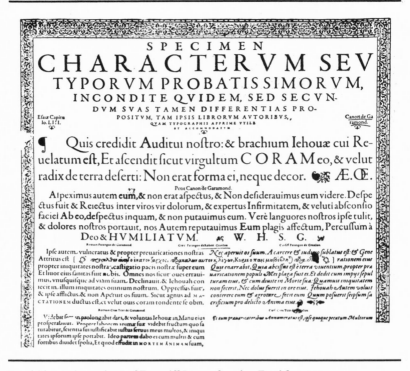

Broadside specimen sheet of Egenolff-Berner foundry, Frankfurt, 1592

at the ATF Library) began her researches into the history of the Garamond types. She discovered in the Bibliothèque Nationale in Paris an unknown copy of the Jannon specimen book of 1621, and published her surprising findings in 1927, under the pseudonym Paul Beaujon. Jannon thus finally received credit for his designs.

When ATF Garamond was completed, in 1917, it set the standard for an international Garamond revival, becoming the hallmark design that has since influenced numerous adaptations, all worth noting carefully. Within a decade all the composing-machine manufacturers had produced copies, varying their interpretations according to the models selected.

In 1920 Frederic W. Goudy became art director of the Lanston Monotype Machine Company, and for the first type under his new responsibility he turned to his own conception of the Garamond design. He elected to follow the Jannon type, although his interpre-

La crainte de l'Eternel eſt
le chef de ſcience: mais les
fols meſpriſent ſapiĕce &

ITALIQVE GROS CANON.

*Car ils ſeront graces enfilees
enſemble à ton chef, & car-
quans à ton col. Mon fils,ſi les*

Specimen of Jean Jannon, Sedan, 1621

tation differed in a number of respects from that of ATF. It is called Garamon*t*, the spelling that appears in several historical accounts of French printing. Goudy later wrote that his delineation was 'not the result of inspiration or of genius on my part, but was merely the result of an attempt to reproduce as nearly as possible the form and spirit of the Garamond letter.'

The next Garamond to be produced issued from the Stempel foundry in Germany in 1924, and it too was made available for the Linotype machine. This type was adapted from the Egenolff-Berner specimen sheet of 1592 and is therefore a copy of an actual Garamond, whereas the aforementioned reproductions are not.

Mergenthaler Linotype Company in 1925 produced a Garamond closely allied to the Stempel cutting but somewhat heavier and not quite so graceful. A little later the firm felt economically obliged to issue a type identical to ATF's standard Garamond, calling the copy

Garamond No. 3. The firm's business sense proved acute, as this type soon became the most widely used of all Garamonds in the United States.

In 1930 R. Hunter Middleton designed for the Ludlow Typograph Company a Garamond also based on the 1592 specimen. Another individualized interpretation, like Goudy's, this is the lightest in weight of all the Garamonds. The distinguished typographer Bruce Rogers greatly admired Middleton's design; he told this writer that he believed it to be one of the best of the modern cuttings of Garamond. Rogers used it in the edition of *Gulliver's Travels* that he designed for the Limited Editions Club in 1950.

GALLIARD

The latest addition to the list of French old-style types was brought out in 1978 by the Mergenthaler Linotype Company. Named Galliard, it is based on a type made by the sixteenth century's Robert Granjon and is the first of its genre to be designed exclusively for phototypesetting. In contrast to the situation when the American Type Founders' Garamond was introduced, in 1917 – Garamond's immediate approval was primarily owing to the few classic types then available – it is too early to predict the reception for Galliard, since to many printers it might at first seem just another roman in a market they believe to be saturated.

The name Galliard stems from Granjon's own term for an 8-point font he cut about 1570. It undoubtedly refers to the style of the face, for the galliard was a lively dance of the period.

This latest venture of Mergenthaler's into the sixteenth century was at the direction of Mike Parker, the firm's knowledgeable director of typographic development. His roots as a typographer go back to the 1950s, when he was on a fellowship from the Belgian-American Educational Foundation working in the Plantin-Moretus Museum in Antwerp. Parker was instrumental in helping the museum set up the procedures by which the identification of the many thousands of matrices and punches owned by Plantin was expedited.

Parker collaborated with a designer eminently qualified to revive a Granjon original, Matthew Carter. As a teenager Carter had been apprenticed to Paul Raedisch, the punchcutter of the Enschedé typefoundry in Haarlem, The Netherlands. Perhaps more important, as the son of Harry Carter, the notable typographic historian, Matthew had received the impetus to study the classical roman letter forms, particularly those of the sixteenth century.

The reader has previously noted that Robert Granjon was highly praised for his italic types, which were used as models for the italic forms of some of the Garamond revivals. But heretofore the only

ABCDEFGHIJK
LMNOPQRSTU
VWXYZ&12345
67890abcdefghijk
lmnopqrstuvwxy
za⌣e⌣n⌣h⌣r⌣t⌣$$¢
$¢ƒ£%ÇŁØÆŒß
çłøæœfictst12345
67890°○★⌣⌣(..!?.————)
ssʿʿ(:;,.:""")
#/‡†§@«»1234567890
[aeilmorst]

Galliard (ITC)

roman of his design that had been adapted for modern use was one that, though a huge success, brought no attention to Granjon, as it was called Plantin, for the printer who had commissioned the original. Quite possibly Granjon would not have recognized that reemergence in 1913 of his Gros Cicero, for it had been appreciably changed to meet the typographic demands of the early twentieth century: the ascenders and descenders were shortened and the strokes thickened to almost monotone weight, to adapt it for the composition of periodicals.

It is a coincidence that the Granjon-based Plantin type, like the much later Galliard, was a roman cut for a modern method of type-setting – one of the first such types. Plantin was designed for the Monotype machine, then achieving its initial popularity in Europe. It has remained an English favorite, possibly because in the post–World War II period, which witnessed the enormous growth of offset lithographic printing, Plantin's lack of strong contrast in thick and thin strokes adapted well to the process (this, of course, was before lithographers had developed the skills in film handling and plate making that made such subterfuge unnecessary). In the United States, Bookman type was the standard for photomechanical reproduction. Plantin later served as the model for Times New Roman, but here the direction of design was fortunately a return to Granjon's standards, even though the type was not recognizable as a Granjon original.

While the designers of the regenerated Garamonds were attempting reasonable fidelity in their copies, Carter preferred simply to bring to Galliard his interpretation of the *spirit* of a Granjon original. Here his broad knowledge of historic printing types bore fruit. In addition, his skill as a punchcutter resulted in a revival that is most sympathetic to its prototype.

Galliard thus possesses the authentic sparkle that is lacking in the current Garamonds. It is a type of solid weight, which will bring good color to the printed page – an asset in offset printing in which the more delicately constructed romans appear to disadvantage. (This has been one of the difficulties encountered by typographers in the selection for photomechanical printing of types originally designed for relief printing: the crispness of the depressed image of relief printing cannot be captured in offset lithography and gravure.) This comparison of printing processes long captured the attention of typographers, particularly in the era 1930–1970. Many and prolonged

ABCDEFGHIJK
LMNOPQRSTU
VWXYZ&1234
567890abcdefghijk
klmnopqrstuvwxyz
a e n t v z $$¢
$¢£f%ÇŁØÆŒßç
łöãæfictspsti234567
890○★ᴜᴠ(.. !?.‹‹›› ‹›#)
ss ci (.;,..!
/‡†§@«»1234567890
[aeilmorst]

Galliard Italic (ITC)

144

ABCDEFGHIJKLMNOPQRSTUV
abcdefghijklmnopqrstuvwxyz
1234567890
ABCDEFGHIJKLMNOPQRSUVX
abcdefghijklmnopqrstuxwxyz
1234567890

Plantin (English Monotype)

were the arguments concerning type selection for the different repro-
ductive processes. Eric Gill, for example, wrote: 'A print is properly
a dent made by pressing; the history of letterpress printing is the
history of the abolition of that dent.' Here Gill is referring to the
twentieth-century concept of the 'kiss impression.' Beatrice Warde,
renowned for championing typographic taste, was fond, in her worldwide lecturing, of comparing relief printing to sculpture, and in fact
recommended that readers feel the impressions on title pages, an advo-
cacy greeted with horror by all librarians within sound of her voice.

The italic of Galliard is particularly felicitous in that the designer
reached back to the feeling of the chancery style, from which Claude
Garamond, in his complementary italic, had departed. The prototype
selected by Carter was a cursive that Granjon had cut for Christopher
Plantin. Galliard italic is a more upright letter than that of Garamond,
demonstrating the former's closer relationship to the chancery forms.

In keeping with current trends in the preparation of fonts for
phototypesetting, Galliard is supplied in four weights. Following the
'normal' boldface adaptation are two additional designs, called Black
and Ultra. Although in Black some semblance of the normal weight
of the roman remains, it seems quite lost in Ultra, but such are the
modern exigencies of typeface marketing which demand the broadest
application for every design. From the standpoint of manufacturing,
the preparation of additional weights is now being simplified by
the computer, which can eliminate many of the laborious procedures

formerly involved. In the case of Galliard, the Ikarus computer program developed by Peter Karow in Hamburg, Germany, has been utilized. Such programs will undoubtedly be increasingly employed in the future rendering of new types, especially those for cathode-ray-tube (CRT) digitized typesetting.

It is a most hopeful sign that a composing-machine manufacturer will promote the design of a new roman type useful in the production of books. Galliard embodies a commitment to the future that is praiseworthy, for it represents the combination of traditional concepts with today's advanced technology.

Many readers of this volume will have noted that it has been set in Galliard.

GRANJON

The type currently called Granjon is one of the best modern recuttings of the original Garamond design. It was produced under the direction of George W. Jones for Linotype and Machinery, the English manufacturer of the Mergenthaler Linotype machine.

During the time that Jones was a director of this firm he was more notably the head of a very fine London printing establishment called the press of George W. Jones at *The Sign of the Dolphin*. That he was a printer of taste is evident from the specimen keepsake of Granjon that he produced in 1931 for Mergenthaler in the United States. It is a distinguished piece of printing and has become a most desirable acquisition for any collection of type specimens.

Robert Granjon's career as a punchcutter lasted from about 1545 to 1588, during which time he cut punches on commission in Paris, Antwerp, Lyons, and Rome. Although he also produced roman types, his reputation is most secure in his skill with italic. Stanley Morison has written of him, 'He is unquestionably the greatest master of Italics of his age, and his Greeks and Romans are not inferior to Garamond's.'

Granjon also designed the cursive Civilité types (1557), and his arabesque fleurons have retained their popularity for decorative typography. Book collectors have long prized the volumes designed by Bruce Rogers that contain the Granjon typographic flowers; no one has used them with quite the élan of Rogers in the decoration of books. Their use will diminish now that hand-composition of single types has become practically obsolete in bookmaking other than by the private presses. Even at the time of Rogers's death, in 1957, very few compositors were allowed the privilege of using these so-called dingbats. But perhaps they will lend themselves to a computer assembling terminal if some enterprising manufacturer cares to write a program for their inclusion in a book composed by a cathode-ray-tube (CRT) typesetting device.

(24△1027) Lower case alphabet, 263 points. Code word, ZAZER

HOW CAN ONE EVALUATE AND

How is one to assess and evaluate a type face in terms of its esthetic design? Why do the pace-makers in the art of printing rave over a specific face of type? What do they see in it? Why is it so superlatively pleasant to the eyes? A good design is always a practical design. And what they see in a good type design is, partly, its excellent practical fitness to perform its work. It has a "heft" and balance in all of its parts just right for its size, as any good tool has. Your good chair has all of its parts made nicely to the right size to do exactly the kind of work that the chair must do, neither clumsy and thick, nor "skinny" and weak, no waste of m ($,.:;'-'?!fiflffffiffl)

ABCDEFGHIJKLMNO
PQRSTUVWXYZ& 1234567890
abcdefghijklmnopqrstuvwxyz

Granjon (Linotype)

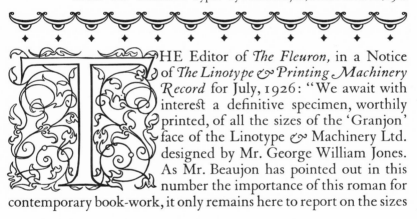

"..... this is a book face worthy to rank with Caslon for usefulness, with Centaur for beauty; sharp enough for publicity, clear enough for a dictionary. For some reason the face is called 'Granjon.' It would seem that Garamont's name having so long been used on a design he never cut is now by stern justice left off the face which is undoubtedly his."

—From "The 'Garamond' Types" by Paul Beaujon, in *The Fleuron*, 1926

THE Editor of *The Fleuron*, in a Notice of *The Linotype & Printing Machinery Record* for July, 1926: "We await with interest a definitive specimen, worthily printed, of all the sizes of the 'Granjon' face of the Linotype & Machinery Ltd. designed by Mr. George William Jones. As Mr. Beaujon has pointed out in this number the importance of this roman for contemporary book-work, it only remains here to report on the sizes

Granjon, in page composed by George W. Jones at *The Sign of the Dolphin*, London

Little is known of Granjon's early life. His father was a printer and publisher in Paris who apprenticed his son to a goldsmith from whom the boy no doubt acquired the degree of skill that eventually made him an outstanding punchcutter.

Granjon began his career about 1525, but his types date from about 1545. In 1547 he cut a nonpareil (6-point), the earliest known cutting of this type size. It was in that year that he took up his father's trade of publishing, continuing until 1551 when it seems that he again became involved in punchcutting and typefounding. In 1556, Granjon went to the great printing center Lyons where he cut types for printers and in a publishing venture of his own produced books set in the Civilité type. A scriptorial letter based on a gothic cursive form, Civilité is believed to be the first type that can be classified as a cursive, apart from the more common italic forms.

Robert Granjon returned again to Paris in 1562, continuing as a typefounder, but by 1565 he had entered a relationship with the scholar-printer Christopher Plantin in Antwerp. Plantin was one of those printers – and they have been legion since – who couldn't resist acquiring new types; upon his death the type in his printing office amounted to some 44,000 pounds, at a value of almost 9,000 guilders. For Plantin, Granjon produced thirty-four fonts of matrices, thirteen of which were noted in the Plantin inventory, along with corresponding punches. In 1578 Granjon was called to Rome by Pope Gregory XIII, where he remained for ten years, cutting numerous 'exotic' – non-Latin-alphabet – types for the Vatican press. He is believed to have returned to Paris in 1590, the year of his death.

When George W. Jones decided that the English Linotype company should have a Garamond, he used for his model the *Historia Ecclesiastica*, printed at Paris in 1582 by Jean Poupy, and composed in a type of Garamond origin. Owing primarily to the fact that several other Garamonds were then in use, Jones elected to reduce the confusion by naming his type Granjon.

His decision prompted Beatrice Warde, in the 1925 *Fleuron* essay on Garamond types, to remark wryly, 'It would seem that Garamond's name, having so long been used on a design he never cut, is now by stern justice left off the face which is undoubtedly his.' Mrs. Warde went on to say that Granjon was 'The first and immeasurably the best of the modern revivals of this letter (the "true" Garamond). . . . This is a book face worthy to rank with Caslon for usefulness, with Centaur for beauty; sharp enough for publicity, clear enough for a dictionary.'

The Jones 'Garamond' was an immediate success as a book type. The Mergenthaler organization in this country very quickly made Granjon available to American printers.

The popularity of Granjon as a book type may readily be attested by the statistics provided by that barometer of type use, the American Institute of Graphic Arts' Fifty Books of the Year Exhibition. From 1927 through 1973 Granjon was used in a total of 135 books, whereas from 1923 through 1973 Garamond in all its other versions combined was selected for 148 books.

SABON

In 1960 a group of German master printers formed a committee to promote the manufacture of a printing type that would be made available in identical versions from three specific sources: foundry type for hand-composition, matrices for machine-casting by Monotype, and matrices for linecasting via the Linotype machine. In addition, it was expected that this new type would 'be both legible and applicable to the various printing processes.'

It is ironic that this rather tall order was issued at a time when all three of these methods of composition were experiencing a serious decline, with the metal casting of type giving way to phototypesetting procedures. But even as late as 1960 – a short time ago when one considers the 500-year history of printing – the adherents of composition in metal type were not to be persuaded that its demise was imminent or at all certain. Naturally, the manufacturers who met with this committee were perfectly willing to fulfill the requirements as stated, seeing them as a boost to business. Furthermore, the specifications were completely rational, in fact long overdue, for it was seldom that a typographer had the opportunity to use a particular style of type that was identical in all the required sizes. The manufacturers of linecasting machines were primarily interested in producing sizes for continuous reading applicable to keyboard composition, and thus the display setting often had to be done with types of somewhat different design, even though they carried the same name. Thus, when representatives of the Monotype, Linotype, and Stempel firms agreed to collaborate in meeting the specifications set before them, their decision was received with much enthusiasm in the printing trade.

Still another desideratum had to be satisfied. The type was to be based on those designs first cut in the sixteenth century by Claude Garamond, but it had to be somewhat more economical in set width (five percent) than existing copies. The reader of this volume will already be aware that there is no dearth of Garamond types on the

9 Die Kunst, ein Buch als Ganzes schön zu gestalten, hat niemals so hoch gestanden wie zu der Zeit der Erfindung des Buchdruckes. Was Gutenberg und seine Genossen im engen Anschluß an die sichere Tradition der gotischen Handschriften geschnitten, gegossen, gesetzt sowie gedruckt haben, hat keiner ihrer Nachfolger daheim oder im Ausland an Kraft und Harmonie übertroffen. Einen weiteren Höhepunkt erreichte die deutsche Buchkunst zur Zeit der frühen Renaissance, als Meister wie Dürer, Holbein und Cranach den auf eignem deutschen Boden ENTSTANDENEN UND ERPROBTEN HOLZSCHNITT FÜR BILDER UND DEN

10 Die Kunst, ein Buch als Ganzes schön zu gestalten, hat niemals höher gestanden als zu der Zeit der Erfindung des Buchdrucks. Was Gutenberg und seine Genossen im engen Anschluß an die sichere Tradition der gotischen Handschriften geschnitten, gegossen, gesetzt sowie gedruckt haben, hat noch kein Nachfolger daheim oder im Ausland an Kraft und Harmonie übertroffen. Einen weiteren Höhepunkt erreichte die Buchkunst ZU DER ZEIT DER FRÜHEN RENAISSANCE, ALS MEISTER WIE DÜRER

2 Die Kunst, ein Buch als Ganzes schön zu gestalten, hat niemals so hoch gestanden wie zur Zeit der Erfindung des Buchdruckes. Was Gutenberg und seine Genossen im engen Anschluß an die Tradition der gotischen Handschriften geschnitten, gegossen, gesetzt sowie gedruckt haben, hat noch kein Nachfolger daheim oder im Ausland an Kraft und Harmonie ÜBERTROFFEN. EINEN GANZ BESONDEREN HÖHEPUNKT

Sabon (Stempel)

market, so this position represented a further challenge to any designer who was selected for the task. The committee naturally entertained the hope that the new face would eliminate the confusing variety of available Garamonds.

Such was the formidable assignment given to and accepted by the eminent German typographer Jan Tschichold, then fifty-eight years of age and a man who had achieved renown in two completely disparate arenas of typography – the avant-garde and the traditional. A son of a painter of letters, Tschichold had expected to follow a similar career, but exposure to typography through his attendance at the Leipzig Akademie and graduate work there under the noted type designer Walter Tiemann brought him into a broader field. In 1924, he visited a Bauhaus exhibition and came away completely converted to the typographic possibilities inherent in the Bauhaus approach to design.

His enthusiasm led to a friendship with Paul Renner, the designer of the Futura types, and further exposure to new trends in design. By 1928, with the publication of *Die Neue Typographie* ('the new typography') – which would influence typographic design for the next generation – Tschichold had established himself in the forefront of the younger European designers who were attempting to reform German typography. But in 1933 the new designs, employing sans-serif types in asymmetric arrangements, were condemned by the Nazis as anti-German. Tschichold therefore took refuge in Switzerland, where except for a short postwar stay in England he remained until his death in 1974.

Ironically, by the midthirties Tschichold himself had begun to have second thoughts about his youthful avowal of the principles expressed in his book. He now believed that the design concept he had so ardently promoted in fact demonstrated, as he later wrote, 'shocking parallels with the teachings of National Socialism and Fascism.' In 1935 he thus published *Typographische Gestaltung* ('typo-

Drawings for Sabon

WHEN JOBS HAVE THEIR TYPE SIZES FIXED QUICKLY
MARGINS OF ERROR WIDEN UNLESS DETERMINING
When jobs have type sizes fixed quickly margins of
error widen unless all determining calculations are
based on factual rather than hypothetical figures.
No variation in the amount of copy can affect the
degree of error once that error has been made. If
When jobs have type sizes fixed quickly margins of
error widen unless all determining calculations are
based on factual rather than hypothetical figures
ABCDEFGHIJKLMNOPQRSTUVWXYZ *ABCDE*

WHEN JOBS HAVE TYPE SIZES FIXED QUICKLY
MARGINS OF ERROR WILL WIDEN UNLESS ALL
When jobs have their type sizes fixed quickly
margins of error widen unless all determining
calculations are based on factual rather than
hypothetical figures. No variation in the total
amount of copy can affect the degree of error
When jobs have their type sizes fixed quickly
margins of error widen unless all determining
ABCDEFGHIJKLMNOPQRSTUVWXYZ *AB*

Sabon, English Monotype

graphic form'), in which he refuted some of the statements in *Die Neue Typographie*. He now taught that good printing had above all to be perfectly legible, 'and, as such, the result of intelligent planning.'

Tschichold's decision to recant his early ideas was not at all well received by his disciples. When he was called a renegade to his own teaching, he answered by asking his critics if they would be happy if he had gone on pretending that he had written a 'faultless book.'

After the war Tschichold's several years in England were spent in overseeing the entire redesign program embarked upon by the Penguin paperback series of books. The establishment of what became a house style was an exhausting undertaking, covering every production detail in the printing of more than six hundred titles, but it was brought off splendidly and greatly enhanced Tschichold's reputation as an outstanding book designer.

In addition to his considerable skill as a typographer, Tschichold brought to his commission for a new 'Garamond' a love of the classic types, such as those of Jenson, Caslon, and Baskerville. He now turned to the famous 1592 specimen sheet of Egenolff-Berner. From it he selected a 14-point roman, Saint Augustine, which in the specimen was attributed to Claude Garamond.

Tschichold by no means attempted a slavish copy of this type. The original irregularities that occurred naturally from size to size – owing to the fact that in the sixteenth century each had to be cut in steel independently – were not allowable in modern typography, in which the pantograph governs the proportions of each size from a master pattern. Tschichold made his drawings to the dimension of twenty times 10-point. (It may be noted that type designers have their individual preferences for drawings; W. A. Dwiggins, for example, drew to ten times 12-point, and Frederic W. Goudy did his originals freehand to seven and a half inches.)

Further restrictions affecting the design were imposed by the

ABCDEFGHIJKLMNOPQ
RSTUVWXYZÄÖÜ
abcdefghijklmnopqrstuvw
xyz ßchckfffififlft&äöü
1234567890 1234567890

Sabon (Linotype)

mechanical requirements of three distinctly different methods of composition – foundry, Monotype, and Linotype. The economic problems of matrix manufacture make it obligatory that character widths be restricted for machine-composition, and though foundry casting presents no such limitation, the foundry version of the projected new type had to conform to the requirements of the other two. The most serious of the restrictions was the Linotype's lack of kerning, since the system of matrix assembly does not allow for projections from the body of a letter. (The Linotype manufacturers could provide kerning only by producing logotype matrices, or two letters on a single matrix, which was the common practice for *f*-ligatures, for which keys were furnished. But other logotypes had to be inserted into the line by hand, thus inhibiting rapid composition, and so kerns were usually dispensed with.) Thus, the new type's design is particularly noticeable in the lowercase *f*: the *f* of the slugcasting machine has always been the means by which the method of composition could be recognized, typographers frequently referring to the unkerned letter as a 'buttonhook.'

For his italic Tschichold chose one that had also appeared on the Egenolff-Berner specimen sheet, where it was attributed to Robert Granjon. Here again mechanical considerations interfered with the aesthetics of letter form. In the linecasting machine each matrix contains either lightface duplexed with boldface or roman (upright) duplexed with italic. Since in single types italic is normally of a narrower set width than roman, the slug-cast italic appears to be letterspaced. In addition, the matrix width interferes with normal kerning (overlapping) common to the italic form. It may be noted that in current automated typesetting this long-criticized feature of machine typesetting has been eliminated.

---

abcdefghijklmnopqrstuvwxyz£1234567890$.,:;"'!?-()[]--—
ABCDEFGHIJKLMNOPQRSTUVWXYZ
ABCDEFGHIJKLMNOPQRSTUVWXYZ&
abcdefghijklmnopqrstuvwxyz1234567890$,:;"'!?()[]
ABCDEFGHIJKLMNOPQRSTUVWXYZ&

Sabon (Monophoto)

The name selected for this first joint venture in typographic harmony was Sabon, which tied the design to its French sixteenth-century origins without adding to the confusion that surrounded such names as Garamond and Granjon. Jacques Sabon was a punch-cutter who had worked in Lyons before going to Frankfurt for employment with Christian Egenolff, who maintained a typefoundry in connection with his printing office. Following Egenolff's death in 1555, his widow asked Sabon for help in running the foundry part of the business. It is also known that Sabon worked at Antwerp for Christopher Plantin.

In 1571, Sabon married Judith Egenolff, the granddaughter of Christian, and through this connection he was able to purchase the foundry itself from Egenolff's heirs in 1572. This marks the real beginning of one of the great typefoundries of the period. Upon Sabon's death, in 1580, Judith married Konrad Berner, who continued the establishment.

In the design of Sabon, Jan Tschichold admirably met the stiff requirements of the German committee of master printers. The design has now been transferred to phototypesetting devices (alas, the non-kerning *f* has been retained in this mode), and the type has continued to grow in popularity. It is used particularly in European printing, where it is beginning to edge out that perennial favorite Bembo – from which, of course, it derives along with all the other Garamond types.

JANSON

One of the most frequently cited examples of the misnaming of a classic type is that of ATF Garamond, in which Jannon, its creator, lost his identity. A similar error of attribution has occurred with the seventeenth-century Dutch old-style type called Janson, a face that has proved its usefulness over the past forty-three years since its revival – indeed, it has become one of the most popular of book types. Determining this design's provenance provides a complicated tale.

Daniel Berkeley Updike, in his *Printing Types* of 1922, discussed the Dutch types in great detail, but failed to properly identify the Janson design, although he described it and showed examples of both the roman and the italic. He simply captioned the illustrations 'Dutch Roman Types. Erhardt Foundry Specimen, Leipsic, 1739.' In the second edition of his book (1937), Updike ascribed the types to the Dutch punchcutter Anton Janson. In addition, he had included the face in the bibliography of his Merrymount Press, published in 1934, in which he discussed a visit he had made to Leipzig during a European tour in 1903. Unaccountably, however, he did not mention that he had purchased 'Janson' types from the Drugulin foundry of that city, which was then in possession of the punches and matrices of the so-called Janson design, a fact noted by Stanley Morison.

Although Updike had purchased 'Janson' fonts as early as 1903, he did not employ them for a book until 1918, even though he had but six roman types in his printing office before 1925. Updike had a great fondness for Caslon, which he selected for about forty percent of his books, and he also had a warm regard for Bell (also called Mountjoye), bought the same year as the Janson. That he did admire Janson, though, is evident from his employment of the letter in what is often considered the finest product of the Merrymount Press, the Book of Common Prayer, printed in 1930, a typographic masterpiece composed entirely in Janson types.

MONOTYPE JANSON
& JANSON ITALIC, No. 401

Many Dutch types were based on those of French origin. For example, although the types of Janson are more precise, narrower (particularly as applied to the roman lowercase), *and show a greater difference between the fine and heavy lines than those of the Frenchman, Claude Garamont, there is never*

Many Dutch types were based on those of French origin. For example, although the types of Janson are more precise, narrower (particularly as applied to the roman lowercase), *and show a greater difference between the fine and heavy lines than those of the Frenchman, Claude Garamont, there is never*

Many Dutch types were based on those of French origin. For example, although the types of Janson are more precise, narrower (particularly as applied to the roman lowercase), *and show a greater difference between the fine and heavy lines than those of the Frenchman, Claude Garamont, there is never*

ABCDEFGHIJKLMNOPQRSTUVWXYZ&
abcdefghijklmnopqrstuvwxyz   fiflffffiffl
$1234567890   .,-:;"!?() $1234567890
ABCDEFGHIJKLMNOPQRSTUVWXYZ&

ABCDEFGHIJJKLMNOPQRSTUVWXYZ&
abcdefghhijklmnopqrstuvwxyz   fiflffffiffl
$1234567890   :;!? $1234567890

TVWY gjpqy   *ATVWY fgjpqy fiflffffiffl*

Janson and Janson Italic (Monotype)

ADhortamur vos fratres, ut abundetis magis,
& in hoc ftudiofe incumbatis, ut quieti fitis,
&propria AGATIS. AD MDCC.

Et fermo ille caro factus eft & commoratus eft Inter
nos & gloriam ejus gloriam quam ut unigeniti egreffi
abcdeffffififflghiklmnopqrfsftfiffiftuxyz A A D D E E H

Biennum eft, & quod excurrit cum rogatui præcellentium non
nullorum Academiæ noftræ Etudioforum indulgerem, vt Adir
ABCD   Fette Text Verfal. A ÆCCDEFIMNRTUV

Deum nemo vidit unquem unigenitus ille filius qui eft fine patris ille

Erhardt foundry specimen of Dutch roman type, Leipzig, c. 1739

One of the earliest descriptions of Janson by a leading typographic historian appears in Stanley Morison's *On Type Faces*, published for the Medici Society in 1923. Here are shown seven sizes, 8- to 36-point. In the introductory essay to this specimen, Morison writes – after discussing the seventeenth-century types purchased by John Fell, Bishop of Oxford, for Oxford University Press – 'An excellent letter of similar spirit but less archaic feeling is to be found in the roman and italic cut by Janson: this Dutch letter is a generation or two later in design and is more regular in its setting.' (Morison was referring to the ragged alignment of the Fell types, approved by many modern typographers but deplored by just as many others.)

However, in another small handbook, entitled *On Type Designs Past and Present* (1927), Morison did not include any remarks about Janson. Nor did the reputable A. F. Johnson of the British Museum in his *Type Designs: Their History and Development*, printed in 1934, a book conceived as an update of Updike's *Printing Types*, although not attempting such broad coverage as the original volumes.

It is scarcely surprising, then, that when both the Mergenthaler Linotype Company and the Lanston Monotype Machine Company

ABCDEFGHIJKLMNOPQRSTU
VWXYZ

abcdefghijklmnopqrstuvwxyz

ﬀﬁﬂ & $£ .,-:;!?'("" 1234567890

ABCDEFGHIJKLMNOPQRSTUV
WXYZ abcdefghijklmnopqrstuvwxyz
ﬀﬁﬂ & $£ .,-:;!?'(" " 1234567890

Janson (Stempel)

announced their revivals of Janson in 1937, most American printers had no choice but to accept the historic information that was disseminated by these firms.

Neither firm could offer many facts to accompany the first specimens of the recuttings. Linotype's statement was simply: '. . . definite information concerning Anton Janson is difficult to obtain.' The Monotype promotional showing – a beautifully designed and produced twenty-eight-page booklet in three colors – contained an essay on Dutch types written by Sol Hess, then associate art director of the company, who had overseen the adaptation. (Frederic W. Goudy was at that time Monotype's art director, but his responsibilities were of a consulting nature, leaving to Hess the everyday decisions in the production of matrices. Hess was therefore quite independent, making a separate contribution to the American typographic scene.) Hess's statement on the Janson specimen echoed that of Mergenthaler: 'Unfortunately, little definite information is to be found concerning Anton Janson and his work.' Both companies, it may be noted, perpetuated the erroneous impression that the types now named Janson had been designed by him. The misconception was sustained into the 1950s by a pamphlet distributed by the German Stempel foundry, of Frankfurt-am-Main, owner since 1919 of the original 'Janson' punches and matrices. The Stempel account says that the types had been created in 'the typefoundry of the famous Dutchman Anton Janson, and show the mark of superior craftsmanship in the firm stems and hairlines.'

During all these early years of confusion concerning its origin, Janson was becoming well known, not so much by commercial printers as by book typographers and collectors. A splendid example of its early use was in Stanley Morison's *Andres Brun, Calligrapher of Sargossa*, hand-set in 1929 for the Pegasus Press of Paris by Giovanni Mardersteig at his Officina Bodoni in Verona and greatly admired for its lovely typography.

As of 1939, however, Morison had become sufficiently curious about the true origin of the type and its designer to take the time to make a more thorough investigation than had heretofore been attempted. He disclosed his findings in an article in *Signature, No. 11*, in a discussion of Leipzig as a typefounding center. Morison proposed that it was the Stempel foundry that had initiated the misconception by attributing to Anton Janson the types that it had acquired from the Drugulin foundry of Leipzig in 1919.

A. F. Johnson, also in 1939, wrote an article for *The Library*, entitled 'The Gout Hollandois,' that shed further light on the mystery, and in *Signature, No. 15*, published in 1940, Morison came to grips with Anton Janson himself, citing information sent to him by a German scholar. None of these essays, however, illuminated the most important missing detail of the Janson type – the name of its designer.

The answer to that question had to await postwar scholarship and was finally supplied by Harry Carter and George Buday in England. Equipped with a photograph of a type-specimen sheet located in the National Library in Budapest (provided by Professor G. W. Ovink of Amsterdam), Carter discovered that the types shown here were the same ones that had reached Leipzig and finally arrived at the Stempel foundry in Frankfurt. The designer of the so-called Janson types, it turned out, was a Hungarian punchcutter named Nicholas Kis (pronounced kish). Carter and Buday published their findings in an article in the British periodical *Linotype Matrix: 18* in 1954, and later produced a definitive account in *Gutenberg Jahrbuch, 1957*, entitled 'Nicholas Kis and the Janson Types.'

Further information on the career of the Hungarian punchcutter

And when this Power of the City shall seem great to you, consider that the same was pur-

chased by Valiant Men ... in imitation of these men, therefore, placing Happiness in Liberty, Liberty in Valour, be forward to

ENCOUNTER THE *Dangers of War*. Such is the City for which these men valiantly fighting have died, and it is fit that every man of you *should be like minded* to undergo any travail for the same.—
Extract from Thucydides, trans. B. Jowett

Ehrhardt (English Monotype)

has been published by Buday in 'Some More Notes on Nicholas Kis of the "Janson" Types,' in *The Library* of March 1974. (The writer, of Hungarian birth but now resident in Britain, gives full credit to Mr. Carter for the identification of the types. Buday's contribution was in the Hungarian-language aspects of the research.)

Nicholas Kis was born in 1650. He took religious orders, and during

☞ THE APPLICATION : This is levelled at that numerous part of mankind, who, out of their ample fortunes take care to accomplish themselves with everything but common sense.

73. *The Old Hound.*

An old Hound, who had been an excellent good one in his time, and given his master great sport and satisfaction in many a chase, at last, by the effect of years, became feeble and unserviceable. However, being in the field one day when the Stag was almost run down, he happened to be the first that came in with him, and seized him by one of his haunches; but his decayed and

85

The Fell type, in *Fables of Aesop*, designed by Bruce Rogers, 1933

his theological studies at the Transylvanian College of Nagyenyed he attained a reputation as a Greek and Latin scholar. After three years as a schoolmaster, he followed the pattern of Transylvanian scholars of his time by traveling to gain experience. It was recommended that he study typography, as knowledge in the field of printing was much needed in Hungary. Kis therefore chose to visit Holland, a center of publishing and printing, and arrived there in 1680.

He managed to secure the services of the well-known punchcutter Dirk Voskens, who agreed to give Kis instruction in the cutting of types for a period of six months, although he informed Kis that nine or ten years would be required to perfect his skill. Kis, however, was apparently an apt pupil, with the result that in a comparatively short time he was in demand as a punchcutter, not only of roman and italic types but also of Greek, Hebrew, and other exotic alphabets. He received international recognition, and printers from several countries requested his punches and matrices as well as his services as a trainer of apprentices.

Kis's reputation continued to grow, resulting in a call from Cosimo de Medici, grand duke of Tuscany, to go to Italy to establish a type-foundry for the ducal court. In coaxing Kis, the duke informed him that he was considered to be the best type cutter in Europe. Kis, however, refused the offer, as he was then planning to go home to give his native land the benefit of his experience.

Kis returned to Hungary in 1690, determined to spend the rest of his life in the service of typography, particularly the printing of beautiful Bibles. Unfortunately, however, the next decade of religious and political upheaval in Hungary, along with personal enmities, frustrated Kis's ambitions and in fact so embittered him that his life was considerably shortened. He died in 1702.

Thus the story was finally out, almost forty years after the type's revival. During this time the availability of Janson for both hand- and machine-composition had very quickly established the face with book designers in Europe and the United States.

Citation of the Fifty Books of the Year Exhibition has become controversial in the past few years, as the American Institute of Graphic Arts, which puts on the show, continues to experiment with the rationale behind it. Nevertheless, the statistics of type use for the books selected cannot fail to indicate the degree of acceptance of certain styles, and in fact are very useful to typographers interested in design trends over the past half century. For example, since 1923 two types in 'The Fifty' stand out above all the rest: Baskerville, the most widely used, and Caslon, a fairly close second (the old reliable Caslon had very little competition in the early days of the show, when there were far fewer good book types available – a factor, indeed, that allowed it to hold its commanding position for a forty-year period).

Janson, as used by Updike, first appeared in The Fifty in 1929, and it is now the third most popular type among these books, having been selected by the designers of more than two hundred works there honored. It is interesting to note that the Dutch old-style types, as represented by both Caslon and Janson, have far outdistanced any other classic-revival type.

Book typographers have long been conscious of the fact that Caslon, unless firmly pressed into the printed page, lacks strong color. Commercial printers have also discovered that in the smaller sizes this type appears anemic when printed on coated papers. In addition, Caslon suffers similarly when printed by offset lithography.

Some of these problems have been corrected by Janson. It maintains the basic unobtrusive character of its Dutch old-style origin, but has a slightly heavier weight, which achieves the close-textured appearance that typographers expect of a book page.

Jack Stauffacher, the California printer whose love for Janson resulted in the production of a beautiful little book about the type, *Janson – A Definitive Collection* (1954), stated the case very well when he wrote: 'It is truly remarkable how these early bookmakers understood the merits of a page amassed in type. The total color of a page was sustained in a harmonious image that blended with the contents. Nothing was inconsistent with the end result of communicating the author's thoughts.'

Janson is available today from numerous sources – in single type (foundry and Monotype), on linecasting machines, and on photo-typesetters. The typographic purists have generally maintained that the version cast by the Stempel typefoundry in Frankfurt is the finest, it being the original font.

These original fonts obtained by Stempel were not complete. Thus in 1951 Hermann Zapf supplied the 24- and 48-point sizes for the foundry, and at the same time redesigned for the German Linotype firm four sizes, 6-, 8-, 9-, and 10-point. Zapf later commented on the difficult task of creating two large sizes that would blend into the overall pattern of the existing fonts, since characteristics vary from size to size when type is cut by hand with the steel punch.

TO THE RIGHT HONORABLE

Henrie Wriothesley

EARLE OF SOUTHAMPTON AND BARON

OF TITCHFIELD

RIGHT HONOURABLE, *I know not how I shall offend in dedicating my unpolisht lines to your Lordship, nor how the worlde will censure mee for choosing so strong a proppe to support so weake a burthen, onelye if your Honour seeme but pleased, I account my selfe highly praised, and vowe to take advantage of all idle houres, till I have honoured you with some graver labour. But if the first heire of my invention prove deformed, I shall be sorie it had so noble a godfather: and never after eare so barren a land, for feare it yeeld me still so bad a harvest, I leave it to your Honourable survey, and your Honor to your hearts content, which I wish may alwaies answere your owne wish, and the worlds hopefull expectation.*

Your Honors in all dutie,

William Shakespeare.

Use of Janson by Bruce Rogers in *The Poems of Shakespeare*, 1940

Linotype Janson was first produced in the United States in 1937 under the guidance of C. H. Griffith, the typographic director of Mergenthaler; he used the Stempel original as the model for this cutting. In the same year Sol Hess undertook for the American Monotype firm a modification of the face, using as a pattern a version in a seventeenth-century book. Both of these revivals found immediate favor with the American printers, even though the types lack some of the crispness of the Stempel foundry version, a factor that is most noticeable in the display sizes. It is, of course, currently offered by manufacturers of phototypesetting machines.

Finally, it may be observed that the Ehrhardt design for the English Monotype Corporation is patterned on the same original as the cuttings of Janson referred to above. A comparison of Ehrhardt and Janson indicates the fascinating differences that may result even between close copies of an original.

15

CASLON

Although infrequently the case, one of the most widely known of all historic printing types indisputably bears the name of its designer, William Caslon. He was an English engraver who cut the face about 1720. It is also an indisputable fact that the reputation of the design has been sullied by too many eulogies on the part of the outstanding typographers of a generation ago – Beatrice Warde, in her 1933 essay 'On the Choice of Typefaces,' mentions the 'almost superstitious regard for Caslon Old Face' that existed at that time.

Contemporary typographers, with the choice of a variety of printing riches far greater than that of their predecessors (if we may take as evidence the bulging current specimen books), are not to be blamed if they express disenchantment with Caslon and the period it seems to represent. Still, their disapproval runs counter to the opinion of the more traditionally oriented type professionals, who point as usual to such printing stalwarts as Daniel Berkeley Updike who in 1922 stated in his seminal *Printing Types*, 'In the class of types which appear to be beyond criticism from the point of view of beauty and utility, the original Caslon type stands first.'

The typographers who grew to maturity before 1930 learned to love Caslon and, more important, acquired expertise in its use. During his formative years the eminent Bruce Rogers employed Caslon in book after book, while Carl Purington Rollins, the estimable Printer to Yale University, acquired an international reputation for his handling of the type. Even on Madison Avenue, the New York advertising typographer Hal Marchbanks was widely known as 'a Caslon printer'; it was he who was responsible for bringing the type out of the library and into the hectic world of commercial and advertising printing.

The result of all this activity by printers who had received their initial inspiration from the English private-press movement – as represented by the Kelmscott, Doves, and Ashendene presses – was to place Caslon today in an ambiguous position. The contemporary

---

Best Act
Rich Girls
KINGDOMS
exporting gold
HEAR VOICES
speaking rapidly
MODERN Machine
helps manufacturing

Caslon No. 471 (ATF)

typographer may very well ignore the design, but at the same time one feels uncomfortable rejecting it out of hand.

Certainly, Caslon is far from forgotten. It continues to turn up regularly in national advertising. All of the manufacturers of photo-typesetting equipment have transferred the type to their film grids for both text and display typography. In 1966, the American Type Founders Company (then practically at the end of its existence as the most important supplier of new types) brought out still another version, Caslon 641, even though the firm already had in its vaults matrices for some three dozen variations on the design.

The original Caslon was devised in the early eighteenth century when a group of London printers and booksellers prevailed upon the young engraver William Caslon to cut for them a font of Arabic-language types for a series of religious tracts then being planned. (Through these tracts, it was hoped, the natives in newly discovered lands would be induced to take up Christianity.) According to one account, when Caslon had finished the task and was ready for proof, he cut his name in pica roman (12-point), in order to identify the proof. It was these few letters of his signature that attracted the interest of his sponsors and which eventually resulted in Caslon's devoting all of his energies to the cutting of non-exotic types.

In that period there was little typefounding being done in England; for some time printers had been dependent on Dutch sources for their types. This was owing largely to the restrictions on printing engendered during the preceding century by the censorial Star Chamber which had severely limited competition in the field. Though by Caslon's time these obstacles had been removed, their effects were still felt in the trade.

The preponderance, therefore, of Dutch types in English printing offices made it almost inevitable that Caslon would be influenced by their characteristics. Indeed, although his types have been praised as the embodiment of English typography, they were in fact modeled on the earlier Dutch forms, albeit better fitted and cast.

Caslon completed the work on his first fonts about 1720, but it was not until 1734 that he issued his first specimen sheet, a broadside that has since been widely reproduced in printing histories and is thus well known to all students of typography. In addition to the roman and italic types, this sheet shows a number of exotics, such as Greek, Hebrew, and Arabic.

The success of these Caslon-designed fonts and the growing repu-

A SPECIMEN

By W. CASLON, Letter-Founder, in Ironmonger-Row, Old-Street, LONDON.

ABCD
ABCDE
ABCDEFG
ABCDEFGHI
ABCDEFGHIJK
ABCDEFGHIJKL
ABCDEFGHIKLMN

French Cannon.

Quousque tan-
dem abutere,
Catilina, pati-

Quousque tandem
abutere, Catilina,
patientia nostra?

Two Lines Great Primer.

Quousque tandem
abutere, Catilina,
patientia nostra?
quamdiu nos etiam
Quousque tandem a-
butere, Catilina, pa-
tientia nostra? quam-
diu nos etiam furor

Two Lines English.

Quousque tandem abu-
tere, Catilina, patientia
nostra? quamdiu nos e-
tiam furor iste tuus elu-
Quousque tandem abutere,
Catilina, patientia nostra?
quamdiu nos etiam furor

DOUBLE PICA ROMAN.

Quousque tandem abutere, Catilina, patientia nostra? quamdiu
nos etiam furor iste tuus eludet?
quem ad finem sese effrenata jac-
ABCDEFGHIJKLMNOP

Double Pica Italick.

Quousque tandem abutere, Catili-
na, patientia nostra? quamdiu
nos etiam furor iste tuus eludet?
quem ad finem sese effrenata jac-
ABCDEFGHIJKLMNO

GREAT PRIMER ROMAN.

Quousque tandem abutere, Catilina, patientia nostra? quamdiu nos etiam furor iste tuus eludet? quem ad finem sese effrenata jactabit audacia? nihilne te
nocturnum præsidium palatii, nihil urbis vigiliæ, nihil timor populi, nihil con-
ABCDEFGHIJKLMNOPQRS

Great Primer Italick.

Quousque tandem abutere, Catilina, pa-
tientia nostra? quamdiu nos etiam fu-
ror iste tuus eludet? quem ad finem sese
effrenata jactabit audacia? nihilne te
nocturnum præsidium palatii, nihil ur-
ABCDEFGHIJKLMNOPQR

ENGLISH ROMAN.

Quousque tandem abutere, Catilina, patientia
nostra? quamdiu nos etiam iste tuus eludet?
quem ad finem sese effrenata jactabit audacia?
nihilne te nocturnum præsidium palatii, nihil
urbis vigiliæ, nihil timor populi, nihil consen-
fus bonorum omnium, nihil hic munitissimus
ABCDEFGHIJKLMNOPQRSTVW

English Italick.

Quousque tandem abutere, Catilina, patientia nos-
tra? quamdiu nos etiam furor iste tuus eludet?
quem ad finem sese effrenata jactabit audacia?
nihilne te nocturnum præsidium palatii, nihil ur-
bis vigiliæ, nihil timor populi, nihil consensus bo-
norum omnium, nihil hic munitissimus habendi se-
ABCDEFGHIJKLMNOPQRSTVU

PICA ROMAN.

Melium, novis rebus studentem, manu sua occidit.
Fuit, fuit ista quondam in hac repub. virtus, ut viri
fortes acrioribus suppliciis civem perniciosum, quam
acerbissimum hostem coercerent. Habemus enim se-
natusconsultum in te, Catilina, vehemens, & grave:
non deest reip. consilium, neque autoritas hujus ordinis: nos, nos, dico aperte, consules desumus. De-
ABCDEFGHIJKLMNOPQRSTVUWX

Pica Italick.

Melium, novis rebus studentem, manu sua occidit.
Fuit, fuit ista quondam in hac repub. virtus, ut viri
fortes acrioribus suppliciis civem perniciosum, quam a-
cerbissimum hostem coercerent. Habemus enim senatus-
consultum in te, Catilina, vehemens, & grave: non deest
reip. consilium, neque autoritas hujus ordinis: nos, nos,
dico aperte, consules desumus. Decrevit quondam senatus
ABCDEFGHIJKLMNOPQRSTVU

SMALL PICA ROMAN. No 1.

(specimen text in small pica roman)
ABCDEFGHIJKLMNOPQRSTVUWXYZ

Small Pica Italick. No 1.

(specimen text in small pica italick)
ABCDEFGHIJKLMNOPQRSTVUWXYZ

SMALL PICA ROMAN. No 2.

(specimen text in small pica roman No 2)
ABCDEFGHIJKLMNOPQRSTVUWXYZ

Small Pica Italick. No 2.

(specimen text in small pica italick No 2)
ABCDEFGHIJKLMNOPQRSTVUWXYZ

LONG PRIMER ROMAN No 1.

(specimen text)
ABCDEFGHIJKLMNOPQRSTVWXYZ

Long Primer Italick. No 1.

(specimen text)
ABCDEFGHIJKLMNOPQRSTVUWXYZ

LONG PRIMER ROMAN. No 2.

(specimen text)
ABCDEFGHIJKLMNOPQRSTVUWXYZ

Long Primer Italick. No 2.

(specimen text)
ABCDEFGHIJKLMNOPQRSTVUWXYZ

BREVIER ROMAN.

(specimen text)
ABCDEFGHIJKLMNOPQRSTVUWXYZ

Brevier Italick.

(specimen text)
ABCDEFGHIJKLMNOPQRSTVUWXYZ

Long Primer Saxon. / Pica Saxon.

Pica Black.

(blackletter specimen text)

Brevier Black.

(blackletter specimen text)

Pica Gothick.

ATTA FNSAK FN IN HIMINAM VEIHNAI
NAMO FEIN QIMAI FINAINASSUS FEINS
VAIKEAI VIAGA FEINS SVE IN HIMINA

Pica Coptick.

ΠΕΝ ΟΥΑΡΟΧ ΕΤ ΟΛΛΟ ΑΤΦΕ ΜΑΡΑ ΠΕ-
ΛΑΙ- ΝΙΚΑΔΙ ΛΕ ΠΕ ΟΥΛΟΝΙΑΥ ΕΡΟΥ ΠΕ ΟΥΟΡ,
ΛΑΤΟΟΤΙ ΟΥΚΑΙ ΠΑΝΟΟΝ ΕΧΕΝ ΦΗΟΥΝΒ ΟΥΟΡ,
ΟΥΝΙΑ- ΑΤΟΟΥ ΠΑΘΗΝΟΥ ΕΜΕΝ ΜΗΝΟΥΥ ε- Ο-

Pica Armenian.

(Armenian specimen text)

English Syriack.

(Syriac specimen text)

Pica Samaritan.

(Samaritan specimen text)

English Arabick.

(Arabic specimen text)

Hebrew with Points.

(Hebrew specimen text with points)

Hebrew without Points.

(Hebrew specimen text)

Brevier Hebrew.

(Hebrew specimen text)

English Greek.

(Greek specimen text)

Pica Greek.

(Greek specimen text)

Long Primer Greek.

(Greek specimen text)

Brevier Greek.

(Greek specimen text)

First broadside specimen of William Caslon, 1734

tation of this most competent English punchcutter no doubt contributed to the lack of appreciation by English printers for the typographic
developments then taking place on the Continent. Exciting things
were happening there, however. Although during much of the 1600s
the Dutch types had dominated European printing, in the last years

Two Lines Great Primer.

Quoufque tandem
abutere Catilina, p

*Quoufque tandem a-
butere, Catilina, pa-*

Two Lines Englifh.

Quoufque tandem abu-
tere, Catilina, patientia
noftra? quamdiu nos e-

*Quoufque tandem abutere
Catilina, patientia noftra?*

Two Lines Pica.

Quoufque tandem abutere,
Catilina, patientia noftra? qu

*Quoufque tandem abutere, Ca-
tilina, patientia noftra? quam-*

Page from specimen book of William Caslon & Sons, 1763

In CONGRESS, July 4, 1776.

A DECLARATION

By the REPRESENTATIVES OF· THE

UNITED STATES OF AMERICA,

In GENERAL CONGRESS ASSEMBLED.

WHEN In the Courſe of human Events, It becomes neceſſary for one People to diſſolve the Political Bands which have connected them with another, and to aſſume among the Powers of the Earth, the ſeparate and equal Station to which the Laws of Nature. and of Nature's God entitle them, a decent Reſpect to the Opinions of Mankind requires that they ſhould declare the cauſes which impel them to the Separation.

We hold theſe Truths to be ſelf-evident, that all Men are created equal, that they are endowed by their Creator with certain unalienable Rights, that among theſe are Life, Liberty, and the Purſuit of Happineſs—-That to ſecure theſe Rights, Governments are inſtituted among Men, deriving their juſt Powers from the Conſent of the Governed, that whenever any Form of Government becomes deſtructive of theſe Ends, it is the Right of the People to alter or to aboliſh it, and to inſtitute new Government, laying its Foundation on ſuch Principles, and organiſing its Powers in ſuch Form, as to them ſhall ſeem moſt likely to effect their Safety and Happineſs. Prudence, indeed, will dictate that Governments long eſtabliſhed ſhould not be changed for light and tranſient Cauſes; and accordingly all Experience hath ſhewn, that Mankind are more diſpoſed to ſuffer, while Evils are ſufferable, than to right themſelves by aboliſhing the Forms to which they are accuſtomed. But when a long Train of Abuſes and Uſurpations, purſuing invariably the ſame Object, evinces a Deſign to reduce them under abſolute Deſpotiſm, it is their Right, it is their Duty, to throw off ſuch Government, and to provide new Guards for their future Security. Such has been the patient Sufferance of theſe Colonies; and ſuch is now the Neceſſity which conſtrains them to alter their former Syſtems of Government. The Hiſtory of the preſent King of Great-Britain is a Hiſtory of repeated Injuries and Uſurpations, all having in direct Object the Eſtabliſhment of an abſolute Tyranny over theſe States. To prove this, let Facts be ſubmitted to a candid World.

He has refuſed his Aſſent to Laws, the moſt wholeſome and neceſſary for the public Good.

He has forbidden his Governors to paſs Laws of immediate and preſſing Importance, unleſs ſuſpended in their Operation till his Aſſent ſhould be obtained; and when ſo ſuſpended, he has utterly neglected to attend to them.

He has refuſed to paſs other Laws for the Accommodation of large Diſtricts of People, unleſs thoſe People would relinquiſh the Right of Repreſentation in the legiſlature, a Right ineſtimable to them, and formidable to Tyrants only.

He has called together Legiſlative Bodies at Places unuſual, uncomfortable, and diſtant from the Depoſitory of their public Records, for the ſole Purpoſe of fatiguing them into Compliance with his Meaſures.

He has diſſolved Repreſentative Houſes repeatedly, for oppoſing with manly Firmneſs his Invaſions on the Rights of the People.

He has refuſed for a long Time, after ſuch Diſſolutions, to cauſe others to be elected; whereby the Legiſlative Powers, incapable of Annihilation, have returned to the People at large for their exerciſe; the State remaining in the mean time expoſed to all the Dangers of Invaſion from without, and Convulſions within.

He has endeavoured to prevent the Population of theſe States; for that Purpoſe obſtructing the Laws for Naturalization of Foreigners; refuſing to paſs others to encourage their Migrations hither, and raiſing the Conditions of new Appropriations of Lands.

He has obſtructed the Adminiſtration of Juſtice, by refuſing his Aſſent to Laws for eſtabliſhing Judiciary Powers.

He has made Judges dependent on his Will alone, for the Tenure of their Offices, and the Amount and Payment of their Salaries.

He has erected a Multitude of new Offices, and ſent hither Swarms of Officers to harraſs our People, and eat out their Subſtance.

He has kept among us, in Times of Peace, Standing Armies, without the conſent of our Legiſlatures.

He has affected to render the Military independent of and ſuperior to the Civil Power.

He has combined with others to ſubject us to a Juriſdiction foreign to our Conſtitution, and unacknowledged by our Laws; giving his Aſſent to their Acts of pretended Legiſlation:

For quartering large Bodies of Armed Troops among us:

For protecting them, by a mock Trial, from Puniſhment for any Murders which they ſhould commit on the Inhabitants of theſe States:

For cutting off our Trade with all Parts of the World:

For impoſing Taxes on us without our Conſent:

For depriving us, in many Caſes, of the Benefits of Trial by Jury:

For tranſporting us beyond Seas to be tried for pretended Offences:

For aboliſhing the free Syſtem of Engliſh Laws in a neighbouring Province, eſtabliſhing therein an arbitrary Government, and enlarging its Boundaries, ſo as to render it at once an Example and fit Inſtrument for introducing the ſame abſolute Rule into theſe Coloni-s:

For taking away our Charters, aboliſhing our moſt valuable Laws, and altering fundamentally the Forms of our Governments:

For ſuſpending our own Legiſlatures, and declaring themſelves inveſted with Power to legiſlate for us in all Caſes whatſoever.

He has abdicated Government here, by declaring us out of his Protection and waging War againſt us.

He has plundered our Seas, ravaged our Coaſts, burnt our Towns, and deſtroyed the Lives of our People.

He is, at this Time, tranſporting large Armies of foreign Mercenaries to compleat the Works of Death, Deſolation, and Tyranny, already begun with circumſtances of Cruelty and Perfidy, ſcarcely paralleled in the moſt barbarous Ages, and totally unworthy the Head of a civilized Nation.

He has conſtrained our fellow Citizens taken Captive on the high Seas to bear Arms againſt their Country, to become the Executioners of their Friends and Brethren, or to fall themſelves by their Hands.

He has excited domeſtic Inſurrections amongſt us, and has endeavoured to bring on the Inhabitants of our Frontiers, the mercileſs Indian Savages, whoſe known Rule of Warfare, is an undiſtinguiſhed Deſtruction, of all Ages,. Sexes and Conditions.

In every ſtage of theſe Oppreſſions we have Petitioned for Redreſs in the moſt humble Terms: Our repeated Petitions have been anſwered only by repeated Injury. A Prince, whoſe Character is thus marked by every act which may define a Tyrant, is unfit to be the Ruler of a free People.

Nor have we been wanting in Attentions to our Britiſh Brethren. We have warned them from Time to Time of Attempts by their Legiſlature to extend an unwarrantable Juriſdiction over us. We have reminded them of the Circumſtances of our Emigration and Settlement here. We have appealed to their native Juſtice and Magnanimity, and we have conjured them by the Ties of our common Kindred to diſavow theſe Uſurpations, which, would inevitably interrupt our Connections and Correſpondence. They too have been deaf to the Voice of Juſtice and of Conſanguinity. We muſt, therefore, acquieſce in the Neceſſity, which denounces our Separation, and hold them, as we hold the reſt of Mankind, Enemies in War, in Peace, Friends.

We, therefore, the Repreſentatives of the UNITED STATES OF AMERICA, in General Congress, Aſſembled, appealing to the Supreme Judge of the World for the Rectitude of our Intentions, do, in the Name, and by Authority of the good People of theſe Colonies, ſolemnly Publiſh and Declare, That theſe United Colonies are, and of Right ought to be, Free and Independent States; that they are abſolved from all Allegiance to the Britiſh Crown, and that all political Connection between them and the State of Great-Britain, is and ought to be totally diſſolved; and that as Free and Independent States, they have full Power to levy War, conclude Peace, contract Alliances, eſtabliſh Commerce, and to do all other Acts and Things which Independent States may of right do. And for the ſupport of this Declaration, with a firm Reliance on the Protection of divine Providence, we mutually pledge to each other our Lives, our Fortunes, and our ſacred Honor.

Signed by Order and in Behalf of the Congress,

JOHN HANCOCK, President.

Attest.
CHARLES THOMSON, Secretary.

Philadelphia: Printed by John Dunlap.

Caslon type in first printing of *The Declaration of Independence* by John Dunlap, Philadelphia, 1776

of the century there took place a most interesting experiment in France, which was to have a long-range effect on the design of printer's types. About 1692 Philippe Grandjean, the French punch-cutter, created for the Imprimerie Royale the famous Romain du Roi, a revolutionary design, the first to be drawn to mathematical principles, that eventually led to the type style now called modern. For though these types were restricted to use by the French royal press, they had considerable influence on the styles developed by the commercial typefounders. One such, Pierre Simon Fournier *'le jeune,'* a younger contemporary of Caslon's, was profoundly impressed by these types and later produced several important variations on them. But despite its impact in Europe, Romain du Roi had little immediate effect on English typefounding, Caslon's excellence in his craft apparently deterring experimentation with new forms in England.

William Caslon died in 1766, but his foundry remained in the family for another century. The last of the Caslons to be active in the firm, Henry William, died in 1874, yet the Caslon name has been retained through subsequent changes of ownership. The firm later was acquired by Stephenson, Blake & Company, of Birmingham, which now appends to its name 'The Caslon Letter Foundry.'

Meanwhile, in the mid-eighteenth century the types of John Baskerville had brought about the changes in English typographic taste that resulted in the eventual decline of the Caslon types. Later in the century the styles of the Didots in France and Bodoni in Italy radically affected European typography, with the result that the old-style types, such as Caslon, which had been dominant for almost three centuries, were soon completely out of favor. In the 1805 Caslon specimen book, for example, not a single old-style type appears.

Then in 1844 Charles Whittingham produced at the Chiswick Press in London *The Diary of Lady Willoughby*, which was set in Caslon. It is this volume that is credited with returning the type to popular esteem, regaining much of the reputation it had earlier enjoyed. By 1900 Caslon was being produced by typefounders on both sides of the Atlantic, and it was ready to be elevated to the unique position that prompted the aforementioned Updike panegyric.

In the United States, Caslon was an historically important type. During the late-eighteenth century it was the principal type of the colonial printers, most of whom depended on English sources for the equipment in their printing offices. When first set in type, the most important document of American history, the Declaration of

So much of the *DIARY* of

LADY WILLOUGHBY

as relates to her *Domeſtic Hiſtory*,

& to the Eventful Period of the

Reign of CHARLES

the Firſt.

Imprinted for LONGMAN, BROWN, GREEN, & LONG-
MANS, *Paternoſter Row*, over againſt *War-
wick Lane*, in the City of
London. 1844.

The Caslon revival as shown in *The Diary of Lady Willoughby*, printed at the Chiswick Press, 1840

Independence, appeared in those types cast by William Caslon. Thus there is an old tradition of enthusiasm for Caslon on the part of American printers, who were largely responsible for its popularity in the years up to the Second World War.

In 1837, the American typefounder Peter C. Cortelyou displayed in

Caslon Old Face

ABCDEFGHIJKLMNOPQRSTUVWXYZÆŒ
QU& 1234567890£$,.:;-!?([
abcdefghijklmnopqrstuvwxyzæœfifffffffiffl&Qu

Old fashioned Ligatures as below
are also available

Uniform figures are also
obtainable if desired

f fb fh ft fi fk fl ffi ffl   1 2 3 4 5 6 7 8 9 0

SMALL CAPS available in all sizes 36 to 6 pt. inclusive

And his half-sisters SARAH THOMPSON and MARY READ.
By payments amounting to nearly £11,000, all other
claimants to the estate were paid off within seven years,
while the freehold land on which the workshops stood
was acquired by the foundry on 29th April, 1845 in the
name of JOHN STEPHENSON. The two remaining heirs,

Caslon Old Face (Stephenson, Blake & Co.)

his specimen book several sizes of a type called simply Old Style, but
which was in fact Caslon, although not at all well produced. But the
great resurgence of Caslon type in the United States can be dated from
1858, when the Philadelphia foundry of L. J. Johnson (later MacKellar,
Smiths & Jordan) brought fonts from England and duplicated them
by manufacturing electrotype matrices, a process by which a founder
could duplicate a competitor's type without cutting punches.

The firm's periodical, *The Typographic Advertiser*, showed thirteen
sizes of Caslon in its July 1859 issue. The type later appeared in
Johnson's 1865 specimen book under the name Old Style No. 1. This
face gained in popularity, so much so that in 1892, when *Vogue*
magazine was restyled in Caslon type, the Johnson version was chosen,
constituting the foundry's largest type order in more than thirty years.
The Caslon revival took a huge leap.

The use of Caslon in *Vogue* was followed by its employment by

A LADY OF QUALITY

Being a most curious, hitherto unknown history, as related by Mr. Isaac Bickerstaff but not presented to the World of Fashion through the pages of *The Tatler*, and now for the first time written down *by*

Frances Hodgson Burnett

New York: From the Publishing House of CHARLES SCRIBNER'S SONS, 153-157 Fifth Avenue. *MDCCCXCVII.*

Caslon typography by Will Bradley in the 1890's

ABCDEFGHIJKL
MNOPQRSTUV
WXYZ 123456789
.,-;:'!?$&

Caslon Openface (ATF)

ABCDEFGHIJKLMNOPQRSTUV
WXYZ abcdefghijklmnopqrstuvwxyz
&$1234567890
Inventiveness tend to assume a wholesome creative mood can go far to produce a specimen book
of his types and borders which will be a posi-

ABCDEFGHIJKLMNOPQ
RSTUVWXYZ &$1234567890
abcdefghijklmnopqrstuvwxyz
Positive revelation of delight to all be-
holders, and an inspiration to typographic
achievement in all users of it. And yet

Caslon Antique (ATF)

some of the nation's best typographers, including Will Bradley who purchased fonts from the Dickinson foundry in Boston in 1895. As an innovative young designer, Bradley further popularized the face. Caslon was therefore an early candidate for the composing machines then being introduced. The Monotype company was the first to make it available in 1903 with a version based on the Johnson type, by then the property of the American Type Founders Company through that firm's amalgamation of the various American typefoundries.

There are now numerous versions of Caslon, all but one of which bear similarity to one another. Caslon Old Face, owned by Stephenson, Blake & Company, is of course the original, but the ATF Caslon 471, based on the Johnson copy, is very close indeed. For advertising printing, ATF shortened the descenders and named the new version Caslon 540, and over decades of newspaper advertising R. H. Macy's department store made 540 practically its private type, at least in New York City.

The last Caslon to mention is that ubiquitous but unrelated Caslon Antique, which possesses no similarity whatsoever to the original. This old reprobate was a victim of bad timing when, late in the 1800s, it was introduced by Barnhart Brothers of Chicago under the name Fifteenth Century. Its negative reception lasted until about 1918, when, with a simple name change to Caslon Antique, it became the most commonly selected type for reproductions of colonial American printing. It is now seen in everything from liquor advertisements to furniture commercials.

Caslon in most systems of type classification is known as an old style (in England it has had the name Old Face, and more recently, in the British Standards System, is listed under 'Garalde'). It represents probably the final development of those romans that were first cut by Nicolas Jenson of Venice in 1470. Among printers interested in type classification, a fairly strong case can be made for calling Caslon a transitional type, as it predates the Baskerville design of 1757. However, most typographic historians have held that Caslon's dependence on the seventeenth-century Dutch forms resulted in a letter with more old-style features than modern. The wedge-shaped serifs of the lowercase characters are a case in point.

Even in the original version, as well as in copies made by the American Type Founders, Monotype, and Linotype, there are inconsistencies in the fitting and the alignment of several letters. Most typographers who work closely with types have learned to be aware

ABCDEFGHIJKLMN
OPQRSTUVWXYZ
abcdefghijklmnopqrstuv
wxyz .,-;:'!? 1234567890

ABCDEFGHIJ
KLMNOPQRS
TUVWXYZabc
defghijklmnopqr
stuvwxyz .,-;:'!?$
1234567890

Caslon Oldstyle No. 540 (ATF)

of such incongruities, particularly in the comparison of sizes. For example, the 24-point Caslon seems to lack the grace of the 18-point, and in relation to the larger sizes appears to be considerably bolder. Owing to this discrepancy, a 22-point was cut in order to provide an in-between size.

ABCDEFG
HIJKLMN
OPQRSTU
VWXYZ
abcdefghij
klmnopqrst
uvwxyz
1234567890

Caslon No. 540

Such variations produce the individuality that has apparently charmed many a typographer unhappy about the regularity of the modern pantograph-designed typefaces. Others, however, take a dim view of such individuality, making it difficult to understand why the type has been a long-lived favorite throughout the world.

But for whatever reason, Caslon persists, offering all the usual variants – bold, condensed, openface, swash – of any successful type. It seems that this design is bound to survive, although even well-informed typographers are hard-pressed to explain why. In a period when so much that is traditional is viewed as suspect, Caslon's enduring popularity is encouraging to any printer admiring the classic forms.

16

BASKERVILLE

The roman types heretofore discussed in this book have been part of the group classified as old style; that is, they are in the spirit of the first roman types developed in Italy between 1470 and 1500. The reader will remember that by the latter date the earlier pen-dominated styles were giving way to the more precisely cut romans of Francesco Griffo. Further modifications took place during the sixteenth century, under the influence of Claude Garamond and his contemporaries. After that the Dutch punchcutters carried out more changes during the next century, so that by the time of William Caslon the old-style letter form, as expressed in a printing type, had reached its final development.

In the last decade of the seventeenth century the first conscious revision of old style occurred in France, with the creation of the fonts for the Imprimerie Royale. These letters, cut by Philippe Grandjean (at the direction of a committee appointed for the purpose by Louis XIV), differed notably from the old-style pattern. The round characters were given a perpendicular axis, as opposed to the incline of the old style, and the serifs were both flatter and sharper, with less bracketing than in the earlier faces. Some authorities have called the Romains du Roi the first modern types, but they seem closer to the transitional classification, which contains features of old style and modern in equal degrees. Whatever theory is followed, however, this French departure from old style greatly influenced designers of printing types during the eighteenth century. There is general agreement that the best-known of these designers, John Baskerville, an English amateur printer and typefounder, be credited with the creation of one of the earliest transitional types.

By every measure, Baskerville's types have demonstrated universal appeal. The proof of this is their present availability throughout the world in the form of single types for hand-composition and for all of the typesetting machines from hot-metal to cathode-ray-tube (CRT).

BASKERVILLE IS OPEN AND CLEAR, WITH DELICATE HAIRLINES AND SERIFS, AND appears to the best advantage when printed on smooth paper stock. The companion italic is very narrow. Both $1234567890 $1234567890

IT WAS A WONDERFUL THING TO CONCEIVE AN IDEA AS REVOLUTIONARY AS that embodied in Lanston's first Monotype and to build it $1234567890 $1234567890

Baskerville (Monotype)

The current popularity of the type is comparatively recent, even though the face was designed more than two centuries ago. The Birmingham printer, underappreciated in his time, would have been delighted to know that his type had won full acceptance in the twentieth century, surpassing in esteem even the well-loved Caslon styles of his own era – which he was consciously trying to improve upon.

John Baskerville was about forty-five years old when he turned to printing as an avocation following an extremely successful decade in the japanning business. Earlier in his life he had been a writing master and had also engraved headstones. In both these capacities he had developed a high degree of skill in the definition of letter forms.

In 1750 Baskerville engaged the services of the punchcutter John Handy and proceeded with ambitious plans for the establishment of a press in which he intended to do fine printing. By 1754 he had progressed to the point of producing a prospectus for his first book, the *Georgics* of Virgil, which finally appeared in 1757. In 1758 Baskerville used the preface of his second book, an edition of Milton, to explain why he had become a printer:

Amongst the several mechanic Arts that have engaged my attention, there is no one which I have pursued with so much steadiness and pleasure as that of Letter-Founding. Having been an early admirer of the beauty of Letters, I became insensibly desirous of contributing to the perfection of them. I formed to my self ideas of greater accuracy than had yet appeared, and

300 Tum duo Trinacrii juvenes, Elymus, Panopefque,
Affueti filvis, comites fenioris Aceftæ.
Multi præterea, quos fama obfcura recondit.
Aeneas quibus in mediis fic deinde locutus:
Accipite hæc animis lætafque advertite mentes:
305 Nemo ex hoc numero mihi non donatus abibit.
Gnofia bina dabo levato lucida ferro
Spicula, cœlatamque argento ferre bipennem.
Omnibus hic erit unus honos. tres præmia primi
Accipient, flavaque caput nectentur oliva.
310 Primus equum phaleris infignem victor habeto.
Alter Amazoniam pharetram, plenamque fagittis
Threiciis; lato quam circum amplectitur auro
Balteus, et tereti fubnectit fibula gemma.
Tertius Argolica hac galea contentus abito.
315 Hæc ubi dicta: locum capiunt, fignoque repente
Corripiunt fpatia audito, limenque relinquunt
Effufi, nimbo fimiles: fimul ultima fignant.
Primus abit, longeque ante omnia corpora Nifus
Emicat, et ventis et fulminis ocior alis.
320 Proximus huic, longo fed proximus intervallo,
Infequitur Salius: fpatio poft deinde relicto
Tertius Euryalus.
Euryalumque Elymus fequitur: quo deinde fub ipfo
Ecce volat, calcemque terit jam calce Diores,
325 Incumbens humero: fpatia et fi plura fuperfint;
Tranfeat elapfus prior, ambiguumve relinquat.
Jamque fere fpatio extremo, feffique fub ipfum
Finem adventabant; levi quum fanguine Nifus
Labitur infelix: cæfis ut forte juvencis
330 Fufus humum viridefque fuper madefecerat herbas.
Hic

Page from *Bucolics and Georgics of Virgil*, printed by John Baskerville, Birmingham, 1757

have endeavoured to produce a Set of Types according to what I conceived to be their true proportion.

The most popular types in England during this period were those produced by William Caslon. Baskerville was at some pains to indicate that he admired the Caslon designs, writing in the same preface:

Mr. Caslon is an Artist, to whom the Republic of Learning has great obligations; his ingenuity has left a fairer copy for my emulation than any other master.

In his great variety of Characters I intend not to follow him; the Roman and Italic are all that I have hitherto attempted; if in these he has left room for improvement, it is probably more owing to that variety which divided his attention, than to any other cause. I honor his merit, and only wish to derive some small share of Reputation, from an Art which proves accidentally to have been the object of our mutual pursuit.

In addition to the design of a new type, Baskerville made a number of other innovations, all of which would today come under the heading of quality control. Although his press, constructed of wood, followed the standard model then employed by English printers, he invented two important changes in its design. First, he made the bed and the platen of machined brass, one inch thick. Next, instead of utilizing a soft packing, which would have produced too deep an impression of his types, Baskerville used a tympan of smooth vellum, packed with superfine cloth. These improvements he discussed in a letter to a contemporary printer: 'I have with great pains justified the plate for the Platten a Stone [bed] on which it falls, so that they are as perfect planes as it will ever be my power to procure. . . .'

Since it was his scheme to produce perfect printing, Baskerville also experimented with the formula for an ink that would not only print blacker and more evenly than existing inks, but would also dry faster, permitting the more rapid printing of the reverse side of the sheet. T. C. Hansard, in his 1825 manual of printing, *Typographia*, stated that the Baskerville ink formula was the first important improvement in that art in more than two hundred years.

Not satisfied with these upgradings of the printing process, Baskerville turned to the papermaker's craft. The paper for printing up to his time was laid paper, in which the lines of the papermaker's mold produced vertical ribs on the sheet. Baskerville attempted to obtain a smoother page by experimenting with the mold. For a mold he obtained a woven screen, which produced a new kind of paper lacking the laid lines; it has since been called wove paper. The first use of it was in the *Georgics*, a book collected today both for its typography and for its paper.

Finally, Baskerville built what was called a smoothing press, consisting of two heated copper cylinders between which was fed each sheet that issued from the press, after the ink had sufficiently dried. This process of flattening the printed image gave the page a plate-smooth finish. And to assure that the inking of all his pages would appear uniform, Baskerville printed extra sheets in order to match pages. Such perfectionism, needless to say, did not endear him to his competitors.

Indeed, the combination of all these features in his method of printing made Baskerville a most controversial figure among the professional printers of his period: he was as roundly damned as he was lavishly praised. In addition, the mixed reception by his colleagues to his high-quality printing was exacerbated both by his amateur status and by his personal eccentricities, notable even in a period of determinedly eccentric behavior.

Daniel Berkeley Updike mentions that, in the words of Macaulay, Baskerville's first book 'went forth to astonish all the librarians of Europe.' Indeed, it was on the Continent that Baskerville achieved his greatest fame, both as a designer of type and as a printer. Professionals and bibliophiles were alike amazed.

The noted French typefounder and inventor of the typographical point, Pierre Simon Fournier, writing in *Manuel Typographique* (1764–66) said of Baskerville and his types: 'He has spared neither pains nor expense to bring them to the utmost pitch of perfection. The letters are cut with great daring and the italic is the best to be found in any English foundry, but the roman is a little too wide.'

A young Italian compositor named Giambattista Bodoni, then working at the Vatican printing office, became so excited about the excellence of Baskerville's work that he determined to travel to Birmingham to meet him. Even across the Atlantic, Benjamin Franklin, the best-known American printer – who had bought six copies of the *Georgics* – became a widely quoted admirer. Nevertheless, in England Baskerville was vilified by his fellow printers.

Despite the many improvements John Baskerville introduced to the art of printing, he did not profit by them. His standards of production were so high that he was unable to compete with the commercial printers for the work of the booksellers (booksellers acted then as publishers), who complained that his prices were two to three

Anno DOMINI 33.

they were, and thou gavest them me; and they
have kept thy word.
7 Now they have known that all things whatsoever thou hast given me are of thee.
8 For I have given unto them the words
[l] which thou gavest me; and they have received
them, [m] and have known surely that I came out
from thee, and they have believed that thou
didst send me.
9 I pray for them: [n] I pray not for the world,
but for them which thou hast given me; for they
are thine.
10 And all mine are thine, and [o] thine are
mine; and I am glorified in them.
11 And now I am no more in the world, but
these are in the world, and I come to thee. Holy
Father, [p] keep through thine own name those
whom thou hast given me, [q] that they may be
one, [r] as we *are*.
12 While I was with them in the world, [s] I
kept them in thy name: those that thou gavest
me I have kept, and [t] none of them is lost, [v] but
the son of perdition; [x] that the scripture might
be fulfilled.
13 And now come I to thee, and these things
I speak in the world, that they might have my
joy fulfilled in themselves.
14 I have given them thy word; and [y] the
world hath hated them, because they are not of
the world, even as I am not of the world.
15 I pray not that thou shouldest take them out
of the world, but [z] that thou shouldest keep
them from the evil.
16 They are not of the world, even as I am not
of the world.
17 [a] Sanctify them through thy truth: [b] thy
word is truth.
18 [c] As thou hast sent me into the world, even
so have I also sent them into the world.
19 And [d] for their sakes I sanctify myself, that
they also might be * sanctified through the truth.
20 Neither pray I for these alone, but for
them also which shall believe on me through
their word;
21 [e] That they all may be one; as [f] thou, Father, *art* in me, and I in thee, that they also may
be one in us: that the world may believe that
thou hast sent me.
22 And the glory which thou gavest me, I
have given them; [g] that they may be one, even
as we are one:
23 I in them, and thou in me, [h] that they
may be made perfect in one, and that the world
may know that thou hast sent me, and hast loved
them, as thou hast loved me.
24 [i] Father, I will that they also whom thou
hast given me be with me where I am; that
they may behold my glory which thou hast given
me: for thou lovedst me before the foundation
of the world.

[l] ch. 8. 28. & 12. 49. & 14. 10. [m] ch. 16. 27, 30. [n] 1 John 5. 19. [o] ch. 16. 15. [p] 1 Pet. 1. 5. Jude 1. [q] ver. 21, &c. [r] ch. 10. 30. [s] ch. 6. 39. & 10. 28. Heb. 2. 13. [t] ch. 18. 9. 1 John 2. 19. [v] ch. 6. 70. & 13. 18. [x] Psal. 109. 8. [y] ch. 15. 18, 19. [z] Matth. 6. 13. Gal. 1. 4. 2 Thess. 3. 3. 1 John 5. 18. [a] ch. 15. 3. Acts 15. 9. Ephes. 5. 26. 1 Pet. 1. 22. [b] 2 Sam. 7. 28. ch. 8. 40. [c] ch. 20. 21. [d] 1 Cor. 1. 2, 30. 1 Thess. 4. 7. Heb. 10. 10. * Or, *truly sanctified.* [e] ver. 11. 22, 23. Gal. 3. 28. [f] ch. 10. 38. & 14. 11. [g] ch 14. 20. [h] Col. 3. 14. [i] ch. 12. 26. & 14. 3. 1 Thess. 4. 17.

25 O righteous Father, [k] the world hath not
known thee: but [l] I have known thee, and
[m] these have known that thou hast sent me.
26 And I have declared unto them thy name,
and will declare *it:* that the love [n] wherewith
thou hast loved me, may be in them, and I in
them.

C H A P. XVIII.

1 *Judas betrayeth Jesus.* 6 *The officers fall to the ground.* 10 *Peter smiteth off Malchus' ear.* 12 *Jesus is taken and led unto Annas and Caiaphas.* 15 *Peter's denial.* 19 *Jesus examined before Caiaphas:* 28 *his arraignment before Pilate:* 36 *his kingdom.* 39 *The Jews ask Barabbas to be let loose.*

WHEN Jesus had spoken these words, [a] he
went forth with his disciples over [b] the
brook Cedron, where was a garden, into the
which he entered, and his disciples.
2 And Judas also, which betrayed him, knew
the place: [c] for Jesus oft-times resorted thither
with his disciples.
3 [d] Judas then, having received a band *of men,*
and officers from the chief priests and Pharisees,
cometh thither with lanterns, and torches, and
weapons.
4 Jesus therefore, knowing all things that
should come upon him, went forth, and said unto
them, Whom seek ye?
5 They answered him, Jesus of Nazareth. Jesus
saith unto them, I am *he*. And Judas also which
betrayed him, stood with them.
6 ¶ As soon then as he had said unto them, I am
he, they went backward, and fell to the ground.
7 Then asked he them again, Whom seek ye?
And they said, Jesus of Nazareth.
8 Jesus answered, I have told you that I am
he. If therefore ye seek me, let these go their
way:
9 That the saying might be fulfilled which he
spake, [e] Of them which thou gavest me have I
lost none.
10 ¶ [f] Then Simon Peter, having a sword, drew
it, and smote the high priest's servant, and cut
off his right ear. The servant's name was Malchus.
11 Then said Jesus unto Peter, Put up thy
sword into the sheath: [g] the cup which my Father hath given me, shall I not drink it?
12 ¶ Then the band, and the captain and officers of the Jews, took Jesus, and bound him,
13 And [h] led him away to [i] Annas first (for he
was father-in-law to Caiaphas, which was the
high priest that same year). *
14 [k] Now Caiaphas was he which gave counsel
to the Jews, that it was expedient that one man
should die for the people.
15 ¶ [l] And Simon Peter followed Jesus, and *so*
did another disciple. That disciple was known
unto the high priest, and went in with Jesus into
the palace of the high priest.
16 [m] But Peter stood at the door without. Then

[k] ch. 15. 21. & 16. 3. [l] ch. 7. 29. & 8. 55. & 10. 15. [m] ver. 8. ch. 16. 27. [n] ch. 15. 9. [a] Matth. 26. 36. Mark 14. 32. Luke 22. 39. [b] 2 Sam. 15. 23. [c] Luke 22. 39. [d] Matth. 26. 47. Mark 14. 43. Luke 22. 47. Acts 1. 16. [e] ch. 17. 12. [f] Matth. 26. 51. Mark 14. 47. Luke 22. 49, 50. [g] Matth. 20. 22. & 26. 39, 42. [h] See Matth. 26. 57. [i] Luke 3. 2. * *And Annas sent Christ bound unto Caiaphas the high priest,* ver. 24. [k] ch. 11. 50. [l] Matth. 26. 58. Mark 14. 54. Luke 22. 54. [m] Matth. 26. 69.

11 Q

Anno DOMINI 33.

Page from *The Holy Bible*, printed by John Baskerville, Birmingham, 1763

ABCDEFGHIJKLMNOPQRSTU
VWXYZ abcdefghijklmnopqrstu
vwxyz .,-;:'!?$&fffififlffl 1234567890
ABCDEFGHIJKLMNOPQ
RSTUVWXYZ abcdefghijk
lmnopqrstuvwxyz 1234567890
.,-;:'!?$&fffififlffffifl

Baskerville (ATF)

times as much as they paid elsewhere for the same kind (though not quality) of work. In 1762, writing to Franklin about his problems in maintaining his printing office, Baskerville stated, 'Had I no other dependence than typefounding and printing, I must starve.' But he persevered, and a year later he produced his masterpiece, a folio Bible printed for Cambridge University. Although indifferently received at its appearance, this edition today is considered one of the finest books not just of the eighteenth century, but since William Caxton established the first English press, five centuries ago.

His beautiful Bible notwithstanding, Baskerville reached the opinion that his hobby of printing was a luxury. He thus spent the rest of his life attempting, fruitlessly, to dispose of his punches and matrices, along with the rest of his printing equipment. It was not until 1779, four years after his death, that his widow was able to find a purchaser, in the person of Caron de Beaumarchais, the French dramatist, who wanted the Baskerville equipment for the printing of an edition of the works of Voltaire. When this work – seventy volumes in octavo and ninety-two volumes in duodecimo – was off the

EARLY PAPERS

INTRODUCTION

THE earliest of the papers in Boswell's hand, which we find to have been preserved at Malahide Castle, takes us back to July 1754 when he was thirteen years of age,—a date four years before that of his first published letter to Temple. We catch for the first time, if only for an instant, an authentic image of Boswell's boyhood: of Boswell in miniature. From that date the present volume extends to August 6, 1763 when, leaving Dr. Johnson on the shore at Harwich, he set forth on his Continental adventure. This day is decisive for Boswell's destiny: the seal is set on the new friendship with Johnson; the die is cast for a legal career; and the journey begun which will lead him to Paoli.

Up to his departure from England the juvenility, which to the last may be considered a distinguishing feature of Boswell's character, is extremely marked. He is still more or less under tutelage, and uncertain as to his profession: it is not until a few months before his departure that he renounces his desire to obtain a commission in the Guards. His Continental studies and travels, culminating in the Tour to Corsica, are an interlude apart, from which he returns with habits of independence, a knowledge of the world and some fixity of ambition. Thus we

Monotype and foundry Baskerville combined in page designed by Bruce Rogers

C'eſt le ſujet de cette Médaille. On y voit Pallas, tenant un Javelot preſt à lancer; le fleuve de l'Eſcauld effrayé s'appuye ſur ſon Urne. La Légende, HISPANIS TRANS SCALDIM PULSIS ET FUGATIS, ſignifie, *les Eſpagnols défaits & pouſſez au-delà de l'Eſcauld.* L'Exergue, CONDATUM ET MALBODIUM CAPTA. M. DC. XLIX. *priſe de Condé & de Maubeuge. 1649.*

Grandjean's *Romain du Roi*, engraved between 1694 and 1714

press at Kehl, Germany, in 1789, Beaumarchais took the punches and matrices to Paris, where he established a typefoundry.

His undertaking was short-lived, however, as he died just one year later. It is not known how many times the Baskerville matrices then changed hands before their eventual acquisition by the Paris typefoundry Bertrand in 1893. Their exalted lineage during this period was neither known nor suspected, but even had it been known, it is doubtful that this would have made much difference to printers. For typographic tastes had undergone numerous changes over the nineteenth century, and the classic letter forms were neither as admired nor as utilized as in earlier times. However, it was at this point, the turn of the century, that the private-press movement was poised to initiate its great regeneration of the art of the printed book.

The revival of the Baskerville types was prompted by the distinguished American typographer Bruce Rogers. While serving as adviser to Cambridge University Press in 1917, Rogers discovered in a Cambridge bookshop a specimen of a type that he instantly recognized as Baskerville. After some typographic sleuthing, he traced the letter to the Fonderie Bertrand in France. When he became printing adviser to Harvard University Press in 1919, he recommended the purchase and use there of the Baskerville types that had been cast from the original matrices.

Thus the type again became known, and when the Lanston Monotype Corporation of London began its program of reviving a number of classic roman types, Baskerville was one of the first to be considered. It was cut in 1923. In 1926 the Stempel typefoundry in Frankfurt, Germany, produced a copy, which was also used by the German Linotype company a year later. Mergenthaler Linotype in England and the United States brought out a version in 1931. Intertype Basker-

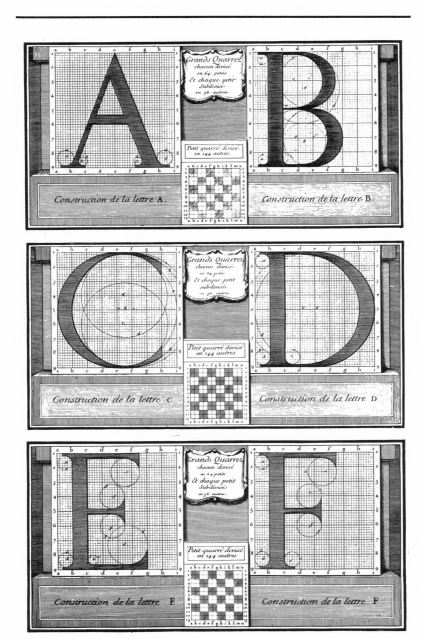

Plate, probably engraved by Louis Simonneau, as a model for the type cut by
Phillippe Grandjean

ville, as well, became available that year. Book typographers rapidly made the revival a resounding success, and they have continued to favor the type.

Produced so generally, before long Baskerville became one of the most widely used types. Making its first appearance in the American Institute of Graphic Arts' Fifty Books of the Year Exhibition in 1925, it has been absent from the annual list just once (in 1927). In three different years Baskerville was used in fifteen selections, and it is now the type that has appeared most frequently in all the books ever selected for exhibition.

In a most generous action, Charles Peignot, representing the Paris typefoundry Deberny et Peignot, the last commercial owner of the historic font, returned the original punches to English soil in 1953, making them a gift to Cambridge University Press, which happily accepted them as representatives of the English national heritage.

The modern recuttings of Baskerville discussed up to this point have all been very close copies of the original, but there is another, quite distinct Baskerville, also well known and deservedly popular, but principally as a display type. In Europe this version is called the Fry Baskerville, whereas in the United States it is more commonly known as Foundry Baskerville.

John Baskerville, though reviled by most English printers in his lifetime, after his death achieved admiration for his types among the typefounders of England. In fact, even before he died (in 1775), some of Baskerville's compatriots were already imitating his work. In 1764 Joseph Fry (a doctor) and William Pine established a typefoundry in Bristol under the direction of the punchcutter Isaac Moore, whose name was given to the firm. Moore then cut a copy of Baskerville's letters, the first showing of it appearing in a 1766 specimen sheet of the foundry. Two other founders of the period also emulated the Baskerville design, Alexander Wilson in Glasgow and the Caslon foundry in London. It is the Fry cutting, however, that has come down to the present day, constantly changing ownership over the years until becoming the property of the famed Birmingham firm Stephenson, Blake & Company, which reissued the type in 1910. In the United States the American Type Founders Company brought out a copy of this face about 1915 in a cutting devised by Morris Benton.

The basic difference between the original Baskerville and the Fry, or Foundry, imitations is in the serif structure, which in the latter is almost needle sharp, as opposed to the flat endings of the former. In addition, the Foundry type has much greater contrast between the thick and thin strokes.

Foundry Baskerville is at its best in the larger sizes, above 18-point. It did not receive much attention in the United States until it became a 'trend' type in national advertising in the 1950s. Since that time it has seen frequent use, in this country mostly for display (to accompany a version made by American Monotype, which was never cast larger than 36-point), and it has been adapted to the phototype-setters. But despite its modern commercial affinity, Fry is nonetheless a rendering of the original, classic Baskerville, so beloved for book composition.

17

BODONI

The numerous types that today bear the name of Giambattista Bodoni are a tribute as much to his reputation as a printer as to his ability as an engraver of punches. Most of them, in fact, tend to be more in the style of Bodoni than exact copies of his letter forms. Nevertheless, the faces that Bodoni cut represent the ultimate development of the Roman letter form as expressed in printing types. Working in the late eighteenth century, Bodoni carried forward the interpretations first rendered by the Venetian punchcutters about 1470 and continued through three hundred years of type design.

During this long period, the stamp of national characteristics had gradually modified the original humanist style of Italy. Garamond in France in the sixteenth century, the Dutch typefounders in the seventeenth, and William Caslon and John Baskerville in England in the eighteenth century all contributed to the ideal of perfection that Giambattista Bodoni held before him in his work. It was Baskerville, in fact, who made the immediate impact on Bodoni, causing the Italian to develop into the most widely admired printer of his time, and to be considered as among the finest in the history of the craft.

Giambattista Bodoni was born in Saluzzo, Italy, in 1740. As a boy, he learned his art from his printer father, in addition to developing skill in the cutting of woodblocks. At the age of eighteen he became a compositor in the Vatican printing office, which possessed a notable collection of types representing most of the world's languages (assembled for the purpose of bringing the Word of God to the lands then being colonized by the Europeans).

Bodoni studied the Oriental languages and was assigned the task of cataloguing the exotics that had originally been cut two centuries earlier by such noted French punchcutters as Granjon, Garamond, and Le Bé, and which by the eighteenth century were in a sad state of pi. It was this assignment that excited Bodoni's interest in the cutting of

ABCDEFG
HIJKLMN
OPQRSTU
VWXYZ
abcdefghijk
lmnopqrstu
vwxyz
1234567890

Bodoni (Monotype 375)

MANUALE

TIPOGRAFICO

DEL CAVALIERE

GIAMBATTISTA BODONI

VOLUME PRIMO.

PARMA

PRESSO LA VEDOVA

MDCCCXVIII

Title Page, *Manuale Tipografico*, Parma, 1818

punches, resulting in his designing several ornaments which received favorable comments from his fellow Vatican compositors.

After serving in Rome for ten years, Bodoni decided to travel to England in the hope of visiting John Baskerville, whose types and books, despite the skepticism of his compatriots, were at the time receiving the hearty approval of European printers and bibliophiles.

But on the very first leg of this journey, at home in Saluzzo, Bodoni became ill. The trip was thus canceled. During his recovery he was sought out by the duke of Parma, who – having founded a library and an academy of art – wanted in addition to establish a fine printing office in the manner of other royal houses in Europe. Bodoni accepted the duke's offer to become its director, and in February 1768 he arrived in Parma to begin the accumulation of materials necessary for establishing a press devoted to fine printing.

The typographical aspects of fine book printing had been in decline during the earlier years of the eighteenth century. Bibliophiles then were more enthusiastic about a book's engraved illustrations and ornaments than the design of its text – the success of a book was judged only by its decoration. With book buyers' attention thus focused, printers had become lax about the selection of type and the quality of presswork. Bodoni was to change this approach radically.

For his first types he copied those cast by Pierre Simon Fournier, the Parisian typefounder whose designs owe their inspiration to the Romain du Roi ordered by Louis XIV for the Imprimerie Royale in 1692. With these types Bodoni produced his first half-dozen books. His admiration for the Frenchman is well illustrated in the first specimen book he printed, in 1771, where he closely imitated the ornamental title pages of Fournier's *Manuel Typographique* of 1764–66.

But the Italian printer soon broke away from his dependence on Fournier. It is probable that he had also become aware of the books then being printed in France by the Didots, whose designs competed with Fournier's. In any case, Bodoni established his own foundry and began to cut punches for types that represented a considerable departure from the ones he had been using.

Bodoni's ideas as a printer and punchcutter are best expressed in his own words. In the preface to *Manuale Tipografico* – his magnificent specimen book, published posthumously by his widow – Bodoni writes: 'It is proper here to offer the four different heads under which it seems to me are derived the beauties of type, and the first of these is regularity – conformity without ambiguity, variety without disso-

ABCDEFGHIJKLM
NOPQRSTUVWXYZ
1234567890

Bokstäverna får sitt sanna behag inte när de skrivas i brådska
och med olust, inte heller när de kommer till blott genom flit och möda,
utan först då de skapas i kärlek och glädje. Giambattista Bodoni

Bodoni (Bauer)

nance, and equality and symmetry without confusion. A second and
not minor value is to be gained from sharpness and definition, neat-
ness and finish. From the perfection of the punches in the beginning
comes the polish of the well-cast letter which should shine like a
mirror on its face.'

D. B. Updike speaks of Bodoni as having two periods. In the first
Bodoni printed with old-style or transitional types, with the addition
of numerous ornaments; in the second he 'depended on his own type
designs and unadorned typography for his effects.' This latter, really
a nineteenth-century style, Updike deplored, calling it 'as official as
a coronation and as cold as the neighboring Alps!' He was not alone
in his criticism. William Morris believed Bodoni's types to be 'shatter-
ingly hideous.' It is nonetheless the later period of the printer of
Parma that represents his great contribution to typography, for it
represented a radical departure from earlier traditions.

Further treating his concept of design, Bodoni wrote of 'the
beautiful contrast as between light and shade which comes naturally
from any writing done with a well-cut pen held properly in the hand.'
The pen referred to is no doubt the chisel-pointed instrument of his
period, rather than the broad pen that had influenced the old-style

ROMAN STUDIO
DAILY WORKER
GUTENBERG
CALIFORNIA
PLEASURE
FRIENDS

Bodoni Title (Bauer)

types. Bodoni thus created in his letters the crisp contrasts of the engraving burin, reflecting a style that was artistically prevalent.

The forty-five years that Giambattista Bodoni spent as director of the Duke of Parma's Stamperia Reale established him as one of the great printers of all time. For Bodoni indeed lived up to his statement 'Beauty is founded on harmony, subordinate to the critique of reason.'

Bodoni's patron certainly had reason to congratulate himself on the founding of a royal press and the selection of its director, who brought worldwide fame to Parma. In response to demand, after 1790 the Duke allowed Bodoni to accept commissions from outside Italy, affording the printer the opportunity to express himself in the typography of other languages, such as German, English, French, and Russian.

The measure of Bodoni's independence, as the duke's printer, from the usual economic strictures of the printing business may be observed from the anecdote told of the French writer Stendhal, who visited Parma and was enchanted with Bodoni's printing. Upon being asked by the printer which of several French Bodoni books he preferred, Stendhal responded that they seemed equally beautiful. 'Ah, Monsieur,' said Bodoni, 'you don't see the title of the Boileau?' The writer confessed that he could see nothing finer in that particular title than the others, at which the printer cried out, 'Ah, Monsieur! Boileau-Despréaux in one single line of capitals! I spent six months before I could decide upon exactly that type.'

Indeed Bodoni did go to great lengths with his typography, sometimes cutting several variations of one size just to fit the copy of a particular title page. An inventory of this output, made in 1840, showed 25,735 punches and 50,994 matrices, an incredible total for one printer when it took upward of four hours to engrave a steel punch. Unquestionably, Bodoni received some assistance in this monumental undertaking, but he was frequently angered when this extraordinary capacity for industry was questioned.

It may be noted that although Bodoni's reputation as a printer and type designer is secure, his standing as a scholarly printer has long been in doubt. This is primarily owing to careless proofreading, and during his lifetime he was criticized, quite logically, on this point.

The Bodoni types were widely copied during the early years of the nineteenth century while the printer was still alive, but most of the imitations were less inspired and more mechanically rigid than the originals. For example, whereas the Bodoni serif in the capitals was of the same weight as the thin stroke but joined with a very slight fillet (bracket) and the lowercase serifs were slightly concave, copies cut by his French rivals, the Didots, featured straight-edged serifs that were unbracketed.

One of the earliest types of the period to imitate the Bodoni letter was cut about 1800 by Justus Erich Walbaum in Germany; a recent writer has called Walbaum's roman 'one of the most important vehicles

ARIEL

What would my potent master? here I am.

PROSPERO

Thou and thy meaner fellows your last service
Did worthily perform: and I must use you
In such another trick: go, bring the rabble,
(O'er whom I give thee power) here, to this place:
Incite them to quick motion, for I must
Bestow upon the eyes of this young couple
Some vanity of mine art: it is my promise,
And they expect it from me.

ARIEL

Presently?

PROSPERO

Ay: with a twink.

ARIEL

Before you can say "come" and "go,"
And breathe twice; and cry "so, so"...
Each one, tripping on his toe,
Will be here with mop and mow....
Do you love me, master? no?

PROSPERO

Dearly, my delicate Ariel...Do not approach,
Till thou dost hear me call.

113

Page from *The Tempest*, printed at the Officina Bodoni, 1924

The mighty * *Orellana*. Scarce the Muse
Dares stretch her wing o'er this enormous mass
Of rushing water; scarce she dares attempt
The sea-like *Plata*; to whose dread expanse,
Continuous depth and wond'rous length of course,
Our floods are rills. With unabated force,
In silent dignity they sweep along,
And traverse realms unknown, and blooming wilds,
And fruitful deserts, worlds of solitude,
Where the sun smiles, and seasons teem in vain,
Unseen, and unenjoy'd. Forsaking these,
O'er peopled plains they far-diffusive flow,
And many a nation feed, and circle safe
In their soft bosom, many a happy isle;
The seat of blameless *Pan*, yet undisturb'd
By christian crimes and *Europe*'s cruel sons.
Thus pouring on they proudly seek the deep,
Whose vanquish'd tide recoiling from the shock,
Yields to this liquid weight of half the globe;
And Ocean trembles for his green domain.

 BUT what avails this wond'rous waste of wealth?
This gay profusion of luxurious bliss?

* *The river of the Amazons.*

12.

Page from Gray's *Complete Poems*, printed by Bodoni, Parma, 1793

of typographic expression in the German language during the 19th century.' In addition, the English type designed in 1791 by William Martin for the Shakspeare Press of William Bulmer has definite Bodoni characteristics, although still maintaining some of the warmth of the transitional style.

Following Bodoni's death in 1813, his widow continued the printing office, producing the great two-volume *Manuale Tipografico* in 1818. This work is rightly considered among the finest specimen books ever produced. In 1842 the Bodoni punches and matrices were sold and placed in the Biblioteca Palatina in Parma; though the library was bombed in 1944, the punches and matrices had fortunately already been moved to a monastery south of the city.

In the twentieth century, interest in the Bodoni types was renewed with a cutting issued by the Italian foundry Nebiolo in 1901. But probably the most important revival of the style was that of Morris Benton for the American Type Founders in 1911. Henry L. Bullen, the printing historian who was ATF's librarian, wrote that Benton had received guidance from Italian sources in his recutting. It is obvious, however, that Benton did not attempt an exact copy of the original Bodoni type, as his version is closer in spirit to the Didot letters; this is particularly noticeable in the unbracketed serifs.

Undoubtedly, the ATF Bodoni influenced subsequent copies produced by the composing-machine manufacturers. The European foundries also produced copies, but they too were inclined to freely adapt the Bodoni idea of high contrast without following through on his details of serif structure.

In 1923, when Giovanni Mardersteig established the Officina Bodoni in Switzerland, he received permission from the Italian authorities to recast some of the original Bodoni matrices. When he moved his private press to Verona in 1927, Mardersteig turned out printing in the spirit of Bodoni's. Later, however, Dr. Mardersteig broke away from his dependence on Bodoni types, designing faces in the fifteenth-century tradition of Italian letter forms, an era to which he was more sympathetic.

Despite his later printing, Mardersteig's original use of Bodoni was instrumental in awakening further interest in the Parma master printer, which resulted in several new cuttings of Bodoni type. Of these the version made available by the Bauer Type Foundry of Frankfurt seems to come closest to the feeling of the original and has thus long been admired.

ABCDEFGHIJKL MNOPQR STUVWXYZ abcdefghijklmnop qrstuvwxyz .,-;:'"!?$& 1234567890

Ultra Bodoni (Monotype)

ABCDEFGHIJKLMNOPQR STUVWXYZ abcdefghijklmnopqrstuvwxyz .,-;:!?""''$&ffffifflffiffl([]) 1234567890

Torino (Nebiolo foundry, c. 1908), a condensed variation on the Bodoni model

ABCDEFGHIJKLMNOP QRSTUVWXYZ

abcdefghijklmnopqrstuv wxyz   .,-;:'"!?$&
1234567890

Bodini Bold (Ludlow), the standard for newspaper headings prior to the introduction of phototypesetting

ABCDEFGHIJKLMNO PQRSTUVWXYZ
abcdefghijklmnopqrstuvwxyz
1234567890

Die Buchdruckerei ist eine so edle und nützliche Kunst, daß man bei denen, welche sie ausüben, einen gewissen Grad von Kultur voraussetzen sollte.

JOHANN FRIEDRICH UNGER

Didot (Ludwig & Mayer)

The standard series of weights in Bodoni includes the variants book, regular, and bold. Only one supplier (Bauer) has ventured into an extra-bold version, which is surprising, since the type lends itself better than most romans to changes in weight without loss of character. There are, in addition, a number of other types that trade on the Bodoni name, including Ultra Bodoni and Poster Bodoni, but these are revivals of nineteenth-century modifications and bear no relation to the prototype.

It is difficult to imagine how advertisers and commercial printers could get along today without Bodoni. It has been used for more display typography than any design other than sans serif. It is also beloved by newspapers: in most American two-paper cities, one will feature Bodoni heads and the other sans serifs. As a book type it continues to fare quite well, particularly in the weight called Bodoni Book.

Although Giambattista Bodoni would probably not willingly claim fatherhood to most of the types currently bearing his name, he would certainly find no fault in still being a household word in the printer's craft two centuries after he began his venture in Parma.

18

BULMER

Type designers, no matter how successful in their art, are all too frequently doomed to a loss of identity in the larger world of print where they have to compete for the limelight with typographers and graphic artists. Certainly, the general reader is seldom aware of the creator of a typeface, or even of the type itself, no matter how well (or perhaps *because* of how well) it performs its function of conveying the author's message. It doesn't appear that the status of the type designer will change, either, even in the printing of books. There is in fact but a single American publisher who has consistently given credit to the type designer: Alfred A. Knopf, by the simple device of including 'A Note on the Type' as a fixture in every book he publishes – upholding the venerable tradition of the colophon – informs the reader about the origins of printing types. And David Godine follows in this tradition.

Many of the great classic types, of course, do bear the names of their creators – Caslon, Baskerville, Bodoni – but even these are known, for the most part, only to printers.

A punchcutter named William Martin is a case in point. He produced a type in 1790 for the English printer William Bulmer that was lavishly praised in its own time and after being recut in the 1920s again became an established favorite. Martin's type was aided immeasurably in its original popularity by being the property of one of the great printers of his period, but there is not much doubt that the type itself contributed largely to the esteem in which it was held. As is often the case, however, the type created by Martin is now known as Bulmer. Be that as it may, twentieth-century printers are fortunate to have it under any name.

With few exceptions, English printing up to the time of John Baskerville was not particularly distinguished. Even after the introduction of Caslon's fine type about 1720, it remained for Baskerville to take the lead in the 1750s by improving the quality of the entire printed product – type, paper, and ink – and, by implication, the press.

Whereas the progress achieved by Baskerville, as we have seen, was duly noted and made use of on the Continent, it was not until after his death in 1775 that English printing generally improved. This was primarily through the accomplishments of three great personalities: the publisher John Bell and two printers, Thomas Bensley and William Bulmer, the three B's of English printing at that time.

William Bulmer, born in 1766, came to London from Newcastle and worked in Bell's printing office before being asked by George Nicol, bookseller to King George III, to aid him in the establishment of a press for the purpose of producing a new edition of Shakespeare. Nicol was a member of a group of artists who had proposed a new 'national' edition of the poet, to be illustrated by British artists and printed in a matter fitting to the hallowed subject. As Nicol was the most knowledgeable in the group about printing, he was charged with selecting the printer.

Bulmer was Nicol's choice. In an advertisement entitled 'A Catalogue of the Pictures,' printed to promote the project, Nicol wrote: 'The Printing is at present under the direction of a Gentleman who had already contributed much to the improvement of his profession, and who will now have the opportunity of showing the World that we can print as well in England, it is hoped, as they do in Parma, Paris, or Madrid.'

The project was undertaken in 1790, the new firm W. Bulmer & Company, The Shakspeare Printing Office, having been established for the purpose. (Note the spelling of Shakespeare, which was followed by Bulmer throughout his career.) The type for the press was cut by William Martin, whose brother Robert had been apprenticed by Baskerville and later was foreman of Baskerville's printing office in Birmingham. It is probable that William, too, had learned punch-cutting in Baskerville's foundry.

The Shakespeare began coming off the press in 1791, but Bulmer then became involved in numerous other projects. He was anxious to 'raise the Art of Printing from the neglected state in which it had long been suffered to continue,' as he forthrightly stated in the preface to his splendidly printed *Poems of Goldsmith and Parnell* of 1795. His recognition of the importance of a fine type in his scheme was indicated when he wrote: 'The whole of the Types with which this work has been printed are executed by Mr. William Martin . . . a very

POEMS

BY

GOLDSMITH

AND

PARNELL.

LONDON:

PRINTED BY W. BULMER AND CO.

Shakspeare Printing Office,

CLEVELAND-ROW.

1795.

Title page, *Poems of Goldsmith and Parnell*, printed by William Bulmer, London, 1795

ADVERTISEMENT

To raise the Art of Printing in this country from the neglected state in which it had long been suffered to continue, and to remove the opprobrium which had but too justly been attached to the late productions of the English press, much has been done within the last few years; and the warm emulation which has discovered itself amongst the Printers of the present day, as well in the remote parts of the kingdom as in the metropolis, has been highly patronized by the public in general. The present volume, in addition to the SHAKSPEARE, the MILTON, and many other valuable works of elegance, which have already been given to the world, through the medium of the Shakspeare Press, are particularly meant to combine the various

Advertisement from *Poems of Goldsmith and Parnell*

THE

DRAMATIC WORKS

OF

SHAKSPEARE.

REVISED

BY GEORGE STEEVENS.

LONDON:

PRINTED BY W. BULMER AND CO.

𝕾𝖍𝖆𝖐𝖘𝖕𝖊𝖆𝖗𝖊 𝕻𝖗𝖎𝖓𝖙𝖎𝖓𝖌-𝕺𝖋𝖋𝖎𝖈𝖊,

FOR JOHN AND JOSIAH BOYDELL, AND GEORGE NICOL;

From the Types of W. Martin.

1791.

Title page of Bulmer's edition of Shakespeare, London, 1791

The Shakspeare Printing Office owes its origin to the publication of that great National Edition of the Works of Shakspeare, which you are now, so much to the honour of our country, happily conducting toward its completion; I

Original version of the italic cut for the Shakespeare Press by William Martin

ingenious young artist who is at this time forming a Foundry, by which he will shortly be enabled to offer to the world a Specimen of Types, that will, in a very eminent degree, unite utility, elegance, and beauty. . . .'

Factors other than an outstanding font of types also contributed to Bulmer's success as a printer. A boyhood friend from his New-castle apprenticeship was Thomas Bewick, the most famous of all English wood engravers, who was prevailed upon to illustrate many of Bulmer's titles. In turn, Bewick could congratulate himself on having so competent a printer. The technique that Bewick employed in making his engravings demanded a high degree of skill for their reproduction, and this he received from Bulmer. Collectors of Bewick cite the Goldsmith-Parnell volume as the best printed of the engravings during Bewick's lifetime, although the artist was seldom happy with the printing of his blocks. It may be added here that Bulmer was also one of the first fine printers to adopt the improved iron press of Lord Stanhope when it became available after 1800. The sturdy frame of this press was a marked advance over the earlier wooden presses, for its metal structure permitted greater precision in the printed image.

An examination of the type that William Martin cut will disclose two strong influences. First, there is the relationship to Baskerville's design, which, while in the tradition of Caslon, had exemplified those characteristics (refined serifs and greater contrast of stroke) that were to result in the type of Giambattista Bodoni of Parma some thirty years later. Second, by the last decade of the eighteenth century the

ABCDEFGHIJKLMNOPQRS TUVWXYZ&

abcdefghijklmnopqrstuvwxyz
fiflffffiffl ..,-'"'':;!?$1234567890%

Bulmer (Monotype)

types of Bodoni were becoming extremely popular (as were those of the Didots in France); in incorporating these styles Martin was obviously following the instructions of George Nicol, who had advertised that the new type would employ 'approved models in imitation of the sharp and fine letters used by the French and Italian printers.'

These Continental faces, with their strong vertical stress and hairline serifs, were the forerunners of the style now called modern. They were so successful that the old-style types on which printers had depended for almost three hundred years became virtually obsolete. But rather than creating just another modern, Martin attempted to bridge the gap between Baskerville and Bodoni-Didot, and he was thus more successful than most of his fellow punchcutters who tried to mix the old-style forms with the modern adaptations.

The Bulmer type designed by Martin is more condensed than Baskerville and has a greater contrast of stroke. The serifs are slightly bracketed, in the manner of the old style, so that although the overall appearance of the design favors Bodoni in its color on the page, it avoids the mechanical starkness of the Bodoni-Didot forms. Typographic historians have praised Martin's type. Even Updike, who had little enthusiasm for the modern styles, wrote of the Bulmer types that 'they were very splendid of their kind.'

After Bulmer's death in 1830, English printing suffered a general deterioration, owing largely to the Industrial Revolution whose mechanizing influence put an end to many fine crafts. An exception is the printing of the Whittinghams, who revived Caslon about 1840,

REFRESHED
Splendid Plays

QUIET FIELDS
Delightful Grove

MUSIC STUDIOS
Proper Atmosphere

Bulmer (ATF)

and of the publisher Charles Pickering. It was not, however, until the closing years of the nineteenth century, with William Morris's revival effort, that attention again turned to the earlier historic types (although Morris himself would in all probability have rejected Bulmer for being too close in spirit to the Bodoni types which he detested).

It remained for Morris Benton, of the American Type Founders

Company, to return the Martin design to popularity. Possibly inspired by the program of the English Monotype firm in its revival of classic types during the twenties – and certainly influenced by ATF's librarian, the typographic historian Henry Lewis Bullen – Benton sought out the books printed by William Bulmer.

Naming this recutting after the printer who had used the type, rather than its designer, ATF issued Bulmer in 1928. The type met with immediate acclaim. During the 1930s it was axiomatic that if a book was hand-set in Bulmer it would make the Fifty Books of the Year Exhibition. Later the type became available for machine-casting on the Monotype in a version based on the Benton copy. It was issued for the linecasting machine in 1953 by the Intertype Corporation.

In the United States Bulmer is today most frequently employed as a display type rather than for continuous reading. When it is used in book printing, it is primarily for title pages and chapter headings, particularly for volumes composed in Baskerville. Bulmer has, however, turned up as the text type for more than thirty-five works in the Fifty Books show since 1934.

Bulmer has now been converted to film and has also been digitized for CRT typesetting. It is to be hoped that this fine old type will be around for a long time. Apart from its beauty, its association with a great period in English printing – specifically, with the names of William Bulmer and Thomas Bewick – is one that can only inspire the designer who turns to it.

19

BELL

The World newspaper of London contained on June 9, 1787, the following advertisement for the publication of a book entitled *The Way to Keep Him*:

J. Bell flatters himself that he will be able to render this the most perfect and in every respect the most beautiful book, that was ever printed in any country. He presumes to promise this excellence from a confidence in the supremacy of his letter foundry which he is now establishing at his own premises and under his own direction. He is at present casting a new type for the purpose on improved principles; and he hopes it will challenge the attention of the curious and the judicious.

John Bell, English publisher and bookseller, had apparently decided to add the craft of typefounding to his many accomplishments. He was to give up the venture just two years later, but not before producing a highly notable typeface, one that continued the tradition of fine English types begun in 1720 by William Caslon and later extended by John Baskerville.

In 1788 Bell announced the opening of 'Bell's British Letter Foundry' in 'an address to the world' in his second specimen sheet. Among his reasons for establishing a typefoundry was that the art of printing was then held in low esteem in England, whereas 'France, Spain, Italy, and Germany are contending for the honours of the Press, under the sanction and encouragement of their respective Sovereigns.'

It is evident that the competition of Continental printers was also disturbing to other English practitioners of this period. William Bulmer, a contemporary of Bell's, wrote in a similar vein in the introduction to one of his books, in which he offered to 'raise the Art of Printing in the country from the neglected state in which it had long been suffered to continue. . . .' The contributions of Baskerville notwithstanding, the English printing trade had permitted the Continental printers to become the typographic innovators and pace setters.

The new type that John Bell was promoting stemmed from the

JOHN BELL

Much admired, these types have presented something of a mystery. Prior to 1926 they were thought to have survived only in this country, as two privately owned 14 point fonts of unknown origin. It awaited discovery of a type specimen of 1788 *in the National Library, Paris, to trace them to the*

ABCCDEFGHIJJKKLMNOPQQRRST
UVWXYZ

ABCDEFGHIJJKKLMNOPQRRSTUVWXYZ
abcdefghijkklmnopqrstuvwxyz

* † ‡ § ‖ ¶ ☞ . , - : ; '' ' ! ? [ ] ( ) £ $ &
ſ ff fi ffi fl ffl Æ Æ æ Œ œ œ
1234567890

AABCDEFGHIJJKKLMNNOPQQR
STTUVVWXYZ
abcdefghhijkklmnopqrstuvwxyz
& $ ct st Æ æ Œ œ ſ ff fi ffi fl ffl . , - : ; ' ! ?
1234567890

Bell (Monotype)

publisher's own advanced ideas on type design. The final result, however, undoubtedly owed a good deal to the very considerable skills of the punchcutter whom Bell had commissioned for the cutting of the type – Richard Austin.

Richard Austin was a talented engraver in wood and metal. This first essay into the creation of a printing type for Bell resulted in a letter of advanced design, particularly in the sharpness of the serifs. Following his association with Bell's British Letter Foundry, Austin continued his career as a punchcutter for both his own and other foundries. Over his lifetime he produced a number of excellent types, including a roman for the Edinburgh foundry of William Miller about 1809 – a letter that was to be most influential in the development of the type that came to be called Scotch Roman.

The essential changes in the Bell type from the pure old-style form were the narrower set width and the more precise serif structure. These elements, along with the stronger contrast of stroke and vertical stress in the round letters, resulted in a type that represented a con-siderable departure from the romans of the period.

Unfortunately, however, Bell's type emerged at a most inopportune period for a letter containing features of the old-style types. The new trend in letter forms – as embodied first in the fonts of France's Firmin Ambroise Didot in 1784, then in those of Italy's Giambattista Bodoni about 1787 – had begun to influence both typefounders and printers throughout Europe, including England. By the end of the century, these so-called modern types were in such demand that typefounders were producing them in quantity, while curtailing their manufacture of old styles.

Thus, John Bell's design, excellent though it was, enjoyed but a short life before it gave way to such modern excesses as Robert Thorne's Great Primer No. 1 and similar blown-up romans by Euro-pean typefounders. The modernized roman also became immensely popular in the United States, where after 1800 it was frequently imitated by newly established American typefoundries.

Nevertheless, though there is little evidence of English printers' turning to the Bell type with any degree of enthusiasm, in the United States it was copied as early as 1792. Indeed, the Boston firm of Belknap & Hall published a newspaper, *The American Apollo*, that was an undisguised imitation of the periodicals from Bell's Apollo Press; this publication followed John Bell's typographic style in every detail. Belknap & Hall also produced a virtual facsimile of the entire

JOHN BELL,

Of the BRITISH LIBRARY, *Strand, London, being engaged in the establishment of*

A NEW

PRINTING LETTER FOUNDRY,

He begs leave to present the Public with a

SPECIMEN of the first

SET OF TYPES

which have been completed under his directions

By William Coleman, *Regulator,*

And Richard Austin, *Punch-Cutter.*

PRINTERS *may be supplied at present with Types agreeable to this Specimen, and afterwards with every other sort which shall be completed by* J. BELL, *however superior they may be, on terms usually observed by other Founders.*

May, 1788.

Announcement of the establishment of John Bell's Letter Foundry, 1788

text of Bell's *The British Album,* to the extent of using Bell's pressmark, though with a change of initials. Another early use of Bell in the United States was in the almanacs published in Washington, Pennsylvania, for the years 1796 and 1797, each of which showed the English face in its title page. In addition, the 1797 edition displayed a typographic border that had been cast at Bell's British Letter Foundry.

Perhaps appropriately – given the original's warmer reception in America than in England (where it was all too quickly forgotten after 1800) – the revival of Bell in our time was partially due to the efforts of a keen and discerning American book publisher, Henry O. Houghton. An ambitious program of book printing that Houghton wished to inaugurate at the Riverside Press in Cambridge, Massachusetts, was his prime reason for a voyage to England in 1864. It was during this visit that he purchased types cast from Bell's matrices, which were then in the possession of the Birmingham foundry Stephenson, Blake & Company.

The Bell fonts were subsequently listed in the catalogue of the Riverside Press – where they were named English Copperplate – but they were little used, except for books written by the Boston author Martin Brimmer. It happened, however, that two young typographers who were later to become world-famous received their initial contact with book production at Riverside: Daniel Berkeley Updike, employed there from 1880 to 1893, and Bruce Rogers, employed from 1896 to 1912. Both of these influential figures in printing therefore became acquainted with the Bell fonts early in their careers.

Rogers so admired the face that he purchased the 14-point size and began to experiment with it in his home, the final result being the setting of two text pages and the title page of a translation of the *Georgics*. In 1899 these samples were selected for showing at the Arts and Crafts Exhibition in Boston (although the book was not published until 1904). Rogers renamed the face Brimmer, since it was through this author's books that he had learned of it. Following the experimental use of Brimmer, Rogers selected it for his second Riverside Press book, *The Rubáiyát of Omar Khayyám*, published in 1900. Thereafter, he employed the face for at least one book a year in the famous Riverside Editions, a series that initiated his reputation as a great designer.

Meanwhile, Updike had embarked on his career at his own Merrymount Press, an undertaking that established him as the finest American printer of his time. Intrigued by the so-called English Copperplate/Brimmer type, he traced its source to Stephenson, Blake, and in 1903 purchased a large casting for Merrymount, renaming the face Mountjoye. He first used it in a privately printed book entitled *Saudades*, by Frances Dabney. The following year Updike selected the font for a fourteen-volume edition of the Bible printed for the R. H. Hinkley Company of Boston. During the next thirty years, Updike produced seventy-six titles in Mountjoye at his famed Boston press.

So little was recalled in England of the original Bell type that when in 1887 the English typefounder Talbot Baines Reed wrote his authoritative text, *A History of the Old English Letter Foundries*, the book contained not a word of information on it. In 1952, when A. F.

ENGLISH ROMAN.

Quousque tandem abutere, Catilina, patientia noſtra? quamdiu nos etiam furor iſte tuus
eludet? quem ad finem sese effrenata jaᶜtabit
audacia? nihilne te noᶜturnum præsidium
palatii, nihil urbis vigiliæ, nihil timor populi,
nihil consensus bonorum omnium, nihil hic
munitissimus habendi senatus locus, nihil horum ora vultusque moverunt? patere tua con
silia non sentis? conſtriᶜtam jam omnum horum conscientia teneri conjurationem tuam
non vides? quid proxima, quid superiore, noc-
te egeris, ubi fueris, quos convocaveris, quid
consilii ceperis, quem noſtrum ignorare ar-
bitraris? O tempora, o mores! Senatus hoc
intelligit, consul vidit: hic tamen vivit. vivit?
imo vero etiam in senatum venit: fit pub-
lici consilii particeps: notat & designat oculis ad cædem unumquemque noſtrum. Nos
autem viri fortes satisfacere reipub. videmur,
si iſtius furorem ac tela vitemus. Ad mortem

A B C C D E F G H I J J K K L M N O P Q Q R
R S T U V W X Y Z Æ Œ

ABCDEFGHIJJKKLMNOPQRRSTUVWXYZÆŒ

abcdefghijkklmnopqrſstuvwxyz

ſtſtſhſiſiffiffiffflflffiffiſiffflſbſkᶜtæœ&.,-;:!?

†§([1234567890])‖‡

Specimen of Bell type, 1788

Johnson revised this monumental work, he added an account of Bell's
contributions.

Meanwhile, in 1931 the type had finally become available to printers
generally. Its revival was due to the efforts of Stanley Morison.

It was during the 1920s that England's Stanley Morison had emerged as an important typographic scholar. His career dated from 1913, when he wrote an article for *The Imprint*, an English typographical periodical that had been founded for the redoubtable purpose of benefiting 'the printing and allied trades, to afford a friendly medium of intercommunication, and to show the place for craftsmanship in the printing trade.'

Following the First World War, Morison took up the practice of typography. In 1922 he was appointed adviser to the Lanston Monotype Corporation of London. Here he was allowed full scope for his varied talents, his principal contribution being the selection of a number of historic types for the innovative program of revivals to be cut for the Monotype machine.

It was by accident that Morison came to add John Bell's type to the Monotype list. In 1926, while doing research at the Bibliothèque Nationale in Paris, Morison happened upon the first specimen of Bell's foundry, no copy of which was then known in England. Morison immediately recognized the type both through its use in the United States by Updike and Rogers and from books produced by William Bulmer, a contemporary of Bell's. Morison, inspired by his discovery, was prompted to the investigations that resulted in the important monograph published in 1930 which returned the name of John Bell to its proper place in the pantheon of English printers.

The reason for the long-term neglect suffered by the original Bell type was the ever-changing typographic taste during the nineteenth century – a factor that has continued to plague even distinguished designs up to the present: many a type has gathered dust in printers' cases because fashion has passed it by. In the instance of Bell, the competition from the more 'modern' Vincent Figgins, who established his foundry in 1792, and Robert Thorne, who began in 1794, was simply too strong. In addition, the growing demand for commercial (or, as the English term them, jobbing) types turned interest away from book types in general, no matter how fine.

Stanley Morison considered Bell to be in fact of the modern classification. Type classification, however, is frequently less than precise, and the term *modern* is a rather general one in regard to letter forms. Most typographers today consider the types of Didot and of Bodoni, with their unbracketed serifs (particularly noticeable in Didot, less so in the original types of Bodoni), as representative of modern. If such is the case, then truly Bell is more a faithful rendition of the

AN

1 A L M A N A C K

FOR

2 THE YEAR 1796,

BEING

3 *Biſſextile; or Leap Year :*

CONTAINING

The uſual ASTRONOMICAL CALCULATIONS, a brief
Account of the UNITED STATES, abſtract from the
CONSTITUTION of PENNSYLVANIA, COURTS of LAW,
Rates of POSTAGE throughout the UNION, LISTS of
the CONGRESS of the UNITED STATES, and of the
OFFICERS of the FEDERAL GOVERNMENT, &c. &c.

ALSO,

Plain and eaſy Rules for the attainment and preſervation
of HEALTH, curious Receipts, Anecdotes, Poetry, a remarkable inſtance of Affection between Brutes, Aphoriſms
on Man, and ſeveral uſeful Tables of Intereſt, Coins, &c.

WASHINGTON:

PRINTED BY COLERICK, HUNTER & BEAUMONT,

PRINTERS AND BOOKSELLERS.

1795.

Use of Bell type in the United States, 1795

so that his necessity, as his pillager well under-stood, was absolute. Again, many others whose indignation will not submit to such plunder, are forced to refuse the assistance, tho' they are often great sufferers by so doing. On the latter side, the lowest of the people are encouraged in laziness and idleness ; while they live by a twentieth part of the labour that ought to maintain them, which is diametrically opposite to the interest of the public; for that requires a great deal to be done, not to be paid, for a little. And moreover, they are confirm'd in habits of exaction, and are taught to consider the distresses of their superiors as their own fair emolument.

But enough of this matter, of which I at first intended only to convey a hint to those who are alone capable of applying the remedy, tho' they are the last to whom the notice of those evils would occur, without some such monitor as myself, who am forced to travel about the world in the form of a passenger. I cannot but say I heartily wish our governors would attentively consider this method of fixing the price of labour, and by that means of compelling the poor to work, since the due execution of such powers will, I apprehend, be found the true and only

[125]

Use of Brimmer type by Bruce Rogers in *The Journal of a Voyage to Lisbon*, Riverside Press, 1902

CHAPTER X

THE HISTORY OF THE PRINTING PRESS

BY

DAVID T. POTTINGER

IN the composing room of a modern printing-office Gutenberg would find himself almost at home; his keen mind would doubtless lead him to comprehend at once what the compositors and the correctors were about. In the pressroom, on the other hand, he would find nothing familiar. Whereas the casting and setting of type, not to mention the idea of type itself, have remained essentially the same as in the earliest days, the methods and principles by which ink is transferred from the printing surface to the sheet of paper have been utterly revolutionized. Gutenberg's presses, according to a very conservative estimate, turned out not more than five hundred sheets in a twelve-hour day, an accomplishment that is equaled in about as many seconds by a newspaper perfecting press of our time. The turning points in the course of this development were so salient as to be easily recognized. The first significant improvements have traditionally been associated with Willem Janszoon Blaeu of Amsterdam and the year 1620. After another two centuries, Earl Stanhope constructed an all-iron press with a series of levers to increase the action of the screw, and in 1816 George Clymer of Philadelphia abandoned the use of a screw entirely. In 1822 Daniel Treadwell of Boston made the first power-driven press of the bed-and-platen type, an invention that was much im-

proved by Isaac Adams of Boston in 1830 and 1836. Meanwhile Friedrich König, a German working in London, invented a flat-bed and cylinder press in 1812–1813. With the introduction of the cylinder the way was open for all the refinements of detail that have resulted in the machines of our own day.

The Fifteenth and Sixteenth Centuries

WHAT the first printing press looked like is, in the absence of contemporary description and of all relics, a matter of conjecture; and even its much later successors were dismissed with only a crude sketch by Moxon, the first English writer on the printer's trade. Robert Hoe, who knew a vast deal about modern presses at least, thought that it was a simple affair embodying the mechanical principle found in the old cheese and linen presses ordinarily seen in the houses of mediæval times. Karl Dieterichs asserts, with much more probability, that the model for it was the papermaker's press, with the fundamental difference that the platen was made to come down with less pressure and with greater steadiness. He has calculated that the platen probably measured about nineteen-and-a-half by fourteen inches, that the diameter of its wooden screw was eight inches, and that as in all later presses up to the end of

323

Bell types as shown in *The Dolphin*, Vol. III, designed by Carl Purington Rollins, 1938

transitional styles, which borrow from both old-style and modern forms, than it is a modern type. Certainly the design is closer to Baskerville, which is widely recognized as a transitional form, than to the so-called classic romans of Bodoni and Didot.

Whatever its classification, Bell deservedly became a popular type for book composition immediately after its revival by the English Monotype firm in 1931. (Stephenson, Blake had fortunately retained the punches and matrices of the original, in the pica size, and this is what Morison used as the model for the Monotype revival.)

Later, a version of Bell was cut by the Lanston Monotype Machine Company in Philadelphia, thus making the type available to American printers. Naturally enough, Bell's availability only for single-type composition has been a restriction in its use in the United States: many American book designers who have wished to employ it have had to substitute a slug-machine type, although they have frequently used Bell in display sizes for title pages and chapter openings.

The first example of the recut Bell was in one of Morison's own books, *The English Newspaper*, published by Cambridge University Press in 1932. Quite possibly the finest American book to be printed from Bell types is the folio *A History of the Printed Book*, edited by Lawrence C. Wroth and published by the Limited Editions Club in 1938. The volume was designed by Carl Purington Rollins and printed at Yale University Press.

It is to be hoped that Bell's transfer to phototypesetting equipment will broaden the use of this fine English type in American typography. In England, where Monotype is still extensively employed, it continues to be widely used.

Stanley Morison

20

OXFORD

Were America's private-press printers allowed the choice of a type that could once again be made available in quantity for distribution into the standard 'California' job cases, it is quite possible that the prime selection would be a design called Oxford.

The rationale of such an option would include its singular appropriateness for American printing and its excellence as a roman letter, not to mention the approbation of some of the finest craftsmen-printers during the last eighty years.

Historically, the choice would be most apt, as Oxford began life as the Roman No. 1 of the first commercially successful American typefoundry, the Philadelphia firm Binny & Ronaldson which opened its doors in 1796. Following several changes of name, the firm in 1867 became MacKellar, Smiths & Jordan, the most important typefoundry of its period. From that dominant position it finally lost its identity when it was amalgamated into the American Type Founders Company in 1892.

Archibald Binny was a Scots typefounder who, with the tools of his trade, had arrived in Philadelphia from Edinburgh about 1795. Here he met an Edinburgh acquaintance, James Ronaldson, whose biscuit bakery in Philadelphia had recently burned down. This was a most timely meeting, as it led to the agreement between the two men to combine their talents in the operation of a typefoundry: Binny would apply his mechanical skills to the craft and Ronaldson his business knowledge to the management of the establishment.

At that time the young American republic was in great need of local sources of printing types. For too long American printers had relied on European supplies, despite the high cost and delays in shipment that had prevented the printing industry from meeting the ever-increasing demands of a rapidly expanding economy. Several attempts had been made to produce types in the United States, but as of 1795 there were no typefounders who could supply printers with a sufficient quantity of type on a regular basis.

After the new Philadelphia firm had opened in November 1796, it issued, on demand, specimen showings of its types, though none of these early samples seems to have survived. It is nonetheless evident that Binny & Ronaldson types were popular, for they began to appear in the printing of the era with increasing frequency. The first specimen book to be produced by the partners did not come out until 1809, almost thirteen years after business was formally begun. Only metal ornaments, however, were displayed in this catalogue; most of them were the illustrations commonly used in advertising, along with mortised borders and headbands. Many of the ornaments had obviously first been cut in wood and presumably were cast as stereotypes at the foundry.

The second specimen book from Binny & Ronaldson, bearing the date 1812, shows several types in addition to piece borders and fleurons. This was the first such catalogue ever to be issued in the United States. In it were listed two roman types, with their accompanying italics, two black letters, a Hebrew, a Greek, and four ornamented styles.

The first roman type, which in the sizes of pica and smaller is labeled 'No. 2,' in the larger sizes is simply styled 'Roman' up to 'Seven Lines Pica' (84-point). This type is a typical modern roman, then very popular in England and Europe; it is illustrative of the degradation of roman letter forms then beginning to take place owing to the rapid industrialization of the printing craft.

The second roman type in the 1812 catalogue, named Roman No. 1, is another matter entirely. Here is a book type that compares favorably with the classic romans. It is a transitional letter; that is, it contains features of both the old styles, as represented by the types up through Caslon, and the moderns which had reached their apogee in the styles of Bodoni and Didot.

Although John Baskerville had, of course, popularized the transitional type styles some forty years before Archibald Binny cut his Roman No. 1, the exact provenance of the Binny design remains uncertain, for very little information has come down concerning Binny's punchcutting before his arrival in the United States.

Born about 1762, Binny must have been apprenticed to a typefounder by 1775 (thirteen was the standard age of a beginning apprentice), and thus he would have practiced his craft for some eighteen years before leaving Edinburgh. Since he was an innovative and resourceful man, it is probable that he was acquainted with the transitional types being cut in England during this period: these included the copies of Baskerville made by the Fry foundry and that of Alexander Wilson, the face cut by Richard Austin for John Bell, and the fonts of William Bulmer that had been cut by William Martin. Of these influential types it is the Austin face to which Roman No. 1 is closest in spirit. Still, lacking documentation, we can only conjecture what Binny was thinking of when he cut his type.

The 1812 Binny & Ronaldson specimen book shows the face in what they called pica (12-point), small pica (11-point), and bourgeois (9-point). Former Princeton University Press typographer P. J. Conkwright, who studied the Binny types in depth stated that the early versions of Roman No. 1 differed from those listed in 1812. He identified, for example, a roman issued before that date, in 14-point (the size then called English), that he believed adhered more closely to the style of the Scottish typefounder John Baine. However, the only 'English' appearing in the 1812 specimen book is the aforementioned modern roman, which 'Paul Beaujon' (Beatrice Warde), writing in *Signature* in 1936, called a 'semi-fat modern of Latin influence.'

The typefounder Baine, who in 1787 had also made the crossing to America, had previously been a partner in Glasgow of the eminent Alexander Wilson, before setting up on his own in Edinburgh. It is not known why, in his seventy-third year, Baine chose to go to Philadelphia to begin a venture. It is suggested, however, that he wished to help establish his grandson in a location that would offer great promise for the future. But the younger Baine showed little inclination to be a founder, and after his grandfather's death in 1790 he decided to sell his interest in the business, finally disposing of it to Binny & Ronaldson in 1799.

The march of progress had by 1812 influenced the Binny & Ronaldson foundry to favor the modern styles. Most of the types they now offered for sale were modern romans. Indeed, the firm used them for the setting of the title page of its specimen book and also the introduction, which declared: 'The very liberal encouragement the Proprietors of this Foundery have received, while it has stimulated their exertions to deserve it, has also put it in their power to extend and improve their establishment on the grand scale, of which this Specimen exhibits a proof; nor shall their endeavours stop here: as they are determined never to relax their assiduity, while there remains any thing useful or

Quousque tandem abutere, Catilina, patientia nostra? quamdiu nos etiam furor iste tuus eludet? quem ad finem sese effrenata jactabit audacia? nihilne te nocturnum præsidium palatii, nihil urbis vigiliæ, nihil timor populi, nihil consensus bonorum omnium, nihil hic munitissimus habendi senatus locus, nihil horum ora vultusque moverunt? patere tua consilia non sentis? constrictam jam omnium horum conscientia teneri conjurationem tuam non vides? quid proxima, quid superiore
ABCDEFGHIJKLMNOPQRSTUVWXY
1234567890

Pica Roman No. 1 as shown in specimen of Binny & Ronaldson, Philadelphia, 1812

ornamental to be added to their Foundery which can be found in the first Founderies of Europe.'

Thus Binny & Ronaldson joined the parade that for the next half century resulted in the virtual extirpation of the old-style types from the printing offices of the world. Nevertheless, because the first modern romans of Binny were not very well designed, it is possible that the founder, in spite of the need to supply the more popular moderns, wished in his fine transitional type, Roman No. 1, to improve on them. In addition, the Bell types had met with some success in Boston and their reception could have influenced Binny in his choice of style. Whatever the derivation, Roman No. 1 certainly is a type that upholds the great tradition of letter forms begun by Baskerville and carried on by Austin and Martin.

In 1815 Archibald Binny sold his share of the foundry to his partner, James Ronaldson, and became a gentleman farmer, taking up residence in Maryland. A year later Ronaldson issued his own specimen book, in the introduction of which he paid tribute to Binny: the types shown were, he wrote, 'the product of [Binny's] genius and labour,' and 'the Letter Foundery owes more of its improvement and simplification to him than to any other individual.'

Ronaldson was here making reference to Binny's mechanical skills, for along with type designing, Binny was credited with inventing the first important improvement in the construction of the hand mold, which doubled the output of the typecaster. Statistics on early output are not reliable, but generally a caster could produce an average of 3,000 characters in each day's work (even this average figure is not dependable, as the length of the working day varied according to season). Binny's improvement consisted in the attachment to the mold of a spring lever that permitted a faster return movement.

Ronaldson also wrote that the 1812 specimen book had been the result of twenty-five years of labor by Binny (which presents the possibility that Binny had begun the accumulation of punches and types even before leaving Scotland). In addition, Ronaldson outlined the improvements in typography that Binny had achieved over his thirty-five-year career, such as the elimination of the long *s*. Ronaldson did add, however:

In the spirit of improvement, some things were carried beyond propriety; but experience alone could discover what was nearest perfection. To your polite attention B. & R. were indebted for specimens of the European improvements as fast as they came to the United States. The example of that quarter, having great influence, and in some cases, strong partialities in its favour, it became necessary for B. & R. to imitate the Europeans, and, in some instances, contrary to their own judgment: examples of this exist in Long Primer No. 2 and Small Pica No. 2.

Ronaldson remained active until 1823, when his brother Richard took over the foundry. His last innovation, in the production of the 1822 specimen book, was the elimination as old-fashioned of the famous quotation from Cicero–'Quousque tandem abutere, Catalina, patientia nostra?'–that had been used by foundries since the days of William Caslon to illustrate straight-matter composition. The quotation occasionally turned up in later American specimen books (for example, in the Alexander Robb volume of 1846), but its use was severely curtailed after Ronaldson dropped it.

After 1822, the year of its final catalogue appearance, the Binny & Ronaldson Roman No. 1 was considered dead. It was not to be revived for seventy years. Two other early American founders, Elihu White and David Bruce, who issued specimen books respectively in 1812 and 1813, also followed the trends by casting only modern romans. But as neither of these men had been trained as a typefounder – as had Archibald Binny – they could not be expected to create styles of type

and this practice continued a long time after the art was introduced into England.

The first essay at printing Greek was made by Fust and Schoeffer, in Tully's Offices, anno 1465. They used only a few characters, and those were very rude. Some were made and introduced into Lactantius's Institutes, printed the same year at a monastery in the kingdom of Naples, which were much better executed than those of Fust and Schoeffer. The Italian printers made use of very decent Greek types about the year 1470 ; and they were brought to a high degree of perfection by the Stephani in Paris, before the year 1540.

About the year 1465, types of a kind of semi-Gothic character, far more elegant than the old German, or the 𝔟𝔩𝔞𝔠𝔨𝔰 used at the present time, were introduced at Venice. They, in shape, approached near to the Roman types, which, in less than two years after, were invented and used at Rome.

The Roman type, which is now, and for nearly two centuries has been, in general use in Italy, France, England, Spain, Portugal, and America, made its first appearance in the capital of his holiness the pope, in an edition of Cicero's Epistolæ Familiares, printed by the brothers Sweynheim and Arnold Pannartz, in 1466. This type was improved in Italy, and brought to nearly its present degree of perfection, as early as the year 1490.

The *Italic* character, anciently called by some *cursive*, and by others *Aldine*, was invented by Aldo Manuzio, at Venice, about the year 1505.

Printing with Hebrew characters, appears to have been first performed at Soncino, in the dutchy

Roman No. 1 as used in *The History of Printing in America*, by Isaiah Thomas, Worcester, 1810

based on a long familiarity with letter forms, as represented by Roman No. 1.

It is surprising that the typographic historian Theodore L. De Vinne, America's first great scholar of the craft of printing, did not recognize Roman No. 1 as a superior type. He certainly was acquainted with *The History of Printing in America* (written and printed in 1810 by Isaiah Thomas, of Worcester, Massachusetts), which affords the best example of the original type, produced under contemporary printing conditions. But, while mainly praising the quality of early American types, De Vinne stated in a lecture (delivered at the Grolier Club in 1885) that 'Their workmanship was good, but not one style of the many they cast can be offered as original or even really characteristic. No one tried to originate new forms or features.'

De Vinne believed that the changes in type styles initiated in the early years of the nineteenth century were due more to the mechanical considerations of printing than to aesthetic ideals. He cited the improved presses, constructed of metal rather than wood, which, together with better ink and finer paper, permitted the use of types with thinner strokes and more refined serifs. Although they printed well in books, these adaptations of the Bodoni-Didot style suffered under the necessarily faster production speed of the ever-growing newspaper industry, thus prompting typefounders – anxious to please their most important customers – to thicken the strokes of their moderns, resulting in the so-called fat-faced romans so sternly condemned by typographers of a later era.

The late-nineteenth-century revival of Roman No. 1 is generally credited to Joseph Warren Phinney. He was a principal in the S. N. Dickinson Type Foundery of Boston at the time of the amalgamation of most American foundries, including Dickinson, into the American Type Founders Company in 1892.

Phinney was a Nantucket boy who became an off-islander when he was apprenticed to a printer on Cape Cod. His period of indenture being interrupted by enlistment in the Union forces in 1864, Phinney subsequently completed his training as a compositor in Taunton, Massachusetts, and then joined the ranks of itinerant printers for three years. By the early 1870s he had returned to the Boston area and was employed in the sales department of the Dickinson firm. It was here that Phinney began his serious involvement with printing types, which resulted in a partnership in the company by 1885.

Upon the formation of ATF Phinney became a vice-president and

full range of sizes from 8 point to 20 point, with all fonts complete, including italic and special characters. Where space is limited the odd sizes, 9 point and 11 point, are particularly useful. *Taylor & Taylor were the first in California to install the Oxford type complete in all available sizes.*

ABCDEFGHIJKLMNOPQRSTU
VWXYZ

ABCDEFGHIJKLMNOPQRSTUVWXYZ &

abcdefghijklmnopqrstuvwxyz

1234567890

&.,;:-'!? [] ()ff fi fl ffi ffl £ $

*ABCDEFGHIJKLMNOPQRST
UVWXYZ*

abcdefghijklmnopqrstuvwxyz

& .,;:-'!? ff fi fl ffi ffl

Oxford (ATF)

manager of the Boston office. It must be presumed that he therefore had some responsibility in the decisions of the new firm concerning the disposal of vast accumulations of punches and matrices, acquired through the consolidation of twenty-three separate foundries.

The largest of these amalgamated foundries was MacKellar, Smiths & Jordan, the firm that had grown out of the original Binny & Ronaldson. Thus, Roman No. 1 must have turned up in the ATF inventory, in which Phinney doubtless played a part. Moreover, as Boston was at that period a center of fine book printing, Phinney probably believed that there would be a market for the revival of the classic Binny type. It is known that he ordered trial castings of the face and issued specimen sheets, in all likelihood to promote the design to the Boston publishers. Unaccountably, the name he chose in place of Roman No. 1 was Oxford, even though one of the Cleveland Type Foundry faces – an advertising style also among the matrices acquired by ATF – already possessed that name. (The Cleveland type later turned up in ATF's 1898 *Desk Book of Printing Types* as Oxford No. 2.)

The recasting of the Roman No. 1 seems to be quite close to the original, an indication that most of the Binny & Ronaldson matrices had survived. And for the replacement of inevitably damaged or missing matrices, the Dickinson foundry was fortunate in having on its staff the punchcutter John Cumming of Worcester, who was fully capable of duplicating Binny's work. Bruce Rogers, who later employed Cumming for the cutting of his Montaigne punches, called him the best punchcutter of his day.

It is a pity that the American Type Founders Company preserved no documentation of its revival of Oxford, particularly concerning matrix replacement. Because of Cumming's duplicating skill, it will probably never be determined how many punches were recut at this time. It is known that no small capitals of the Roman No. 1 were available from Binny & Ronaldson, so that those in ATF's Oxford were undoubtedly cut by Cumming; they follow the standard cap font in all respects except for the Q, which is supplied as a kerned letter. In addition, Oxford offered the long *s* and its ligatures, which had been eliminated in the 1812 Binny & Ronaldson catalogue. (It had, in fact, been a boast of Ronaldson's that the foundry had taken the lead in dropping this old-fashioned character. But as Phinney no doubt was reviving Roman No. 1 as a 'period' type, he must have felt printers would request the long *s* for colonial reproductions.)

Oxford thus became available in 1892, although it is difficult to find specimens of it or evidence of its early use. The new type was not even advertised. In 1895 ATF printed its Blue Books, followed in 1896 by the first 'Collected' specimen book, showing many of the older American types and the foundries from which they came. But though Phinney was active in the production of these catalogues, particularly the 'Collected' book, neither of them lists Oxford. How, then, did printers learn about the face? One must assume by word of mouth.

An early admirer of Oxford was Bruce Rogers, who was hired by the Cambridge, Massachusetts, Riverside Press in 1896. In 1900, having begun his full-time work as a book typographer, he was asked to head a department for special book production, and in this capacity he first made use of Oxford in 1905. In 1907 he began employing it more regularly.

Daniel Berkeley Updike, proprietor of Boston's Merrymount Press, had always expressed his enthusiasm for Oxford, although he did not acquire fonts until 1906 and did not actually use them until 1910. By 1932, however, when he published a bibliography of the first forty years of his press, he had employed it in more than forty titles. Unfortunately, he doesn't disclose how he became acquainted with the face or why, after buying it, he waited four years before using it.

In the chapter on early American specimens in his *Printing Types* of 1922, Updike took issue with the statement of Binny & Ronaldson in 1812 concerning the grand scale on which they conducted their foundry. He averred there was little grand about the enterprise except its pretensions, but he did, late in the book, list Oxford with those types 'that seem indisputably standard, on which there is no possibility of going astray: or, if I may call them, "types of obligation."' As Caslon and the nineteenth-century Scotch were the only other faces in this category, this was praise indeed.

Updike also wrote: 'For books where the old-fashioned air of Caslon would be too obtrusive, and yet which call for a letter more interesting in design than the somewhat bald Scotch face, there is nothing better [than Oxford].' He ended the paragraph by calling Oxford a type 'of great distinction.' The proof of Updike's assessment was that he had selected it as the face in which to hand-set both volumes of his monumental book, which made *Printing Types* itself the best single source for future scholars on the appearance of the revived Roman No. 1.

Collectors interested in acquiring books composed in Oxford can also turn to the work of Edwin and Robert Grabhorn, the San Fran-

*vers Caractères Vignettes et Fleurons des Fonderie et Stéréo-
typie de L. Léger, Graveur, neveu et successur de P. F. Didot,*
which, according to its compiler, represented the results of
twenty-five years' labour. The ornaments and borders are
distinctly light in effect, black backgrounds having mostly
disappeared (*fig.* 324). The types, less excellent than the
ornaments, are still in the Didot style.

An extremely characteristic showing of types in popular
use in the first fifty years of the nineteenth century is made
in the *Specimen Typographique de l'Imprimerie Royale.* These
two folio volumes (I, 1845; II, 1851), display a number of
fonts modelled on the Didot plan, and also make a distinguished showing of exotic fonts by Jacquemin. An index at
the end of the first volume tells who cut the various types
displayed—Firmin Didot, Marcellin Legrand, and Léger
Didot figuring among their designers; while among ancient
fonts are those from Garamond, the Propaganda and Medici offices, and Savary de Brèves.

The Didot foundry remained in the possession of the
family until sold by Ambroise Firmin Didot, when its types
became part of the Fonderie Générale of Paris. In this house
were consolidated the establishments of Firmin Didot, Molé,
Crosnier, and Éverat. The 1839 specimen of the Fonderie
Générale, issued by E. Tarbé, who presided over it, shows
text types in the "classic" Didot style, and many of the ornaments designed to accompany them—as well as *vignettes*
in the "romantic manner" which are very characteristic of
that time and very amusing in this. Another important specimen of the Fonderie Générale, then managed by Biesta,
Laboulaye & Cie, issued in 1843, showed, in addition to the
collections mentioned, those of Lion, Tarbé, and Laboulaye
Frères. The preliminary *Avis* supplies references by which
the types cut by different designers may be identified. The

Use of Oxford in *Printing Types*, by Daniel Berkeley Updike, Merrymount Press,
Boston, 1922

cisco printers. The Grabhorns first used the type (most appropriately) in *Early Printing in America*, their thirtieth book, published in 1921. The innovative brothers evidently were very fond of the type, for it then turned up in fifty-two other titles that bore their imprint. After Edwin's death in 1968, Robert continued the press, selecting Oxford for seven more titles, and when he and Andrew Hoyem combined forces as Grabhorn-Hoyem, it turned up yet again in four books.

Another well-known San Francisco printing firm, Taylor & Taylor, also promoted Oxford. In 1939 the company claimed that it was the first printer in California to offer the type in all the available sizes.

During the thirties and forties Oxford gained a host of friends, but its availability as a type for hand-composition only – and in a limited range of sizes – manifestly diminished its appeal to publishers. This situation was then rectified by a collaboration between Princeton University Press and the Mergenthaler Linotype Company.

In 1943 Princeton commenced the publishing of all of the papers of Thomas Jefferson, an enormous project, which is still expected to take decades to complete. P. J. Conkwright, then Princeton's director of design, had long been interested in early American typefounding, and Binny & Ronaldson in particular. Citing that this foundry's formative years were during Jefferson's presidency, Conkwright proposed Roman No. 1 as an excellent choice for the text of the papers.

It so happened that C. H. Griffith, who headed Linotype's type-design department, was also a longtime admirer of the Binny face and had actually put in a great deal of thought on the possibility of converting Roman No. 1 for machine-composition. It was thus agreed that Linotype would provide fonts for the Jefferson project, issuing the design under the name Monticello.

Another fine printer, Fred Anthoensen, of Portland, Maine, also thought highly of Roman No. 1/Oxford. He therefore supplied Griffith with specimens of printing on various papers of the sizes of Oxford in his possession. In addition, Griffith studied the five-volume edition of *Marshall's Life of George Washington*, printed in Roman No. 1 between 1804 and 1808, in order to acquaint himself with the appearance of the type under original printing conditions.

Rather than simply copying the original, Griffith took into consideration such factors as the heavy appearance of its lowercase, due to excessive use of the ink balls on the hand press; Griffith therefore had to thicken the capitals slightly, so that they would not be disproportional. He also made note of the redesign of several characters

ijprnmdblhk

These enlarged letters reveal the rather lively variation in serif treatment and bracketing which contribute to the inherent readability of Monticello. Note the subtle distinction in treatment of the i, r, n and k, among other letters. ¶ Transitional in character, MONTICELLO embodies in its letter-structure certain design characterisitics of Baskerville and Scotch, along with some of the movement and informality of Caslon. Its inspiration was the pica size of the celebrated Binny and Ronaldson Roman No. 1, cut by Archibald Binny in Philadelphia about 1796. The *Italic*, originally cut as a companion of the pica roman, was discarded in favor of the small-pica design, which discriminating authorities regard as superior. ¶ Each of the half dozen sizes of Linotype MONTICELLO (7 to 14 point) was drawn separately and modelled on the original pica design. The careful grading for optical harmony, so essential for mixing sizes in contemporary printing, is apparent at a glance at the inside spread. Here the refinement characters and *Recut Italic* provided for discriminating typography are also detailed.

LIST OF MAJOR CHARACTERS AVAILABLE

ABCDEFGHIJKLMNOPQRSTUVWXYZ&

ABCDEFGHIJKLMNOPQRSTUVWXYZ&

ABCDEFGHIJKLMNOPQRSTUVWXYZ&

abcdefghijklmnopqrstuvwxyz gjpqy Long Descenders

abcdefghijklmnopqrstuvwxyz gjpqy

abcdefghijklmnopqrstuvwxyz Recut Italic

1234567890$£,.:;'-'?!()*†‡¶§[]%

1234567890$£,.:;'-'?!()†‡¶§[]%*

Monticello (Linotype)

in the Oxford revival, possibly owing to matrix damage or loss (whether or not these were among the 1892 replacements cannot now be determined).

The first volume of *The Papers of Thomas Jefferson* was published in 1950, and it was promptly selected for inclusion in the Fifty Books of the Year Exhibition of 1951. By sheer coincidence, another selection in that show was Jacob Kainen's *George Clymer and the Columbian Press*, in the Typophile Chapbook series, which was hand-set in Oxford. Since then, however, the Roman No. 1 design has not turned up in this annual exhibition.

At about the time that Monticello was beginning to be used, Oxford, itself a revival, had a tiny revival of its own, thanks to the efforts of Steve Watts. Having retired in the early 1950s after a lifetime with ATF in several positions, including manager of the typefoundry, Watts continued to be happily occupied with printing. He prevailed upon his former employer to resurrect the matrices of Oxford and cast him twenty complete fonts which he then offered to friends in what he called 'kittypot' casting. The huge corporation, of course, would never have undertaken the sale of the type to small purchasers, so Watts now made it possible for private-press operators to acquire a limited number of fonts of a type that had previously been considered most desirable but completely unobtainable.

Roman No. 1 in its Linotype Monticello incarnation has been very well received, becoming a standard type for the text of books of every description. With further conversion to film and CRT, it is probable that this earliest American contribution to the large-scale manufacture of first-class book types will prove an enduring success.

To end this account on an upbeat note, it is a most happy circumstance that the Oxford matrices are now safely in the possession of the Smithsonian Institution. There they reside with countless others that several years ago were saved from destruction when interested typographers persuaded ATF to withdraw its plan to melt them down for brass and instead offer them to the museum as a national legacy.

21

CALEDONIA

The nineteenth century has long been considered by traditionally oriented printing historians to have been a period of aesthetic decline. According to this viewpoint, we are led to believe that little significant printing was produced between that of William Bulmer (1757–1830) and the artist William Morris (1834–96), and that the only era of printing worth remembering is the one, four hundred years ago, when the printed book was the primary product of the press. Although it is true that the nineteenth century is not particularly noted for fine printing, the innovations of industrialization can by no means be disregarded – and indeed, they made their own contributions to the art.

Technologically, in fact, the nineteenth century was one of the most exciting periods that printers have ever known, particularly in the United States. Every phase of the craft was being subjected to the scrutiny of inventive minds, and it was then that the first steps were taken to bring the industry to its present stage of automation. The typefounders were emerging from their status as mere suppliers of types for straightforward, relatively unimaginative printing: they began to produce distinctive faces that could be utilized to advertise the myriad manufactured goods that were being churned out by the Industrial Revolution. That art departments of the founders obviously had a glorious time developing these new types may be readily observed in the numerous catalogues that were prepared during that era of typographic innovation. Nevertheless, a survey of these same specimen books does show that very little space was given to text types, indicating that they were of secondary importance to the foundries, even though, ironically, they represented the bulk of the foundries' production. Types for continuous reading were most used in sizes much smaller than is common today. Possibly the difficulty of supplying distinction to 6- and 8-point types discouraged both designers and founders. By contrast, the development of modern advertising seemed to spark a competitive urge among typefounders who found aesthetic expression in the profusion of display types that, reinforcing this effort, were in continual demand throughout the century. Another factor, and one based on economics, was the high initial cost to the printer of acquiring a sufficient supply of text sizes, compared with the fewer fonts display type required.

The grand period of the classic roman types – the types of fine book printing – was past. Caslon and Baskerville and their derivatives were sadly neglected. Bodoni and Didot had made their impact, the sorry effects of which demonstrably changed roman types popular after 1800, whose forms were not at all comparable to the originals.

The finest early types combining the spirit of old style with that of the Bodoni-Didot forms dated from the end of the 1700s. Cut by Richard Austin for John Bell, this deservedly popular letter was printed at the Shakspeare Press of William Bulmer. Although the Bell and Bulmer types themselves were used primarily by their originators, the concept they represented of combining features of both old style and modern became well established. Numerous foundries in England and the United States developed standardized letter forms of this nature for straight-matter composition.

But by midcentury there no longer existed the demand for anything but the lighter and more condensed variations of Bodoni-Didot. Although printers of the twentieth century find these types dreary and monotonous, they presented to printers of the time a logical expression of typographic distinction. Dissenting from this view, however, was Theodore Low De Vinne (1828–1914), the first important American typographical historian, who, as a practicing printer, was also at the forefront of technological innovation. With this 'bi-focal' perspective, De Vinne termed the modern romans 'effeminate,' and in his *Plain Printing Types* (1900) articulated the growing opposition of experienced printers to such faces.

The best-designed of all the nineteenth-century romans were those produced in Scotland by Alexander Wilson and the firm of William Miller. The term *Scotch face* was first given to a type cut by Wilson for the S. N. Dickinson Foundery in Boston about 1837. However, the present-day type called Scotch Roman stems from the Pica Roman No. 2 of Miller & Company; it was cut (according to T. C. Hansard) about 1809 by Richard Austin for an edition of Dryden edited by Sir Walter Scott. A number of characters were redrawn, including the lowercase *t* – which was given the flat top reminiscent of the Didot

abcdefghijklmnopqrstuvwxyz
ABCDEFGHIJKLMNOPQRSTUVWXYZ
1234567890$ £ & ÆŒ
ABCDEFGHIJKLMNOPQRSTUVWXYZ&
1234567890

or steel; recently he has been drawing them greatly enlarged so that **the machine** may engrave them for him, and now he is starting to work with film so that his letters may be set photographically. However he works, *the purpose of a book-type does not change.* Apparently this discipline keeps the serious designer of book-types within the broad tradition. The conservative nature of book-type design has obvious advan-

abcdefghijklmnopqrstuvwxyz
ABCDEFGHIJKLMNOPQRSTUVWXYZ
1234567890
1234567890$ £ &
ÆTŒ

Caledonia (Linotype)

design – but the revision did not extend to the overheavy capitals. It was this recutting of Roman No. 2 that was copied by the New York foundry, Farmer, Little & Company, and which in turn became the model for the Mergenthaler Linotype Company's Scotch Roman. The English Monotype firm followed the same style in 1907, but in

1920 it revised it yet again. This fifth version stands today as the best extant reproduction of the Miller & Company type of 1813.

With the advent of machine-typesetting, the Scotch letter remained in favor, and up to the 1930s it was widely used for both book and commercial printing. But following the appearance of numerous revivals of the classic typefaces it declined in popularity. The basic fault of the American version of Scotch, in the opinion of most typographers, lies in the excessively bold capitals which present an uneven appearance in a book page. But though it has never been considered a beautiful letter, its large x-height and open counters contribute greatly to its legibility.

It was a combination of these factors that prompted the Mergenthaler Linotype Company in the late 1930s to plan a replacement for Scotch Roman. The firm persuaded William A. Dwiggins of Hingham, Massachusetts, to explore the redesign of the face in order to make it more adaptable to contemporary typographic ideas. Dwiggins had already produced the sans-serif Metro series for Linotype, in addition to the esteemed Electra, a book type with distinctly modern features. Both designs had established him as a type designer of solid accomplishment and considerable promise.

Dwiggins had good credentials as a graphic artist – calligrapher, illustrator, book designer – which he had gained before his exposure to type design. Born in Martinsville, Ohio, in 1880, he had been a student of Frederic W. Goudy's at the Frank Holme School of Illustration in Chicago. When Goudy moved his Village Press to Hingham in 1904, he persuaded Dwiggins to accompany him. Shortly thereafter, Goudy continued on to New York City, but Dwiggins remained in Hingham until his death on Christmas Day, 1956.

For more than half a century this 'black and white–smith,' as Dwiggins called himself, proved to be one of the most versatile designers of his time. As a book designer he was one of the best, attested by hundreds of volumes bearing his inimitable style and particularly those embellished with his stencil decorations. Unquestionably, he helped raise the standards of trade-book design which comprised the bulk of his work (as opposed to the production of limited editions).

In 1928 Dwiggins wrote *Layout in Advertising*, probably the best text on the subject that had ever been published in America. Despite some ephemeral material, much of this book continues to be valuable to contemporary designers, for it is written with style and without dogma.

BASKERVILLE AND SCOTCH

mnliptjohf ldonegia

DIDOT AND SCOTCH

mfupjoiat tfnade

MARTIN AND SCOTCH

amnifeupt etnapr

On the trail: *The final effort:*

hamilent mhnjuf

amulet pi dbosrt ag

mhnjup

. . . the final effort: h

Steps in the development of Caledonia

   When offered the challenge of improving Scotch Roman, Dwiggins began by drawing each character of the new font to the size of 120-point. A number of these letters were put through Linotype's design department, and trial matrices were manufactured from which type was cast and proofed. From these results Dwiggins – after 'living'

PICA—*Old Style.*

Founts of any weight with or without Italic.

SCENES IN SOUTH AFRICA.—As you penetrate into a secluded valley in South Africa, the white washed farm houses gradually unfold themselves, scattered at short intervals along the skirts of the hills, each mansion surrounded by plantations of oak and poplar, intermingled with groves and

SMALL PICA—*Old Style.*

Founts of any weight with or without Italic.

SCENES IN SOUTH AFRICA.—As you penetrate into a secluded valley in South Africa, the white washed farm houses gradually unfold themselves, scattered at short intervals along the skirts of the hills, each mansion surrounded by plantations of oak and poplar, intermingled with groves and avenues of orange and lemon trees, and with orchards producing in exuberance almost every va-

LONG PRIMER—*Old Style.*

Founts of any weight with or without Italic.

SCENES IN SOUTH AFRICA.—As you penetrate into a secluded valley in South Africa, the white washed farm houses gradually unfold themselves, scattered at short intervals along the skirts of the hills, each mansion surrounded by plantations of oak and poplar, intermingled with groves and avenues of orange and lemon trees, and with orchards producing in exuberance almost every variety of fruit, European and Tropical ;—while,

BOURGEOIS—*Old Style.*

Founts of any weight with or without Italic.

SCENES IN SOUTH AFRICA.—As you penetrate into a secluded valley in South Africa, the white washed farm houses gradually unfold themselves, scattered at short intervals along the skirts of the hills, each mansion surrounded by plantations of oak and poplar, intermingled with groves and avenues of orange and lemon trees, and with orchards producing in exuberance almost every variety of fruit, European and Tropical;—while, amidst and around the whole, appear the extensive and well dressed vineyards, sloping

Scotch types, in the specimen of Miller & Richard, Glasgow, 1876

When, in the course of human events, it becomes necessary for one people to dissolve the political bands which have connected them with another, and to assume, among the powers of the earth, the separate and equal station to which the laws of nature and of nature's God entitle them, a decent respect to the opinions of mankind require that they should declare the causes which impel them to the separation. We hold these truths to be self-evident: That *all men are created equal; that they*

ABCDEFGHIJKLMNOPQRST
1234567890

When, in the course of human events, it becomes necessary for one people to dissolve the political cal bands which have connected them with another, and to assume, among the powers of the earth, the separate and equal station to which the laws of nature and of nature's God entitle *them, a decent respect for the*

ABCDEFGHIJKLMNOP
1234567890

First showing of ATF Scotch Roman, 1909

When jobs have their type sizes fixed
quickly margins of error will widen
When jobs have the type sizes fixed
ABCDEFGHIJKLMNOPQRSTU

When jobs have type sizes
ABCDEFGHJKLMNOR

The bank recognizes this claim as quite valid
and just, so we are expecting full payments
The invitations were printed in jet black
ABCDEFGHJKLMNOPQRSTUVWXYZ

Scotch Roman (English Monotype)

with the proofs for a few days – decided whether he was on the right
track, and then proceeded to redraw, in pencil outline, his own working
drawings to a size of ten inches. Rudolph Ruzicka, another American
artist of note, called Dwiggins's approach an unparalleled *tour de force*
of type design.

'Why modify Scotch?' Dwiggins had asked. He did admit that
there was a 'wooden heaviness' about the type – particularly after
it had gone through so many recuttings since its first appearance –
and his impulse was to redesign the face in the feeling of the early
nineteenth century when Scotch had first surfaced. This, however,
proved to be unsatisfactory. 'It appears that Scotch is Scotch,' he
wrote, 'and doesn't stay Scotch if you sweat the fat off it.'

He next looked carefully at the antecedents of Scotch, the types of
Baskerville, Bodoni, and Didot. But any restyling of that eighteenth-
century triumvirate turned out to be 'merely a rehash.' He then studied
the Bulmer type, and it was here that he found the inspiration that
when applied to the basic structure of Scotch Roman resulted in one
of the most admired book types ever produced in the United States.

SCOTCH-ROMAN

THIS is the face and the size of the type selected by Messrs. Charles Scribner's Sons for their Kensington edition (octavo) of Thackeray's Novels, Poems, and other work, in thirty-two volumes. It was also used by them for Miss Hapgood's translation of the Novels and Stories of Iván Turgénieff in seventeen volumes, in large octavo. The typographical appearance of these limited editions was commended by discerning book reviewers as entirely satisfactory and as a wise return to the simplicity of early nineteenth-century printing. Of this size we have two pairs of cases for roman, and roman and italic matrices for linotype machines.

Measurement in 12-point ems

CAPITALS . 20½
SMALL CAPITALS 14
Lower-case . . 12½
ITALIC CAPS 21⅛
Italic lower-case 12¾
123456789 *234567890*

Books are not made for show.

BOOKS are written to be read and read easily, without discomfort or annoyance. The conditions of printing that favor easy reading are plain types, clear print, and freedom from surprises. Any peculiarity in the letters or in their arrangement that turns aside the reader from following the written thought is a surprise and an annoyance. It was not for a study of the caprices of a designer of letters, or of the ingenuity of the compositor who has rearranged types by new or old methods, that the book was bought. The reader reads for information or for amusement, but not for the study of typographical eccentricities. ¶ Of this size we have two pairs of cases for roman, and roman and italic matrices for linotype machines.

Measurement in 12-point ems

CAPITALS . . . 14¾
SMALL CAPITALS . . 10
Lower-case . . . 10
ITALIC CAPS . 16¾
Italic lower-case . 11
1234567890 *1234567890*

10-point. Farmer

Scotch Roman as shown in specimen book of the De Vinne Press, 1907

The new face, ready by 1941, was given the ancient name of Scotland, Caledonia.

About the only character in the font that is still recognizable as Scotch Roman is the lowercase *t*, which retains its Didot roots in its lack of a beginning serif. The Caledonia capitals are greatly improved over those of Scotch by being shorter than the lowercase ascenders, thus allowing them to blend easily with the lowercase. There are no quaint or trick characters in Caledonia. The type therefore measures up to the first requirement of a successful book type: that nothing interfere with the ideal relationship of reader to text.

No statistics are available on the number of books set in Caledonia each year, but the type is the first choice of many publishers. The index of the Fifty Books of the Year Exhibition does provide some information – the design now ranks fifth in popularity among the books chosen for that show; as its first appearance was only in 1941, this indicates how quickly the type has risen to eminence. (It is interesting to note that old Scotch Roman itself has been used for more than seventy-five books in the exhibition since 1923, an excellent showing in its own account.)

In addition, in the important area of paperback-book production Caledonia vies with Times Roman as the most widely used type for the setting of mass-market editions. This is a real tribute to its outstanding legibility even under the most trying of printing conditions.

CEX 22 XD

CHELTENHAM

The history of American typefounding really begins with the firm established in Philadelphia in 1796 by the two Scotsmen we have already met in chapter nineteen, Archibald Binny and James Ronaldson. Their company eventually became MacKellar, Smiths & Jordan, the largest and most successful of the nineteenth-century typefounders. During that century there were upward of seventy-five different manufacturers of printing types, for the burgeoning typefounding trade could scarcely keep up with the demand for the printed word. By the 1890s an enormous number of types had been designed and produced in an effort to satisfy that market. With the further development of typesetting by machine, which came into its own at the turn of the century, the number of types available to American printers had proliferated to the point where a volume of encyclopedic proportions would have been necessary to list and display them all.

Of this vast output over a period of 180 years, one type seems to stand above all the rest as the embodiment of type design that is thoroughly American: Cheltenham. (Its very English name was of course far too rich for the practicing typos, who simply called it Chelt – the independent-minded American compositors seldom bothered with the niceties of literary pronunciation, as in their rendering of *bourgeois*, the old term for 9-point, always 'burjoys.') Cheltenham is, in all probability, the most widely known type designed in the United States.

One of the reasons for the fame of Cheltenham – or notoriety, as some practitioners would have it – is that for more than half a century it has been a most controversial typeface. In the post–World War II era, when its use declined, it became the subject of numerous articles in printing-trade periodicals, most expressing divided opinions on its pedigree as a good letter form or its usefulness as a typeface.

During the 1920s, when advertising typography came into its own, the typefounders expended a great deal of effort on the creation of

253

ABCDEFGHI
JKLMNOPQR
STUVWXYZ
abcdefghijklm
nopqrstuvwxy
z 1234567890
.,-;:""!?&$

Cheltenham Bold (ATF)

types specifically for that market. The new professionals, feeling themselves especially knowledgeable about what constituted a 'good' typeface, habitually denigrated Cheltenham – even though for the preceding two decades the agency typographers could scarcely have managed without it. To attract these demanding consumers, the manufacture of printing types became extremely competitive.

The typography of the twenties enjoyed its own version of the Jazz Age; exotic letter forms proliferated, and most of them, fortunately, lasted for only brief duration. Rivaling the Americans were the European foundries, eager to cut into this big market, particularly after the innovations of the Bauhaus had made the American advertising profession aware of the advantages of typographic sophistication.

With all the fancy competition, Cheltenham's plain-Jane features stood little chance, and it became fashionable to relegate Chelt to the country printshop. Most ad typographers were extremely pained if a client pushed the matter, such as by praising the type's 'rugged characteristics.' This was borne out by the late Stevens L. Watts, who spent his career with the American Type Founders Company, retiring as manager of the typefoundry. Himself an ardent advocate of Cheltenham, he stated at one time that 'to publicly call a man a Cheltenham printer would be on a par with telling a master mariner to go and buy a farm.'

Yet back in 1902, when ATF brought out its first version of Cheltenham, the type became a veritable gold mine for the foundry, eventually being produced in more than two dozen variants. There was not a printing office in the land that didn't proudly accommodate one or more fonts of Chelt. Nevertheless, even during this heyday the use of Cheltenham was always questioned by those designers seeking a reputation for typographic savoir-faire. One of the typographic gods of the period, Douglas C. McMurtrie, put it succinctly: 'The appearance of most magazine and commercial printing will be improved by the simple expedient of denying any variants of the Cheltenham design to compositors.'

The original development of the type remains a matter of conjecture, typefounders' records being as casual as they are. The chronicle of Cheltenham is additionally obscured by its simultaneous introduction to the trade by both ATF and Mergenthaler Linotype.

What is definite, however, is that the face was first conceived as a book type by Bertram Goodhue, a considerable American architect who also happened to be active in the production of the semimonthly *Chap Book*, founded in Cambridge, Massachusetts, in 1894. Goodhue, always interested in the graphic arts, had already cut the Merrymount type for D. B. Updike's press of the same name and had executed for

THE CHELTENHAM FONT

¶ It is in characters not differing in any material item from these (the designer trusts) that this new font will be cut.

THE CHELTENHAM TYPE

Quaint enough will be this type lacking exactly what chiefly gives the Italic, its qualities of dash & zip; i.e. the kerns. J.

Original sketches of Cheltenham by Bertram Grosvener Goodhue

printers numerous designs in the spirit of the Kelmscott Press artist Edward Burne-Jones.

Also connected with the *Chap Book* project was Ingalls Kimball of the Cheltenham Press, a New York printing firm. At Kimball's suggestion, Goodhue prepared a type for the private use of the press. Goodhue later sold the design to the Mergenthaler firm, while retaining his right to the single-type version. In 1902, ATF also purchased the design.

It was Goodhue's intent to create a book type in which legibility would be the dominant element. He therefore designed an alphabet of rather monotonous construction, including serifs similar to the Clarendon styles of fifty years earlier. It was in the treatment of the ascenders and descenders that Goodhue's premise was most evident. Believing that the upper half of a line of type is the more important for recognition, the designer lengthened the ascenders and shortened the descenders of the letters. This feature also allowed for economical composition, since leading could be dispensed with, even in longer-than-average lines. Goodhue's theory has been borne out by more recent studies of typographic legibility, but Cheltenham nevertheless

SCARE
Just Held

FENCED
Clear Bend

DESIGNER
Useful Letters

First showing of Cheltenham by American Type Founders Co., 1903

was not to become a popular type for straight-matter composition as employed in books and periodicals. It was as a display type that it would develop its reputation, primarily because of the large number of variants that appeared during the next two decades.

Cheltenham Oldstyle	CHELTENHAM BOLD EXTRA CONDENSED TITLE
Cheltenham Wide	Cheltenham Bold Extended
Cheltenham Medium	Cheltenham Extrabold
Cheltenham Bold	Cheltenham Inline
Cheltenham Bold Condensed	Inline Extra Condensed
Cheltenham Bold Extra Condensed	Inline Extended
Cheltenham Bold Outline	Cheltenham Medium Expanded
Cheltenham Oldstyle Condensed	Cheltenham Medium Condensed
Cheltenham Italic	**Chelt Extrabold Shaded**
Cheltenham Medium Italic	*Cheltenham Bold Italic Shaded*
Cheltenham Bold Italic	Cheltenham Bold Shaded
Cheltenham Bold Condensed Italic	

The Cheltenham "family" of Types, c. 1918

By the turn of the century, ATF had shaken off the growing pains it had been enduring as the new typefounding conglomerate of the early nineties: the growls from the trade about the 'Type Trust' were dying out. Under dynamic new leadership, the firm was about to embark on a great period in the marketing of types. Although earlier styles – notably De Vinne and Philadelphia Lining Gothic – had proved the success of the so-called 'family' idea in printing types (variants in both weight and width), it was with Cheltenham that the theory really blossomed. By 1915 Morris Benton, ATF's director of type design, had cut twenty-one variations of the original Cheltenham, and the name was now almost a household word, certainly reaching far beyond the confines of the nation's composing rooms.

The Linotype firm, beginning about 1904, eventually brought out ten Cheltenham variants plus special advertising figures. The Monotype company followed with fifteen varieties of Cheltenham, Ludlow Typograph Company produced thirteen, and a dozen variations were marketed by the Intertype Corporation. Thus by 1920 every American supplier of printing types was producing Cheltenham. It was inevitable that its style would dominate the period's typography.

Foreign typefounders quickly followed suit, selling Cheltenham

A HAPPY FACE IS A FACE
THAT GIVES JOY, AND THE
CHELTENHAM—*SO APT,*
SO FITTING—IS THIS KIND

IT is undoubtedly the *most popular type face* that has been brought out in recent years. Judging by the *satisfaction* with which it was received the design was a most *fortunate* one, and it came at an opportune time measured by the demand which immediately sprang up. Scarcely had the *American Type Founders Company* finished the *fourteen sizes* in the *Cheltenham Oldstyle series* when requests came for an *Italic series* to go with it. The present series of *Cheltenham Italic* was the result. Its introduction met with an *immediate success,* and orders came in from the largest publishers and job printing offices, until now it is hardly possible to pick up a publication of any merit without a showing of the complete series of both the *Cheltenham Oldstyle* and the *Cheltenham Italic* being prominently displayed therein. A still further demand necessitated designing the other Cheltenhams shown on following pages. In fact, many among the most prominent advertisers in the country have *requested* that this face be the one used to *display their matter* as it so fittingly challenges the eye of the reading public. The distinguished character of the *Cheltenham family* is so pronounced that the first glance reveals a design of decidedly unusual character that shows *qualities never before attained* in any other type face. *It is in a class by itself.* In

Cheltenham Oldstyle and Cheltenham Italic in combination

cutting the other *Cheltenhams* to complement the *Cheltenham Oldstyle* the same lines that gave distinction to the first series were followed, and all have been as satisfactory as the original one. The *Cheltenham* family has been the type sensation of the year, and their necessity in every properly equipped printing plant is quite apparent

A typical Cheltenham advertisement by ATF, 1906

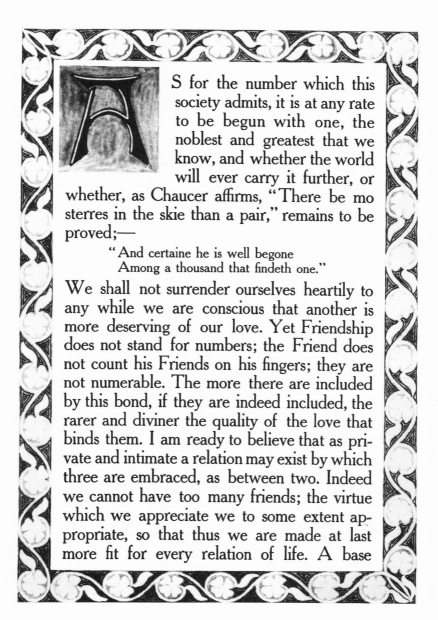

AS for the number which this society admits, it is at any rate to be begun with one, the noblest and greatest that we know, and whether the world will ever carry it further, or whether, as Chaucer affirms, "There be mo sterres in the skie than a pair," remains to be proved;—

> "And certaine he is well begone
> Among a thousand that findeth one."

We shall not surrender ourselves heartily to any while we are conscious that another is more deserving of our love. Yet Friendship does not stand for numbers; the Friend does not count his Friends on his fingers; they are not numerable. The more there are included by this bond, if they are indeed included, the rarer and diviner the quality of the love that binds them. I am ready to believe that as private and intimate a relation may exist by which three are embraced, as between two. Indeed we cannot have too many friends; the virtue which we appreciate we to some extent appropriate, so that thus we are made at last more fit for every relation of life. A base

Cheltenham as used in Thoreau's *Friendship*, Roycroft Press

Goodhue's earliest book decorations were made while he was still in New York before his association with Ralph Adams Cram in the firm of Cram, Wentworth & Goodhue in Boston, where he was drawn into the companionship of a group of young men interested in good bookmaking, and where he produced those fine drawings which are found often in the publications of Copeland & Day, and less often in those of other publishers. Many very beautiful book decorations, as well as a distinguished fount of types, were designed for D. Berkeley Updike in the early days of the Merrymount Press.

Cheltenham medium used as a book type in Goodhue biography

under several different names. The English firm Stephenson, Blake & Company called it Winchester; English Monotype listed it as Gloucester; and a Dresden foundry named it Pfeil Antiqua. Steve Watts loved to tell of a version he found in a Japanese specimen book called Chentury Bold.

Two or three American founders, still outside the ATF fold, picked up the type while it was in its prime, so even up to the present it is possible to run across fonts of Inland Foundry's Kenilworth or Western Foundry's Chesterfield in the cases of country printers.

By any name, Chelt is going to be around for a long time. Naturally, it has been transferred to the phototypesetting devices and is therefore continuing its life in that medium. Undoubtedly, given typography's addiction to type trends, Cheltenham will have its ups and downs, but whenever a vigorous, legible display face is needed, this type will prove as useful as ever. And though it is rarely selected for books, Time-Life Books recently made an interesting experiment in choosing Cheltenham for its series on the Old West: Cheltenham Medium is employed for the text of each volume, thus being returned to Bertram Goodhue's original reason for designing it.

BOOKMAN

The revival of historic printing types is a continuing process which in many instances can be attributed to nothing more than a search for novelty. Obviously, display type with its function of catching the eye is more subject to such resurrection than is book type. Occasionally, however, a face that serves both media is subject to a regeneration.

Bookman is a case in point. About 1968 this turn-of-the-century typeface was selected for an advertising campaign of United Airlines, appearing in all the important consumer magazines. Exactly what prompted the use of Bookman is problematical, but perhaps the fact that the font featured a number of decorative letter variants met the particular requirements of the type director of the advertising agency. The restoration also coincided with a small rebirth of art nouveau in advertising circles, and given Bookman's roots in that style, it no doubt appeared to be a logical choice.

Bookman has had a curious history, which can be likened to that of Cheltenham; that is, it has been both damned and praised at the same time. Every instance of its use over the years could almost guarantee controversy. Daniel Berkeley Updike, dean of typographic orthodoxy in the United States, did not even mention it in any of his books. Yet fellow-Bostonian William A. Dwiggins, one of the best of American graphic designers, considered Bookman a candidate for 'reasonable human perfection' as a display type, and very close to that standard for 'grace in the mass.' Another New Englander of great typographic accomplishment who agreed with Dwiggins was Carl Purington Rollins, Printer to Yale University. He considered the design 'a simple and honest and self-effacing type.' Among the most charming editions of *Walden* is the one Rollins designed for the Heritage Press in 1939, in which he coupled Bookman with the wood engravings of Thomas W. Nason to create an almost perfect match of type and illustration.

Another distinguished use of Bookman was in the *Tom Sawyer*

REGARD

New Shop

QUESTION

The Job Office

RANCH BAR

Signal *of* Quality

MODERN & CHIC

Great displays typify

Bookman Oldstyle (ATF)

Benevolent Members
GENEROUS
Granite Received Monthly
MONUMENTS
International Societies Celebrate
DEMONSTRATION
Frolicsome Excursionists in Snowstorms
LOVINGLY WAITING

Old Style Antique of MacKellar, Smiths & Jordan foundry

printed by Elmer Adler in 1930, which received the accolade of being chosen for the Fifty Books of the Year Exhibition. Going still further back, a wide use of Bookman occurred about 1900, when Elbert Hubbard decided that it was about as close as he could come to the typographical style of William Morris, whom he emulated at his Roycroft Press. In thousands of rural American homes the Bookman-composed Roycroft volumes, bound in suede, represented the ultimate of sophistication in the accumulation of a modest library.

However it was its commercial use that kept Bookman active as a standard type during the first quarter of this century. When a designer of that time was confronted with reproduction by offset lithography or gravure, the specification of Bookman seemed *de rigueur* – it didn't appear necessary (or possible) to bother with typographic niceties when faced with the imprecision of early photomechanics, so the rugged Bookman was the choice for any such printing processes in which hairlines were reproduced haphazardly if at all. For many years the best example of this approach was the weekly edition of *Collier's* printed by the gravure process.

In 1925 J. L. Frazier, longtime editor of the *Inland Printer* and

ABCDEFGHIJKLMNOPQRSTUVWXYZ
abcdefghijklmnopqrstuvwxyz
(&$1234567890£.,;:'"""-!?) 1234567890
cAAAAABBᴄCCᴄᴅDᴅEEEᴇEFFF
GᴄGHHH'ᴛᴛᴛᴛᴛᴊKᴋKᴋKᴋKᴋKᴋLLᴛᴛL
MᴛMMMᴛMMᴛNᴛNᴛNᴏOPᴛPᴏPᴏQᴏQᴏQᴏQQ
RᴛRᴛRᴛRRRᴛSS ᴤSTTTᴛᴄUUᴄUᴄUᴄVVᴄVᴄVV
WᴄWᴄWWᴄWXXXXᴄyᴄᴄYᴄYYZZ&ᴄ&ᴄ&ᴄ&?
aᴄabbcddᴄddᴄeeeeffffgᴄgᴄghhᴛhᴄhhᴛhhbiᴛiᴛjᴄj
kᴋkkᴋkᴋkᴋkᴋ.lllᴛlᴛmᴛmᴛmnnᴛnᴛnᴛooᴄpᴄbbpqᴛ.pᴛrᴛrssᴄgᴄs
tᴛtᴛtᴛuuᴛvᴛvᴛwᴄᴄwwxxᴄᴄxᴄᴄxᴄᴄxxxyᴄyᴄzᴛzzz

Photo version of Bookman, with swash variants

the typographic authority for a majority of small printing shops, surveyed the advertising in four national magazines of that year for type use. He discovered that out of 404 ads, 125 were composed in Caslon and 78 in Bookman (he didn't disclose the number set in Cheltenham, but quite possibly it was the other 201, that being the state of advertising typography in 1925 just prior to the advent of the 'Jazz Age' types and the sans-serif revolution generated by the Bauhaus).

Theodore L. De Vinne in *Plain Printing Types*, which was published in 1900 (and is still an excellent source of information on types), discussed some of the reasons for the popularity of heavy faces for book composition at the turn of the century. He stated that the book critics had 'rightfully complained of a deficiency in blackness of ink in recent [nineteenth-century] books' – this comment, of course, echoes the fundamental criticism of William Morris when he established the Kelmscott Press. The reason for the 'deficiency in blackness' in the 1800s is articulated in 'Nineteenth-Century Reactions Against the Didone Type Model' (in *Quarendo*, 1976), by the astute typographic historian Professor G. W. Ovink of Amsterdam. Ovink pointed out

A USEFUL TYPE
For Variety Of Fine
printing and $67890

UNIFORMITY
Was The Motive
in the creation of

VERY NICE
In Books, Ads
and job work

IN ADS IT
brings sales

New Bookman, designed for Monotype by Sol Hess

that the modern faces had become increasingly condensed, and that 'a reaction against these crawling masses of heavy, parallel lines was inevitable.'

It was the exigencies of mid-nineteenth-century typography that had called for complementary types of greater weight than possessed by the standard old styles. This situation resulted about 1858 in the cutting by the Scottish foundry Miller & Richard of a type that was named Old Style Antique. The first American firm to produce a similar face was MacKellar, Smiths & Jordan, which issued its Old Style Antique in 1869. Many other typefoundries followed suit within the next few years, making Old Style Antique one of the most popular designs. Tracing the transition of Old Style Antique to Bookman is particularly confusing, partly because of the reorganization of the many American foundries into the American Type Founders Company in 1892 and the subsequent amalgamation of matrix production into a single standard.

It appears, however, that Wadsworth A. Parker is responsible for the name Bookman, about 1900, and it is the Old Style Antique No. 310 of the Bruce Foundry that became the ATF version of Bookman. (Parker had had the responsibility of producing the specimens for the Bruce Foundry, and he continued in the same capacity at ATF.) He is also credited with the innovation that has undoubtedly contributed to Bookman's current popularity – the addition of the swash characters and logotypes to both the roman and italic fonts. The italic supplied to Bookman is an oblique, or sloped, roman style, which retains some of the legibility of the roman when used in the mass; this departure from the normal italic is a feature that endeared Bookman to many typographers confronted with copy containing an abundance of italic.

The earliest ATF showing of the type, under the name Bookman Roman, occurs in the *American Line Specimen Book*, of 1903. The italic was initially shown in a supplement to that volume, issued in 1905.

Old Style Antique continued in use for many years, thanks to a mechanical improvement added to the Linotype machine about 1900. This was the duplex (two-letter) matrix, which could contain both a roman and an italic, thus simplifying the composition of roman and italic type in the same line. However, in the typography of newspapers italic is not widely used in the news columns, editors preferring boldface in its place. Confronted with this requirement, the Mergenthaler firm supplied an Old Style Antique as the second character on

CHAPTER X

The two boys flew on and on, toward the village, speechless with horror. They glanced backward over their shoulders from time to time, apprehensively, as if they feared they might be followed. Every stump that started up in their path seemed a man and an enemy, and made them catch their breath; and as they sped by some outlying cottages that lay near the village, the barking of the aroused watch-dogs seemed to give wings to their feet.

"If we can only get to the old tannery before we break down!" whispered Tom, in short catches between breaths, "I can't stand it much longer."

Huckleberry's hard pantings were his only reply, and the boys fixed their eyes on the goal of their hopes and bent to their work to win it. They gained steadily on it, and at last, breast to breast, they burst through the open door and fell grateful and exhausted in the sheltering shadows beyond. By and by their pulses slowed down, and Tom whispered:

"Huckleberry, what do you reckon 'll come of this?"

"If Dr. Robinson dies, I reckon hanging 'll come of it."

"Do you though?"

"Why, I *know* it, Tom."

Tom thought awhile, then he said:

"Who'll tell? We?"

"What are you talking about? S'pose something happened and Injun Joe *didn't* hang? Why he'd kill us some time or other, just as dead sure as we're a-laying here."

"That's just what I was thinking to myself, Huck."

"If anybody tells, let Muff Potter do it, if he's fool enough. He's generally drunk enough."

Tom said nothing—went on thinking. Presently he whispered:

"Huck, Muff Potter don't *know* it. How can he tell?"

"What's the reason he don't know it?"

"Because he'd just got that whack when Injun Joe done it. D' you reckon he could see anything? D' you reckon he knowed anything?"

"By hokey, that's so, Tom!"

"And besides, look-a-here—maybe that whack done for *him!*"

"No, 'tain't likely, Tom. He had liquor in him; I could see that; and besides, he always has. Well, when pap's full, you might take and belt him over the head with a church and you couldn't phase him. He says so, his own self. So

it's the same with Muff Potter, of course. But if a man was dead sober, I reckon maybe that whack might fetch him; I dono."

After another reflective silence, Tom said:

"Hucky, you sure you can keep mum?"

"Tom, we *got* to keep mum. *You* know that. That Injun devil wouldn't make any more of drownding us than a couple of cats, if we was to squeak 'bout this and they didn't hang him. Now, look-a-here, Tom, less take and swear to one another—that's what we got to do—swear to keep mum."

Bookman as used in Pynson Printers edition of *The Adventures of Tom Sawyer*, New York, 1930

the matrix. In later years, of course, it became necessary to design a proper matching boldface for more sophisticated use, but the use of the term *antique* for this purpose continued for the earlier styles which were not modernized.

The two-letter matrix, though accepted as a practicality, was never approved of by typographers. Normally an italic is of narrower set width than a roman, as a comparison of alphabets of single type will disclose. But a slug-machine italic had to be the same width as the roman as it occupied the same matrix. The italic therefore appeared deficient. In the matter of boldface, a similar difficulty was apparent, as normally the bold letter would be wider than the normal weight. Nevertheless, in the United States typesetting by the slug machine became the main method of composition, so the two-letter matrix was employed. The advent of phototypesetting will alleviate some of the earlier mechanical constrictions of the older machines, but no doubt there will still be problems in maintaining purity of letter form.

Bookman today is generally thought of as a type for advertising and commercial use. Present typographic taste in book design being what it is, it is doubtful that the old-style antiques will ever return to general favor. In the future, therefore, we can expect to continue to see Bookman mostly in advertising. And given the vagaries of that world, it is difficult to predict when Bookman may be returned to honest retirement.

TIMES ROMAN

Of all the typefaces developed during the past seventy years, Times Roman is the one most frequently singled out as typifying the twentieth century. The design is currently available to printers from all the standard sources – foundry type, Monotype, Linotype, Intertype, and Ludlow – in addition to most of the phototypesetting machines, both keyboard and hand-operated. Times Roman has even been digitized for the cathode-ray-tube typesetters. It is a universal type.

The design of the font is credited to Stanley Morison, the noted English typographic historian, who was asked by the management of *The Times* of London to restyle that newspaper in 1929. The circumstance that prompted this move was Morison's brusque article 'Newspaper Types: A Study of *The Times*,' which was written for a special number of that paper devoted to twentieth-century printing issued on October 29, 1929. In it Morison severely criticized *The Times* for being both badly printed and typographically out of date. The commission to redesign it was a challenge that pre-empted his censure.

In his article Morison had said that the *Times*'s typeface (a nineteenth-century modern roman) was 'cut off from the mainstream of typographic endeavour.' Continuing, he stated, 'For, whereas the history of the craft is that of letter-cutting and founding as applied to the printing of books, the history of newspapers is that of mechanical development of the typesetting machine and the power press – the newspapers being left untouched, either by the aesthetic movement of the nineties or the arts and crafts movement represented by William Morris.' At a meeting of a committee of important staff members of the newspaper, Morison went on to say that in his opinion the types employed for *The Times* should 'be brought to the standard obtaining in the average book as brought out by London publishers.'

It so happened that during the 1920s there had been an increasing interest in the study of legibility factors in type design on the part of both typographers and psychologists. There also existed a wide

ABCDEFGHIJKLMNO
12345 PQRSTUVWXYZ 67890
abcdefghijklmnopqrstuvwxyz
ABCDEFGHIJKLMNO
12345 PQRSTUVWXYZ 67890
abcdefghijklmnopqrstuvwxyz

Times New Roman (English Monotype)

divergence of opinion on whether continued research in the legibility of printing type should follow aesthetic or mechanical concepts. One of the most important of the early studies of the subject had recently been published, by His Majesty's Stationery Office, R. L. Pyke's *The Legibility of Print* (1926).

A further stimulation to Morison's thinking was the 1926 cutting in America of Ionic by the Mergenthaler Linotype Company. Ionic was the first of a series of so-called legibility types produced for newspaper use. It had immediate and enormous success, for it was designed specifically to meet the mechanical requirements of modern newspaper production.

As early as the last decade of the nineteenth century, the noted American printer Theodore L. De Vinne and Linn Boyd Benton of the American Type Founders Company had jointly produced a 'type for a purpose' in the Century design, created for the specialized printing requirements of *Century* magazine. The Cheltenham type of Bertram Goodhue, issued by ATF in 1902, was also originally conceived as a legibility type for the printing of books. In addition, the French Alphonse Legros and the English J. C. Grant in their authoritative manual on the mechanics of typesetting, *Typographical Printing Surfaces* (1916), included a chapter on legibility. All of this activity in the area of typographic legibility provided impetus to the perception that the style of *The Times* was due for a complete revision.

efforts which this has involved to the British nation, coming as they did after the losses resulting from the War, constitute, in the view of his Majesty's Government, a strong claim to consideration on the part of the United States Government.

5. The Increase in the Burden

His Majesty's Government also call attention to the changes of circumstances which have increased the burden of their obligations.

In the first place the British debt is expressed in terms of gold, but the burden on the British people is measured in terms of sterling. The payment due on December 15 is owing to this circumstance increased from £19,750,000 to approximately £30,000,000.

In the second place the average wholesale price index in the United States of America during the period when the debt was incurred was 189, and is now under 94 (taking 1913 as a basis in each case). The debt therefore represents to-day in terms of goods not less than twice the amount which was borrowed.

In the third place the effect of the American Tariff has been to restrict the import of the manufactured goods which the United Kingdom produces. In 1923 when the British War Debt was funded, the War Debt annuity amounted to £33,000,000, or approximately half the value of the British domestic exports to the United States (£60,000,000). From 1933 onwards the annuity in respect of the War Debt would amount at present rates of exchange to approximately £60,000,000; whereas the British domestic exports to the United States of America this year are not likely to exceed £16,000,000.

The imports into the United Kingdom from the United States show an equally remarkable fall from £211,000,000 in 1923 to £59,000,000 in the first nine months of 1932. The total trade between the two countries from the time of the Funding Agreement has fallen from about £300,000,000 a year to £100,000,000.

6. Economic Reactions of Resuming War Debt Payments

The United Kingdom has up to the present generally been the best customer of the United States, but, if War Debt payments had to be resumed, the very heavy adverse balance of visible trade between the United Kingdom and the United States of America (£78,000,000 in 1931) would have to be reduced by adopting measures which would further restrict British purchases of American goods. To the extent, therefore, that payments were resumed to the United States Treasury a definite loss must follow to the United States producer.

Moreover, his Majesty's Government would also have to guard against the effects which would follow if the unique facilities offered by the British market to the world's goods were used by the other debtors of America to obtain sterling which they would then sell across the

WASHINGTON VIEWS

DISCUSSIONS AT WHITE HOUSE

THE EFFECT ON CONGRESS

FROM OUR OWN CORRESPONDENT

WASHINGTON, DEC. 1

A copy of the second British Note was sent at 8.30 this morning to the residence of Mr. Stimson and by him was at once taken to President Hoover at the White House. Mr. Mills, Secretary of the Treasury, was summoned into conference there and the Note was discussed at length. Later in the morning Mr. Stimson went to the State Department, where he was joined by the British Ambassador. It was then announced that the text of the Note would be given to the Press soon after the Stock Exchange was closed for the day.

There is no reason to doubt that Mr. Stimson was able to convey to Sir Ronald Lindsay the conclusions which Mr. Hoover had reached and to indicate in general the nature of the President's recommendations to Congress next week, as these may have been affected by the arguments of the British Government. It is common knowledge that, independently of their presentation by London, these arguments are in a large sense found convincing not only by Mr. Hoover, but by all those whose executive position here gives them a knowledge of and a concern in the world situation. What effect the British Note, the recommendations Mr. Hoover will make, and the growing mass of opinion favourable to friendly adjustment will have upon Congress is still doubtful almost to the point of despair.

AGRICULTURISTS' VIEWS

It is true that some hold to the belief that a deeper impression was made upon those members of the Senate Finance and House Ways and Means committees who were called in by the President some time ago than could discreetly appear in the statement of views issued by Mr. Hoover soon after they had left him. If this is so these gentlemen have signally failed to make this evident. It is true also that the agricultural interests, for the relief of

RENT CONTROL

CHANGES IN NEW BILL

RIGHTS OF TENANT AND LANDLORD

From Our Parliamentary Correspondent

Important changes in the present law of rent restriction and control are contained in the Government's new Rent and Mortgage Interest Restrictions (Amendment) Bill, the text of which will be issued to-day. It is hoped to obtain a second reading before the Christmas recess.

The Bill carries out the main recommendations of the report of the Departmental Committee which sat during the life of the Labour Government under the chairmanship of Lord Marley. It recognizes that private enterprise has now caught up with the demand for the best type of houses which were controlled under the original legislation. It is rapidly catching up with the second type of house, for the better-class artisan, but it has not yet solved the problem of providing cheap houses for the lowest-paid sections of the community. Where houses of this type are decontrolled the rent may jump up to 80 per cent. above the pre-War figure, and the Government recognize that for these houses full control must continue.

PLAN FOR FIVE YEARS

The Bill accordingly proposes that there shall be immediate decontrol of houses with a rateable value which in 1931 was more than £45 in the Metropolitan Police District, £35 in the rest of England and Wales, and £45 in Scotland. A period of six months will elapse before mortgages on these houses are decontrolled. Houses with a rateable value between £20 and £45 in the Metropolitan Police District, £13 and £35 in the rest of England and Wales and £26 5s. and £45 in Scotland will still be subject to decontrol when they become vacant. Houses with a rateable value below these figures will cease to be decontrolled when they become vacant, but houses which are already decontrolled will remain decontrolled. A register will be kept by local authorities of houses falling within these limits which are already decontrolled, and if a landlord does not register a house within a specified time it will be treated as controlled. The Bill will remain operative for five years, and if it is not renewed rent restriction will then come to an end.

Times New Roman as used in *The Times* (London) edition of December 2, 1932

Part of the popularity enjoyed by Linotype Ionic, a design of Clarendon origin, was due to its rich color, a feature contrasting favorably with the rather anemic modern romans then widely used in newspapers. Morison disapproved of these romans, believing that the 'colorful' juxtaposition of stroke differences as represented by the

---

old-style letter forms was preferable to the monotony of the antique style.

In his report to the publisher Morison wrote:

The Times will not be recommended to introduce anything remotely resembling the aesthetic faces of the private press movement of the 19th century, nor one of the mass production faces which American newspapermen have recently brought out, but rather . . . by articulating the problem of a new type with relevant detail of past and present practice, to assist the Committee towards the adoption of a font which shall be English in its basic tradition, new, though free from conscious archaism or conscious art, losing no scintilla of that 'legibility,' which rests upon fundamental ocular laws, or that of 'readability,' which rests upon age-long customs of the eye.

There have been several accounts of the provenance of Times New Roman, the name of the type created for the restyling of the newspaper. Morison is, of course, listed as its designer, but it is obvious that since he was not a draftsman he could not have drawn the type himself. Rather, he brought his ideas to an artist, who prepared the drawings from which the type was cut.

Although Morison had commended what he called the technical superiority of Ionic, he stated that for the *Times*'s purposes it would be more productive to redesign a nineteenth-century modern type albeit with an approach similar to Ionic's. It is therefore perplexing that he in fact turned to the old-style form once he was charged with preparing a new type. One must assume that in arriving at his decision Morison was impressed by R. L. Pyke's praise in his legibility report for three Monotype faces, two of which were old-style. Whatever the case, Morison selected Monotype Plantin 113 as the model for the new newspaper type.

Morison then asked Victor Lardent, an artist employed in the *Times*'s advertising department, to study a photographic copy of a page printed by Christopher Plantin, the sixteenth-century Antwerp printer. The type shown on this page had been identified as a Robert Granjon cutting and had already been used as the source of Monotype Plantin. Lardent worked up alphabets from this model, which were subsequently revised by Morison until his desired effects were attained. Basically, these were maximum legibility and economy of space, displaying the salient attributes of the finest book types.

The design that emerged from the Morison-Lardent collaboration resembles its Plantin model in outline, but its sharp serifs and higher degrees of contrast lend it a sparkle never achieved by Monotype

Plantin. As the type already employed by the newspaper was called Times Old Roman, the revision became simply Times New Roman. American manufacturers of the type have dropped the 'New.'

On October 3, 1932, *The Times* appeared in its new typeface. The newspaper held exclusive rights to the type for just one year, after which the design was released for copies produced by the Linotype and Intertype firms.

The new face was very successful for *The Times*, but it never gained popularity with other newspapers, particularly in the United States. The reason for this lies in the procedures of newspaper production. *The Times* was unique in its use of newsprint that was a good deal whiter (and, of course, more expensive) than that of other periodicals; the paper held a stronger impression than lower-quality newsprints, carrying more ink on the page. To most newspaper publishers such printing was a luxury not to be imitated. Thus Times Roman, which for its success required higher-quality newsprint, never replaced the standard legibility types in American newspapers. But it soon came into favor as a type for book and commercial printing.

Writing in 1953, Stanley Morison said of his design, now flourishing outside the world of newsprint: 'Morris would have denounced the heresy of the original cutting immediately. As a new face it should, by the grace of God and the art of man, have been broad and open, generous and ample; instead, by the vice of Mammon and the misery of the machine, it is bigoted and narrow, mean and puritan.' Contemporary critical opinion, nevertheless, favors Morison over Morris (although it should be pointed out that without Morris's impact on the consciousness of printers, there would have been relatively few with sufficient typographic sophistication to have an opinion of any kind concerning type designs).

Perhaps an indication of the value of Times Roman as a book type of the first order was its purchase by the extremely conservative D. B. Updike of the Merrymount Press in Boston, who became the first American printer to employ the design. Indeed, Updike's own last book – *Some Aspects of Printing, Old and New*, published in 1941 (the year of his death) – is set in the Morison type.

The American use of Times Roman increased when David Silve, as consultant to the Crowell-Collier Publishing Company, recommended the face for the restyling of the firm's magazines. The December 1941 issue of *Woman's Home Companion* accordingly published a spread in Times New Roman (set by the Merrymount Press), and by August

behind a change of type face, serious for any newspaper, are doubly so for a journal of this scope.

Fortunately, in addition to its individual experience, *The Times* could draw upon a rich fund of knowledge derived from the comprehensive printing supplements which it issued in 1913 and 1930, and the special supplement dealing with the printing of books which was presented with its *Literary Supplement* of October, 1928. With such an accumulation of data it was possible to design with some confidence the three new body founts, 5½, 7, and 9 point ; to design, also, a complete series of heading founts ; and to prepare every detail in Printing House Square.

The new designs, controlled by the specific requirements of the case, differ from the text and heading founts of every other press, or newspaper, or book printer in the world. " *The Times* New Roman " (as it is called) *is* new ; but while it is an innovation, it is also something of a reaction. The " modern " type characteristic of the English newspapers is, as has been said, a version. of the design which, invented between 1780 and 1790, came to full development between 1800 and 1820. By the time Queen Victoria ascended the throne it had completely supplanted, whether in books or in newspapers, the early Georgian " old face " cut by William Caslon and used in *The Times* until November, 1799. Caslon's design stems directly through Garamond to a roman first used by Aldus in 1495. " *The Times* New Roman " possesses many structural features to be found in this distinguished archetype. Nevertheless, it is not exactly an " old face," for its sharp serifs are tokens of " modern face." It is a newspaper type—and hardly a book type—for it is strictly appointed for use in short lines—*i.e.*, in columns. A modified design will be cut for book-work. Typographical pundits will probably classify the design as a " modernized old face." Ordinary

---

Times New Roman used as a book type in *Printing the Times*, by Stanley Morison

ABCDEFGHIJKLM *NOPQRSTUVWX*
abcdefghijklmno *pqrstuvwxyz*

Plantin (English Monotype)

1942 the entire magazine employed the type. Following suit were the *American* magazine in October and *Collier's* in December.

However, the wide use of Times Roman in American printing did not take place until the close of the Second World War. Since then it has been chosen primarily for commercial printing, magazines, and books (a few newspapers use it, but it has never been able to compete with other legibility types designed for ordinary newsprint). Its popularity constitutes solid proof of Morison's dictum 'For a new font to be successful, it has to be so good that only very few recognize its novelty.'

The universality of the acceptance of Times Roman has in turn served to enlarge its usefulness. The English Monotype firm has adapted the type to Greek and Cyrillic, provided long descenders for book work, added several weights, and supplied the countless extra characters necessary in the various printing specialties but so rarely provided in types brought out for general use.

Alas, despite all this, *The Times* in 1972 abandoned the type it had spawned. The paper went over to a new letter, named Times Europa, which lends itself more favorably to the newest methods of newspaper production – phototypesetting and web-offset reproduction.

NEWSPAPER TYPES

In the days before a Baltimore mechanic-watchmaker named Ottmar Mergenthaler invented the machine that industrialized typesetting in 1884, most nineteenth-century newspapers were composed in typefaces that can be loosely termed modern romans.

The origins of such types stemmed from the innovations in the latter years of the eighteenth century of Giambattista Bodoni in Italy and the Didot dynasty of printers in France. By 1800 English typefounders were beginning to produce types resembling these Continental styles but with an admixture of Caslon and Baskerville. The resulting adulteration was not at all distinguished, but the types were reasonably legible in the sizes called nonpareil, minion, brevier, and bourgeois (today referred to as 6-, 7-, 8-, and 9-point), those sizes commonly used for newspaper composition.

The modern romans also bore up well under the wear and tear of printing on newsprint, a low-grade paper, and readily survived the rigors of stereotype molding for both newspaper and book printing. By the mid-nineteenth century the stereotype duplicate plate was a great help to the book printer, who always seemed to be running out of type in his cases. Its wide use probably precluded a more rapid development of the composing machines, since types lasted longer when it was not necessary to print directly from them. In fact, Mergenthaler first experimented with a typesetter that produced a stereotype molding, but it was not until the development of the rotary press, in the 1860s, that stereotyping became common in the larger newspaper offices.

Typographic historians have tended to disregard the newspaper typefaces. Since inventive inspiration in the great expansionist period of the post–Civil War era was diverted in printing to mechanical devices, the aesthetics of type design were rarely considered. Thus, most book types and newspaper fonts appeared to have almost identical characteristics, hardly enhancing the heritage of classic letter forms. And as their parentage was somewhat suspect, they have generally been left out of the standard histories. Daniel Berkeley Updike, for example, in his *Printing Types* (1922), speaks of newspaper types exactly once (in a description of the specimen sheet of Alexander Wilson & Son, the Glasgow typefounding firm). He did, however, mention the first stereotyped book, printed in London in 1804, which was set in a type he termed modern and was clearly a forerunner of the newspaper types appearing later in the century.

Theodore L. De Vinne in his *Plain Printing Types* (1900) describes the typical stubby serifs and few kerned letters resulting from the requirements of molding wax or plaster. These factors, naturally enough, worked against the continuation of the Bodoni-Didot tradition of strong contrast and hairline serifs. Book and newspaper printers were beginning to demand more utilitarian styles to meet the exigencies of an increasingly mechanized industry.

De Vinne, who was an innovative practical printer in addition to being a typographic scholar, also believed that the replacement of the hand presses by cylinder presses had contributed to the printers' decline in enthusiasm for the long ascenders and descenders of the Bodoni styles. He wrote that such types 'could not properly resist the force applied' by the advanced press equipment then coming into wide use. So the tendency of both typefounders and printers during most of the nineteenth century was to steer clear of aesthetic complications in printing production. This resulted, unfortunately, in the development of letter forms that, despite their poor designs, eventually became standard for the composition of continuous reading material.

That these letters were characterless, truly anemic, in appearance seemed to matter very little. Possibly because of their lack of individuality, they were designated by number rather than by name, even after naming type designs had become a common practice. A numbering system also made it easier for a founder to market a copy of a competitor's type; so Minion No. 2, for example, was reissued as Minion No. 5.

A concurrent blandness permeated the typographic output of straight-matter types in the 1840s. Visual relief depended on the development at this time of the myriad display types of kaleidoscopic variety that characterize for us nineteenth-century typography. Indeed, the constant demand for decorative display faces made their

WHEN, in the course of human events, it becomes necessary for one people to dissolve the political bands which have connected them with another, and to assume, among the powers of the earth, the separate and equal station to which the laws of nature and of nature's God entitle them, a decent respect to the opinions of mankind requires that they should declare the causes which impel them to the separation. We hold these truths to be self-evident, that all men are created equal ; that they are endowed by their Creator with certain unalienable rights ; that among these, are life, liberty, and the pursuit of happiness. That, to secure these rights, governments are instituted among men, deriving their just powers from the consent of the governed ; that, whenever any form of government becomes destructive of these ends, it is the right of the people *to alter or to abolish it, and to institute a new government, laying its foundation on such principles, and organizing its powers in such form, as to them*

ABCDEFGHIJKLMNOPQRSTUVWXYZ
1234567890

WHEN, in the course of human events, it becomes necessary for one people to dissolve the political bands which have connected them with another, and to assume, among the powers of the earth, the separate and equal station to which the laws of nature and of nature's God entitle them, a decent respect to the opinions of mankind requires that they should declare the causes which impel them to the separation. We hold these truths to be self-evident, that all men are created equal ; that they are endowed by their Creator with certain unalienable rights ; that among these, are life, liberty, and the pursuit of happiness. That, to secure these rights, governments are instituted among *men, deriving their just powers from the consent of the governed ; that, whenever any form of government becomes destructive of these ends, it is*

ABCDEFGHIJKLMNOPQRSTUVWXYZ
1234567890

WHEN, in the course of human events, it becomes necessary for one people to dissolve the political bands which have connected them with another, and to assume, among the powers of the earth, the separate and equal station to which the laws of nature and of nature's God entitle them, a decent respect to the opinions of mankind requires that they should declare the causes which impel them to the separation. We hold these truths to be self-evident, that all men are created equal ; that they are endowed by their Creator with certain unalienable rights ; that among these, are life, liberty, and the pursuit of happiness. That,

ABCDEFGHIJKLMNOPQRSTUVWXYZ
1234567890

Century Roman (ATF, c. 1898)

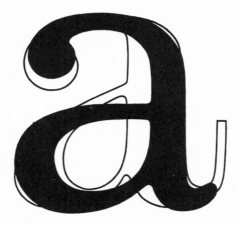

Linotype Excelsior superimposed upon Roman No. 2, showing larger counter-spaces to reduce ink-trapping in high-speed printing

production the most profitable aspect of the foundries' business and reinforced the neglect of the text types.

It is no wonder that in 1890 William Morris, in righteous indignation, turned the clock back some four centuries, at least as far as book types were concerned. As an antidote to blandness, he promoted the use of solid (albeit ungainly) black-letter types. But though the Morris revival definitely affected book and commercial typography, the newspaper printers remained aloof from innovation, maintaining their adherence to the well-established 'modern' roman. A rationale for this was that the heavier, or bolder, types in the small sizes used for editorial content were subject to ink-trapping in the counter-spaces. In addition, the newer types were not as narrow, and economical, as the existing romans.

At first mechanized typesetting increased the reliance on the plainer types. With the successful launching of Mergenthaler's machine in the 1880s, and the need to supply it with types in matrix form, his company very early turned to the modern romans already available from the typefounders under several names and numbers. When the Intertype machine was developed in 1912, the numbered types received similar attention. In fact, both of these firms today still show in their

ABCDEFGHIJKLMNOPQRSTUV
WXYZ abcdefghijklmnopqrstuvw
xyz .,-;:'!?$&fffififlffiffl() 1234567890
ABCDEFGHIJKLMNOPQR
STUVWXYZ abcdefghijklm
nopqrstuvwxyz 1234567890
.,-;:""!?$&fffififlffiffl()

Century Expanded (ATF)

catalogue several of the styles that originated during that dry period
of the mid-nineteenth century. The emphasis then, of course, was
not on the introduction of new types, but – as expressed in the
company literature – on supplying 'a complete type foundry' in a
single machine.

In the area of magazine printing, greater artistic scope was permitted. De Vinne worked with the American Type Founders Company
in the 1890s to develop what was probably the earliest type designed
for a specific purpose: the Century typeface for *Century* magazine.
In this instance, the result was highly successful, the product being
the popular Century family of types. Noting the high quality of
printing presses and paper then becoming available, De Vinne proposed thickening the thin lines of the modern romans and beefing up
the serifs, in order to get away from what he termed the feebleness
of the existing typefaces. He maintained, however, the economical
narrow width of the periodical type. In the development of Century,
De Vinne collaborated with Linn Boyd Benton of ATF.

The magazine's publishers, cognizant of the economies of a narrower face, were greatly pleased with the type when the first issue of
Century appeared in 1896. A somewhat wider-set version than the

An American newspaper management once vividly expressed a great truth about text types when they said 'people are tired of type that mumbles'. They were announcing an increase in the size of their journal's body type. Size alone does not, however, determine readability, or general ease of reading, especially in terms of quantity of narrow-column matter. Other factors are (i) reproduction: the type must print clearly even when stereotyped and rotary-machined, which means that it has to have a clean and open cut; (ii) colour: the drawing of the letter should be strong enough to avoid greyness, even with thin inks at high speeds, while retaining sufficient contrast between the thick and thin strokes to beat monotony; (iii) proportion: the height/width relationship should be oblong, not square, and the body of the type (x-height) must not seriously encroach on the ascenders, those upper distinguishing strokes which perform an essential optical function. By the

l.c. alphabet 115 pts; figs ·055″

An American newspaper management once vividly expressed a great truth about text types when they said 'people are tired of type that mumbles'. They were announcing an increase in the size of their journal's body type. Size alone does not, however, determine readability, or general ease of reading, especially in terms of quantity of narrow-column matter. Other factors are (i) reproduction: the type must print clearly even when stereotyped and rotary-machined, which means that it has to have a clean and open cut; (ii) colour: the drawing of the letter should be strong enough to avoid greyness, even with thin inks at high speeds, while retaining sufficient contrast between the thick and thin strokes to beat monotony; (iii) proportion: the height/width relationship should

l.c. alphabet 123 pts; figs ·062″

Linotype Excelsior

An American newspaper management once vividly expressed a great truth about text types when they said 'people are tired of type that mumbles'. They were announcing an increase in the size of their journal's body type. Size alone does not, however, determine readability, or general ease of reading, especially in terms of quantity of narrow-column matter. Other factors are (i) reproduction : the type must print clearly even when stereotyped and rotary-machined, which means that it has to have a clean and open cut; (ii) colour : the drawing of the letter should be strong enough to avoid greyness, even with thin inks at high speeds, while retaining sufficient contrast between the thick and thin strokes to beat monotony; (iii) proportion : the height/width relationship should be oblong, not square, and the body of the type (x-height) must not seriously encroach on the ascenders, those upper distinguishing strokes which perform an essential optical function. By the

l.c. alphabet 114 pts; figs ·055″

An American newspaper management once vividly expressed a great truth about text types when they said 'people are tired of type that mumbles.' They were announcing an increase in the size of their journal's body type. Size alone does not, however, determine readability, or general ease of reading, especially in terms of quantity of narrow-column matter. Other factors are (i) reproduction: the type must print clearly even when stereotyped and rotary-machined, which means that it has to have a clean and open cut; (ii) colour: the drawing of the letter should be strong enough to avoid greyness, even with thin inks at high speeds, while retaining sufficient contrast between the thick and thin strokes to beat monotony; (ii)

l.c. alphabet 127 pts; figs ·062″

Linotype Ionic

An American newspaper management once vividly expressed a great truth about text types when they said 'people are tired of type that mumbles'. They were announcing an increase in the size of their journal's body type. Size alone does not, however, determine readability, or general ease of reading, especially in terms of quantity of narrow-column matter. Other factors are (i) reproduction: the type must print clearly even when stereotyped and rotary-machined, which means that it has to have a clean and open cut; (ii) colour: the drawing of the letter should be strong enough to avoid greyness, even with thin inks at high speeds, while retaining sufficient contrast between the thick and thin strokes to beat monotony; (iii) proportion: the height/width relationship should be oblong, not square, and the body of the type (x-height) must not seriously encroach on the ascenders, those upper distinguishing strokes which

l.c. alphabet 120 pts; figs ·059″

An American newspaper management once vividly expressed a great truth about text types when they said 'people are tired of type that mumbles'. They were announcing an increase in the size of their journal's body type. Size alone does not, however, determine readability, or general ease of reading, especially in terms of quantity of narrow-column matter. Other factors are (i) reproduction: the type must print clearly even when stereotyped and rotary-machined, which means that it has to have a clean and open cut; (ii) colour: the drawing of the letter should be strong enough to avoid greyness, even with thin inks at high speeds, while retaining sufficient contrast between the thick and thin strokes to beat monotony; (iii)

l.c. alphabet 129 pts; figs ·062″

Linotype Paragon

An American newspaper management once vividly expressed a great truth about text types when they said 'people are tired of type that mumbles'. They were announcing an increase in the size of their journal's body type. Size alone does not, however, determine readability, or general ease of reading, especially in terms of quantity of narrow-column matter. Other factors are (i) reproduction: the type must print clearly even when stereotyped and rotary-machined, which means that it has to have a clean and open cut; (ii) colour: the drawing of the letter should be strong enough to avoid greyness, even with thin inks at high speeds, while retaining sufficient contrast between the thick and thin strokes to beat monotony; (iii) proportion: the height/width relationship should be oblong, not square, and the body of the type (x-height) must not seriously encroach on the ascenders, those upper distinguishing strokes which perform an essential optical func-

l.c. alphabet 112 pts; figs ·055″

An American newspaper management once vividly expressed a great truth about text types when they said 'people are tired of type that mumbles'. They were announcing an increase in the size of their journal's body type. Size alone does not, however, determine readability, or general ease of reading, especially in terms of quantity of narrow-column matter. Other factors are (i) reproduction: the type must print clearly even when stereotyped and rotary-machined, which means that it has to have a clean and open cut; (ii) colour: the drawing of the letter should be strong enough to avoid greyness, even with thin inks at high speeds, while retaining sufficient contrast between the thick and thin strokes to beat monotony; (iii) proportion: the height/width relationship should

l.c. alphabet 118 pts; figs ·062″

Linotype Corona

HOW IS ONE TO ASSESS AND EVALUATE A TYPE FACE IN TE
OF ITS ESTHETIC DESIGN? WHY DO THE PACE-MAKERS IN T
How is one to assess and evaluate a type face in terms of its esthetic
design? Why do the pace-makers in the art of printing rave over a
specific face of type? What do they see in it? Why is it so superlatively pleasant to their eyes? **Good design is always practical design.**
And what they see in a good type design is, partly, its excellent practical fitness to perform its work. It has a "heft" and balance in all of
its parts just right for its size, as any good tool has. Your good chair has
all of its parts made nicely to the right size to do exactly the work that
the chair has to do, neither clumsy and thick, nor "skinny" and weak,
no waste of material and no lack of strength. And, beyond that, the
chair may have been made by a man who worked out in it his sense
of fine shapes and curves and proportions: it may be, actually, a work
of art. The same thing holds for shapes of letters. And your chair, or
your letter (if a true artist made it) will have, besides its good looks, a
suitability to the nth degree to be sat in, or stamped on paper and read.
That explains, in a way, why the experts rave over the fine shapes of
letters; but it fails to explain wherein the shapes are fine. If you seek
to go further with the inquiry, theories will be your only answer. Here
is a theory that the proponent thinks may have sense in it: Fine type
letters were, in the first place, copies of fine written letters. Fine written letters were fine because they were produced in the most direct
and simple way by a tool in the hands of a person expert in its use, by
a person, moreover, who was an artist, i.e., a person equipped to make
sound judgments about lines, curves, proportions, etc. The artist of
that moment when printing was invented who furnished the fine
written patterns for type was (luckily for printing) working at the
How is one to assess and evaluate a type face in terms of its esthetic
design? Why do the pace-makers in the art of printing rave over a
specific face of type? What do they see in it? Why is it so superla-

---

Linotype Opticon

original cutting was later marketed by ATF as Century Expanded.
This design, now available for most typesetting machines, has proved
its worth; over the past seventy-five years it has remained a favorite in
both commercial printing and advertising typography.

Nevertheless, none of this magazine activity had any immediate impact on newspaper text, where the debased Bodoni-Didot types of the 1800s continued to dominate the news columns into the twentieth century. Surprisingly, though, in the advertising columns of newspapers a typographic rejuvenation had already taken place between 1875 and 1900; that alone so much affected the appearance of newspapers that one publisher, discussing the phenomenon with his colleagues, declared: 'But, gentlemen, this is not journalism; this is bill-posting!'

Moreover, along with the visual stimulation in the ad alley had come a change in the style of headings in the editorial section.

Cheltenham, available as of 1902, and its multiple variants took over as a standard headline style in American newspapers, and to this day it remains conspicuously with us in the daily edition of *The New York Times*.

It was not until the 1920s that American newspaper publishers, finally aware of the concept of typographic legibility, began to consult the composing-machine manufacturers about it. The firms, of course, were delighted to comply with any request that would create a new market for matrices. It was accordingly discovered that one of the problems with the spindly types then used by newspapers was partly the fault of the dry-molding of stereotypes, which required heavier pressures than the obsolescent wet-matrix process. High-speed rotary presses were also to blame for poor presswork. Indeed, the incessant demand for greater production by publishers of large city dailies where competition was keen had for too long been an element deteriorating the legibility of newspaper types.

In response to the awakened interest in types specially adapted to newspapers, the designers at Mergenthaler Linotype Company began a series of experiments with new letter forms. After four trial fonts they came up with a modified 'Clarendon' style – a throwback to the 1850s, but nonetheless considerably different from the maligned modern romans. Called Ionic No. 5, this new type was of large x-height and had shortened ascenders and descenders and solid, bracketed serifs. In addition, the letter was of almost monotone color. Cut, as were all Linotype faces from 1915 to 1950, under the direction of C. H. Griffith, Ionic was completed about 1925. First used by *The Newark Evening News* (N.J.), Ionic was a resounding success. Within a year it had been adopted by some 3,000 newspapers all over the world.

One would think that such popularity would have established Ionic as the standard newspaper type for years to come. But the manufacturers readily saw that the concept of typographic legibility had opened up possibilities for profit that could go far beyond just one type. The firms supplying the newspaper market therefore further experimented with innovative faces for newspapers. As legibility was also currently receiving considerable attention from both reading psychologists and typographers, Mergenthaler sponsored research in this field in the hope that the findings could be translated into the production of other lucrative types.

The results were not long in arriving. Five years after the intro-

ABCDEFGHIJKLMNOPQRSTUV
WXYZ 1234567890
abcdefghijklmnopqrstuvwxyz

ABCDEFGHIJKLMNOPQRSTUV
WXYZ 1234567890
abcdefghijklmnopqrstuvwxyz

ABCDEFGHIJKLMNOPQRSTUV
WXYZ 1234567890
abcdefghijklmnopqrstuvwxyz

British Linotype Olympian

duction of Ionic, a new face appeared in what was to become Linotype's Legibility Group. This was Excelsior, which incorporated several features of Ionic but in addition solved another problem that was then becoming apparent in newspaper production.

In a new high-speed rotary press installed in Philadelphia, the ink rollers had been melting from friction heating. It became necessary to supply hard rubber rollers, which were less resilient than the defective composition rollers and also tended to drag over the stereotype plate, filling the counter spaces of the types with ink. This ink-trapping difficulty was partially solved in Excelsior by opening up the counters of the letters thus affected.

In any discussion of newspaper typefaces, it is of interest to note the gradual increase over a long period in the sizes used for editorial

Ideal was one of the first type faces designed especially for ease in reading under adverse conditions. Its legibility in small or larger sizes is unequaled. Ease of reading is a major consideration in the choice of a type face where masses of words are required. In basic form, Ideal is not unlike Century Expanded, yet it has a more even line, with hairlines that are heavier and serifs that are sturdier. It has a lateral look as opposed to Century Expanded's vertical appearance. It sets slightly wider, but its word count is high.

In design, Ideal has a precise and delicate balance between just enough shading to afford reader interest and little enough to prevent such mechanical difficulties as broken or filled-in letters. Its characters are wide and its counters open. Its color is rich and even. Its high word count is an important consideration in the printing of masses of words in relatively narrow columns. Ideal does not require leading for legibility. Although it is most widely used on book papers and newsprint, it retains its legibility on any stock. Assisted by its exceedingly clear italic and bold, it has an almost limitless versatility, and combines well with practically any other face which is based on a modern roman structure.

Ideal is the result of Intertype's scientific research and experimentation. It was designed for readability, proportioned for legibility, and constructed for durability.

Small types are a serious problem, especially when being used in large masses for reference works, textbooks, law and financial printing, or for newspapers or publications which have to be read hastily and often in poor light. This type face is fitly named Ideal, because it has everything that it takes to make a type face ideal under such varying conditions.

Ideal is available in a complete range of small sizes up to and including 14 point. Ideal Bold is a well designed companion, insuring good contrast between the light and the bold when used with each other. It is also available in a wide range of unit font sizes and alphabet lengths, designed especially for automatic teletype operation. A specimen showing of the 8 point size for use in $11\frac{1}{2}$ and $11\frac{1}{4}$ pica column measure is included in a folder contained in pocket of this booklet.

Intertype Ideal

---

columns. Until the present century, 6-point was standard, and it was not until the studies made in the 1920s that the need to enlarge this size became apparent. Ionic was originally offered in $6\frac{1}{2}$-point, its large x-height giving the type the appearance of the 8-point size. By 1931, when Excelsior arrived, the standard size became 7-point.

By the midthirties other technical difficulties peculiar to newspapers were being examined. For example, American newspapers that,

Design must follow function, and a type face created specifically for newspaper usage rarely is satisfactory for book work and commercial printing. Rex is the exception. Its elements were scientifically blended to suit the requirements of the Milwaukee Journal for whom it was developed. Both Ideal and Regal rival Rex only by providing a larger letter in a given space.

Because of the roundness of the Rex letters, they appear to be wider than those of Ideal or Regal. The alphabet length of Rex, however, is actually shorter than either and, therefore, Rex's word count—line for line—is more favorable. This rotundity of design is also an asset in rapid reproduction processes because it affords remarkably open counters that are free from filling-in. There are no sharp points to break off; the serifs have square ends that are delicately bracketed. Rex has an economic sturdiness of practical use as well as of size.

Rex's lower case letters are reduced in body size, but the height of the capitals is maintained. The capitals, however, have a slightly narrower letter and a thinner stroke so that they blend harmoniously with the lower case into an even grey tone. The delicacy of treatment is pronounced in the bold capitals where it lends restraint to their inherent power and legibility.

Rex has long ascenders and descenders, and it is these which make the face that rarity among news type faces that are also suitable for book printing. They endow it with the feeling of refinement and the smoothness of tone so essential to a fine book page.

Although cut for use in editorial and classified pages of newspapers, Rex is excellent for use in advertising where character count is important. It is becoming increasingly important for all-around use in both book and publication fields where legibility is a factor because of a limited amount of space.

Those who specialize in the printing of college textbooks, law briefs and large masses of reading where space is a problem will find Rex an excellent choice because it is easy on the eyes.

Alert typographers will find that Rex is especially adaptable to usage in financial reports, price and parts catalogs. This feeling is brought about by the contrasting height of the lower case letters in proportion to the figures.

Rex is available in 5, 6, 7, 7½, 8, 10, 12, and 14 point with bold. Roman with italic and small caps is made in 6, 7, 8, and 10 point sizes only. Rex is also duplexed with Franklin Gothic in 4 and 5 point sizes.

Intertype Rex

for economic reasons, were using European newsprint complained that the paper was less absorbent than the American variety, and that Excelsior was printing 'too thin.' To rectify the problem, the designers at Mergenthaler thickened the stems and serifs, though keeping the general style of Excelsior intact. A third legibility type thus emerged, and was christened Opticon.

The great growth in the 1920s of tabloid newspapers also brought

Regal is not just one man's idea of a legible type face. It is, rather, a development of type legibility in which many individuals have had a part. Made originally for the *Chicago Tribune*, in accordance with suggestions from that newspaper, Regal is a scientific blending of elements designed to meet various requirements. Before being chosen by the *Tribune*, and after exacting comparative tests which included a vote among *Tribune* employees, Regal was selected by both type and eye experts.

Regal was developed not only for readability, but created to serve a fast reading, fast moving public and so constructed to stand rough treatment of stereotyping. Two versions of Regal were created and are available in all popular sizes, duplexed light with bold face, light with italic and small caps, and in addition, duplexed with other desirable faces. Regal No. 2 is slightly larger in lower case body height than its companion, Regal No. 1, and is also designed wider. Both sizes are well opened up in design to insure good stereotyping and to prevent smudging from accumulations of ink within the closed letters. Both are excellent types for gravure and offset printing because they reproduce sharply and cleanly.

Although one news type looks pretty much like another to the average reader, there are important differences which even the inexpert eye can see when columns set in different types are placed side by side. It is said that the difference between Regal and other popular news type faces is less than one-thousandth of an inch. Yet this difference that is so small it can be seen only under a powerful microscope, is easily apparent in a side-by-side comparison.

Designed expressly for the editorial and classified columns of a newspaper, Regal is widely used in other fields. It is an ideal choice for book work and for magazine pages. It lends an authoritative look to factual statements in advertising. Regal is legible with or without leading. Because it is a scientifically designed roman face, it combines well with many other faces.

Regal is also available in a wide range of unit font sizes and alphabet lengths, designed especially for automatic teletype operation. Specimens of sizes and alphabet lengths are included in a folder contained in pocket of this booklet.

Intertype Regal

problems. Ink coverage for large areas of halftones tended to flood the counters of the types used for the text. Mergenthaler met this challenge with a type named Paragon, designed to print sharply and cleanly under the specialized printing requirements of the tabloid.

A fifth legibility type named Corona, also from Mergenthaler, once again solved a technical difficulty – the distortion produced by stereotype-matrix shrinkage. In addition, Corona's design filled the

Imperial is an exclusive Intertype face designed from the ground up for narrower newspaper columns and modern news setting techniques. It was designed by Edwin W. Shaar specifically to *preserve word count,* to *reproduce clearly* and *sharply* and provide *maximum legibility* under these conditions.

The design of a text face affects the basic "color" or overall appearance of a newspaper page. The establishment of the *weight* of Imperial was the first and *paramount* consideration from the very beginning of the design. Based upon exhaustive studies of typecasting procedures, presswork, stereotyping, ink and newsprint, the designer carefully tailored every element of Imperial to meet the most exacting demands of the discriminating publisher. It has an inherent strength of design combined with a fine balance of white to create a clean, vigorous page.

Imperial is by all tests a legible face. It has a distinctly clean look, presenting a pleasant, *even color in mass* on newsprint. Its carefully planned, close fitting design enables the eye to see word pictures rather than single letters.

Very slim wedges of white are forced into the anatomy of the letters (spaces that might otherwise fill with ink); counters are scooped clean to avoid ink traps; the contrast of thick and thin strokes is reduced to minimize possible damage to the letters by rough treatment in stereotyping and the rigors of faster printing methods.

Imperial is pleasing in design, modern in spirit, with perhaps ever so slight a bow to the best features of tried and proven transitional faces. *It is not a revision, redesign or an adaption* of an old face.

Imperial Bold closely follows the character of the light face in design; has ample color for emphasis and is in *complete harmony* with its companion. This was accomplished not merely by increasing the width of thick and thin strokes but by adept formation of curves and serifs, thereby sidestepping the heavy-handed, fat look that affects all too many of our bold faces.

Imperial is in no way limited in use to newspapers alone. It may be used to excellent advantage in textbooks and magazines, and will lend vigor to the factual statements of advertisements and job printing.

Imperial is also available in a wide range of unit font sizes and alphabet lengths, designed especially for teletype operation. Specimen showings of most-used sizes and alphabet lengths are included in a folder contained in the pocket of this booklet.

Intertype Imperial

request of a particular publisher for a new 'dress' (style) for his paper; the face had to be aesthetically arresting but at the same time have a more economical character width than the type then in use. Produced in 1941, Corona quickly became the most widely employed of all newspaper types in the United States. Fully half of American papers now use Corona for text composition.

During this whole period Linotype's Brooklyn competitor in the

ROYAL

This example of Intertype's new typeface ROYAL is set in the 9 point size. Royal owes much of its clarity to generous x-height and slightly elongated form. **The bold face is equally successful.** A complementary italic is in preparation. Excellent word count.

Intertype Royal

manufacture of a slugcasting typesetter, the Intertype Corporation, was also involved in the production of legibility types. As the latter had been established in 1912 by an association of newspaper publishers, the firm had always been sympathetic to the specialized typographic requirements of journalism.

The news types that emerged from Intertype strove for objectives similar to those of Linotype. Ideal (1928), the first Intertype legibility design, followed the concept of Ionic with its Clarendon-style serifs and monotone strokes. Intertype's advertising department then apparently decided that there was (or should be) a majestic aspect to its newspaper types, and henceforth all of its legibility faces were given 'royal' names.

Regal came into being about 1935, specially designed for *The Chicago Tribune*. It was voted in by the employees of the newspaper and presumably also received the approval of the *Trib*'s monarch, the redoubtable Colonel Robert Rutherford McCormick. Regal followed the pattern established by Linotype's Excelsior in being a slimmed-down version of a previous design – in Regal's case, Ideal. A third Intertype legibility font, Rex, appeared in 1939. Designed for *The Milwaukee Journal*, Rex was also more condensed than its predecessors.

In 1957 Edwin Shaar, director of typography for Intertype, produced Imperial, another close-fitting legibility letter that became one of the firm's most successful types. It was adopted by numerous newspapers, including *The New York Times*, which changed over from Ideal in 1967. The standard size for *The Times* is 8½-point, continuing the forty-year trend toward larger body sizes in American newspaper types.

Another Shaar design, Royal, became available in 1960. It follows the concept of Corona and it, too, has been widely adopted by the world's newspapers.

The basic character in a type design is determined by the uniform design characteristics of all letters in the alphabet. However, this alone does not determine the standard of the type face and the quality of composition set with it. The appearance is something complex which forms itself OUT OF MANY DETAILS, LIKE FORM, PROPORTION,

Melior (Linotype)

The premier 'newspaper' type of the century, Times Roman, although designed for the prestigious *Times* of London, has enjoyed little success on Newspaper Row in the United States. Its use in America has been as a book and commercial type, presenting one case where a legibility type has transcended its original purpose. The printing procedures and materials of most U.S. newspapers do not permit the use of a type featuring strong contrast of stroke and fine serifs. As discussed earlier, Times Roman is a luxury design. But the recent growth of web-offset in the newspaper field, along with the replacement of stereotype plates by photomechanical plates in the newer relief presses, will perhaps allow for the greater use of more aesthetic roman types in newspapers of the future.

Another postwar legibility type is Melior, designed by Hermann Zapf for the German newspaper market. This type, too, has been bypassed by American papers, but like Times Roman it has achieved considerable renown as a commercial type of distinction.

All of the types discussed so far have been in the transitional classification; that is, types that display characteristics of both old-style and modern faces. However, two English type designers have recently turned away from the transitional, producing types of purely old-style and purely modern derivation.

Walter Tracy, typographic manager of Linotype and Machinery, the British Linotype affiliate, in 1969 designed a legibility face that was named Linotype Modern. The type approaches the vertical stress of the Bodoni-Didot models, but without the thinning of light strokes or serifs. This is somewhat similar to W. A. Dwiggins's Electra, a book type that was also conceived in terms of legibility.

More recently, England's Matthew Carter, the designer of Galliard, has turned his attention to a news face based on old-style forms, with their oblique stress. Named Olympian, this type revives some of the Aldine-French-Dutch ideas of letter form. It was designed and produced at Mergenthaler Linotype.

Carter brings to such work, in addition to his familiarity with punchcutting, a mastery of the intricate technology now required to create a type compatible with the newest high-speed typesetting devices. Designers of newspaper types have always encountered technical needs that are incompatible with typographic aesthetics. The introduction of the Teletypesetter, for example, brought the factor of unit widths, or 'sets,' to slug-machine characters, and this design restriction continued with the multiplicity of keyboard functions of phototypesetting machines. In considering this limitation along with all the other technical exigencies of a newspaper type, Carter appears to have been most successful. Indeed, Olympian, like Times Roman, could very well be useful beyond the confines of the newsroom. However, with complete automation via the computer, the designer is no longer limited to arbitrary letter widths.

In the fifty years of development of the newspaper legibility types, perhaps the only constant has been the demand for ever larger sizes in the editorial columns. That Olympian is standardized at 9-point bears out Carter's observation that statistically twice as many papers are set in that size as in the next most popular size, 8½-point.

Newspaper types are rarely selected for book typography, but they nonetheless constitute a significant group of faces, if only because so many people read them. It is therefore important that outstanding designers continue to turn their attention to the production of such types, trying to come to grips with the aesthetic restraints that seem concomitant with every technical innovation.

26

FRANKLIN GOTHIC AND THE TWENTIETH-CENTURY GOTHICS

When the late Stevens Watts was manager of the American Type Founders' foundry, he was fond of saying that 'while types come and go, Franklin Gothic goes on forever.' The type was a perennial best seller, and over the past seventy years it has been one of the best-known representatives of a style of type notable for its multiplicity of forms, the modern gothics. These faces are not, despite their name, gothics – at least in the traditional understanding of the term. And Franklin Gothic is doubly misnamed, having no historical relationship to Benjamin Franklin.

If anyone can be blamed for the gothic misnomer it is perhaps the corporate body of the Boston Type and Stereotype Foundry, which back in 1837 issued a new series of types without serifs under the name Gothic. Probably it was the bold weight of this type that prompted the designation. In any event, the Boston firm was the first foundry in America to introduce a serifless design then attaining great popularity in Europe, particularly England and Germany.

In the post–World War II era, when sans-serif types dominate the typography of the marketplace, it is difficult to recall that typefounders up to the beginning of the nineteenth century sought to please only book printers. It was the Industrial Revolution, of course, that brought to printers, as to manufacturers, countless changes and the introduction of extra-bold types, called fat faces, patterned somewhat akin to the Didot and Bodoni styles. These were welcomed for their display value by printers specializing in the production of broadsides, handbills, and posters.

The impact of the new commercial types evidently stimulated William Caslon IV – of the famous English typefounding family – in 1816 to offer experimentally a monotone type without serifs under the name Two-Line English Egyptian. This 28-point type, produced in capitals only, was the first sans serif to be purveyed as a printing type.

ABCDEFGHIJKLMNOP
QRSTUVWXYZ abcdef
ghijklmnopqrstuvwxyz
.,-;:"'!?   1234567890

ABCDEFGHIJKLMN
OPQRSTUVWXYZ
abcdefghijklmnopq
rstuvwxyz
.,-;:   1234567890

Franklin Gothic (ATF)

Caslon's design did not meet with immediate support, primarily because its introduction coincided with that of the well-received square-serif faces currently being issued by competing typefoundries. But by 1825 the German firm of Schelter and Giesecke was also offering a series of condensed sans serifs, which included lowercase characters. Then, in 1832, three English foundries brought out additional sans-serif types. One of these firms, that of William Thorowgood, termed the style 'grotesque,' a classification that is still standard in Britain for the sans-serif types that originated in the nineteenth century.

By 1850 all of the world's typefounders were issuing sans serifs in an endless, and confusing, variety of weights and widths. This

CASLON JUNR
LETTERFOUND

The sans serif type of William Caslon IV, c. 1816

venezianischer
Porträtmalerei

Sans serif lowercase of Schelter & Giesecke, c. 1825

MARCHES

Early American sans serif of George Bruce, c. 1853

typographic overkill continued until metal types were largely super-seded by film fonts in the past few decades.

When the American Type Founders issued Franklin Gothic in 1905, it didn't seem that the company needed another gothic. For after ATF had been formed in 1892 – as an amalgamation of many American typefoundries – the new firm issued a specimen book that showed about fifty gothic types. Some of these types had such color-ful names as Turius, Altona, Octic, and Telescope, but most of them were simply numbered. Many of the faces were difficult to distinguish, but all of the widths now common in gothic series were represented, from extra-condensed to extra-extended.

297

When ATF's Morris Benton became fully involved in type design, about 1902 (when he was thirty), he began cutting the Franklin Gothic series. In this he was no doubt influenced by the German production of sans-serif type, for in 1898 the Berthold foundry in Berlin had produced the Akzidenz series (later known to American printers as Standard) which had proved very popular and inspired the cutting of Reform Grotesk by Frankfurt's Stempel in 1903 and the Venus series by the Bauer foundry, also of Frankfurt, in 1907.

Franklin Gothic is an excellent example of a traditional early-nineteenth-century sans-serif letter which retained certain features common to roman. For example, the lowercase *a* and *g* are normal roman characters, and in all of the letters there occurs a thinning of stroke at the junction of rounds to stems. Some of the contrast of roman letters also persists, although the overall appearance is mono-tone. The weight of stroke of Franklin Gothic is heavy, or what modern practitioners call extra-bold. It should be pointed out that there has never, alas, been any consistency in the terminology for the thickness of a stroke; such unquantified designations as *light*, *thin*, *medium*, *bold*, *heavy*, *extra-bold*, *ultra-bold*, and *semi-bold* indicate the difficulty faced by typographers in type recognition and description.

Benton finished designing Franklin Gothic in 1902, but it did not appear until about 1905. (The years in which typefaces were drawn frequently differ from their dates of issuance. Unfortunately, the records of the manufacturers have rarely survived, making it extremely difficult to affix accurate dates.) In 1905 a condensed variant was drawn, and in 1906 an extended one – the latter was abandoned at the time and not cut until 1953, as Franklin Gothic Wide, following the great revival in the fifties of these early gothics. An extra-condensed version was also produced in 1906. Benton completed his contribution to the Franklin Gothic family with the drawing in 1913 of an italic for the original face and in 1914 of a condensed shaded modification.

The monotone structure of the gothics readily lends itself to a variety of weights in which a type designer can maintain both a uniformity of style and his original concept. In merchandizing their wares, typefounders learned to take advantage of this fact by suggesting to printers that they required two or three *weights* (light, bold, etc.) for each style of type, along with several *widths* (extended, condensed, etc.). The printer was then urged to purchase these variations in series, that is, all of the sizes cast for each family variant.

Such marketing procedures were just beginning to emerge during

ABCDEFGHIJKLMNOPQRSTUVWXYZ 1234567890
abcdefghijklmnopqrstuvwxyz .,-;:'!?$&

ABCDEFGHIJKLMNOPQRSTUVWXYZ
abcdefghijklmnopqrstuvwxyz
.,-;:'!?$& 1234567890

Alternate Gothic No. 1 (ATF)

the period 1900–1910, as an inspection of any typefounders' catalogues will disclose. A very successful example was the dissemination of the Cheltenham design, but it was with the serifless types that this approach to manufacture and selling came to fruition.

It was with the gothic types that early in the present century foundries began exploiting the concept of offering types in a variety of weights and widths. For example at ATF Morris Benton drew a condensed gothic named Alternate Gothic cast in three widths differentiated by number but all narrower than normal. Since Franklin Gothic was an extra-bold type, Alternate Gothic was designed as a normal boldface. To fill out Benton then cut Lightline Gothic and News Gothic, the latter being a medium-weight letter. The success of this venture is evident, since all of these styles remain in use in photographic or digitized versions of the original designs.

Successful from the start, ATF's original twentieth-century gothic was eventually adapted by all the composing-machine manufacturers, and more recently it has been transferred to film. The fact that Franklin Gothic survived the impact of the geometric sans serifs during the period from 1926 to 1950 – in addition to the revival of its contemporary competitors, Venus and Standard – warrants the conclusion that Morris Benton, even in his early efforts as a type designer, possessed the skill to create a printing type that could withstand obsolescence.

Indeed, up to 1950 the geometric unserifed types, as represented by Futura, dominated commercial printing. But by midcentury a re-action against them had begun to reduce their effectiveness: Futura was damned as being too cold for modern tastes – the word of critical disapprobation being *mécanique*, 'mechanical,' as used by the Swiss typographers, who were the vanguard of a search for a new typography that fitted the needs of a postwar generation. It was not to be expected that the younger designers would sponsor a return to the roman letter, although their elders were buoyantly anticipating such a gesture. Instead, the sans-serif ideal was reaffirmed, but the form embodied a return to an earlier tradition rather than to that of the geometric unserifed types of the turn-of-the-century 'gothics.'

Perhaps resurrecting these gothics seemed more efficient to the typefounders than taking the time to commission new designs. Thus,

ABCDEFGHIJKLM
NOPQRSTUVWXY
Z abcdefghijklmno
pqrstuvwxyz 1234
567890   .,-;:'!?$&

News Gothic (ATF)

ABCDEFGHIJKLMNOPQRSTUVWXYZ
abcdefghijklmnopqrstuvwxyz
(&$1234567890£¢.,:;"''''-*%/!?)$1234567890

Lightline Gothic (ATF)

ABCDEFGHIJKLMN
OPQRSTUVWXYZ
abcdefghijklmnopqrstu
vwxyz 1234567890
.,-;:'!?$&

Standard (Berthold)

from the Bauer foundry came Venus, circa 1906, and Berthold reissued the even older Akzidenz Grotesk, which was renamed Standard for the English and American markets. The first series of Venus to reach the United States was the extra-bold extended group, and it precipitated an explosion in the use of wide types, which in turn spread to gothics of all widths. Such was these types' impact on American advertising designers that for a time most of the German freighters making the westerly Atlantic crossing were ballasted with Venus and Standard types. The appearance of the types fortuitously coincided with a design trend then touching every object from furniture to automobiles: wide and squat was in.

ABCDEFGHIJKL MNOPQRSTUVW XYZ abcdefghijkl mnopqrstuvwxyz 1234567890 .,-;:'!?$&

Venus Bold (Bauer)

For two or three years Venus and Standard had the market to themselves, with typographers vehemently disagreeing as to which was superior. ATF in the United States attempted to meet the competition with aggressive promotion of its Benton gothics, but it was a losing battle, for the German types possessed a greater range of compatible series. More important, Venus and Standard were sold as single-type families, thus assuring the typographers of their effectiveness in a comprehensive advertising campaign. In the meantime, new approaches were being sought by the typefoundries, eager to promote and prolong this regeneration of the early serifless letter forms.

In the mid-1950s all this activity came to a boil, with nearly every supplier of printing types peddling redesigned gothics to a trade already saturated with the earlier models. The appeal was made, therefore, to the printer's customer – often an advertising agency – rather than to the printer himself, and the solicitation was explicit in its offer of typographic sophistication.

In 1953 Adrian Frutiger, a twenty-five-year-old Swiss designer and former compositor, was invited by the Paris typefoundry Deberny et Peignot to assist in the selection of types to be used for the Lumitype phototypesetting machine, the European version of the American Photon machine, which the foundry was manufacturing under license. Before this assignment Frutiger had been experimenting with a uni-

ABCDEFGHIJKLMNOPQRST UVWXYZ
abcdefghijklmnopqrstuvwxyz
(&$1234567890¢.,:;"-*%!?)
$1234567890¢

Eurostyle Bold (Nebiolo)

ABCDEFGHIJKL MNOPQRSTUVW XYZ abcdefghijk lmnopqrstuvwxyz .,-;:!? 123456789

Univers 65 (ATF-Deberny Peignot)

fied series of gothic types in which a single designer controlled every facet of their construction. At Deberny et Peignot the opportunity to produce such a design was provided, resulting in the type named Univers, first distributed in 1957. The name was anticipatory, but the style did become available to printers in forms other than for photo-composition, for the foundry itself produced the type in metal for its own market and, by agreement with the American Type Founders

Company, for sale in the United States. Arrangements were soon concluded with the Monotype Corporation of London to transfer Univers to the Monotype.

Univers represents a most ambitious program of integrated type design, for Frutiger brought to the task a highly developed skill in letter design. As a critic of the Futura concept of sans-serif construction, he sought to modify its severe strokes yet stay within the serifless boundaries. In discussing his ideas Frutiger said, 'A purely geometric character is unacceptable in the long run, for the horizontal lines appear thicker to the eye than the vertical ones; an O represented by a perfect circle strikes us as shapeless and has a disturbing effect on the word as a whole.'

But what is undoubtedly the most unusual contribution of Frutiger to the marketing of printing types was his defiant attempt to simplify typographic nomenclature. Rather than employ the ordinary imprecise designations of weight and width, he organized his entire design plan of twenty-one series into a logical 'palette,' by which each variant received a number that instantly identified its structure. The palette consisted of six vertical and six horizontal rows; the extended versions occupied the vertical rows, diminishing in width from left to right; and the weights were categorized horizontally, the lightest at the top and the heaviest at the bottom.

For the first time, Frutiger's palette for printers brought a rational approach to the difficulties of describing the various type weights and widths, always an area of debate among practitioners. Though not applicable to many other types, the palette clearly differentiated the numerous gothic and sans-serif faces, with their multiplicities of stroke and variations of width. Unfortunately, however, Frutiger's idea never caught on; when printers put Univers into their cases, they compared the weight of each series with that of the geometric sans serifs and applied the weight of the latter to the new type. The type-specimen books of different printers therefore varied considerably from one another, to the great confusion of customers. And, in the Monotype version, Frutiger's numbers conflicted with the font number assigned by the company to all of its types and so the palette was discarded. Thus, a worthy attempt to bring order to the chaotic designation of type weights and widths was allowed to fail.

Univers met with competition when it was introduced – 1957 was a halcyon year for the new gothics, three others also emerging from the drawing boards. Mercator was cut by the Dutch typographer

ABCDEFGHIJKLMNOPQ RSTUVWXYZ abcdefghij klmnopqrstuvwxyz .,-;:'!?$& 1234567890

Helvetica (Hass-Stempel)

Dick Dooijes for Typefoundry Amsterdam. Folio was produced by Germany's Bauer foundry, and a type named Neue Haas-Grotesk issued from the Swiss Haas'sche foundry, of Basel. The following year, Aldo Novarese, at the Nebiolo foundry in Turin, produced a gothic family named Recta. Neither Recta nor Mercator made an impact in the United States, but Folio and Neue Haas-Grotesk certainly did.

Folio, designed by Konrad Bauer and Walter Baum, benefited from the promotion of the excellent sales agency that Bauer had long retained in this country. It also became available for the linecasting machine when adopted under a royalty agreement by the Intertype Corporation.

Neue Haas-Grotesk, designed by Max Miedinger, was cut for Linotype by the German Linotype firm, which named it Helvetica. And the Stempel foundry entered into an arrangement with Haas'sche to manufacture the type for export, again under the name Helvetica.

By the early 1960s, when the manufacturers of all these competing types had brought their production up to encompass the innumerable series involved, there was, of course, intense rivalry in their promotion. Each design had its adherents, and it was fairly simple to start an argument among typographers concerning the efficacy of each style. The older type professionals naturally recalled the period, thirty years earlier, when the geometric sans serifs had been subjected to similar polemics; at that time, a single design – Futura – received by far the most enthusiastic approval and became the dominant form. Among the neo-gothics, Helvetica has received greatest attention by adver-

ABCDEFGHIJKLMNOPQRS TUVWXYZ
abcdefghijklmnopqrstuvwxyz
(&$1234567890¢£.,:;'""-*%/!?)

$1234567890¢%/

Folio (Bauer)

ABCDEFGHIJKLMNOPQR STUVWXYZ
abcdefghijklmnopqrstuvwxyz
(&$$1234567890¢.,:;'-*/!?[]«»)

Mercator (Amsterdam)

ABCDEFGHIJKLMNOPQRST UVWXYZ&
abcdefghijklmnopqrstuvwxyz
12345678

Record Gothic (Ludlow)

tising-agency designers, and up to the present it is the most widely used of them all. The more traditional typographers are mystified by this preference, believing that the subtleties of difference among these styles are so slight that an intelligent judgment of them is impossible.

It is evident that the admiration for Swiss typographic design in general was an additional attraction in the selection of Helvetica as the best representative of that style. In any case, the use of Helvetica has spread from advertising into the world of publishing, where it turns up frequently for the setting of textbooks of every description – thus violating long-established precepts concerning typographic legibility.

Notwithstanding the impact of the rejuvenated gothics, the older forms still are very much in evidence at every hand. It would therefore appear that Franklin Gothic will be selected by future designers whose great-grandfathers would have nodded their approval.

27

CLARENDON AND THE
SQUARE-SERIF REVIVAL

The development of the group of types called square serif parallels that of the gothics. Both forms represented the typefounders' answer to the challenge of the nineteenth century: to find a new typographic expression for industrialized society. As with the gothics, the square-serif results were uneven, depending as they did on the skill of the founder and the interpretation of the designer.

The earliest square-serif attempts to meet the demands of the new entrepreneurs – from peddlers to industrialists – had resulted in the modification of the late-eighteenth-century Continental types, especially those of the Didots in France (these have survived to the present but generally under the name Bodoni). It was believed that thickening the main stem of a letter while reducing the weight of the serif would create the maximum boldness required by this rapidly expanding market. Such a rationale produced the numerous types that were labeled 'fat-face' during the first decade of the nineteenth century. The English typefounder Robert Thorne is ordinarily credited with the introduction of such a letter, one that was destined radically to affect the marketing of founders' typefaces, merchandizing that had heretofore been concerned primarily with the printing of books.

Within just twenty years the fat faces were joined by the sans serifs and the square serifs, and never again did typefounders emphasize the production of types for continuous reading, realizing that the production of display types would henceforth be more profitable. Although they continued to manufacture text types in quantity until the development of typesetting machines in the late 1800s, their enterprise after 1820 was directed toward the display faces.

The first square-serif type to be introduced was the Antique of London's Vincent Figgins Foundry, turning up in the 1817 catalogue of that firm in four sizes. These were capital fonts only, of monotone construction, in which the serifs were unbracketed and of the same

ABCDEFGHI JKLMNOPQR STUVWXYZ

abcdefghij klmnopqr stuvwxyz

1234567890

Clarendon Bold (Haas)

weight as the stems. The square serifs outshouted the contemporary fat faces on the printed page, since the heavy serifs contributed to the overall boldness of the character, making it perhaps the blackest ever cast in printing type. But in the contrast of stem weight many of the early sans-serif and square-serif fonts were not at all consistent. For example, in the Antiques of Figgins three are monotone and in one, the four-line pica size, a discrepancy in the thickness of stems and serifs is evident.

R. THORNE

£126780

diminishing

Six-Lines Pica Egyptian of the Thorowgood foundry, 1821

ABCDEFGHIJKLMNO PQRSTUVWXYZ&,;:.'

Two-lines Pica Antique of the Figgins foundry, 1817

Robert Thorne, whose Fann Street Foundry in London specialized in the production of display types, undoubtedly was aware of the Antiques of Figgins, and of their potential. Although he was in poor health at the time, Thorne began to work on several sizes of a similar design. It would appear that it was Thorne who applied the term *Egyptian* to the square-serif types, for upon his death in 1820, the inventory of his foundry listed six sets of 'Egyptian'; his successor, William Thorowgood, issued a specimen book the same year that exhibits these faces. There is, however, a good deal of confusion concerning terminology during this period. For instance, the foundry of William Caslon IV had shown in its 1816 specimen book a single size of sans-serif caps that was called Egyptian and represented the first instance of a sans-serif letter in a typefounder's catalogue. Throughout the nineteenth century the logical designation of such types remained a perplexing problem, and as late as 1907 the difficulty had still not been resolved. That year as venerable a typographic historian as Theodore Low De Vinne listed in his splendid specimen book all of the square serifs under the heading 'Antique, Ionic, Doric, Etc.'

The provenance as much as the use of the term *Egyptian* is obscure. Most authorities agree that it was the coincidence of the emergence of the square-serif types with the popular interest in Egypt following the Napoleonic conquest (which opened the country to archaeological study, along with large-scale plundering of its artifacts) that gave the design its name. There have been attempts to compare the structure of the square-serif letter to Egyptian architecture, but it is more reasonable to assume simply the natural appropriation of a name that had attracted wide attention, similar to the interest in the Tutankhamen exhibitions of the 1970s.

Whatever the derivation of their name, Egyptian types were extremely successful and by 1840 they were being manufactured in

ABCDEFGHIJKL
MNOPQRSTUVW
XYZ abcdefghijk
lmnopqrstuvwxyz
1234567890
.,-;:"'!?$&–

Craw Clarendon (ATF)

audacia tua? nihilne te nocturnum præsidium palatii, nihil urbis vigiliæ, nihil timor £1234567890 METROPOLITAN IMPROVEMENT.

Two-Lines English Clarendon of the Thorowgood foundry, 1848

great variety, the foundries competing with one another in the production of such variants as open, shadow, outline, reversed, and compressed. Another innovation in the type catalogues at this time was the exhortation to printers to adopt the new forms. Prior to the nineteenth century, specimen books had simply exhibited printing types in dignified array, with the quotation from Cicero – 'Quousque tandem abutere, Catilina?' – that had been inaugurated by William Caslon in 1734. Other than a magisterial introductory statement such as, 'We beg to inform the printer . . .,' the founders believed a hard-sell approach to be unnecessary.

The new texts of the specimen books were a result of the industrialization of the printing craft. Increasing numbers of printers in the nineteenth century were engaged in the production of the ephemera of the marketplace – the placards, broadsides, tickets, proclamations, and notices that constituted the daily work of what in England became known as jobbing printing, a term shortened in the United States to job printing – and the many new types created for this work needed advertising. (There is also little doubt that the new fraternity of compositors was unschooled in Latin.) By midcentury the foundries were aggressively catering to the trade, their advertising suggesting the most desirable uses of the numerous new display types. Such promotion flowered during the present century, when the typefounders employed first-rate typographers and maintained their own printing plants, which specialized in the production of admirably planned specimen books, many of which were devoted to but a single type. These pieces have today achieved status as collectors' items.

By 1830 the Egyptian types had spread to France, Germany, and the United States, and the versions, differing in many respects, depended on the interpretation of the punchcutters. The pressures of increased production interfered with aesthetic considerations, a factor that noticeably affected the design of Egyptian lowercase forms. As the first square serifs were cut in capitals only, a weight was applied to the stems that could not be adequately maintained in the transfer to lowercase; an examination of the few lowercase alphabets cut for the early Egyptians reveals the awkwardness of many of the characters. In addition, a similar difficulty may be noted in the maintenance of the monotone boldness of the capitals. The designers of the early gothics had encountered corresponding problems resulting in long delays in preparing acceptable lowercase fonts.

Whereas the new breed of commercial printers was most enthusiastic about the Egyptians, the more traditionally oriented practitioners deplored these styles. For a contemporary criticism of the 'modern' typography, it is interesting to turn to the famous printer's manual *Typographia*, published in England in 1825 by Thomas Curson Hansard.

Instrumental Examination
REMARKABLE

Expecting Northeastern Storms
SIGNAL SERVICE

Harmonious Condition Destroyed by Legislators
RESERVED ADMINISTRATION

French Clarendon as shown in ATF Specimen Book, 1896

Normally approving of the industrialization of printing – especially the technological advances – Hansard was outraged by what he considered the typographical excesses of his time. Of three contemporary display letters that he condemned, one was a black letter and two were Egyptians. In this early critique of the job types, Hansard first censured the fat faces and then added: 'To the razor-edged fine lines and ceriphs [*sic*] of type just observed upon [the fat-faced types], a reverse has succeeded, called "Antique," or "Egyptian," the property of which is, that the strokes which form the letters are all of uniform thickness! – After this, who would have thought that further extravagance could have been conceived? . . . Oh! sacred shades of Moxon and Van Dijke, of Baskerville and Bodoni! what would ye have said of the typographic *monstrosities* here exhibited, which Fashion in our age has produced?'

But Hansard's criticism had no apparent effect on the popularity of the new type styles. As far as printers were concerned, the types met the requirements of the era and provided the means by which they could trumpet their typography to a new market waiting to be exploited.

With the multiplication of the Egyptians by the foundries, gradual changes were introduced which altered somewhat the structure of the letter. In the early models the serifs had generally been unbracketed – that is, they lacked the normal joining stroke, or fillet – but by the 1830s some Egyptians appeared with slightly bracketed serifs, though no consistency may be observed in this practice. And by 1845 a new form had emerged, under the name Clarendon.

The Fann Street Foundry, in London, is credited with the introduction of the first Clarendon. This type's initial appearance was as a condensed letter, and unlike the Egyptians it was issued as a text type rather than for display purposes. Furthermore, it was designed to accompany a roman type as a related boldface, to provide emphasis where required. In order to blend with the roman, the serifs were bracketed and a degree of contrast was applied to the stroke widths.

The Clarendon design is ascribed to Robert Besley, who had joined William Thorowgood at the Fann Street firm in 1838. It will be remembered that it was Thorowgood who had helped to popularize the Egyptians. From a surprising beginning as a typefounder in 1820 – a calling for which he had had no training – Thorowgood a year later had parlayed a big win in the national lottery to an appointment as Letter-Founder to His Majesty. The foundry rapidly grew to include

Greek, Hebrew, Russian, and German types, and in 1828 it absorbed the foundry of Dr. Edmund Fry with its numerous exotic styles.

Besley was no doubt assisted in the design of Clarendon by the skilled punchcutter Benjamin Fox. It so happened that in 1845 England's designs-copyright amendment act came into being, which permitted registering a typographic design for a three-year period. But when Clarendon, the first type to be so registered, became an overwhelming success, the protection was soon violated, with competing firms seeking to take advantage of the type's popularity. Besley was acrimonious in his denunciation of this plagiarism, a problem, as discussed earlier, that afflicts the industry to the present day.

There is little information concerning the origin of the name Clarendon. De Vinne in *Plain Printing Types* (1900) notes that the type was first made for the Clarendon Press at Oxford University, 'to serve as a display letter in a mass of text-type, and for side headings in dictionaries and books of reference.' English sources do not support this theory of the type's having been explicitly manufactured for the Clarendon Press, but they do recognize that the name may well refer to that press. In England *Clarendon* subsequently became synonymous with *boldface* as a description of weight, as it is described in the *Oxford English Dictionary*.

Whatever the derivation of the name, the Clarendon design was a huge commercial success. By 1850 Besley was advertising the virtues of the font as follows:

The most useful Founts that a Printer can have in his Office are Clarendons: they make a striking Word or Line either in a Hand Bill or a Title Page, and do not overwhelm the other lines: they have been made with great care, so that while they are distinct and striking they possess a graceful outline, avoiding on the one hand, the clumsy inelegance of the Antique or Egyptian Character, and on the other, the appearance of an ordinary Roman Letter thickened by long use.

The idea of using a boldface character for emphasis rather than an italic became well established with Clarendon, a practice that remains common in commercial printing, principally newspapers. When the duplexed, or two-letter, matrix was developed for the Linotype machine, about 1900, the second letter was invariably an 'antique' (Clarendon-style), when not an italic. Later on, of course, the composing-machine manufacturers developed complementary bold variants for many of their popular roman styles and so were not dependent on a standardized boldface.

ABCDEFGHIJKLMNOPQRST UVWXYZ&
abcdefghijklmnopqrstuvwxyz
1234567890

Karnak Medium (Ludlow)

INTERTYPE matrices excel in type 12345
INTERTYPE matrices excel in type 12345

Cairo and Cairo Bold (Intertype)

Clarendon thus began as a bold condensed type, but it was soon appearing in an expanded version and even as a lightface letter. By the 1850s it was internationally recognized as a utilitarian addition to the commercial composing room. Besley's expanded variant became the model for German cuttings as well as for the Clarendons that appeared in the catalogues of the Bruce Foundry in New York, and the Cincinnati Foundry – the first American firms to issue the type.

For the balance of the nineteenth century the Clarendons and the Egyptians, by whatever name they went, continued to thrive and were generally more popular than even the gothics. Although the decorated letters and scripts took up much of the attention of the design departments of the foundries – leaving little time for experimentation in modifying the existing square-serif types – for some fifty years (from about 1820 to 1870) the square serifs played a dominant role in everyday typography. Nicolete Gray, in *Nineteenth Century Ornamented Types and Title Pages* (1938), wrote that the Egyptians as developed by the English punchcutters represent the most brilliant typographic expression of the century. But in his *Printing Types* (1922), Daniel Berkeley Updike reduces the achievement to but one reference of less

Inspired Singer
DISTINGUISH

Urgent Note
FINANCIER

Reinforce
EXPORT

Beton (Bauer)

than a sentence: '. . . a kind of swollen type-form in which all the lines of a letter were of nearly equal strength. . . .' (In a footnote he expressed even greater disdain for the form.)

In the United States most of the foundries produced square serifs. When the American Type Founders Company was formed – out of some two dozen separate foundries – the first 'Collected' specimen book of the amalgamation, issued in 1896, showed twenty-six varieties under such names as Ionic, Clarendon, Antique, French Clarendon,

AAABCDEFGHIJJKKLMN
OPQRSTUVWXYZ&ÆŒ
a a b c d e f f g h i j k k l m n o
p q r r s t t u v w x y y z æ œ
$ 1 2 3 4 5 6 7 8 9 0 .,-':;!?

Rockwell Antique (Monotype)

ABCDEFGHIJKLMNOPQ
RSTUVWXYZ abcd
efghijklmnopqrstuvwxyz
.,-;:!?''"$&$¢ 1234567890

Stymie Bold (ATF)

and Doric. But in 1906, in the 1,180-page ATF specimen book, just ten square serifs were listed, none of which was Clarendon. And in the 1923 catalogue this list had been reduced to only six examples of the genre, again with the name Clarendon missing. The Barnhart Brothers & Spindler specimen book of 1925, the last large-scale American type catalogue, exhibited five square serifs of which two were called Antique and three Clarendon.

When a revival of the square-serif style occurred in the 1930s, it followed the same pattern as the regeneration of the gothics that had taken place in the 1920s when the geometric sans-serif forms had emanated from the experimental typography of the Bauhaus movement. Simply stated, the square-serif revival consisted of the addition of serifs to the Futura model.

The first such type to be produced was Memphis, cut in 1929 by

Rudolf Wolf, then head of Stempel's design department in Frankfurt. Memphis was sold in the United States through Melbert Cary, Jr.'s Continental Typefounders Association under the name Girder – an inspired choice for a period when in most American cities the steelwork of the new skyscrapers was very much in evidence. For two or three years there was a great flurry of activity in the production of the geometric square serifs, most of which were given names connoting their 'Egyptian' origin. In 1930 Georg Trump drew City for Berlin's Berthold foundry, but it was not available in this country until 1936, again as a Continental Typefounders import. For the Bauer foundry, Heinrich Jost cut Beton in 1931, and the Paris foundry Deberny et Peignot offered Pharaon by 1933, with the English Stephenson, Blake & Company tagging along with Scarab about 1937.

ABCDEFGHIJKLMNOPQRSTUVW
XYZ abcdefghijklmnopqrstuvwxyz
1234567890 äöü ß .,-:;!?()„"»«'&/ §†*

Memphis Bold (Linotype-Stempel)

ABCDEFGHIJKLMN
OPQRSTUVWXYZ..!?
adcdefghijklmnopqrs
tuvwxyz1234567890

City Bold (Berthold–Continental Typefounders Assoc.)

The American type manufacturers, already menaced by furious competition from the Europeans in the production of the sans-serif faces, responded quickly to the new challenge but with little apparent enthusiasm. The Intertype Corporation cut Cairo in 1931, and Mergenthaler Linotype, by arrangement with Stempel, began to advertise Memphis, thus competing with Girder, the same type. In 1931 R. Hunter Middleton started work on the long series of square serifs named Karnak, which he drew for Ludlow Typograph. At American Type Founders a shortcut was taken by digging into the vaults and coming up with Litho Antique of circa 1910; a few characters were redesigned to bring that face into conformity with the current trend. Rather than checking the gazetteer for yet another Egyptian-sounding name, ATF's advertising department wistfully named the face Stymie, in the hope, unfulfilled, that their entry would curtail the enthusiasm of their competitors. Lanston Monotype Machine Company in Philadelphia followed ATF's lead by also resurrecting an older type, Rockwell Antique, but soon thereafter adopted ATF's Stymie, by agreement with the foundry, to capitalize on Stymie's acceptance (even if competitors' enthusiasm remained undiminished).

For the balance of the 1930s all the suppliers were busily filling out their square-serif series, but at the same time they were being careful not to neglect the Futura models that continued to dominate advertising typography. Of the geometric square serifs, Beton, of the Bauer foundry, proved the most popular, but all of these types suffered somewhat in comparison with the sans serifs, since the serifed geo-

---

QUALITY COLOR
Zero is the figure

P. T. Barnum (ATF)

ABCDEFGHIJKLMNOPQRSTUVWXYZ
ÆŒ&1234567890£$,.:;-'!?ABCDEFGHIJ
abcdefghijklmnopqrstuvwxyzæœfiffflffiffl

ABCDEFGHIJKLMNOPQRSTUVWXYZ&
ÆŒ1234567890£$,.:;-"!?(ABCDEFGHIJ
abcdefghijklmnopqrstuvwxyzœœfifffiffiffab

Consort and Consort Italic (Stephenson, Blake & Co.)

metric pattern was not compatible with the design of the numerous variants required by the advertising typographers, whose demands ruled the market for new typefaces.

After World War II the emergence of the earlier gothics, particularly the extended series, spurred another wave of interest in the Egyptians, but this time the emphasis was on the Clarendon style. In 1951 the English foundry Steven, Shanks & Son revived three series of Antique, the second of which was a true Clarendon, in addition to an Antique Expanded. In the same year the Scottish foundry Miller & Richard offered Egyptian Expanded, the Haas'sche foundry in Basel revived an excellent Clarendon cut by Hermann Eidenbenz, and the Bauer firm brought out Fortune, called Volta in Germany.

In 1953 Stephenson, Blake returned to the original punches of the Fann Street Foundry for the type that it reissued as Consort, adding an italic and a boldface, and in 1960 the Monotype Corporation of London brought out New Clarendon. The American Type Founders Company commissioned the talented typographic designer Freeman Craw to produce a new type on the Clarendon model, which was marketed in 1956 and became a great success. Those printers who resisted the move to the Clarendons based their objections on the similarity of these faces to the ubiquitous Cheltenham design.

The Clarendon revival of the 1950s was by and large restricted to foundry types, although some of the styles did become available for composition by the display phototypesetting devices. There appeared to be little interest in the transfer of the Clarendons to the larger film machines.

One other style of Clarendon has retained its popularity from the nineteenth century, the so-called circus letter, which was cut by many

ABCDEFGHIJKLMNO
PQRSTUVWXYZ
abcdefghijklmnopqrstuvwxyz
1234567890

ABCDEFGHIJKLMNO
PQRSTUVWXYZ
abcdefghijklmnopqrstuvwxyz
1234567890

Fortune Bold (Bauer)

ABCDEFGHIJKL
abcdefghijklmnop

MNOPQRSTUVWXYZ
qrstuvwxyzfifffffifffiffl&,.!

ABCDEFGHIJKLMNOPQR
abcdefghijklmnopqrstuvwx
yzæœ&,.:;-!'[(£$1234567890

Consort Light (Stephenson, Blake & Co.)

of the early founders under the name French Clarendon. In this style the slab serifs are overemphasized for display purposes, which has naturally limited its usefulness as a general type. The restoration of this face began as early as 1938 and had no relation to the later Clarendon revival. Stephenson, Blake offered its version, called Play-bill, and Typefoundry Amsterdam produced Hidalgo the following year (Hidalgo was cut in only a capital alphabet, by S. Schlesinger). In the United States the form is best known as P. T. Barnum, an ATF resurrection of the 1950s that has seen frequent albeit circumscribed use.

28

OPTIMA AND THE
HUMANIST SANS-SERIF TYPES

Type designers have made numerous attempts to create a sans-serif type that could be considered both beautiful and utilitarian. It was the latter requirement that had shaped the sans serifs that were originally produced early in the nineteenth century, but the prosaic typographic needs of the Industrial Revolution brought forth types containing features of little aesthetic interest.

For the better part of a century, sans-serif types tended to be unimaginative renditions of roman letter forms, although it was discovered that their monotone characteristics did allow for variations of weight and width that would have been more difficult to achieve with their roman counterparts. In Europe these sans serifs were termed 'grotesque' and in the United States 'gothic' quite soon after their introduction. This unfortunate nomenclature was probably due to their weight, which indeed was similar to that of the black letter – the truly gothic fifteenth-century forms – but the term also expressed the disdain of printers for the early serifless typefaces.

This attitude changed abruptly during the 1920s when the Bauhaus typographers selected the sans-serif structure as the most expressive icon of their functionalist ideals. But the types of geometric construction that emerged from the Bauhaus experiments were, of course, considerably removed from the so-called gothics and thus served, in fact, to further alienate typographic designers from the older style. Meanwhile, the traditional typographers, particularly those who espoused the post-Morris canons, severely criticized the geometric typefaces, censuring them as gross caricatures of roman letter forms and as both unreadable and illegible.

Unquestionably, the nineteenth-century gothics were plain letters. In most instances – the traditionalists notwithstanding – the new geometric styles were considered a great improvement over them, particularly by typographers who appreciated the asymmetric designs of

ABCDEFGHIJKL MNOPQRSTU VWXYZ

abcdefghijklmno pqrstuvwxyz

1234567890

Optima (Stempel)

the Bauhaus. But the idea persisted in some circles that it might also be possible to combine the forms of roman and sans serif in an aesthetically acceptable type.

One of the first type designers to experiment along such lines was R. Hunter Middleton, then a young man producing types for the Ludlow Typograph Company in Chicago. In 1929, when interest in the sans serifs was at its peak, Middleton drew Stellar, which thus became the first new sans serif to be produced in the United States.

LEIPZIG SPRING FAIR 1936

ROOM XII

PRINTING MACHINERY SHOW

Offenbach design of Rudolf Koch for Klingspor foundry

In its lightface weight, Stellar has much to commend it as a reasoned attempt to blend the spirit of a graceful roman type with a serifless structure. But its appearance at the very moment when American typographers were captivated by such geometric types as Futura and Kabel militated against any success it might have enjoyed.

In Europe, the German Rudolf Koch, who had designed the Kabel series of geometric sans serifs, now turned to a sans serif of roman inspiration and drew Offenbach. This was a pen-drawn roman, and though it was widely admired, its lack of a lowercase alphabet restricted its use.

A decade after the introduction of the geometric types of the 1920s, there occurred a slight reaction to their overuse. The American Type Founders Company accordingly accepted the design for a romanized sans serif brought to the firm by a young American named Warren Chappell, who had studied with Rudolf Koch in the early thirties. The resulting type, Lydian, was introduced in 1938 and was an immediate success. It was highly regarded as a display and advertising type for twenty years after its introduction. Chappell supplied a very legible oblique italic, which he followed with a chancery italic drawn for the bold weight only. The design has been transferred to the film composers and is still in wide use.

But during the 1950s a sans serif emerged that gripped the attention of typographers as the most satisfying blend to date of the best features of both the roman and the sans-serif structures. This was the Optima design of Hermann Zapf.

Zapf – now the most prolific of the world's type designers as well as the most widely known – first began to think of such a type in 1950. He has written, 'The type of today and tomorrow will hardly be a faithful recutting of a 16th century roman of the Renaissance, nor the original cutting of a classical face of Bodoni's time – but neither will it be a sans serif of the 19th century.' He was familiar with Italian inscriptional lettering and, along with other typographers who have admired the fifteenth-century sans-serif characters on the tombs in Florence's Santa Croce, he was entranced by their classic forms. Inlaid in green marble in the floor of that church, these circular inscriptions were cut about 1530; they are the product of sensitive artists attempting to vary the existing roman styles. Zapf had also made sketches of the inscriptions on the fourth-century Arch of Constantine in Rome.

Another source of serifless inscriptions is the Schiattesi tombstone

ABCDEFGHIJKLMNOPQRSTU
VWXYZ   abcdefghijklmnopqrs
tuvwxyz   1234567890
.,-;:"!?$&

Lydian (ATF), designed by Warren Chappel for American Type Founders Co.

ABCDEFGHIJKLMNOPQRSTU
VWXYZ&
abcdefghijklmnopqrstuvwxyz
1234567890

ABCDEFGHIJKLMNOPQRST
UVWXYZ&
abcdefghijklmnopqrstuvwxyz
1234567890

Stellar (Ludlow), designed by R. Hunter Middleton for Ludlow Typograph Co.

in Rome, dated 1423. Here designers can readily observe a possible inspiration for the twentieth-century letters drawn by the English Edward Johnston and the later adaptations in England by Eric Gill.

In several other Italian inscriptions, dated 1423 and 1430, the letters are unserifed but have strong thick-and-thin contrast. It is this style, sharing equally the best features of the roman letters and the sans serifs, that inspired Hermann Zapf to begin experiments that resulted in one of his most successful types. He began his Optima designs in 1952 and spent some six years in their development.

In 1954, while working on this project, Zapf took the suggestion of Monroe Wheeler, of the Museum of Modern Art in New York, and began to consider adapting his developing letter as a book type. He thereupon changed the proportions of the lowercase, and by means of photography (working with Ed Rondthaler at Photolettering, Inc., in New York), he tested the suitability of the design for continuous-reading application. The capitals of Optima, as Zapf has stated, follow the proportions of the Trajan Column inscriptions, which date from A.D. 113 and serve as the best model of Roman majuscules.

Zapf also said that Optima is the first German type not based on the standard baseline alignment established in 1905. Zapf writes: 'This base line is too deep for a roman, as it was designed for the high x-height of the Fraktur and Textura letters. Thus, too many German types have ascenders which are too long and descenders which are too short. The proportions of Optima Roman are now in the Golden Section: lowercase x-height equalling the minor and ascenders–descenders the major. However, the curved lines of the stems of each letter result from technical considerations of type manufacturing rather than purely esthetic considerations.'

All of these details under Zapf's sure hand have been successfully attended to, with the result that Optima is today widely used not only for display composition but also for continuous reading, for which its contrast of stroke makes it more adaptable than the mono-tone sans-serif types. The regular and the medium weights show to best advantage the classic principles called upon by the designer. In the variants of the face, the semi-bold and the black, the nineteenth-century gothic characteristics seem to dominate, although these weights are meant to be complementary to the regular one.

Optima was first manufactured in 1958 in a foundry version by Stempel of Frankfurt, and shortly thereafter in linecasting matrices by America's Mergenthaler. It made its debut that year at the Drupa exhibition in Düsseldorf. Like all popular new types (particularly those of Zapf), Optima has been widely pirated for use with competing photographic typesetting systems. It is now sold under several names, and the results are frequently very unhappy.

In a discussion with the writer, Zapf admitted a preference for Optima over his other types, but he has also observed in print that a father should not have to select a favorite among his daughters! If left to his own devices, Zapf would have called the type, in a straightforward manner, New Roman, but the marketing staff at the foundry insisted on naming it Optima. By any name, it is a splendid addition to the resources of twentieth-century typographers.

In 1929, when the geometric sans-serif types revolutionized commercial printing, the emphasis in their development was quite different from that of roman types. For traditionalists the new styles, no matter how functional, were still without any aesthetic merits. The astute Stanley Morison said of this period that 'typography was in a *cul-de-sac* and life could only be wrung from the letterforms by torture.' Daniel Berkeley Updike had not given consideration even to the nineteenth-century gothics in his monumental *Printing Types* of 1922. Indeed, in the chapter 'The Choice of Types' he asked, 'And what are the types we ought not to want – which have no place in any artistically respectable composing-room?' He then proceeded to name the outlaws, lumping sans serifs with fat-faced romans, hairline types, and almost all ornamental types. In the second edition of this text, published in 1937, the typographic pundit was confronted with the sans-serif explosion. But of it he merely said that he had nothing to add or take away from his original remarks, 'save that if sans serif fonts must be had, the medium Futura of Paul Renner or the Gill Sans may be used.'

In 1929 William A. Dwiggins became involved with a sans-serif typeface. Following a conversation on the subject with Dwiggins's cousin Laurance B. Siegfried (a distinguished figure in American printing until his death in 1978), Mergenthaler's Harry Gage visited Dwiggins at his home in Hingham, Massachusetts. There ensued some correspondence, with the result that Dwiggins was engaged to draw a sans-serif type for Mergenthaler.

Dwiggins, then forty-nine, had a solid reputation as a book designer, calligrapher, illustrator, and advertising typographer. As a young man he had studied lettering with Frederic W. Goudy in Chicago and later produced a number of designs for Updike's Merrymount Press. His connection, as of 1926, with Alfred A. Knopf's

Stencils —— Somebody is sure to try this pretty
soon, sans-serif — a mechanically finished C. S.
body-letter of good shape

Binder rate bp

These are experimental – not perfected – but there
is an idea lurking in this somewhere.

tram and und

lc X 12 pt   could be close-fitted
and still legible

> too heavy

stems 0.013

Districted DID

immoderate fgh

too close fitting

bad
gap

g not up to weight

too much condensed, not evident

Modelled sans-serif that might be interesting
intended to be close-fitted – experimental drawing WAD March 21 1929   lc X 14 pt

Drawing for humanist roman by William A. Dwiggins, 1929

publishing firm resulted in the design of hundreds of books that established Dwiggins as the indisputable leader in American trade book design.

Mergenthaler's interest in the production of a sans-serif type was to satisfy the requests of its customers; to supply a type in the Futura mode to be made available in matrix form. The collaboration with Dwiggins was most successful: from it came the popular type family Metro, cut in 1929, which is still used in newspaper typography.

W. A. Dwiggins was happiest with traditional forms, but his lively imagination and whimsical approach to design freed his thinking from the conservatism expressed by so many contemporary type designers. Whereas his old teacher, Goudy, was a purist in letter design who never fully accepted the technical modifications of manufacturing, Dwiggins felt that he had a good deal to learn from the engineers responsible for the transfer of drawing to matrix; moreover, he thoroughly enjoyed working with them.

Although Dwiggins had satisfactorily met the demands of the Mergenthaler firm, he was also eager to generate a sans-serif type along somewhat different lines. This letter would be far removed from dependence on geometric principles or the concepts of the nineteenth-century gothics. In fact, what Dwiggins really wanted to design was a sans-serif type with a humanist structure.

Since the center of the sans-serif revival was in Europe, Dwiggins at first investigated the possibility of designing such a type for a European typefoundry. Working through Melbert B. Cary, Jr., president of the Continental Typefounders Association – an import house connected with a number of the European firms – he prepared a few drawings to demonstrate his tentative ideas. Shortly after this, however, Dwiggins decided that the Atlantic Ocean was too formidable a barrier for effective type design and so abandoned his hope of finding a European foundry.

The stats of the sketches Dwiggins made for Cary are contained in the Melbert B. Cary, Jr., Graphic Arts Collection at the Rochester Institute of Technology. Dated March 1929, the drawings show a sans-serif type with definite roman characteristics. Dwiggins had prepared these sketches in his own preferred manner, by cutting stencils for stem weights, curves, arches, and so on, and 'getting a focus' by combining related elements of letter anatomy. This is also the procedure he employed in constructing the elements of his inimitable ornaments, used with such success in his book design.

Several years later, when Dwiggins had become more involved in the design of types, particularly for book composition, he changed his method, drawing letters with a brush or pen to a size of ten times 12-point. In this he followed the style of his former teacher, Fred Goudy, who also drew freehand to a large size.

In the drawings prepared for Cary, Dwiggins noted, 'Somebody is sure to try this pretty soon, san-serif [*sic*] – a mechanically finished o.s. body-letter of good shape. These are experimental – not perfected – but there is an idea lurking in this somewhere.'

So when Mergenthaler Linotype approached Dwiggins for a sans serif, the designer immediately thought of his earlier ideas. Unhappily the firm was not prepared to break new ground. Though its customers were persistently demanding a 'new' sans serif, of course what they really wanted was a geometric style in the pattern of Futura. Dwiggins, always practical, bowed to the unavoidable requirements of the marketplace. His Metro design therefore followed the Futura idea in the capitals, though departing from it in the lowercase; Rudolf Koch, another traditional type designer, had done the same with the Kabel type. Dwiggins had earlier commented on the geometric sans serifs: 'They are fine in the caps and bum in the lowercase. I don't know if you can make a Gothic that is good in the lowercase, but we might try.'

Once the Metro design was launched, Dwiggins again turned to his dream of a sans serif with classic proportions and style. The earliest evidence of this continuing interest that the writer can discover appears in a letter dated January 4, 1930, addressed to C. H. Griffith, at that time assistant to the president of the Mergenthaler Linotype Company. Here Dwiggins states: 'I shall send you a few more characters of that experimental face of mine. [Harry] Gage took down to you some stencils of a modelled san [*sic*] serif that you were to try experimentally but it has been side-tracked. I have a hunch that it may be important (listening to the whispers among the younger set), and maybe it would be well to dig it out and look at it.'

During the next three years Dwiggins produced numerous drawings for a humanist sans serif, and Mergenthaler produced matrices for a sufficient number of characters to obtain a realistic idea of the final appearance of the design. But after several attempts to evolve a satisfactory style (all of which were, in Dwiggins's phrase, 'drowned' by the manufacturer), the company turned to other matters. Dwiggins, however, persisted. By 1931 he was back at the drawing board, and he wrote to Mergenthaler:

It seems that I can't keep away from the 'modelled san-serif,' [*sic*] partly because I think there is something valuable to be done along that line, and partly because the 'young ones' keep howling for a face, sanserif, [*sic*] that can reasonably be used for body-matter in a book.

I enclose the latest effort, which I send with no suggestion that it be cut, but that you lay it in the portfolio and take a look at it now and then.

One of the secrets of success in such a face would be great finesse in fitting. With no cerifs [*sic*] the exact relation between black mark and white paper becomes even more important than with usual characters. For every two black bands of a given weight, there is just right white to go with them, e.g., in rules scheme. I think these san-serifs [*sic*] could be fused into a correct color by finding out just that right white interval. If it were formed between straight stems the round letters could be brought into position to meet it, couldn't they? I should suppose that there is a formula that controls that: if the m, n, interval is so much, the m, o, interval will be so much?

The straight-stem interval in Met Black and Met Medium struck me as very well calculated.

Mergenthaler finally got around to cutting a few characters of this type, labeling them '12-point Experimental No. 63.' On May 24, 1932, Griffith wrote Dwiggins as follows:

Dear Bill:

Experimental No. 63 Modelled Sans Serif. Further to your comments on the above and in answer to your query I am frankly of the opinion that Experimental No. 63 can be nothing else than a 'stunt' face. At the moment I cannot bring myself to the point of feeling that it has any immediate sales value; or perhaps I should say that I do not regard it of sufficient importance to interfere with the development of Electra or the development of your ideas with regard to a face on the Scotch base.

On the other hand I cannot get away from the feeling that there is an important place somewhere for a Modelled Sans Serif and I do not think that we should let it get away from us altogether. Two or three young designers who have recently returned from a sojourn in Germany have told me that our German contemporaries are searching for a model of this kind and that it is a live topic of discussion. They all seem to feel that the key to the solution of the problem is just around the corner; but they are unable to find it. I recall that you used the identical expression a year or so ago. I heard it again today from a young man who had just returned from a year's study in Germany with Dr. [Rudolf] Koch. So let's not drop it altogether.

Dwiggins replied to what was beginning to appear to be Lino-type's final rejection of the whole concept of the modeled sans serif:

Your comments are entirely correct. For myself I am not awfully thrilled. In spite of the clamor of the 'young' typographers, I doubt if a san-serif [*sic*] body letter will work. This one looks flea-bitten – like a hand-lettering plate that had been over-etched. Metroblack and Metromedium carry the eye on

A a B b C c   A a B b C c

Albertus Light 534   Albertus 481

A B C

A B C D E F G H I J K L M N O P Q R S T U
V W X Y Z & £ 1 2 3 4 5 6 7 8 9 O

Albertus Titling 324

A B C D E F G H I J K L M

Albertus Bold Titling 538

Albertus, designed for English Monotype by Berthold Wolpe, 1932

the line because of the thickness of the stems. It seems that anything with lighter stems than Mblack and Mmed. requires the cerif [*sic*] stroke to carry the line. Metrolight, e.g., doesn't work as a body face at all well.

I will follow your lead as to further experiments with No. 63. If you think it worthwhile, there are things that are plain to be done. My query would be: can it be anything else than a 'stunt' face? If a stunt face looks like sales to you, good enough, let's go. But don't let's go on my account. 'Within me is more.'

Attached to this letter in the files of the Griffith-Dwiggins corre-spondence, at the University of Kentucky, is a handwritten note from WAD, dated May 27, 1932, which might very well be the final comment on a humanist sans-serif type by one of the greatest of American type designers and graphic artists: 'On the strength of your comments I will not let the idea die. Using that last experiment as a point of departure, I'll try some more twists. But as you say, do Electra stuff, etc., first. If it is possible to make a sans serif body-letter that the American public can read without noticing the fact that it is reading, we are the ones who can do it. Yes?'

The idea did not perish but what did come to an end was the opportunity for William A. Dwiggins to accomplish something that was very close to his heart – a sans-serif type based on humanist roman forms.

The 'modelled sans serif' that Dwiggins so hoped to produce was finally and superlatively drawn as Optima by the thirty-four-year-old Hermann Zapf in 1952. In 1969, the writer showed Zapf the Dwiggins drawings in the Cary Collection, and they were a revelation to him. Zapf could only shake his head at the coincidence of inspiration between himself and Dwiggins, thirty years and four thousand miles apart. Zapf fully agrees that the success of a printing type depends on numerous factors other than the skill of a designer, and proper timing is one of the most essential. The Dwiggins experimental sans serif, like Middleton's Stellar type, is a case in point.

William A. Dwiggins

29

FUTURA AND THE
GEOMETRIC SANS-SERIF TYPES

The types that Americans call gothic and that Europeans call grotesque were the first serifless letters to achieve popularity as printing types. Now, more than a century and a half since their introduction, their appeal has not diminished in the eyes of most typographic designers. Naturally there have been several dips in the curve of these styles' acceptance, but they continue to flourish and fulfill a substantial niche in the typographic requirements for commercial printing.

The specimen books of the nineteenth-century typefounders were brimming with gothics, and when the family concept of providing various weights and widths for one face became established – after 1900 – it seemed that these types would continue their domination of commercial printing. In the midtwenties, however, the gothics experienced a setback, which was to last for a quarter of a century. This was a result of the influence of the German school of design (encompassing the Bauhaus), from which emerged an approach to structuring serifless letters that captured the imagination of the younger typographic designers. The typeface that expressed *die neue Typographie*, 'the new typography,' was Futura.

But though Futura made a definite impact upon its introduction in 1926, it was not the first sans-serif type to depart from the gothic model – there were antecedents that had influenced its design. Probably the most important of these was the alphabet drawn by Edward Johnston for the London Underground Railway in 1916. Johnston was an outstanding teacher of calligraphy, who in 1906 had published *Writing and Illuminating and Lettering*, a work that held great authority in England and Germany and is still considered probably the most influential book on lettering ever published.

The Johnston Underground Alphabet – still in use – represented a departure from the nineteenth-century gothic letters. Whereas these gothics had been primarily serifless modifications of roman forms,

ABCDEFG
HIJKLMNOP
QRSTUV
WXYZ

abcdefghi
jklmnopqrstu
vwxyz
1234567890

Futura Medium (Bauer)

ABCDEFGHIJKLMNOP
QRSTUVWXYZ
abcdefghijklmnopqrst
uvwxyz
1234567890&£

The "Underground" type of Edward Johnston

abcdefghi
jklmnopqr
stuvwxyz
a   dd

Herbert Bayer's experimental Universal typeface, 1925

Johnston, with compass and straightedge, created monotone characters of geometric construction. Utilizing his profound knowledge of
traditional letters, he produced an alphabet that had far greater legibility than the earlier sans-serif forms.

The Johnston approach to sans-serif lettering was to come to
fruition in the type of the fine English designer Eric Gill. Named Gill
Sans, this face was cut by the Monotype Corporation in 1928 and

rapidly became the most widely used serifless type in Great Britain. As the American Monotype firm refused to offer the Gill type for the American market, it received limited use here with the result that the Continental sans serifs became dominant.

In Germany just before the First World War there had been a movement to discard conventional ideas in typography. Its spokesman, Jakob Erbar, believed that the type that would best express the new concepts would have to be a serifless letter. The world conflict delayed the spread of Erbar's ideas, but after the war their effect was enhanced by the Johnston alphabet, giving further impetus to the reform movement.

In 1919 the Bauhaus school, under the direction of the architect Walter Gropius, brought to fruition some of the untried theories of design – particularly those related to architecture – that had previously only been discussed. Function and form became the key words of the philosophy of this new design, whose focus was the elimination of the Victorian 'gingerbread' decoration on buildings and the substitution of pure line. Applied to type, this approach could only result in clean sans-serif characters. And what could be more appropriate than constructing these characters with compass and straightedge?

The timing of the sans-serif experiments coincided with a period that many observers of typography considered deplorable. Blackness reigned supreme, in such faces as Cooper Black, Ultra Bodoni, and Broadway. Complementary to the heavy types were rules of equal weight, with dingbats and cubes to match. Thus, the functional movement, with its clean lines and geometric distribution of white space, offered a most dynamic contrast to the existing styles. Indeed, American typographers had been experimenting with the asymmetric designs of the neo-Bauhaus period before Futura became available. And since the resulting designs – being based on the extra-bold types then popular – were appalling, the advent of the German sans serifs by contrast sparked even greater enthusiasm for geometric sans serifs.

The first type to emerge from this philosophy was a sans serif designed by and named for Jakob Erbar. Produced in 1926, this type should be recognized as the initiator of 'the new typography,' but it was followed closely by another design, Futura, that appeared to most observers to be superior in every way. Futura captured the imagination of typographers worldwide and thus robbed its predecessor of its claim to being 'the first.'

Futura was created by Paul Renner, a book designer and founder

Original concept of the Futura design by Paul Renner

of the Masters' School for German Printers in Munich. As originally conceived, Futura represented what can only be termed an abstraction of the idea of the roman letter. The capitals were more traditional than the lowercase characters, and they followed more closely the features of the earlier gothics, although they were of monotone and geometric construction. But in drawing the lowercase, Renner's obvious enthusiasm for 'form follows function' resulted in a font in which several letters became caricatures of classic minuscules.

Renner offered the design to the Bauer Typefoundry of Frankfurt, which recommended a number of changes based on its long experience in producing printing types. The design as it is now recognized was completed in 1927. The major changes, made in the lowercase characters, brought them closer to the accepted forms. The type became enormously successful and instigated a sans-serif renaissance that quickly spread from Europe to the United States.

At the same time that Futura was under development, the most widely known and respected German type designer, Klingspor's Rudolf Koch, was also preparing a geometric sans serif, ultimately named, for the export market, Kabel. Appearing the same year as Futura, Kabel was also heartily received.

As Koch was in every sense a traditional designer – who had cut many of the punches of his earlier types by hand – he evidently found it more difficult than did Renner to depart from the normal roman forms. For example, in Kabel the lowercase *a* is in the standardized roman pattern, as are *g* and *t*. The *e* reaches back to the Venetian period in its retention of the slanted crossbar. It is in the capitals that Kabel holds more closely to the geometric style, although several letters are unique among the sans serifs in having slanted stroke endings.

In the cap font Futura is a surprisingly simple design of plain block letters with no remarkable individual characters other than perhaps the *Q*, whose tail is a diagonal that is longer inside the counter space than outside it. It may be noted that the caps are shorter in height than the ascenders of the lowercase, a feature of practical value in German-language printing in which there are so many capitals. The lowercase alphabet utilizes the perfectly round *o* as the base for seven other characters, which are changed with the mere addition of a stroke to create *a*, *b*, *d*, *e*, *g*, *p*, and *q*.

Together Futura and Kabel were received by the more progressive typographers in the United States as harbingers of a whole new world of typography. Some traditionalists, as could be expected, took an entirely different view – one of them called the faces 'block letters for block-heads.' It was probably the combination of geometric sans-serif types with the asymmetric design that was most disturbing to the conservative typographers. But the movement could not be halted or even slowed. The excitement greeting the debut of the geometric sans-serif types in the United States prompted the American manu-facturers of type and matrices to take immediate steps to counter the competition from the German foundries. By 1930 this had been accomplished, but since accurate records of the dates of introduction of these designs do not exist, it is difficult to determine the exact sequence of presentation. The fact remains, however, that within

THOSE
desirable

Characters in Font

A B C D E F G H I J
K L M N O P Q R
S T U V W X Y Z
& ◆ « » ₵ . , - ' : ; ! ? ( ) ◖◗ ◖
$ 1 2 3 4 5 6 7 8 9 0
a b c d e f g h i j k l
m n o p q r s t u v
w x y z ch ck ft ff fi fl

Kabel Light

343

ABCDEFGHIJKLMNOPQRSTUVWXYZ
abcdefghijklmnopqrstuvwxyz
(&$1234567890¢£.,:;'""--·--·*%/!?[]«»)

three years of the arrival of the German types, all American manufacturers had produced competitive styles.

The Intertype Corporation entered the sans-serif derby with the
Vogue series, created for the fashion magazine of the same name.
Designed anonymously, Vogue superficially resembles Futura. The
response to Futura of two of the other manufacturers of linecasting
machines – the Mergenthaler Linotype Company and the Ludlow
Typograph Company – was the production of independently designed
sans-serif styles. Mergenthaler turned to one of the finest graphic
designers of our time, William A. Dwiggins.

A year previously, Dwiggins had written a great book on the subject of typography, entitled *Layout in Advertising*. In this volume he
had discussed the legibility of types and stated: 'Gothic in its various
manifestations has little to commend it except simplicity. It is not
overly legible, it has no grace. Gothic capitals are indispensable, but
there are no good Gothic capitals; the typefounders will do a service
to advertising if they will provide a Gothic of good design.'

Dwiggins received an immediate response from Harry L. Gage, at
Mergenthaler, who requested that Dwiggins define good design in a
gothic, illustrate it, and then cut it for the Linotype. This Dwiggins
proceeded to do, and from then on he was, in addition to all of his
other roles, a type designer.

Linotype's sans serif was named Metro, and the first series to
be drawn was the bold weight called Metroblack. The subsequent
variants of the series were drawn by the firm's design department
under Dwiggins's supervision. Metro is at its best in the capitals,
which represent the same approach as that of Edward Johnston to his
alphabet for the London Underground. In the lowercase several
characters depart from the geometric principles, such as the *e* in its

HOW IS ONE TO ASSESS AND EVALUATE A TYPE FA

How is one to assess and evaluate a type face in terms of its esthetic design? Why do the pace-makers in the art of printing rave over a specific face of type? What do they see in it? Why is it so superlatively pleasant to their eyes? *Good design is always practical design.* And what they see in a good type design is, partly, its excellent practical fitness to perform its work. It has a "heft" and balance in all of its parts just right for its size, as any good tool has. Your good chair has all of its parts made nicely to the right size

ABCDEFGHIJKLMNOPQRSTUVWXYZ&
ABCDEFGHIJKLMNOPQRSTUVWXYZ&
abcdefghijklmnopqrstuvwxyz 1234567890 ($,.:;'-'?!)
abcdefghijklmnopqrstuvwxyz 1234567890 ($,.:;'-'?!)

Metromedium (Linotype)

thin crossbar and the *f*, *j*, and *t* in their peculiar slabbed-off stroke endings.

A successful individualized approach to the redesign of a gothic – which has sold very well for Linotype, particularly in the newspaper field – Metro is nonetheless scarcely a face in the Futura pattern, and it was later felt that a closer copy of Futura was needed. This was supplied in conjunction with the American Type Founders Company when Spartan, an almost identical copy of Futura, was brought out in the early 1930s.

Another rendition of the Futura design was created by R. Hunter Middleton, typographic director of Ludlow. Like Dwiggins, Middleton was intrigued by the sans-serif idea, and he, too, went his own way. When he introduced it in 1929, Middleton called Stellar 'a modification of the Futura severity,' although, like Metro, it was a considerable remove from Futura, actually resembling a humanist sans serif, a form that would garner attention thirty years later. Under pressure from its customers, Ludlow felt it necessary in 1930 to pro-

ABCDEFGHIJKLMNOPQRSTUVWXYZ

abcdefghijklmnopqrstuvwxyz

&.,:;!?'""'-()¢$1234567890%

Spartan Medium (ATF)

ABCDEFGHIJKLMNOPQRSTUVWXYZ

abcdefghijklmnopqrstuvwxyz

&.,:;!?"-·❖$1234567890

Bernhard Gothic Medium (ATF)

ABCDEFGHIJKLMNOPQRST
UVWXYZ

abcdefghijklmnopqrstuvwxyz

(&$1234567890.,:;"--!?+[])

Tempo Bold (Ludlow)

vide a type closer to Futura, and thus brought out its Tempo series, also drawn by Middleton.

Meanwhile, the American Type Founders Company had contracted for a sans-serif type with Lucien Bernhard, a German artist who had come to the United States in 1923, having earlier produced several types for the Bauer Typefoundry in Germany. In 1929, the series called Bernhard Gothic was introduced. Displaying his skill as an imaginative designer of posters, Bernhard brought the same flair to his sans-serif type, prompting an instant acceptance by printers dependent on foundry types.

But despite the success of Bernhard Gothic, ATF was also compelled by competition from the European foundries to make available for American printers a sans serif that was closer to Futura. As mentioned above, this decision to satisfy the market resulted in the joint undertaking with Mergenthaler to bring out Spartan.

The Lanston Monotype Company in Philadelphia, in its desire quickly to provide a geometric sans serif, adapted Koch's Kabel design, naming it simply Sans Serif. But during the middle 1930s, under the direction of Sol Hess, this firm also bowed to the inevitable and manufactured its own copy of Futura, which it called Twentieth Century.

It may be noted that Monotype also asked Frederic W. Goudy, in 1929, to produce a sans serif. He acceded to this request somewhat reluctantly and, like his fellow-American designers Dwiggins and Middleton, turned away from the German style. The type that emerged, Goudy Sans, was disappointing to the Monotype firm, though it was nonetheless produced. Goudy later wrote of it, 'I attempted to give to my type a definite expression of freedom and a personal quality not always found in this kind of a letter.'

The Intertype Corporation was the only American firm to enter into an arrangement with the German Bauer foundry to produce Futura for machine-composition, and it was given permission to apply the original name to its cutting.

With the availability of Futura in either the original or the numerous copies, it may be seen that the geometric sans serif came into its own during the 1930s. Although there have been a few periods when the nineteenth-century gothic types have returned to favor, the Futura style has remained possibly the most popular of all the sans-serif types for the past half-century.

ABCDEFGHIJKLMNOP QRSTUVWXYZ abcd efghijklmnopqrstuvw xyz 1234567890

20th Century Bold (Monotype)

ABCDEFGHIJKLMNOPQRSTUVW XYZ&
abcdefghijklmnopqrstuvwxyz fiflfffffiffl
1234567890£

Gill Sans Bold (English Monotype)

Eric Gill

30

SCRIPT, CURSIVE
AND DECORATED TYPES

The examination of any current type-specimen book will invariably disclose a large number of faces designed to imitate some form of handwriting. The catalogues of the nineteenth century also listed numerous examples of such written forms, though they were mostly restricted to the styles that had been developed by seventeenth- and eighteenth-century writing masters, and all were written with a steel pen. The modern scripts differ from those of the last century by their bewildering variety of structure, which stems primarily from the use of several instruments – the broad pen, the steel pen, and the brush (surprisingly, this is a very late development in the design of cursive printing types, coming only within the last half century). That scripts are types selected for specialized use precludes any particular script style from achieving favored status among typographers. Decorative letters, to be discussed later in the chapter, are similarly restricted in modern typography.

It is a simplification to state that all printing types descend from writing styles, but once the fifteenth-century book hands had been transferred to metal types, they followed a line of development that can be continuously traced over the past five centuries, an evolution now solidly documented by typographic historians and bibliographers. The documenting of these types has been made easier for well over half of that period by the hegemony of *book* production as opposed to more ephemeral printed matter. Until the nineteenth century, books remained the major product of the printer. By the beginning of industrialization, the traditions of roman, italic, and black-letter types had been well established; the slight changes in form forged by commercial necessity during the first three centuries of printing were readily assimilated, thereby simplifying their arrangement into a comfortable system of typographic nomenclature.

Under pressure to cater to the new industrial age's requirements, typefounders after 1800 were stimulated into frenetic competition (with often disastrous financial results). Theirs was a passionate search for profitable novelty, which frequently took the form of scripts and decorated types. Contributing to this effort were the new mechanical changes invented for the founding of printing types – after almost four hundred years of technological lethargy – which finally provided the means by which founders could both vastly increase their output and improve the quality of their product. The two-piece hand mold gave way to the Pivotal Typecaster patented in 1838 by David Bruce, Jr., a New York typefounder. This device permitted the production of 100 to 175 characters per minute, depending upon size, as opposed to the 400 to 500 per *hour* of the most skillful hand-caster. Several hand operations still had to be performed after casting, but by 1888 Henry Barth, of the Cincinnati Type Foundry, had perfected a casting machine that delivered completely finished types at the rate of about 250 per minute. The Barth machine is essentially the same caster that is now used by all typefounders.

Another factor contributing to the typefounders' increasing interest in producing extravagant new display types was the development of stereotyping, a method by which whole pages of type could be molded into lead printing plates. Since it was no longer necessary to print from actual types, the types could be redistributed after the molding operation. Although continued molding did cause some wear, the damage was far less than that of printing, and types lasted longer. Faced with a shrinking market for book and magazine type, the founders turned their attention to display and special-purpose types.

One of the most important mechanical developments to affect typefounding and the creation of fancy types was the invention of a method whereby matrices could be made by the electrotyping process. This practice bypassed the cutting of punches, allowing a foundry readily to duplicate a competitor's type by simply purchasing a font and then molding each character in wax and obtaining by electro-deposit a copy from which to manufacture a set of matrices. Perfected in 1845 by Edwin Starr in Philadelphia, the method initiated the pirating of printing types on a large scale. It also contributed greatly to the difficulty of identifying a type, as the same design, reproduced by many foundries, frequently appeared under a dozen different names.

The final major contributor to the multiplication of new types was the matrix-engraving machine. Invented by Linn Boyd Benton in 1885, this device eliminated the need for hand-cutting a steel punch.

C esareum cecinisse ... , Romeq3 ruinam
E t Macedum clarus succumbat Honorius armis .
S , gemitu commota pio, votisq3 suorum
F lebilibus , diuina darel clementia talem
F rancorum Regem : toto radiaret in orbe
H aud mora vera fides , et nostris fracta sub armis ,
P arthia Baptismo renouari posceret vltrò.
Q ueq3 diu latuit effusis moenibus alta
A d nomen Christi Carthago resurgeret , et quae
S ub Carolo meruit Hispania soluere poenas ,
E rigeret vexilla crucis , gens omnis et omnis
L ingua Iesum cantret , et non inuita subiret
S acrum sub sacro Remorum praesule fontem.

Finis Libri quinti.

Argumentum Libri septi.

S eptus Alexandrum lupu Babylonis et auro
  Corruptum ostendit, castrensia munera certis
D istribuit numeris, armato milite fines
z rios Ingressus, Sizigambis liberat vrbem,
E t Madatem precibus à moenibus eruta sumat
I nclita persepolis, mouet occursus miserorum
T urbatum Regem, Darius discrimina martis
R ursus inire parat, hic seditio patricidas
S eparat à Dario, Sed eos Innata simultas
A cceptos reddit, et pectora credula placat.
M ec fatum mutare valent decreta patronis.
                                      C   Liber

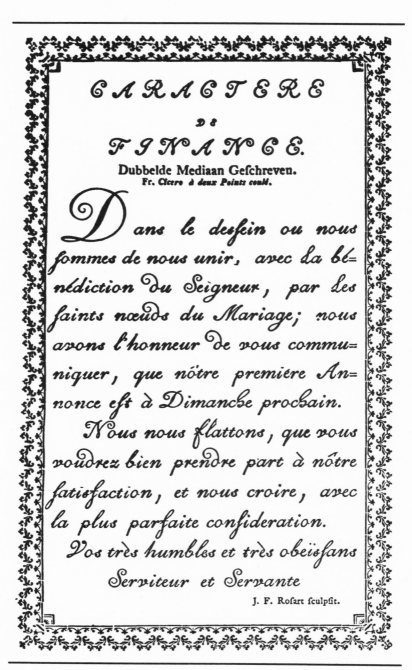

CARACTERE
DE
FINANCE.

Dubbelde Mediaan Geschreven.
Fr. Cicero à deux Points coulé.

D ans le dessein ou nous sommes de nous unir, avec la bé= nédiction du Seigneur, par les saints nœuds du Mariage; nous avons l'honneur de vous commu= niquer, que nôtre premiere An= nonce est à Dimanche prochain.

Nous nous flattons, que vous voudrez bien prendre part à nôtre satisfaction, et nous croire, avec la plus parfaite consideration. Vos très humbles et très obeïsfans Serviteur et Servante

J. F. Rosart sculpsit.

Rosart's Caractére de Finance, Enschedé foundry, 1768

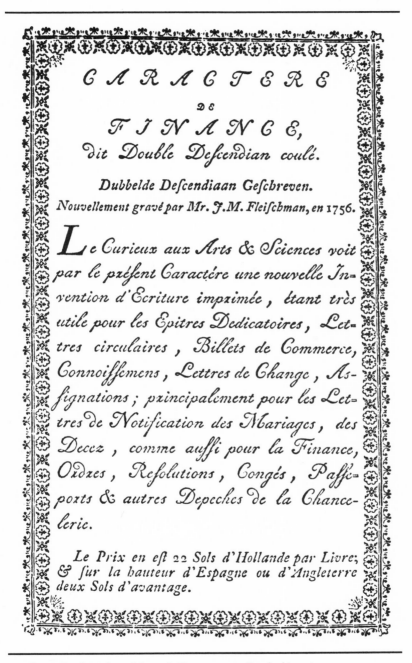

CARACTERE
DE
FINANCE,
dit Double Descendian coulé.

Dubbelde Descendiaan Geschreven.
Nouvellement gravé par Mr. J.M. Fleischman, en 1756.

Le Curieux aux Arts & Sciences voit par le présent Caractére une nouvelle Invention d'Ecriture imprimée, étant très utile pour les Epitres Dedicatoires, Lettres circulaires, Billets de Commerce, Connoissemens, Lettres de Change, Assignations; principalement pour les Lettres de Notification des Mariages, des Decez, comme aussi pour la Finance, Ordres, Resolutions, Congés, Passeports & autres Depeches de la Chancelerie.

Le Prix en est 22 Sols d'Hollande par Livre; & sur la hauteur d'Espagne ou d'Angleterre deux Sols d'avantage.

Fleischmann's adaptation of Rosart's Finance types, Enschedé, 1768

The long period of mechanization from the nineteenth into the twentieth century was so turbulent that typefoundries never again regained their earlier complacency. It was a frenzied, demanding, and highly competitive time, a period in which bankruptcy and amalgamation became quite common. The great majority of the innumerable types marketed during this century have long been forgotten, although some have recently been resurrected both by type collectors and by phototypesetters.

The reader of this book has been confronted with a confusing diversity of typographic terminology, for no single system of type classification exists. And script types, because they derive from a profusion of handwriting styles, are even more difficult to classify than others. In describing these types two terms are used almost interchangeably: *script* and *cursive*. Many typographers prefer to call a type a script only if it has joining characters, and a cursive if the characters are separate. But there is a general lack of agreement in usage; manufacturers themselves are quite indiscriminate in their names. Beyond this imprecision, the diversity of writing styles over the past five centuries further complicates the classification. Under such circumstances, it is reasonable and safe simply to resort to terms of historic accuracy.

The first type to be based on cursive, or informal, writing is the italic of Aldus Manutius (1500–1). Within thirty years, the French punchcutters adapted this italic form as a complementary companion of roman type, and it is so used to the present time. Because of this roman connection, italics are not considered scripts, even though their derivation is the same as the styles called script. About 1524 Vicentino degli Arrighi brought to metal types the chancery cursive writing, a style that today is used primarily as the complementary italic for a number of romans based on the Italian Renaissance letter forms. Yet another complication exists in arriving at a rational terminology, since printers have rarely agreed with the nomenclature used by Latin paleographers. For example, Berthold Louis Ullman, in his authoritative study *Ancient Writing and Its Influence*, refers to the 'humanist script' as the model for all printing types, thus making no distinction between the structure of letters. As noted in the chapter on the Arrighi types, the italic form developed from the font first used by Aldus in 1501, and within two decades became a complementary form to roman, never classified as script despite the obvious relationship of form.

Credit for the first cursive type is generally given to the French punchcutter Robert Granjon, who made a type based on the gothic cursive book hand that had been in use for several centuries in northern Europe before the invention of printing. Harry Carter, the English historian, has written that Granjon called this style *lettre françoise*, and that several French typefounders of the period also knew it by that name. It was related to the *bâtarde* form of black-letter type, although it was certainly more freely written. The first use of the Granjon cursive was in *Dialogue de la Vie et de la Mort*, by Innocenzio Ringhieri, printed at Lyons in 1557. Its second appearance, the following year, was of greater importance, as it was used in *La Civilité Puerile*, written by Erasmus as a 'grammar' of manners for children. Reprinted innumerable times in later centuries, and always with the same style of type, the title became synonymous with the type: Civilité. Granjon received the exclusive rights to his type for ten years, and by 1562 had printed some twenty books in it. But just two years after its appearance, it already had been copied by Parisian printers.

Civilité reached Scotland by 1571 and was being used by English printers some five years later. Called Secretary in Great Britain, it was employed primarily for legal printing until the eighteenth century. Civilité types were available from founders in France and the Low Countries until the nineteenth century in much the same form as the sixteenth century. Deberny et Peignot of Paris offered an excellent version, last shown in its catalogue of 1926.

Currently there are several cursives that bear some relation to the Granjon type. Morris Benton cut a letter for the American Type Founders Company in 1922 that received the name Civilité, but it lacks the strong gothic character of the original. The most widely used adaptation is Ernst Schneidler's Legend, introduced by the Bauer foundry of Frankfurt, Germany, in 1937. Legend immediately caught the fancy of the advertising typographers, who adopted it, curiously, to depict the exotic atmosphere of the Near and Far East, rarely selecting it to suggest the spirit of its place of origin, northern Europe of the high Middle Ages. Even closer to this spirit than Legend is Rhapsodie, designed by Ilse Schüle in 1951 for Frankfurt's Ludwig & Mayer foundry.

The 1950s was an extremely active period for the cutting of script types, possibly the most productive ever, in which more than sixty different designs issued from the various typefounders. Several of these types bore traces of the black-letter cursive form, notably

Ondine of Deberny et Peignot, designed in 1954 by Adrian Frutiger, and Georg Trump's Palomba, manufactured by C. E. Weber in Stuttgart about 1955. Neither of these scripts, however, was widely available or used in the United States.

The chancery writing of the early sixteenth century – which inspired such beautiful italic types as Arrighi, Narrow Bembo, Deepdene, and Palatino – has also been adapted for independent script faces, mostly of bold weight, used principally for display purposes. The broad-pen influence is noticeable in two such adaptations that have both enjoyed considerable popularity in this country: Lydian Cursive, drawn by Warren Chappell to accompany his broad-pen Lydian series, in which the standard italic is an oblique, or sloping, roman; and Rondo, designed in 1948 by Stefan Schlesinger and Dick Dooijes for the Amsterdam Typefoundry. A third type containing chancery overtones is Raleigh Cursive, designed in 1929 by Willard T. Sniffin for the American Type Founders, and enjoying considerable success with the smaller commercial printers.

During the last half of the sixteenth century the principles that had been expounded in 1522 by Arrighi in his writing manual of the chancery style, *Operina*, became controversial among the writing masters. For example, Giovanni Francesco Cresci, a calligrapher employed by the Vatican Library, was critical of the chancery style as being 'slow and heavy' and too pointed, and he also found fault with the writing instrument of the earlier period, preferring a more rounded and flexible point. He believed that letters should be rounder and also advocated the joining of characters. The English historian of calligraphy James Wardrop has said of Cresci that he exemplified such concepts as 'Overboard with geometry; overboard with edged pens: let us get back to handwriting, handwriting that flows.' In 1570 Cresci published *Il Perfetto Scrittore* ('the perfect writer'), in which he argued for such reforms. From that time the more commercial standards of writing came into favor, and the classic traditions of the chancery hand went into a long decline.

By the mid-seventeenth century the position of the writing master, the teacher of calligraphy, dominated that of the scribe, the practicing penman, so that calligraphy influenced commercial writing styles. During this period three different hands were developed in France and began to appear in the writing manuals. *Ronde* is an erect script deriving from the Civilité of the sixteenth century but written with lighter strokes, thus deemphasizing the gothic influence. Apparently emanating from the financial writing rooms, *ronde* has also been called *financière*. The second style was termed *lettre italienne* and is attributed to Lucas Materot, who worked in the papal office at Avignon and produced a copybook in 1608. This is a hand of joined letters, which lent itself to rapid writing and became a model for what later was to be called English round hand, or copperplate. Along with these smoothly flowing script hands came a tendency to apply the embellishments, or decorative flourishes, that were eventually to diminish the scripts' practicality for commercial purposes. The third style, called *coulée*, is a modification of *ronde*, being somewhat rounder and simpler to write and consequently more suitable for business writing.

Typographical copies of these written scripts first appeared about 1643, cut by Pierre Moreau, a French calligrapher who had turned to printing, first using engraved plates and then from actual types. The English historian A. F. Johnson refers to the Moreau types – appearing in eleven books between 1643 and 1648 – as *bâtardes italiennes*. The full development of the scripts as printing types came during the eighteenth century when a number of notable punchcutters turned to their production. Pierre Simon Fournier cut a *bâtarde coulée* in 1742, and in 1753 J. F. Rosart at the Dutch Enschedé foundry of Haarlem made a *caractère de finance*, which Stanley Morison called 'singularly ugly'; Morison deplored the decision of Giambattista Bodoni to copy it later in the century. The noted German punchcutter J. F. Fleischmann cut a much improved copy of the Rosart type for Enschedé.

The *ronde* remains alive today as a printing type in but few versions, although during the nineteenth century it was a standard French script. In fact, American foundries generally applied the name French Script to the style. In its 1906 catalogue, ATF first exhibited a *ronde*, called Tiffany Upright and designed by Morris Benton. The face's name was subsequently changed to Typo Upright and it became a standard for social printing, remaining popular up to the present. The English firm of Stephenson, Blake has an identical type named Parisian Ronde. Both of these are later versions of the Rondes Modernes originally cut by France's Deberny et Peignot.

By the close of the seventeenth century the writing masters were slowly abandoning the more ornate forms, bringing an end to the capricious directions taken by the earlier penmen. By the start of the eighteenth century writing hands were more disciplined and practical, as can be seen in examples of writing books of the time. In 1712, the Englishman Charles Snell published the *Art of Writing* in which he censured his fellows for the superfluous decoration of scripts. George Bickham's *Universal Penman*, published in parts between 1733 and 1744, is the best single source of information concerning the variety of contemporary English writing hands. In this beautiful engraved book, still available in reprint, appears the script now called English Round-hand, which became the model for hundreds of script types (though mostly of inferior design) during the nineteenth century, some of which have survived in modified form into our own time. The English Roundhand became standardized throughout Europe, being called in France *écriture anglaise*, in Italy *scrittura inglese*, and in Germany *englische Schreibschrift*. The typographic form of the round hand is also an English contribution, initiated by the typefounder Thomas Cottrell, who cast it into type in 1774.

Through the influence of scores of copybooks, round hand had spread to every part of the world by the mid-nineteenth century. It was the recognized standard for penmanship, not only in businesses but also in schools. Under such names as Spencerian and the more utilitarian American Palmer Method, generations of children were systematically taught to hate handwriting – the central 'R' of a questionable philosophy of education – with the obvious result that most adults never acquired the ability to write legibly, much less beautifully.

The conversion of the true copperplate scripts to printing types required both great skill of design and rigorous craftsmanship in execution. Not only the close fitting of the characters but their inclination, on the order of about thirty-five degrees, presented a stiff challenge to the ingenuity of the typefounder. Since it was not possible to cast such a letter on a standard square type body, a variety of methods were used to produce an angled body that could support the extending letters and provide the interlocking of characters to assure tight fitting. Founders solved the problem in a number of ways. When the mechanization of typesetting brought economic upheaval to the type-foundries, founders took some comfort in the fact that at least one style of type could not be produced in any way but by a skilled craftsman – it was not until the arrival of the phototypesetting devices that it became possible to set script types other than by hand-composition. But the price to the foundry was slow production, which could be afforded only by charging the printer at least fifty percent more for copperplates than for normal types.

The manufacture of copperplate scripts continued unabated until the outset of the Second World War. Few scripts of other origin

DOUBLE PICA SCRIPT.

We hold these Truths to be self=evident: That all Men are created equal; that they are endowed by their Creator with certain unalienable Rights; that among these are Life, Liberty, and the Pur= suit of Happiness: that, to secure these Rights, Governments are instituted among Men, deriving their just Powers from the Consent of the Governed; that when= ever any Form of Government becomes destructive of these Ends, it is the right of the People to alter or to abolish it, and to institute new Government, laying its Foundation on such Principles, and organizing its Powers in such Form, as to them shall seem most likely to effect their Safety and Happiness. Declara= tion of the Congress of the United States of North=America, July 4, 1776.

D. & G. BRUCE, New-York, 1820.

Early American roundhand script type, cut by George Bruce, c. 1820

encroached on their popularity. In its 1906 specimen book the American Type Founders Company listed eight different copperplates, and in both the 1912 and the 1923 catalogues ten varieties were listed. But it was in Germany that the greatest number was produced: by the 1930s some seventy-five copperplates were advertised, mostly for German printers and not for export.

The use of copperplate scripts was primarily restricted to social printing whose style had been traditionally initiated by the engravers, with a spillover into legal forms. Every printer had at least one such style to offer customers, and in most instances this represented the only script type in his cases. From 1920 the predominant American copperplates were ATF's Typo Script and Typo Script Extended (originally called Tiffany Script), both drawn by Morris Benton. As of 1908 a boldface copperplate had been offered. In 1923, in the final large catalogue to be issued by ATF, a medium-weight variant appeared, named Bank Script. The three weights enabled advertisers to use the formal scripts even for newspaper advertising. In England Stephenson, Blake did not begin such a program until the 1950s, with their medium-weight Youthline Script, followed by Copperplate Bold.

That the round hand continues to intrigue type designers is evident in this era of phototypesetting. In 1966 the Englishman Matthew Carter returned to the eighteenth-century copybook of the writing master Charles Snell. From this source, for use in the Mergenthaler Linofilm, Carter drew a type that was named Snell Roundhand and which once again brings to a script type the controlled skills of an experienced penman. Freed of the necessity of conforming to a physical body of type, the Carter design is successfully sympathetic to the copperplate ideal.

As already mentioned, by the late 1920s the script letter forms of all varieties were returning to favor. With very few script types available, the advertising agencies employed hand-lettering artists to supply styles and meet specific orders. Frequently such occasional letters would attract attention, inspiring job printers to make demands on the founders for similar styles. Advertising budgets could readily cover the cost of making photoengravings of single words or lines, but the printer's budget could not – the printer needed types, and this requirement once again created a market for typefounders' scripts.

In 1925 Lucien Bernhard, a German designer resident in the United States, drew a cursive in the tradition of the *ronde* but with ascenders three times the length of the descenders, accompanying an extremely

ABCDEFGHIJKLMNO
PQRSTUVWXYZ
Q Ien opt

abcdefghijklmnopqrstuvwxyz

(&$1234567890¢£.,:;""''-*%/!?)

Rondo Bold (Amsterdam)

ABCDEFGHIJKLMNOPQ
RSTUVWXYZ

abcdefghijklmnopqrstuvwxyz

(&$1234567890¢.,:;""''-%!?)

Thce's ss t thtt

Brush (ATF)

short x-height. The capitals, however, were round and full, and this combination was sufficiently intriguing to make the type an international success. In 1927 ATF brought out a reasonably close likeness of Bernhard Cursive, named Liberty. The rising interest in the script forms received additional impetus from a vigorous quill-drawn design from the experienced hand of Germany's Rudolf Koch. Named Holla and drawn in 1932, its cutting was completed after Koch's death in 1934. Holla exerted a strong influence on the design of script types issued later.

Also affecting the script faces after 1930 were the geometric sans-serif types. As none of the available scripts seemed to be visually comfortable with the unadorned letter forms, lettering artists discarded the orthodox styles and turned to new forms. Brush-lettering seemed to meet the new demands more satisfactorily than pen-drawn characters, allowing greater freedom and informality and thus ushering in

ABCDEFGHIJKLMNOP
QRSTUVWXYZ

abcdefghijklmnopqrstuvwxyz

(& $1234567890.,:; ' " " =!?)   H Sh Th ffifl

Bernhard Cursive (Bauer)

ABCDEFGHIJKLMNOPQ
RSTUVWXYZ
abcdefghijklmnopqrstuvwxyz
æ do'c œ ß nd rd st th

(& $1234567890¢£.,:; " " -–— —·*%/[]!?)

Snell Roundhand (Linotype)

A B C D E F G H I J K L M N O P Q R S T U V W X Y Z abcdefgh ijklmnopqrstuvwxyz ., -;: '/!?$& 1234567890

Kaufmann Bold (ATF)

what might be termed the era of brash-brush script lettering, which still remains the dominant form. Early examples of these scripts are remembered with nostalgia by postwar typographers: Bernhard Brushscript, Signal Black, Keynote, Mandate, Kaufmann Bold, Hauser Script, Grayda, and Brush. Of these, Brush has most successfully survived the passage of time, remaining popular despite strong competition for over forty years.

During the past half century there have been several interesting efforts on the part of type designers to modernize the copperplates. In 1933 a New Yorker, Howard Trafton, drew such a letter. Marketed by the Bauer typefoundry of Germany, Trafton Script became the most popular such type of the thirties. A face of similar derivation, Coronet, designed by R. Hunter Middleton of Chicago, was produced in 1937 by the Ludlow Typograph Company. In 1933 the German designer M. Wilke drew a series for the Berthold foundry called Ariston, which had just penetrated the American market when the war interfered with its distribution. Hermann Zapf tackled the problem about 1947. Of the opinion that the true copperplate scripts were not typographic, he attempted to capture their spirit but within the restrictions of a normal type body, and his solution was a script that lacks the connecting strokes and excessive kerning of the copperplate. The type was issued in 1952 under the name Virtuosa I. The following year Zapf simplified the capitals in Virtuosa II, and in 1957 he added a

ABCDEFGHIJKL
MNOPQuRS
TUVWXYZ
ÄÖÜ Th
abcdefggghijklmnopqurstuvwxyyz
chckffffififlftllndngßttz
1234567890 IVX
.,-:;!?„" »«()' & §†* $£

Virtuosa II (Stempel)

Enterprising Diplomatist

Bulgaria Imported Biplanes

Delightful Saxophone Orchestra

Raleigh Cursive (ATF)

ABCDEFGHIJKLMNOPQRS
TUVWXYZ
abcdefghijklmnopqrstuvwxyz
&$1234567890.,:;'!?   LThTuofhrrso'sdt

Typo Upright (ATF)

ABCDEFGHIJKL
MNOPQRSTUV
WXYZV $1234567890
abcdefghijklmnopqrstuvwxyz

Typo Script (ATF–Linocraft)

ABCDEFGHIJKLMN
OPQRSTUVWXYZ abcdef
ghijklmnopqrstuvwxyz 1234567890
.,=;:.!?"',/s$&

Commercial Script (ATF)

ABCDEFGHI
JKLMNOPQR
STUVWXYZ
abcdefghijklmnopqrstuvwxyz
&.,:;.,!?''ó=$1234567890

Bank Script (ATF)

boldface version. This series was most successful, contributing to the esteem in which Zapf is held by the world's printers. In 1955, no doubt spurred by the favorable reception accorded Virtuosa, the Berthold foundry produced Boulevard, cut by G. G. Lange.

This discussion of the transfer of handwriting styles to printing types ends on a rather predictable note. Many of the script types of the past century and a half have been conscious attempts to perpetuate the best standards of penmanship. But scripts produced in our era tend to go in the direction of ordinary twentieth-century handwriting, a far remove indeed from the refinement of the old writing masters. One example: in 1953 the French typographer Roger Excoffon prepared for the Olive foundry, of Marseilles, Mistral, a cutting quickly made available on the Anglo-American points-system type body and distributed by the Amsterdam Continental agency. To the amazement of the purist, it became an instant best seller, primarily because it is such an uncanny example of the current 'hand' of Everyman. Truly outrageous for a printing type, Mistral represents an extreme of typeface eccentricity, and for just that reason it has been received with delight by most practitioners although it is debased as much as any script can be while still remaining useful for the dissemination of information, the *raison d'être* of every printing type.

ABCDEFGHIJK
LMNOPQRS
TUVWXYZ&

abcdefghijklmnopqrst
uvwxyz $1234567890

Legend (Bauer)

ABCDEFGHIJKLMNOPQR
STUVWXYZ&
$1234567890
abcdefghijklmnopqrstuvwxyz

Lydian Cursive (ATF)

Brazil and Other Countries were exporting to Portugal pottery impregnated with a delicate and fragrant perfume. Europe had a constant market

An Invitation is most cordially extended to Printers and Other Persons interested in the Typographic Library and Museum, which was established to honor and perpetuate the memory and deeds

Civilite (ATF)

A B C D E F G H I J K L M N O P Q R S T U V W X Y Z

Are you feeding your child protein foods?

Decorator colors in most lovely sheets

Wanted! New Spring Shoes

Rhapsodie (Ludwig & Mayer)

ABCDEFGHIJKLM
NOPQRSTUVW
XYZ& abcdefghijklmnopqrstuvwxyz
$1234567890

Trafton Script (Bauer)

ABCDEFGHIJKLMNOPQRS
TUVWXYZ&

abcdefghijklmnopqrstuvwxyz 1234567890

Coronet (Ludlow)

ABCDEFGHIJKLMNOPQRSTU
VWXYZ& $1234567890
abcdefghijklmnopqrstuvwxyz

Mistral (Olive)

THE DECORATED TYPES

Ever since people gave shape to letters, they have rarely been content to allow their creations to remain pure in form. The urge for personal embellishment is eternally irresistible. The books produced during the medieval period bear witness to the capacity of the scribes, the rubricators, and the illuminators to paint, ornamentalize, and by all the aesthetic skills at their command enrich the letter forms. Indeed, the survival of many of the ancient texts has depended at least as much on the appeal of their decoration as on their content. With the invention of printing such practices were continued, though in this less personal medium at a diminished rate. During the incunabula period – 1455 to 1500 – the printers allowed space in their pages for the artists to decorate and beautify. When this custom was discontinued in the sixteenth century, printers supplied their own, printed decorations, in the form of initial letters, borders, tail-pieces, and fleurons, all of which perpetuated the tradition of page adornment.

It was not until late in the seventeenth century that the concept of embellishing the initial in the normal roman letters was investigated by typefounders in cast metal types. The earliest decorated type to survive from this period is Union Pearl, an italic cut by the Grover Foundry of England in about 1690; the matrices for this letter have come down to Birmingham's Stephenson, Blake & Company, from which the type may still be purchased. But it was not until the middle years of the eighteenth century that the ornamented letter became common, owing primarily to the French founder Pierre Simon Fournier. His *Manuel Typographique* of 1764 exhibits a number of ornamental letters that seem to have been partially inspired by his preoccupation with the numerous fleurons he had designed, all shown in profusion in this remarkable specimen book along with examples of their use in borders, title pages, and headbands.

The Fournier departure from the production of standard romans and italics was quickly followed by his competitors. The fine 1768 catalogue of the Enschedé foundry of Haarlem is indicative of how quickly the festooned letters caught the imagination of the typefounders. In many instances such decoration was not casual embellishment, however, but rather it was integral to the letter, taking the form of a shadow effect, or the addition of a white line to the heavier stem of the letter or of a florid pattern to the main stroke. In such cases the letter retained its original classic form. Discussing Fournier,

J. F. ROSART.

J. F. Rosart's shadowed letter, ca. 1759

JACQUES FRANÇOIS ROSART.
MATTHIAS ROSART.

J. F. Rosart's lettres fleuragées, ca. 1768

IZAAK
ET
JOHANNES
ENSCHEDÉ.

Enschedé's shadowed script, Double Capitale Financier, engraved by J. F. Rosart, 1768

LA VEUVE DECELLIER.

Double Mediaan Fleuragée, engraved by J. F. Rosart, and one of the finest of all lettres fleuragées

18th century decorative types cut by J. F. Rosart for Enschedé foundry, 1759–68

Daniel Berkeley Updike relaxed his normal conservatism and wrote in *Printing Types* (1922), 'And to all these fonts he added series of varied ornamental letters and shaded letters (*lettres grises*), and very delightful they were.' For Updike such a statement was practically a panegyric – one that was not repeated about the decorated types of the following century.

After 1800 the English typefounders took over the ornamented letter, which seemed to them the ideal expression of the industrialization transforming the venerable printing craft into a humming modern business. By 1850 Continental and American foundries were also strenuously turning out the decorative types, but in the avaricious competition that ensued, the letter forms degenerated, often losing all relationship to the classic models that had survived up to that time. During the last half of the nineteenth century the American typefounders took the lead in the production of the ornamented display types.

It was, as indicated, owing to the rampant commercialism in ephemeral printing of the 1800s that the ornamented letter radically

Fournier's decorative types, 1764

The Moſt Ancient Engliſh Types

The Union Pearl newly caſt for the Fleuron from the original matrices formerly in the poſſeſſion of the Grover Foundry (eſtabliſhed London circa 1674) by the preſent owners, Meſſrs. Stephenſon, Blake & Co. Limited, Sheffield and London, 1927.

A B C D E F F G Ç H I J K L M N
O P Q Qu R S T T U V W X Y Z
a b c d e f g h h i j k l l m n o p q
r s t u v w x y z ſ ſh ſt &

Union Pearl, the earliest decorative type, c. 1690

departed from the charm of the eighteenth-century styles. However, prior to the development of the decorated fat faces early in the nineteenth century, several English founders offered inline/outline versions of the classic romans. William Caslon IV as early as 1784 produced an extremely handsome three-dimensional rendering of his Old Style, which set a high standard of accomplishment and in the twentieth century has stimulated founders to follow suit. Inlines were cut for many of the basic roman series of the revived classic types, such as Garamond, Goudy Old Style, Bodoni, Cochin, and Eusebius, and

abcdefghijklmnopqrstuvwxyz
ABCDEFGHIJKLMNOPQRSTUVW

Campanile (MacKellar, Smiths & Jordan, 1879)

ABCDEFGHIJKLMNO

Lavinia (Boston Type Foundry, c. 1840)

ABCDEFGHIJKLMNOP
QRSTUVWXYZ &.!×$*£

Helvin (c. 1870)

ABCDEFGHIJKLM
NOPQRSTUVWXYZ&

Buffalo Bill (Johnson & Co., c. 1845)

abcdefghijklmnopqrstuvwxyz
ABCDEFGHIJKLMA

Bijou (MacKellar, Smiths & Jordan, 1883)

ABCDEFGHIJKLM
NOPQRSTUVWXYZ
&$1234567890

Modernistic (ATF)

ABCDEFGHIJKLMNOP
QRSTUVWXYZ
abcdefghijklmnopqrstuvwxyz
(&$1234567890.,;: '' "" -!?* <>) ‡

Lilith (Bauer)

during the 1930s this practice was continued with such new types as
Lutetia, Romulus, Erasmus, and Egmont. Typefounders have, in fact,
continued to produce fine variants up to the present. Examples are
the beautiful font of capitals called Castellar, drawn for English
Monotype in 1957 by John Peters, and Cristal, another alphabet of
capitals, cut for Deberny et Peignot in 1955 by Rémy Peignot.

There have also been several revivals of early inline faces, such
as Fry's Ornamented, first cut by Richard Austin about 1796, and
Enschedé's Rosart, which appeared in 1759, from the hand of J. F.
Rosart. Modern printers therefore are well equipped with three-
dimensional letters designed on classical lines for fine book printing.

Had the realm of the decorated type not been invaded by the
excessive commercial demands of the new class of industrial entre-

ABCDEFGHIJKL MNOPQR
STUVWXYZ (&.„°°°⁶⁹₌)

Fry's Ornamented (Stephenson, Blake & Co.)

ABCDEFGHIJKL
MNOPQRSTUVWXYZ
(&$1234567890¢.,:;"'-«»*%/!?)

Cristal (Deberny et Peignot)

ABCDEFGHIJKL
MNOPQRSTUVWXYZ
&$1234567890£.,:;"-/!?

Sapphire (Stempel)

preneurs, it is quite possible that the ornamented letter would have
been further developed within the tradition of the book. But the
pressures of competition among the various typefounders brought
about the extremes of design that contributed to the low esteem
in which the genre has been held by most typographical historians.
Another factor, of course, was the emerging practice by the mid-
nineteenth century of the manufacture of matrices by electro-deposit,
an invention that promoted a wave of plagiarism; it had been discovered that the fat faces, the grotesques, and the square serifs readily
lent themselves to embellishment, since the boldface weights provided

ABCDEFGHIJKLM
NOPQRSTUVWXYZ
(&$1234567890¢
...;; °°°°°-*°%/!?)

Profile (Haas)

ABCDEFGHIJKLMNOPQR
STUVWXYZ ..;;""""==/%!?()
(&$1234567890¢

Prisma (Klingspor)

a broad surface for decoration, so that these faces were accordingly modified and decorated. But for the immoderation it is quite possible that Updike might have accepted the necessity for such creations and included the ornamented letter in *Printing Types*. Instead he was outraged by the appendages applied to the roman letter and by the typefounders' preoccupation with typographic extravagance. The proper Bostonian thus placed practically the entire output of ornamental letters under sentence as 'types we ought not to want – which have no place in any artistically respectable composing room.'

Fortunately, given their neglect by Updike, Nicolete Gray has thoroughly documented the development of these marketplace typefaces in her most authoritative *Nineteenth Century Ornamented Types and Title Pages*, first published in 1938 and completely revised in 1976. Far from inveighing against the crassness of the era, Gray says of it, '19th century ornamented type design and jobbing printing are one of the folk arts of early industrial society and reflect aspects of its

ABCDEFGHIJKLMN
OPQRSTUVWXYZ &
$1234567890£.,:;''''''''''''----.
/·/!?«‹›» À Á Ä Â ÆÇŒÈ
ÉÈÊÌÍÏÎÒÓÖÔÙ ÚÜÛ

Trump Gravure (Weber)

ABCDEFGHIJK
LMNOPQRSTU
VWXYZ .,-;:''!?&

Caslon Openface (ATF)

ABCDEFGHIJKL
MNOPQRSTUV
WXYZ &

Bodoni Bold Paneled (Monotype)

ABCDEFGHIJKLMNOPQRS
TUVWXYZ ff fi fl ffi ffl
abcdefghijklmnopqrstuvwxyz
(&$1234567890¢.,:;'"-*%/!?)

Bodoni Open (ATF)

ABCDEFGHIJKLMNOPQ
RSTUVWXYZ
abcdefghijklmnopqrst
uvwxyz
{&$1234567890.,:;'"-!?—}

Cooper Hilite (Barnhart Brothers & Spindler)

ABCDEFGHIJKLMNOPQR
STUVWXYZ
abcdefghijklmnopqrstuvwxyz
(&$1234567890¢£.,:;"''"-*/!?)

Goudy Handtooled (ATF)

ABCDEFGHIJKLMNOP
QRSTUVWXYZ
abcdefghijklmnopqrstuvwxyz
(&$§1234567890c.,:;'""––%/!?)

Goudy Text Shaded (Monotype)

culture in a way which is historically illuminating.' Certainly this period of typographic inventiveness deserves further study as an exciting and innovative interval in printing history, placed as it is between the end of the book's influence on the world of print and the return of the classic influence after 1900.

While at first glance it would appear that the classification of decorative typefaces is a procedure fraught with difficulty, in actuality most of the styles can be easily recognized by their basic structure, such as old style, modern, square serif, and sans serif. A number of terms are used to describe them: inline/outline, in which a white line runs the length of the stem; shaded, in which the stems are screened with either dots or lines; patterned, in which a floriated design is added; dimensional; cameo, in which the letter is outlined in reverse on a solid background; and embellished, in which the shape of the letter gives way to flamboyant additions.

There are of course many designs that owe nothing to the past. These employ novelty to attract attention to themselves and by extension to the message of the words. Although the traditionalist may deplore such letters, it must be recognized that every promotional printing type need not aspire to the heights of typographic aesthetics and legibility to fulfill its fundamental purpose of engaging the reader's attention. For such reasons the ornamental typefaces, in either classic or rococo form, will continue to be employed. Printers enjoy an unending flow of both styles from the manufacturers, especially considering the ease with which hand-lettering may now be transferred directly to film fonts with no mechanical restrictions.

CRX 31 XRD

TYPE MAKING
FROM PUNCH TO COMPUTER

The term *type designer* is of fairly recent origin, having been practically unknown until the late years of the nineteenth century. This is not to say that type was not 'designed' during the four hundred years following Johann Gutenberg's invention, but rather that until the present century the designing of type was not a distinct, prestigious profession within the confines of typefounding. Even today, despite the respect for the title, the calling rarely brings affluence to the practitioner. Indeed, most twentieth-century type designers have found it necessary to seek permanent employment in other fields to indulge in the 'luxury' of drawing letters for printing types.

The more fortunate of the fellowship have been those who have made a permanent connection with a typefounder or a manufacturer of typesetting machines. In the United States, for example, Morris Benton spent his whole career – almost fifty years – on the staff of the American Type Founders Company, as did Sol Hess with Lanston Monotype and R. Hunter Middleton with Ludlow Typograph. Frederic W. Goudy managed a certain amount of independence by maintaining his own workshop, but from 1920 to his death in 1947 he also received a monthly stipend from Lanston as the firm's art director. The types designed by these four men far outnumber those produced by all the free-lance type designers of their era. Nevertheless, the latter group was well accepted by the manufacturers and in fact greatly encouraged to create new faces.

The independents were also engaged in a variety of non-type-designing jobs, though most of this work was in some way connected with the graphic arts. It is fortunate that they were encouraged by the manufacturers, since many excellent types have issued from their drawing boards. Today resident type designers of established reputation are rarely found in manufacturers' offices; they prefer the freedom to broaden their design work. And in the future it is probable not only that the free-lance designer will be encouraged, but that this person will hold a dominant position in the production of types: most firms will continue to employ knowledgeable draftsmen for the everyday handling of the innumerable tasks in the production of fonts of type – whether by the hot-metal or the cathode-ray-tube method – but in all likelihood the important new faces will come from the independent type designers, most of whom maintain studios and engage in a broad range of design activity.

The supply of good type designers will probably remain stable and may even grow, as indicated by the burgeoning interest in calligraphy. While the availability of young designers familiar with classic letter forms is a heartening development, it is most unlikely that such ability will be combined with a similar perception of the technical problems connected with the translation of drawing to finished type. In this realm the designer connected with a foundry or a manufacturer has, needless to say, a distinct advantage. The free-lance designer, to be most effective, must make the effort to acquire knowledge of the *technology* of type production, which over the past two decades has undergone revolutionary changes. It is because of this necessity for technical understanding that this survey will undertake to trace the evolution of the *making* – as distinct from the designing – of printing types from the very beginning.

Theodore Low De Vinne wrote of Johann Gutenberg: 'He was the inventor of typography, and the founder of modern printing, who made the first adjustable type mold.' This statement appeared in *The Invention of Printing*, published in 1876 and still one of the most authoritative sources on the origins of the invention of movable type. Most experts in De Vinne's time and since have more or less agreed with him – although there is also a considerable body of opinion of the opposite persuasion – and given the lack of documentation of that fifteenth-century incunabular period it is unlikely that credit will ever be awarded to anyone other than Gutenberg. By mutual agreement, the world's printers celebrated the 500th anniversary of Gutenberg's contribution in 1940, consecrating that date as the inaugural of their craft.

Indeed, despite the absence of even a single record fully describing the procedures by which the first type was made, theorists during the past century have produced hypothetical treatises about Gutenberg's invention. One of the most common presumptions is that carved wooden letters were joined into words and lines and held together

Punch and matrix as shown in De Vinnes's *Plain Printing Types*, 1900

with string; a variation of this theory is that the cutting of wood punches, in conjunction with a sand mold, produced cast type. Still another hypothesis is the early utilization of an alphabet carved in a woodblock (such as an abecedarium) and then cast into a thin lead plate, on which the characters were cut out and mounted on wooden shanks.

The authoritative English typographic historian Harry Carter, after a lifelong examination of the early documents of printing practices, has stated that he sees nothing to controvert the judgment that from the beginning punches, matrices, and molds were used to make type. He cites the fact that punches bearing letters or symbols had been developed well before the appearance on the scene of Johann Gutenberg, and that engravers of coins and seals and even jewelers were competent in such work. Precise molds were also required for the making of arms and armor.

The earliest account of the making of type appears in *Dialogues François pour les Jeunes Enfans*, printed by Christopher Plantin at Antwerp in 1567. This is a child's encyclopedia and in it the punch, the matrix, and the mold are described – a description that largely applied until the close of the nineteenth century. It is unfortunate that the *Dialogues* was written for children and thus contains virtually no technical details that would have provided invaluable insight into the craft of punchcutting. Moreover, as Stanley Morison has written,

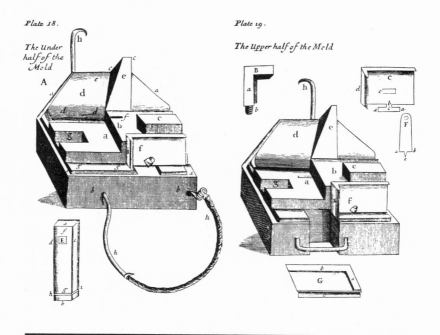

The Type mold, from Moxon's *Mechanick Exercises*, 1683

'If ever the Dialogue was clear and easy reading to the parents of Plantin's time, it is hardly so today to any of us' (Morison's statement appears in the foreword of *Calligraphy and Printing in the Sixteenth Century*, a translation edited by Ray Nash in 1964).

Imperfect as the *Dialogues* account is, it tells us that the punch was 'a long piece of steel with whatever letter is wanted cut or engraved on the end.' The next step in typefounding as detailed by Plantin (the probable author as well as printer of the work) was: 'When it is finished they strike it in copper and so make a matrix, which is simply an impression of the letter that has been struck in, like the mark made by a seal in sealing wax.' The mold is described, vaguely, as 'an assemblage of several parts, which makes all the letters alike, being, as they say, of one fount.'

Not until 1683, with Joseph Moxon's *Mechanick Exercises*, did a fuller description of typemaking appear. (The first account written by an actual typefounder would not be published until 1764, when Pierre

Simon Fournier issued his *Manuel Typographique*.) Moxon devotes an entire chapter to 'Letter-Cutting,' and in the preface states: 'Letter-cutting is a Handy-Work hitherto kept so conceal'd among the artificers of it, that I cannot learn any one hath taught it any other; But every one that has used it, Learnt it of his own Genuine Inclination.'

Moxon does not explain where he himself learned the craft. It is known that while in Holland he had visited Christoffel van Dyck, the most proficient punchcutter of the period. In addition, as a printer Moxon must have been acquainted with the London typefounders, and presumably he learned some of their procedures from conversations with them. In 1669 he had issued a proof showing seven sizes of roman type and three of italic, which he had personally cut (possibly these types were produced covertly for his own use, since at the time but four typefounders were licensed to practice in England). On the strength of this experience in cutting types, Moxon has left a very complete account of every step of production, describing all the tools required and then proceeding to an all-embracing explanation of every step of typemaking. Moreover, three chapters of *Mechanick Exercises* are devoted to 'Mold-Making,' 'Sinking the Punches,' and 'Casting of Letter,' making this first technical treatise on typefounding such a solid document that it served as the standard dissertation on the subject through the nineteenth century.

To return to the fifteenth century, Gutenberg unquestionably took many years to perfect his invention of movable type. As may be determined from court records, he was certainly experimenting with type prior to 1440, although he probably did not begin the production of his Bible until 1452. When printing spread throughout Europe during the following two decades, each printer had to acquire the various skills of typefounding by himself or else train a craftsman for this purpose – there were no typefounders as such. By the end of the century typefounding began to emerge as a separate craft, particularly the typecasting (the least-skilled founding job), but punchcutters were still in short supply.

We know so little about the early typemakers that no generalization about their training is possible. Apparently some of them had been scribes, for such an activity provided competence in the creation of letter forms. But, as we have discovered, the calligrapher, adept with pen or brush, is not necessarily as dexterous with file and graver. For example, when Arrighi decided to produce a printing type he did not cut the punches himself. In the present century such a distinguished type designer as Frederic W. Goudy never cut punches, nor did any of his contemporaries other than Rudolf Koch and Victor Hammer.

The modern concept of type designing, unknown during the first four centuries of typefounding, fell under the category of punchcutting. The punchcutters whose names we know were all men with great facility for the creation as well as the rendering of letters. The creative proficiency needed for type designing is not, it should be pointed out, an automatic outgrowth of the skills of the metal worker – the majority of the early punchcutters doubtless relied on design suggestions made by the printers, who knew exactly what kind of types they wanted for their work. And the names of mediocre designers and punchcutters have almost entirely disappeared.

Throughout the sixteenth century there continued to be few punchcutters, and these were in great demand. It was during this period that typefounding established itself as an operation distinct from the printing office. The numerous skilled operations involved in the manufacture of type had always placed a burden on the master printer, who was already fully occupied with the production of books. Eventually, the separation of the crafts became an economic necessity, owing to the long training and experience required for cutting punches, driving and justifying matrices, constructing molds, and casting type. Moreover, once a printing office had accumulated a reasonable supply of type, there was little work for the resident founders.

Even with the growth of typefounding as a separate institution, the number of punchcutters remained fairly constant. Since all that was required to enter the founding business was a reasonable supply of matrices, some founders dispensed with punchcutters altogether, which further preserved punchcutting as an exclusive craft. Nicholas Kis, the Hungarian who journeyed to Holland to learn the art about 1680, was lucky to obtain six months of instruction from Dirk Voskens, who granted this training only because Kis was a foreigner – Voskens later remarked that he would not consider teaching his calling to one of his own nation for a 'hundred thousand florins.' Such was the attitude of most punchcutters throughout their long period of dominance in type design, a prominence not ending until the late nineteenth century. As recently as 1855 the English founder Vincent Figgins II remarked, 'The art had been perpetuated by a kind of Druidical or Masonic induction from the first.'

As to the traditional making of a type, the steps were relatively few. The operation began with the punch, whose basic appearance

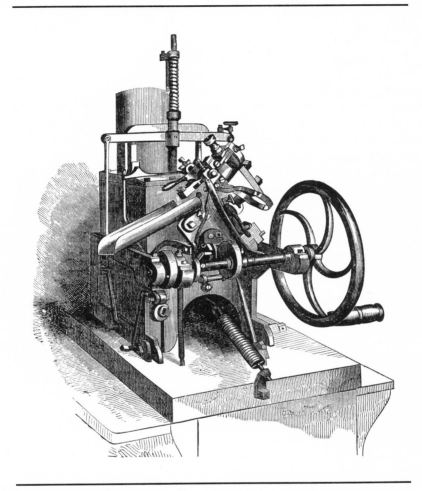

Bruce's typecasting machine

varied little from place to place except in size. It was a bar of steel about two and a half to three and a half inches in length and a quarter inch square (for 12-point or smaller). The cutting of the bar was performed while the steel was in an annealed state, after which it was hardened before being driven into the matrix. The character to be cut was scribed into the upper flat surface of the punch. This was followed, with certain letters, by driving in a counterpunch. Here practice varied, as some cutters preferred to tool the counters by hand. During the various stages of cutting, the craftsman made smoke proofs to check his progress, a test easily accomplished by holding the face of the punch over a candle flame and using the soot deposit to obtain progressive proofs. The entire cutting process was most exacting and could not be hurried – completing a single punch depended on the skill of the engraver, but a minimum of four hours was required for a good punch. Cutting an entire font was therefore a long and laborious task, particularly when languages employed many ligatures and accented letters sometimes adding up to more than two hundred characters. It is not known when the practice of cutting accents separately came into use, though it is described by Fournier. This procedure saved a great deal of time, as a shoulder was cut into each matrix to allow the positioning of the accent before the striking of the matrix, eliminating the need for separate accented letters.

The second step in typefounding was the striking, or driving, of the matrix, which was a bar of copper or soft iron (or nickel or brass as of the nineteenth century) about one and three-quarters inches long, three-eighths of an inch thick, and as wide as necessary to incorporate the character. The punch was driven into the matrix to a specific, carefully controlled depth, whereupon it had to be justified, that is, filed and trimmed so that all of the characters of the font had standard space at the head and sides to assure proper alignment and fitting. Again, these procedures required considerable judgment and skill. The worker executing this job was called a justifier, and he was not necessarily the punchcutter who might or might not drive his own matrices. Before the emergence of independent typefounders, the punchcutter controlled his creative output by retaining his punches and selling only his strikes (matrices).

The final step of production was the casting of the type itself in type metal. The mold – which most authorities view as the crux of the invention of printing – is of fixed dimensions in reference to a specific size of type, but it can be readily adjusted to allow for the various thicknesses, or widths, of the letters which make up a font of type. The height-to-paper – the size of the type character from its base to its face – was a constant within any one shop (although it changed from place to place), but the point size of the letter varied, as did the character width. This last dimension made the type mold unique, distinguishing it from molds for the casting of coins, medals, and the like. A separate mold was required for each size of type.

The matrix was positioned in the mold and held in place by a spring. The caster held the mold in his hand and poured molten metal into it, at the same instant jerking it upward to assure a cast of solid metal. The mold was then opened and the character removed. At its foot a jet of metal projected, which was later removed, following which each character was 'dressed.' This final operation, performed by the least-skilled worker in the foundry, consisted of planing the bottom of each letter to remove the burr caused by the breaking of the jet, and the rubbing of each side of the cast character to remove 'flash' at the edges, resulting from casting difficulties or, as was often the case, improperly driven matrices. The rate of production in hand-casting was slow; depending on the size of type, between 2,000 and 4,000 casts were made each working day.

The alloy of type metal in the earliest days of printing was softer than in later times. Tin was used in greater quantity than it is today, as documented by early colophons. Being expensive and soft – resulting in type that was easily bent in the smaller sizes – tin was replaced by the end of the sixteenth century by lead as the principal metal in the alloy. Harry Carter cites the analysis made of types cast at the Plantin printing office about 1580 (the types are preserved because of having been inserted in woodblocks): they are 82 percent lead, 9 percent tin, and 6 percent antimony, with the balance copper. Carter compares this analysis with that of twentieth-century foundry type, which is about 60 percent lead, 15 percent tin, and 25 percent antimony, and includes a trace of copper. Until commercial typefounding emerged in the late sixteenth century, many of the types were too soft to withstand constant wear. This may account for some bad printing. As Harry Carter has pointed out, the sharpness and durability of type depend upon good (and strong) metal. Such metal, that has the least shrinkage in cooling and reproduces the punch most precisely, is dependent upon the proper proportions of tin and antimony.

Until the nineteenth century all types were manufactured much as described above. Modifications in the basic method were individual and dependent upon the craftsman's skill and enterprise. But after 1800, primarily as a result of industrialization, the various typefounding operations were rapidly improved.

The first innovations increased the output of the hand mold by fifty percent and more by applying a spring-pump feature that facilitated a faster return motion. In the 1830s the pivotal caster appeared almost simultaneously in the United States, England, and the Continent. The best-known version (patented in the United States in 1838 by David Bruce, Jr.), hand-operated and later power-driven, turned out 100 to 175 types per minute. These types still had to be hand-dressed, as it was not until about 1890 that the modern typecasting machine, producing completely finished types at twice the rate of the pivotal devices, was developed. The ultimate machine of this kind was the Wicks Rotary Typecaster, patented in England about 1900, which cast 60,000 characters per hour up to 11-point. By that time, however, keyboard typesetting machines had proved completely successful and obviated the need for foundries manufacturing great quantities of type for hand-composition. From then on the founders became more and more involved in producing the display types not yet practical for the keyboard machines.

The last phase of the industrialization of typefounding did not occur until 1884, with the invention of the matrix-engraving machine by the Milwaukee typefounder, Linn Boyd Benton. There was, however, an interim development in midcentury that had preceded this machine – the electrotyped matrix. Invented by the American founder Edwin Starr about 1845, the matrix substituted the steel punch with one made of lead, allowing for both a much simpler procedure of cutting and even the use of an existing type character. The letter was molded in wax and by the standard electrotyping technique a copper shell was made, which became the basis for a matrix. It was this new opportunity to use existing types that upset typefounders everywhere, subjecting as it did their most successful designs to the plagiarism of competitors. The smaller foundries, never adequately staffed with skilled punchcutters, could use Starr's method to easily produce any of the current styles (marketing the faces under different names perhaps assuaged their consciences).

It was the Benton matrix-engraving machine that finally displaced the punchcutter from four centuries of dominance. Essentially a pantograph device, it bypassed the need for a steel punch by simply engraving a matrix from a pattern plate made from a drawing of a letter. Ironically, this invention came at exactly the same time as the Mergenthaler Linotype machine, which freed the printer from the need to compose types by hand. Benton further assured the demise of the foundry by selling the use of his machine to the Mergenthaler firm, which paradoxically converted it to engraving steel punches, insuring that matrices could be stamped out by the millions for the new typesetting machines.

Type designing underwent radical changes with the development of the Benton machine. Now the designer needed only to draw an

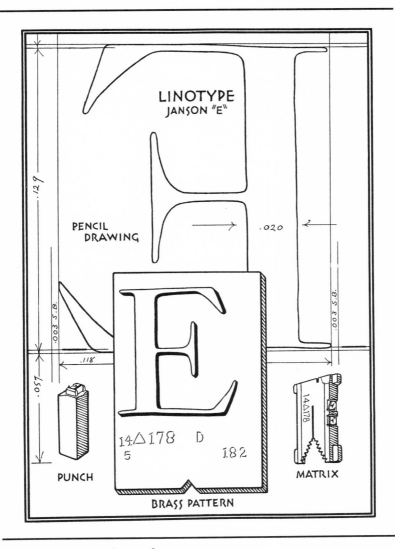

Sketch of Linotype matrix manufacture

alphabet to the size of about an inch, whereupon it was removed to another of Benton's devices, the 'delineating' machine, which was also a pantograph. The operator traced the original drawing to a greatly enlarged scale and, in the inventor's words, this person was 'also enabled, by various adjustments, to change the form of

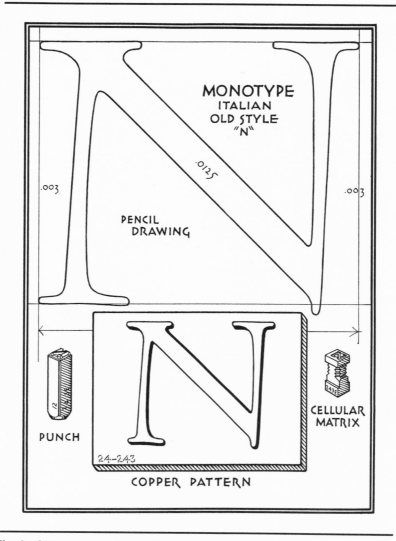

MONOTYPE
ITALIAN
OLD STYLE
"N"

.0125

.003   .003

PENCIL
DRAWING

N

PUNCH

24--243

COPPER PATTERN

CELLULAR
MATRIX

Sketch of Monotype matrix manufacture

the pencil tracing in such a manner that it becomes proportionately more condensed or extended, and even italicized or back-sloped.' Apparently this pantograph was so novel in construction that a patent was refused on the grounds that the application described a mechanical impossibility; Benton had to demonstrate the device to be granted

Punchcutter at the Bauer foundry

a patent. The enlarged drawing was next reduced to a smaller size, again by pantograph, this time being transferred to a metal plate containing a coating of wax, through which the line was completely traced. This plate was then electrotyped, thus providing a pattern plate for the matrix-engraving machine. From it, all sizes of a design

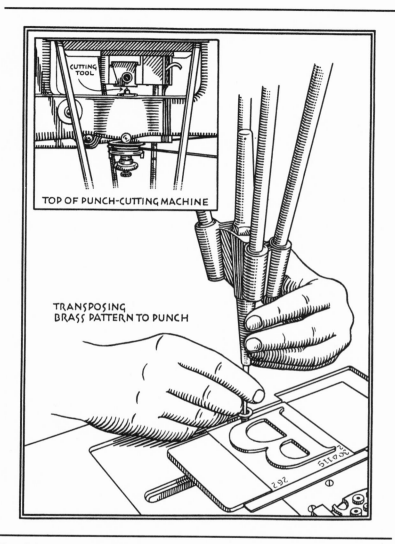

Use of the punchcutting machine

could be cut. Benton said of this method that it was superior to cutting handmade punches in both accuracy and uniformity. He boasted of its ability to cut letters that could be read only by a microscope – too small even to print. Adjustments were possible that enabled the operator to engrave the letters proportionally more extended or

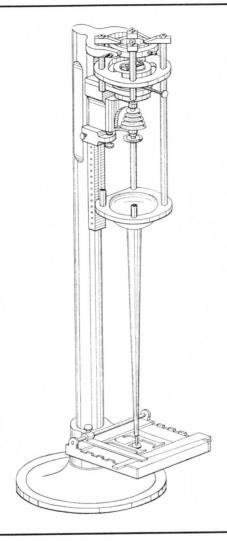

The mechanical punchcutting machine of Linn Boyd Benton, c. 1885

condensed, and lighter or heavier in face than the pattern, adaptations necessary, the inventor believed, 'for the production of a properly graded modern series containing the usual sizes.'

The Benton pantograph was an enormous success and was soon adopted, in one form or another, by all typefounders. European firms

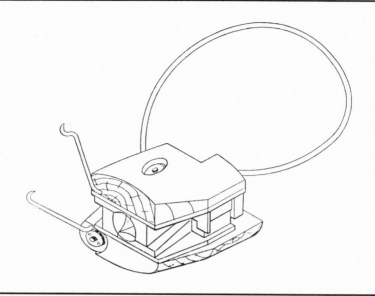

Typefounder's hand mold

retained punchcutters' services until very recently, but during the past seventy-five years the vast majority of new types have been cut by the pantograph-engraved matrix. The composing-machine manufacturers depended absolutely on the Benton-produced punch for stamping matrices, a process demanding precisely engineered punches to insure identical matrix replacement.

Since the pantograph principle was adopted there has never been complete uniformity among founders or typesetting-machine manufacturers concerning the numerous steps necessary to convert the drawing of a letter to an engraved matrix or punch. In most instances, however, the procedures vary only slightly, and at that, primarily out of aesthetic considerations, as governed by the transfer of a freely drawn character to one that may be mechanically restricted. In the case of the Mergenthaler Linotype Company, the type designer's work is sent to the mechanical-drawing department, which produces large engineering drawings for each size of type to be manufactured; the company claims that precise corrections are made, down to .00025 inch, in order to assure the proper proportion of lines, curves, and strokes in a given point size of type—most other firms are satisfied with three or four drawings for the whole range of types. The master drawings are converted to pattern plates by pantograph, from which the punches are cut on the Benton machine. These operations differ only in small degree among the other composing-machine manufacturers. The American Monotype company, for example, produced a pattern plate by a photoengraving made from the working drawing. At the Ludlow Typograph Company, R. Hunter Middleton, the director of typography, was also the firm's principal type designer and was thus able to control the various steps in ways impossible for outside designers. He personally made the working drawings on polystyrene film, which had excellent dimensional stability. The drawings were then photographed on zinc for the pattern plates.

In light of the diverse steps endemic to type production, it may be seen how a designer's original concept could be altered during execution. Whereas the punchcutter who designed type was always in control of every 1 ·ter he cut, the modern type designer has discovered that what emerg_s from the manufacturing process often differs considerably from what went in. In many cases, needless to say, the designer is not at all sympathetic to the limitations placed on his creations by the techniques of production. It may be assumed that some of the changes in an original drawing have been made because the designer ignored or was unaware of the restrictions of the manufacturing process, or even of the use to which the design was to be put. But sometimes, too, the whim of the in-house supervisor has subtly modified a curve here and there, to the obvious annoyance of the artist.

It is interesting in this respect to compare the responses of two very fine American type designers to the vagaries of the manufacturing operations. William A. Dwiggins, whose excellent types were all drawn for the Mergenthaler Linotype Company, maintained a cordial relationship with the firm through the vicissitudes of twenty-seven years and eleven types. His attitude is best summed up in a sentence from a letter written to artist Rudolph Ruzicka in 1937: 'I haven't any complaint to make about the staff's French curves and straight-edges.'

On the other hand, Frederic W. Goudy, who after more than twenty years as an independent type designer made a connection with the Lanston Monotype Machine Company, became quickly disillusioned with Monotype's drawing department. Since Goudy drew all of his types freehand, he could not appreciate the technical difficulties of converting his drawings to the large-scale matrix production. Therefore, though retaining the title of Art Director until his death, Goudy established his own workshop in his home in Marlborough, New York, purchasing all of the equipment necessary to produce matrices and cast type. After he learned to cut his own matrices, however, Goudy tempered his earlier criticism. He did not agree, for example, with Rudolf Koch that the engraving machine was a means of displacing craftsmanship and that type designers should oppose its use. Goudy wrote, 'The important point is to recognize where handwork ends and machine work begins.' As Goudy's most prolific period occurred after his decision to cut his own types, it is apparent that he found the pantograph to be compatible with his ideals as a type designer.

Another twentieth-century type designer who held strong views concerning the hand versus the machine approach to type design was the Dutchman Jan van Krimpen, of Enschedé, in Haarlem. His position was that of the skeptic – even cynic – as illustrated in a report he sent to Stanley Morison in 1956, entitled 'On preparing designs for Monotype faces so as to prevent arbitrary encroachments from the side of the drawing office on the designer's work and intentions and otherwise inevitable disappointments at the designer's end.' Readers who wish to pursue van Krimpen's strongly individual views on the design of printing types are referred to *Jan van Krimpen: A Letter to Philip Hofer on Certain Problems Connected with the Mechanical Cutting of Punches*, most competently edited, with an introduction and commentary, by John Dreyfus (David R. Godine/The Houghton Library, 1972). This account summarizes the complex relationship between an artist and an industrial process.

The age of the hand-cut punch lasted for almost 450 years, but the mechanical cutting of punches seems to have just about run its course in less than a century. Technological changes in the post–World War II era have had a profound effect on typesetting procedures, resulting in a massive shift from dependence on metal types to the employment of photomechanical means to produce typographic images.

At first glance, phototypesetting would appear to remove many restrictions encountered by type designers previously confronted with the transfer of handwritten forms to the caprices of matrix manufacture and subsequent mechanical composition. In some instances, improvements were readily noticeable, such as the proper kerning of letters and close fitting of italics, neither of which was economically feasible on linecasting equipment, although excellent fit was possible on the Monotype. Along with these improvements, however, numerous complications were introduced in the transition to film. The enlargement or reduction in size from a master font was a constant problem; so was the difficulty of fitting characters not physically juxtaposed, as is type cast from matrices whose fit has been carefully determined by the type designer. Film exposure could distort the image, chemical deterioration occurred during development, and matching densities for patch corrections remained a perennial dilemma. These are but a few of the problems encountered in changing from metal to film, not to mention the vagaries of the complex electronic typesetting equipment.

Outweighing these drawbacks, however, are the many advantages in designing type for film. Artists can very quickly see the results of their efforts, as the laborious and time-consuming manufacture of punches or matrices has been eliminated. Changes of form can thus be made economically, freeing the designer from having to accept results that formerly would have been too costly to revise. It is also now possible to carry through to production many experimental types which earlier would have remained on the drawing board.

Ironically, however, though such freedom is welcome, it comes at a time when there are fewer well-trained type designers than ever to take advantage of it. This is owing to the infiltration of nonprofessionals into the world of type design. Numerous manufacturers have entered the field of electronic typesetting, and their engineers, though proficient in the construction of machines and systems, are often unequipped to judge letter forms. In the new era of modern typesetting, spawning devices that have enormous output capability, the tendency is to downgrade such traditional typographic concepts as the correct fitting of letters and the spacing of words. The touch of a key can allow the operator to either minus-space or plus-space in order to justify a line, and this decision, if wrong, can severely reduce legibility. It may readily be seen, then, that the new freedom of the type designer may not always result in positive typographic solutions. Thus, a wide gap currently exists between the technology's almost astonishing potential for excellence and the supply of traditionally oriented practitioners who are skilled in the construction of letter forms. Indeed, it is ironic that a machine with sophisticated abilities may be subjected to the caprice of an operator who lacks any basic understanding of fundamental typographic practices.

The phototypesetting machines' design has gone through two

Sketch of coordinates in digitizing a type

Example of coordinates used to define 18-pt. characters in Autologic APS-5 typesetter

Conversion of a letter into a grid pattern

Digitization is a technique by which the analog (continuous) property of a letter is converted into a grid pattern, or series of numbers.

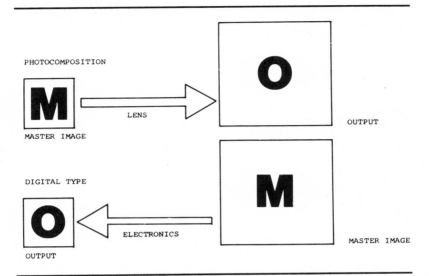

PHOTOCOMPOSITION

MASTER IMAGE

LENS

OUTPUT

DIGITAL TYPE

OUTPUT

ELECTRONICS

MASTER IMAGE

Procedures for coding a letter for digitization

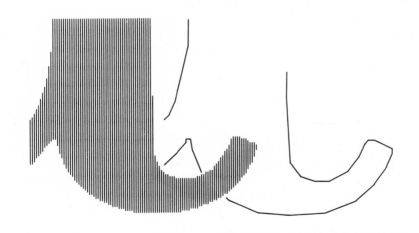

Storage of master information for digitizing type is done at a large print size, whereas the physical limitations of optics require that a film master be produced at the smallest point size.

There are four techniques of coding or representing typographic shapes: dot by dot, vertical strokes, straight line segments, and straight-line/arc segments.

phases and is now into a third. The earliest devices followed quite closely the concept of the hot-metal typesetters. Later they were improved by the adaptation of electronic principles, allowing for more rapid output and more complicated responses. The equipment of this second phase is now dominant in the typesetting field, but a very recent advance – the third phase – appears to offer the greatest advantages yet encountered in the manufacture of typesetting machines. This new group benefits from the application of computers capable of astounding output speed. More important, from the standpoint of type design, these machines do not require fonts in the shape of grids or disks, but rather can store the most intricate letter forms in computer memory.

Traditional computer readout has been in the shape of all-capital 'stick' characters, which compared with printing type are not at all legible. But the computer is also capable of reproducing the most beautiful fonts ever used by printers. The ability to deliver the elegant types depends on the amount of storage and memory available in the computer and on the refinement of the letter construction, which in turn depend on the quality of the computer and the software – a matter of economics.

The preparation of letters for computer storage is called digitizing. Digital type may be defined as a set of coordinates for each letter, to be stored in memory and produced by a computer printer or typesetter on photographic film or paper. The font of type is generally stored on a magnetic disk and is electronically called up in any size required. The process of digitizing can be decribed in six steps: 1) artwork is prepared; 2) it is then scanned for transfer to magnetic disk or tape; 3) the scanning process provides digital representations of the characters, which are now called raw data; 4) the raw data are edited in a graphics terminal, which displays the characters for evaluation and correction or modification; 5) after the editing, master font sizes are generated from the data obtained; and 6) finally a disk is manufactured, containing fonts conforming to the specialized needs of the purchaser.

Among recent developments in the digitizing of type fonts is the Ikarus system. This German computer program has drastically cut the time to digitize type, and which, properly used, represents a tool of tremendous significance to the type designer. In addition to the process of digital transfer, the device has unique capabilities for the modification of an original design, such as the converting of a typeface to additional weights of stroke and change of width, all of these steps being closely integrated by the designer on a video screen.

The computer is the most advanced typographic product yet to appear; it would seem to be the culmination of almost five and a half centuries of progress in the transfer of the scribal hands to the printed page. Engineers have thus provided the means for printers to continue enriching the heritage they have provided humankind. Now the responsibility falls on the printers to control the new technology and make it serve the great legacy of their time-honored craft.

Diagrams of counter-punching by Rudolf Koch

SHELDON·LUTETIA·SPECTRUM

ROMANEE·ROMULUS·ANTIGONE

CANCELLERESCA·BASTARDA·ETC.

JAN VAN KRIMPEN

TYPOGRAPHICUS·IN·URBE·CUI·NOMEN·HAARLEM

Jan van Krimpen

BIBLIOGRAPHY

This bibliography attempts to list many of the books, past and present, in
print and out of print, that may be of use to scholars in
the field and other interested readers.

General books on the history of printing and bookmaking

BALSTON, THOMAS. *The Cambridge University Press Collection of Private
Press Types: Kelmscott, Ashendene, Eragny, Cranach.* Cambridge: Cambridge
University Press, 1951.

BARKER, NICHOLAS. *Stanley Morison.* Cambridge, Mass.: Harvard University Press, 1972.

BENNETT, PAUL A. *Books and Printing: A Treasury for Typophiles.* Cleveland:
World Publishing Company, 1951.

BLUMENTHAL, JOSEPH. *The Printed Book in America.* Boston: David R.
Godine, Publisher, and Dartmouth College Library, 1977.

———. *Art of the Printed Book, 1455–1955.* Boston: David R. Godine, Publisher, in association with The Pierpont Morgan Library, 1973.

———. *Typographic Years: A printer's journey through a half century 1925–1975.*
New York: Frederic C. Biel, 1982.

BLUNT, WILFRID. *Sweet Roman Hand: Five Hundred Years of Italic Cursive
Script.* London: James Barrie, 1952.

BÜHLER, CURT. F. *The Fifteenth Century Book.* Philadelphia: University of
Pennsylvania Press, 1986.

CARTER, THOMAS FRANCIS. *The Invention of Printing in China and Its
Spread Westward.* Revised by Carrington Goodrich. New York: The Ronald
Press Co., 1955.

CHAPPELL, WARREN. *A Short History of the Printed Word.* New York:
Alfred A. Knopf, 1970. (Reprint in paperback by David R. Godine, Publisher, 1980.)

CHAYTOR, H. J. *From Script to Print.* Cambridge: W. Heffer & Sons, 1945.

CLAIR, COLIN. *A History of Printing in Britain.* London: Cassell, 1965.

———. *A History of European Printing.* London, New York, San Francisco:
Academic Press, 1976.

DAY, KENNETH. *Book Typography, 1815–1965*. London: Ernest Benn, 1966.

DE VINNE, THEODORE L. *The Invention of Printing*. New York: Francis Hart & Co., 1876.

———. *The Practice of Typography*. 4 vols., New York: Oswald Publishing Co., 1921.

———. *Notable Printers of Italy During the Fifteenth Century*. New York: The Grolier Club, 1910.

Fleuron, The: A Journal of Typography. Edited by Oliver Simon (1923–25) and Stanley Morison (1926–30). Seven vols., London: At the Office of the Fleuron (vol. 1–4); Cambridge: At the University Press (vol. 5–7), 1923–30. Reprint, Westport, Connecticut: Greenwich Reprint Corporation, 1960.

Fleuron Anthology. Chosen and with a retrospectus by Sir Francis Meynell and Herbert Simon. Boston: David R. Godine, Publisher, 1979.

GILL, ERIC. *An Essay on Typography*. Boston: David R. Godine, Publisher, 1989.

GOLDSCHMIDT, E. P. *The Printed Book of the Renaissance*. Cambridge: At the University Press, 1950.

IVINS, WILLIAM M., JR. *The Artist and the Fifteenth Century Printer*. New York: The Typophiles, 1940.

MCKITTERICK, DAVID, ED. *Stanley Morison & D. B. Updike: Selected Correspondence*. New York: The Moretus Press, 1979.

MCMURTIE, DOUGLAS C. *The Book: The Story of Printing and Bookmaking*. 3rd edition. New York: Oxford University Press, 1943.

MORISON, STANLEY. *German Incunabula in the British Museum*. London: Victor Gollancz, 1928.

NASH, RAY, ED. *Calligraphy and Printing in the Sixteenth Century*. Antwerp: The Plantin-Moretus Museum, 1964.

NESBITT, ALEXANDER. *The History and Technique of Lettering*, 2nd edition. New York: Dover Publications, 1957.

OSWALD, JOHN CLYDE. *Printing in the Americas*. New York: The Gregg Publishing Co., 1937.

ROGERS, BRUCE. *Paragraphs on Printing*. New York: William E. Rudge's Sons, 1943. (Facsimile edition, paper. New York, Dover Publications, Inc., 1979.)

SAVAGE, WILLIAM. *The Art of Printing*. London: Longman, Browns, Green, and Longmans, 1841.

SIMON, HERBERT. *Song and Words: A History of the Curwen Press*. Boston: David R. Godine, Publisher, 1973.

STEINBERG, S. H. *Five Hundred Years of Printing* with a foreword by Beatrice Warde. Middlesex, UK; Baltimore, Md.: Penguin, 1955.

TARG, WILLIAM. *The Making of the Bruce Rogers World Bible*. New York: 1979.

UPDIKE, DANIEL BERKELEY. *In the Day's Work*. Cambridge, Mass.: Harvard University Press, 1924.

WROTH, LAWRENCE C., ED. *A History of the Printed Book, Being the Third Number of the Dolphin*. New York: The Limited Editions Club, 1938. Rpt., Westport, CT, Greenwood Reprint Co., 1970.

Books with material on individual typefaces or type designers

ARMSTRONG, ELIZABETH. *Robert Estienne, Royal Printer*. Cambridge: At the University Press, 1954.

BEMBO, PIETRO. *De Ætna*. Postscript by Giovanni Mardersteig. Verona: Officina Bodoni, 1969.

BENNETT, PAUL A. *Postscripts on Dwiggins*. 2 vols. New York: The Typophiles, 1960.

BENTON, JOSIAH HENRY. *John Baskerville, Type-Founder and Printer, 1706–1775*. New York: The Typophiles, 1944.

BINNY AND RONALDSON. *The Specimen Books of Binny and Ronaldson, 1804–1812*. Introduction by Carl Purington Rollins. New Haven: The Columbiad Club, 1936.

BLUMENTHAL, JOSEPH. *Bruce Rogers: A Life of Letters, 1870–1957*. Austin, Texas: W. Thomas Taylor, 1988.

BUDAY, GEORGE. 'Some More Notes on Nicholas Kis of the "Janson" Types.' London: *The Library*, March, 1974.

CARTER, HARRY, AND GEORGE BUDAY. 'Nicholas Kis and the Janson Types.' *Gutenberg Jahrbuch, 1957*.

CARTER, SEBASTIAN. *Twentieth Century Type Designers*. New York: Taplinger Publications, 1987.

CHAYT, STEVEN & MERYL, EDS. *A Ludlow Anthology*. Winter Haven, Fla.: Anachronic Editions, 1986.

CLAIR, COLIN. *Christopher Plantin*. London: Cassell & Co., 1960.

DREYFUS, JOHN. *The Work of Jan van Krimpen*. Haarlem, The Netherlands: Joh. Enschede en Zonen, 1952.

———. *Bruce Rogers and American Typography*. New York: Cambridge University Press, 1959.

DWIGGINS, WILLIAM A. *Mss by WAD*. New York: The Typophiles, 1947.

Fine Print on Type: the Best of Fine Print Magazine on Type and Typography. San Francisco: Fine Print Publishers, 1988.

FRUTIGER, ADRIAN. *Type, Sign, Symbol*. Zurich: ABC Edition, 1980.

GILL, ERIC. *A Book of Alphabets for Douglas Cleverson Drawn by Eric Gill*. Wellingborough, Eng.: Christopher Skelton, 1987.

GOUDY, FREDERIC W. *A Half-century of Type Design and Typography, 1895–1945*. 2 vols. New York: The Typophiles, 1946. (2nd edition retitled *Goudy's Type Designs. New Rochelle, 1978. 1 vol.*).

GRANNIS, CHANDLER B., ED. *Heritage of the Graphic Arts; A Selection of Lectures Delivered at Gallery 303, New York City, Under the Direction of Dr. Robert L. Leslie*. New York and London: R. R. Bowker Co., 1972.

HAIMAN, GYORGY. *Nicholas Kis: A Hungarian Punch-Cutter and Printer 1605–1702*. San Francisco: Jack Stauffacher/The Greenwood Press, 1983.

HANDOVER, P. M. 'Black Serif,' *Motif: 12* (Winter, 1964).

HARLING, ROBERT. *The Letter Forms and Type Designs of Eric Gill*. Boston: David R. Godine, Publisher, 1976.

HUTT, ALLEN. *Fournier: The Compleat Typographer*. London: Frederick Muller, 1972.

Janson: A Definitive Collection. San Francisco: The Greenwood Press, 1954.

KOCH, RUDOLPH. *The Little ABC Book of Rudolf Koch*, a facsimile of *Das ABC Buchlein*, with a memoir by Fritz Kredel and a preface by Warren Chappell. Boston: David R. Godine, Publisher, 1976.

MARROT, H. V. *William Bulmer and Thomas Bensley*. London: The Fleuron, 1930.

MCLEAN, RUARI. *Jan Tschichold*. Boston: David R. Godine, Publisher, 1975.

MORAN, JAMES. *Stanley Morison: His Typographic Achievement*. New York: Hastings House, 1971.

MORISON, STANLEY. *John Bell, 1745–1831*. Cambridge: At the University Press, 1930.

————. Edited by Brooke Crutchley. *A Tally of Types*. 2nd edition. Cambridge: At the University Press, 1973.

RANSOM, WILL, ED. *Kelmscott, Doves, and Ashendene: The Private Press Credos*. New York: The Typophiles, 1952.

Robert Hunter Middleton: The Man and His Letters. Chicago: The Caxton Club, 1985.

ROGERS, BRUCE. *The Centaur Types*. Chicago: October House, 1949.

SCHOLDERER, VICTOR. *Johann Gutenberg, the Inventor of Printing*. London: The Trustees of the British Museum, 1963.

SHAVER, NEIL, ED. *A Goudy Memoir*. Council Bluffs: Yellow Barn Press, 1987.

STRAUS, RALPH AND ROBERT K. DENT. *John Baskerville: A Memoir*. Cambridge: Printed at the University Press, 1907.

TRACY, WALTER. *Letters of Credit: A View of Type Design*. Boston: David R. Godine, Publisher, 1986.

Victor Hammer: Artist and Printer. Lexington, KY: The Anvil Press, 1981.

William Morris and the Art of the Book. New York: The Pierpoint Morgan Library, 1976.

ZAPF, HERMANN. *About Alphabets*. Cambridge, Mass.: M.I.T. Press, 1970.

————. *Hermann Zapf*. Hamburg: Maximillian-Gesellschaft, 1984.

————. *Hermann Zapf and His Design Philosophy*. Chicago: The Society of Typographic Arts, 1987.

Books on type and letterforms

CARTER, HARRY, AND H. D. L. VERVLIET. *Civilité Types*. Oxford: The Oxford Bibliographical Society, 1966.

CARTER, HARRY. *A View of Early Typefounding, Up to About 1600*. Oxford: At the Clarendon Press, 1969.

DE VINNE, THEODORE L. *Historic Printing Types*. New York: The Grolier Club, 1886.

————. *Plain Printing Types*. New York: The Century Co., 1900.

ETTENBERG, EUGENE. *Type for Books and Advertising*. New York: D. Van Nostrand Co., 1947.

FAIRBANK, ALFRED, AND BERTHOLD WOLPE. *Renaissance Handwrit-*

ing. Cleveland and New York: The World Publishing Co., 1960.

GRAY, NICOLETE. *The Art of Lettering*. Boston: David R. Godine, Publisher, 1986.

GOUDY, FREDERIC W. *The Alphabet and Elements of Lettering*. New York: Dover Publications, Inc., 1963.

JOHNSON, A. F. *Type Designs: Their History and Development*. 2nd ed. London: Grafton & Co., 1959.

————. and PERCY H. MUIRE. ED. *Selected Essays on Books and Printing*. Amsterdam: Van Gendt & Co.; New York: Abner Schram, 1970.

KAPR, ALBERT. *The Art of Lettering; the History, Anatomy, and Aesthetics of the Roman Letter Forms*, Munich, London, New York: K. G. Saur, 1983.

KELLY, ROB ROY. *American Wood Type 1828–1900*. New York: Van Nostrand Reinhold Co., 1969.

LAWSON, ALEXANDER S. *Printing Types: An Introduction*. Boston: Beacon Press, 1971.

————. and A. PROVAN. *100 Type Histories*. 2 vols. Arlington: National Composition Association, 1983.

LINDEGREN, ERIC. *ABC of Lettering and Printing Types*. New York: Museum Books, Inc., 1964.

MORISON, STANLEY. *'Black-Letter Text.'* Cambridge: At the University Press, 1942.

————. and HARRY CARTER. *John Fell, The University Press and the 'Fell' Types*. Oxford: At the Clarendon Pess, 1967. (Facsimile edition, New York: The Garland Press, 1981.)

————. *Letter Forms, Typographical and Scriptorial*. New York: The Typophiles, 1968.

————. Edited by David McKitterick. *Selected Essays on the History of Letter-Forms in Manuscript and Printing*. Cambridge: Cambridge University Press, 1981.

OSLEY, A. S. *Scribes and Sources: Handbook of the Chancery Hand in the Sixteenth Century*. Boston: David R. Godine, Publisher, 1980.

POORE, TAYLOR. *Graphic Arts ABC; Volume 2, San Serif. Historical Development by R. Hunter Middleton*. Chicago: Poole Bros., Inc., 1949.

REED, TALBOT BAINES. *A History of the Old English Letter Foundries*. Edited by A. F. Johnson. London: Faber & Faber, 1952.

SILVER, ROLLO. *Typefounding in America, 1787–1825*. Charlottesville: University Press of Virginia, 1965.

SMITH, DAN. *Graphic Arts ABC; Volume 1, Square Serif*. Chicago: A. Kroch & Son, Publisher, 1945.

ULLMAN, BERTHOLD LOUIS. *Ancient Writing and Its Influence*. Cambridge, Mass.: M.I.T. Press, 1969.

UPDIKE, DANIEL BERKELEY. *Printing Types, Their History, Forms, and Use: A Study in Survivals*. 2nd ed. Cambridge, Mass.: Harvard University Press, 1937. (Facsimile edition in paper. New York: Dover Publications, Inc., 1980.)

WARDROP, JAMES. *The Script of Humanism*. Oxford: At the Clarendon Press, 1963.

ZAPF, HERMANN. *Manuale Typographicum: 100 Typographic pages with quo-tations from the past and present on types and printing in 16 different languages, selected and designed by Hermann Zapf.* Cambridge, Mass.: The M.I.T. Press, 1970.

Technical descriptions of type-founding and treatises on type design

AVIS, F. C. *Edward Philip Prince, Type Punchcutter.* London: F. C. Avis, 1967.

CARTER, HARRY, ED. AND TRANS. *Fournier on Typefounding.* London: Soncino Press, 1930.

The Computer and the Hand in Type Design: Proceedings of the Fifth ATypI Working Seminar, Part I. In: "Visible Language," Vol. xix, no. 1 (Winter 1985).

DWIGGINS, WILLIAM A. *WAD to RR: A Letter About Designing Type.* Cambridge, Mass.: Department of Printing and Graphic Arts, Harvard College Library, 1940.

GILL, ERIC. *A Book of Alphabets for Douglas Cleverdon Drawn by Eric Gill.* Wellingborough, England: Christopher Skelton, 1987.

GOUDY, FREDERIC W. *Typologia: Studies in Type Design and Type Making.* Berkeley and Los Angeles: University of California Press, 1940.

HOPKINS, RICHARD L. *Origin of the American Point System for Printers' Type Measurement.* Terra Alta, W. Virginia, 1976.

KOCH, PAUL. 'The Making of Printing Types.' In *The Dolphin*, vol. 1. New York: The Limited Editions Club, 1933.

LAWSON, ALEXANDER. *Anatomy of a Typeface.* Boston: David R. Godine, Publisher, 1990.

LEGROS, L. A., AND J. C. GRANT. *Typographical Printing Surfaces.* London: Longmans Green & Co., 1916. (Facsimile edition. New York: The Garland Press, 1980.)

LEWIS, JOHN. *Anatomy of Printing: The Influence of Art and History on its Design.* New York: Watson Guptill, 1970.

MARROT, H. V., TRANS. *G. B. Bodoni's Preface to the Manuale Tipografico of 1818.* London: Elkin Mathews, 1925.

MIDDLETON, ROBERT HUNTER. *Making Printers' Typefaces.* Chicago: The Black Cat Press, 1938.

MOXON, JOSEPH. *Mechanick Exercises on the Whole Art of Printing, (1683–84).* Edited by Herbert Davis and Harry Carter. London: Oxford University Press, 1962. (Paperback reprint, 1978. New York: Dover Publications, Inc.)

VAN KRIMPEN, JAN. *On Designing and Devising Types.* New York: The Typophiles, 1957.

———. *A Letter to Philip Hofer on Certain Problems Connected with the Mechanical Cutting of Punches.* Cambridge, Mass.: Department of Printing and Graphic Arts, Harvard College Library; Boston: David R. Godine, 1972.

Catalogues of type, and identification aids

BERRY, W., JOHNSON, A. F., AND W. P. JASPERT. *The Encyclopedia of Typefaces.* 4th ed. London: Blanford Press, 1983.

GRAY, NICOLETE. *Nineteenth Century Ornamented Typefaces.* Berkeley and Los Angeles: University of California Press, 1976.

HUTCHINGS, R. S. *A Manual of Decorated Typefaces.* New York: Hastings House, 1965.

———. *A Manual of Script Typefaces.* New York: Hastings House, 1965.

McGREW, MAC. *American Metal Typefaces of the Twentieth Century.* New Rochelle: The Myriade Press, 1986.

MERRIMAN, FRANK. *A.T.A. Type Comparison Book.* New York: Advertising Typographers Association, 1965.

PERFECT, CHRISTOPHER AND GORDON ROCKLEDGE. *Rockledge's International Type-Finder: The Essential Handbook of Typeface Recognition and Selection,* New York: Frederick C. Beil, 1983.

Bibliographies and dictionaries of typefounders and printers

ANNENBERG, MAURICE. *Type Foundries of America and Their Catalogs.* Baltimore and Washington: Maran Printing Services, 1964.

BERRY, W. TURNER AND A. F. JOHNSON. *Catalogue of Specimens of Printing Types by English and Scottish Printers and Founders, 1665–1830.* New York: Garland Publisher, Inc., 1983.

MARDERSTEIG, GIOVANNI. *The Officina Bodoni: An Account of the Work of a Hand Press 1923–77.* ed. and trans. by Hans Schmoller. Verona, Italy: Edizioni Valdonega, 1980.

RINGWALT, J. LUTHER. *American Encyclopaedia of Printing.* Philadelphia: Menamin & Ringwalt, 1871. (Facsimile by Garland Publishing, Inc., 1981)

INDEX

Page numbers in italics indicate illustrations.

Vale type, 50
Van Dyck, Christoffel, 385
Vatican Library, 124
Venus type, 298, 299–300, 301, 302, *302*
Verard, Antoine, 23
Verard Textura type, 23–24
Vicentino, Ludovico. *See* Arrighi, Ludovico degli
Vicenza type, *87*
Village Letter Foundry, 13, 117
Village Press, 113, 246
Village type, 50
Virgil of Aldus, 60, 86
Virtuosa type, 363–65, *364*
Vogue (periodical), 177–78, 344
Vogue type, 344
Voiage and Travaile of Sir John Maundevile, Kt., The, 29–32
Volta type, 321
Voskins, Dirk, 165, 386

Walbaum, Justus Erich, 202–5
Walden (Thoreau), Heritage Press (1939) edition of, 262
Walker, Sir Emery, 49, 50, 65
Warde, Beatrice Becker [pseud. Paul Beaujon], 92, 145; on Caslon type's reputation, 169; on Garamond types, 137–38, *149*; "The Garamond Types" by, *149*; on Jones' Granjon type, 150; Linotype matrix sketch by, *391*; Monotype matrix sketch by, *392*; "On the Choice of Typefaces" by, 169; punchcutting machine sketch by, *394*; on Roman No. 1 type, 231
Warde, Frederic, 71–72, 95–97, 99, 102
Wardrop, James, 89, 124
Watts, Stevens L., 242, 295; on Cheltenham type, 255
Way to Keep Him, The, 218
W. Bulmer & Company. *See* Shakspeare Printing Office
Wechel, Christian, 132

Wedding Text type, 28, *34*
Wells College, 35, 40
Western Type Foundry, 68, 261
Wheeler, Monroe, 329
White, Elihu, 233
Whittingham, Charles, 175, 215; *Diary of Lady Willoughby* produced by, 175, *176*
Wicks Rotary Typecaster, 390
Wiebking, Robert, 67, 71
Wilhelm Klingsporschrift, 31
Wilke, M., 363
William, Henry, 175
Wilson, Alexander, 102, 194, 231, 244
Winchester type, 261. *See also* Cheltenham type
Wolf, Rudolf, 318–19
Wolff, Kurt, 99
Wolpe, Berthold, 335
Woman's Home Companion (periodical), 274
Worde, Wynkyn de, 23
Word processing, 8
World, The (newspaper), 218
Wove paper, 187–88
Writing and Illuminating and Lettering (Johnston), 92, 122, 337
Wroth, Lawrence C., 228

Yale University Press, 169, 228
Youthline Script type, 360

Zainer, Günther, 21
Zapf, Hermann, 120–28, *128*; adaptation of types to varied printing processes by, 123; calligraphy of, 121, *122*; Goudy and, 122; International Typeface Corp. and, 128; Janson types redesigned by, 166; plagiarism of, 126–27; sources of twentieth century sans-serif letter and, 327–28
Zell, Ulrich, 21
Zeno type, 102–5, *103*, 106

Anatomy of a Typeface

was set in Galliard, a typeface designed by Matthew Carter and introduced in 1978 by the Mergenthaler Linotype Company. Based on the types created by Robert Granjon in the sixteenth century, Galliard is the first of its genre to be designed exclusively for phototypesetting. A type of solid weight, it possesses an authentic sparkle that is lacking in the current Garamonds. The italic is particularly felicitous and reaches back to the feeling of the chancery style, from which Claude Garamond's italic departed.

Printed by Maple-Vail Book Manufacturing Group,
Binghamton, New York, on Glatfelter
Offset Smooth Eggshell.